SPIRIT WARS

Pagan Revival in
Christian America

PETER JONES

WinePress Publishing  *Mukilteo, WA 98275*

and

Main Entry Editions *Escondido, CA 982025*

Unless we are mistaken . . . the twentieth century . . . is to witness a gigantic conflict of spirits. . . . More serious and fiercer than ever before, the conflict is between the old and new worldview.
- Hermann Bavinck, Christian theologian, 1901

There was some primary warfare going on . . . an archetypal battle between principalities and powers . . . and I willed to go all the way in this death battle.
- Mary Daly, ex-Roman Catholic nun, eco-feminist pagan witch, 1968

The Goddess has returned: Magic is afoot.
- Californian bumper sticker, 1995

We women are going to bring an end to God.
- Naomi R. Goldenberg, Jewish feminist, 1979

I call out for protection of the Goddess's people from the wrath of right-wing fundamentalists and their God.
- Wendy Hunter Roberts, pagan priestess, 1993

DEDICATION

To that wonderful group of people,
affectionately known as the *Jones Tribe*:

Eowyn, Stasie, Julien, Myriam, Tessa, Zoé and Toby

ACKNOWLEDGMENTS

I wish to thank:

- my students, who have stimulated my thinking about Gnosticism and its lessons for today;

- my colleagues at Westminster Theological Seminary in California, who have constantly encouraged and inspired me. I especially acknowledge the help of Professors Dennis Johnson and Steven Baugh who, in teaching my courses for a semester, enabled me to give my complete attention to research;

- Dr. Mark Futato, my Old Testament colleague, who in our collaboration in a seminar we offer to churches, *Following Christ in the New Age,* has sharpened my thinking about the Bible's teaching on creation, ecology and sexuality;

- the library staff for their competent help; my secretary, Mrs. Jackie Vanden Bos, for her invaluable assistance beyond the call of duty;

- John DeFelice for his original translations from the Coptic of the Gnostic texts cited in this volume;

- my wife, Rebecca, who as expert editor, stylistic critic and astute theologian, as well as constant encourager, friend and helper, has allowed this project to progress from endless unworked paragraphs and notes into a finished, readable text.

TABLE OF CONTENTS

Part One:
The Origin and Purpose of the New Spirituality

Part Two:
Anatomy of an Apostasy

AUTHOR'S NOTE

The discovery in 1945 of a whole library of ancient Gnostic Coptic texts in Nag Hammadi, Egypt, revolutionized the modern study of early Christianity. Instead of second hand reports from the Church Fathers, we now possess some fifty texts, written by the early Gnostic teachers themselves.

These precious documents immediately became the object of political and academic intrigue. Hans Jonas, the leading authority on Gnosticism of a generation ago, complained of "a persistent curse of political roadblocks, litigations and most of all, scholarly jealousies and 'firstmanship' (a veritable *chronique scandaleuse* of contemporary academia)." James Robinson, director of the English translation, *The Nag Hammadi Library in English* (Harper, 1977) characterizes the discovery period (1945-70) as dominated by the European "monopolists." Elaine Pagels, modern popularizer of Gnostic theology and spirituality, in her best-selling book *The Gnostic Gospels* (Random House, 1979), speaks of the deliberate suppression of the texts, not only in ancient times, but also since their recent rediscovery. Quoting another well-known European expert, she hails the first complete translation by Harper and Row in 1977 as the event which has brought to an end "personal rivalries . . . and pretensions to monopolize documents that belong only to science, that is to say, to all."

When I began research for *Spirit Wars*, as a sequel to my short book *The Gnostic Empire Strikes Back* (P&R, 1992), I continued to note the striking parallels between the ancient heresy of Gnosticism and the spirituality of New Age thinking and the post-modern worldview. These translations represented direct access for me as a scholar and for my readers, some of whom, while not professional Bible students, have bought these translations for themselves. Clearly this translation is doing its job, making these texts available "to all."

Following academic etiquette, I requested permission to cite the English translations. I was puzzled when permission was denied. No commercial considerations were suggested, no legal objections were raised, no other reasons were given. I was obliged to commission a Coptic scholar to make original translations of all my citations. Why was I not included in the "all"? Readers will draw their own conclusions.

One thing I have done — like the New Testament writers and Church Fathers of old — is to present the Gnostic system as a heretical, apostate distortion of the Faith once delivered to the saints. In an age of relativism and tolerance, such an approach has become politically and religiously incorrect. I also oppose what I judge to be an orchestrated attempt in Christian liberal circles to propose this distortion both as a valid, alternate, even superior expression of early Christianity and as a new lease on life for innovative spiritual seekers at the twilight of Western Christendom.

For my part, I have to wonder if this denial of permission constitutes a minor but revelatory skirmish in the growing reality of *Spirit Wars*.

John Lennon was an old school chum. Simple fellows, with little intellectual sophistication, we never spoke about religion or philosophy. Instead, we listened to Bill Haley and the Comets over fish and chips in a greasy spoon "chippy" on Penny Lane — strictly against the rules of traditionalist Quarry Bank High School For Boys, where we enjoyed education for all the wrong reasons. At sixteen, John left Quarry Bank to go to the Liverpool Arts School. I stayed on for "A levels" and went to University. We never met again.

History is funny. As everybody knows, John became a mega star, and converted to New Age Hinduism. Hardly anyone knows that I became a committed orthodox Christian and taught New Testament Greek in French to future pastors of the old Huguenot church in the South of France for eighteen years. But our lives once again became strangely intertwined.

In 1991, with great reluctance, I left my adopted land and church, to accept a teaching post in Southern California. The culture shock shook a few synapses loose in my brain. When they came together again, I made the connection that Lennon had made years earlier between ancient Gnosticism and New Age spirituality. In "The Mysterious Smell of Roses," a chapter in an anthology of his writings, *Skywriting by Word of Mouth*, published after his death, Lennon made a most unusual affirmation for someone not trained in theology or philosophy: "It seems to me that the only true Christians were (are?) the Gnostics who believe in self-knowledge, i.e., becoming Christ themselves, reaching the Christ within."[1]

As jocular high-school pals sitting together in a two-seater desk, we never imagined that divergent interpretations of an obscure Christian heresy would put us on opposing sides in the war of the worlds. Were Lennon alive today, he would certainly be a leader of the neo-pagan, pseudo-Christian camp that this book seeks to describe and unmask. I discovered Gnosticism as part of my graduate studies. But how did Lennon, with no formal training beyond a two-year technical school, come to know about such arcane matters of ancient Church history? There is clearly more to life than meets the eye!

Is There A Problem?

Michael Kinsley, as co-host of CNN's news comment program, *Crossfire*, recently said: "What could be more absurd than the idea that genuine anti-Christian prejudice is a major force in American politics?"[2] Kinsley finds it absurd to think that a deliberately anti-Christian agenda might motivate recent changes in society. Such changes are surely the result of the natural evolution of the democratic process. Journalist Robin Abcarian, married with child, recently voted for a gay candidate as secretary of state for California; a vote for tolerance and civil rights.[3] She was not consciously voting against Christians.

Journalists like Kinsley and Abcarian have no personal vendetta against Christians. Nor do most Americans, in spite of a media elite that brands committed believers as bigots and homophobes. Tolerance, dialogue and civil exchange are the order of the day. The terminology of spiritual battle has gone the way of "Onward Christian Soldiers," in our politically correct churches of peace and love. Relativity, compromise and civility without principle have replaced the antithetical, black and white thinking of Scripture. But, like it or not, warfare exists from the beginning, as God declares to the serpent and the woman concerning their opposing historical progeny: "I will place enmity between . . . your seed and her seed."[4] In our time, that warfare has broken cover. Kinsley, in spite of warm personal feelings, remains disturbingly uninformed.

From behind the oak doors of impeccable suburban homes and the surgically sterile partitions of abortion clinics the blood of our people cries out. The battle for the soul of this nation and of Western civilization rages unchecked. This is no video game of the mind that returns the player to reality when the quarter runs out. Homes and marriages, like unborn babies, are torn to shreds in a culture heralded as the epitome of enlightened civilization. America, defender of the great values of Western Christian culture is staggering, critically wounded by a radical ideology of "empowering," pro-choice, personal autonomy.

Ideas matter. Ideology becomes political program. On center stage in the war theater that touches every one is the battle of *worldviews*. A worldview is what people think when they are least aware — while watching T.V. or reading the paper. It is at this unconscious level that the struggle is most crucial.

At the threshold of the third millennium, two radically opposed ways of understanding human nature and the universe vie for allegiance. One defends the truth, the other the diabolical lie. One follows the God of the Bible, the other follows the goddess of paganism. Today's revolutionaries have launched their stealth weapon, "tolerance," which has quietly wound its way past our defenses to strike at the heart of the culture. It blasts the opposition with guilt-inducing accusations of intolerance while slick propaganda leaflets, proposing the pernicious and irrational teaching that *all is relative*, float down on the warm breezes of unity.

The secret weapon, like my stupid dog, is all bark and no bite. How can proponents of tolerance be intolerant? How can relativists make the truth claim that all is relative? Nevertheless, until the church and the society stop throwing up their hands in defeat before the pop-gun, the revolution will continue. In time of war an army cannot be "tolerant" of the invader. The religious left wants the label of demonizing bigotry stuck on anyone who does not buy its worldview. But when emotive rhetoric fades, we must ask how a Christian can tolerate error or the church an ideology that denies every element of her faith.

Their hands on the levers of power, forces with a blue-print for a social and spiritual experiment stand poised, ready to introduce a revolution that defies imagination. The American Revolution sought to eliminate taxation without representation. The French Revolution imagined Paris without aristocrats. The Russian Revolution dreamed of the disappearance of employers and private property. The Nazi Revolution hoped to rid the world of inferior races. The twentieth century American Revolution promises a society *without patriarchy*, that is, without the traditional family structure, and, in the long run, without God the Father, creator of heaven and earth.[5]

This revolution penetrates every home and soul, redefining sexuality, spirituality, God, religion, and revelation. The new world order turns everything we have known on its head — good becomes evil, homosexuality the preferred sexual expression, and the traditional family a minority structure.

The juggernaut of Marxist expansion came to an earth-shaking halt in 1989, as the desire for freedom burst the prison walls of the Eastern bloc, and the "cold war" became a memory. A pleasant lull in the war games has created premature disarmament, both in the physical and spiritual realm. While some in the church are awake, many sleep on, unaware of the "Game of the Century" flickering across the screens of their lives.

Like two hockey players poised over the puck, ready to force it in one direction or another, two religious faiths, the only two, battle for the spirit and the mind of the modern world. The "game" no longer pits the dark forces of atheistic humanism and godless materialism against the spirituality of the "Christian" West. The present contest is between two powerful spiritualities; Christian theism /God the Father, and pagan monism/ the Mother goddess.

If the teams in this "face-off of the soul" had different colored shirts, the game would be easier to follow. Alas, one team seeks to win by making all the shirts grey and, in the confusion, steals the puck to score the winning goal. Only a close look shows that the teams differ in style of play and direction. Choose sides, for the puck is your soul and the game is a spiritual battle to the death.

PART ONE

THE ORIGIN
AND PURPOSE
OF THE NEW
SPIRITUALITY

CHAPTER 1

THE BIRTH OF
THE RELIGIOUS LEFT

The Sixties ended before the turn of the decade, but the seeds of change had
been planted.
   -Marilyn Ferguson, author, *The Aquarian Conspiracy*[1]

The social movements of the 1960s and 1970s represent the rising culture,
which is now ready for passage into the solar culture.
   -Fritjof Capra, New Age physicist and Professor at UC, Berkeley[2]

Conceived in the Sixties, Born in the Nineties

On November 3, 1992 the people of the United States voted
into the most powerful position on earth a president who had
smoked pot, dodged the draft, and espoused the sexual morals of the
hippie revolution. The anti-establishment, flower-power children of the
Sixties entered the halls of political power in the nineties. Politics will
never be the same again.[3] Hippies, now with short hair and three piece
suits, squat in the White House — legally.[4] In the nineties, the world
witnessed "The Second Coming of the 60s,"[5] and President Bill Clinton,
he who had "breathed that (60s) era's heady atmosphere, and inhaled
deeply,"[6] became, in his capacity as social head of the nation, a metaphor for our times.

New Age mystics like Ferguson and Capra analyze the impact of
the Sixties with chilling accuracy. Says Ferguson, "The values that

had powered the movement of the Sixties could not be institutional-ized without a shift in cultural assumptions. *As consciousness changes, the world changes"* [emphasis mine].[7] The change has occurred. Ameri-cans not only tolerate but have institutionalized divorce, abortion, homosexuality and feminism. This has happened because *the religious consciousness of America has changed.*[8] Calls to strengthen the family, clear the streets of crime, make sex safe and abortion rare, and to beef up educational standards[9] go unheeded. Those who cling to patriotic optimism that a sensible nation will pull itself together one more time may be the most disappointed. The new consciousness cannot hear the calls for reform because it is deaf to anything but revolutionary spiritual and social change. How has this metamorphosis of the Ameri-can psyche come about?

More prophet than comedian, one journalist observed that the mix of piety and popular culture in the Clinton presidential inaugural celebrations in January, 1993 convinced her that she was present at "the birth of the Religious Left."[10] Everyone is acquainted with the Religious Right, but the Religious Left . . . ?

"**This is our time**,"[11] proclaimed President and Mrs. Clinton as they entered the White House. But just whose time is it? The new-look first couple who claimed this time symbolized not primarily a political party but the maturing fruit of the Sixties counter-culture revolution. Here is a new kind of religious commitment that can in the same breath — or at least in the same week — sing Gospel songs with genuine tears and promote the new morality of abortion and homosexuality. Southern Bap-tist presidential tears also spill in deep spiritual communion with the Buddhist Dalai Lama, whom Clinton found "a most remarkable man." The Tibetan Buddhist leader reminded the President that he was now "the most important man in the world."[12]

"**Our time**" is Marianne Williamson, author of the best selling book, *A Return To Love: Reflections on the Principles of 'A Course in Miracles.'*[13] Williamson is a hard-core New Age believer and popular-izer. She writes the laudatory preface toKen Carey's book, *The Third Millennium.* Carey writes this book under the influence of a voice "speaking to me" belonging to "a spirit-being in the eternal fields of light." Carey testified that as he wrote he "felt as if something enor-mous were looking through my eyes." His "revelations" are radically New Age and anti-Christian, but Williamson heartily approves. This is her time. She is one of the spiritual advisers of the first lady Hillary Clinton, with whom she often lunches. She has dined at the White House and slept in the Lincoln Bedroom.[14]

"Our time" is Jean Houston, a leading New age feminist guru, author of books such as *Godseed* and *The Hero and the Goddess,* and co-founder of the Foundation for Mind Research. She is a board member of the Temple of Understanding that is connected with the occult Theosophical Society and whose goal is the promotion of a one-world religion. Jean Houston was a leading participant at the *Parliament of the World's Religions* in Chicago in 1993, one of whose sponsors was the Theosophical Society. Her lecture, which the present author attended, described in classical New Age globalist terms a new day "being called forth by an evolution in . . . spiritual practice." She went on: "We are on the brink of the planetary person, who represents a whole new order of capacities and consciousness necessary for sacred stewardship of the earth."[15] Such new spiritual "capacities" intrigue old-style social-gospel liberals from main-line denominations. White House spokesman Neil Lattimore denied that they were seances, but it has recently been acknowledged by official sources that in 1995 Jean Houston led the United Methodist first lady, Mrs. Clinton, in "imaginary conversations" with figures of the past such as Eleanor Roosevelt and Hindu peace activist Mahatma Gandhi. "We have to draw strength from wherever we can to make it from day to day," said White House Chief of Staff, underplaying the enormity of these revelations. Surely Nancy Reagan's dalliance with popular astrology pales into insignificance compared with Hillary Clinton's "reaching out and searching hard,"[16] away from her Christian roots into the powerful pagan core of the new Religious Left's occult spirituality.

"Our time" is the appointment of twenty-seven practicing homosexuals in the Clinton administration and, behind them, the rise to power of the homosexual lobby in every area of society, including the mainline churches.

"Our time" is the "pro-choice" abortion forces whose power ensured that the President would veto the 1996 bill outlawing the horrendous procedure known as "partial birth abortion," even though this legislation was supported by the vast majority of both houses of Congress, and the veto was condemned by all eleven living past presidents of the Southern Baptist Conference, President Clinton's denomination.

"Our time" is the radical feminists surrounding the first lady. Their influence monopolized the American representation both at the U.N. Conference on World Population in Cairo in 1993 and at the Beijing Conference on Women in 1995. Certain radical alumnae from Mrs. Clinton's *alma mater,* Wellesley College in Massachusetts, were a major force in Beijing and in the formulation of the Platform for Action, the conference agenda that refuses to recognize the normativity of heterosexuality and of the two-parent heterosexual family. Such women see themselves as constituting "a critical mass," and believe that to spread this ideology throughout the globe is "truly Wellesley's mission."[17]

"Our time" is the twenty-one White House staffers who "entered a special testing program because of recent illegal drug use."[18] From the kinky margins of society and the minuscule intellectual elites, this new view of the world has, in the last four years, moved front and center stage.

The Great March From Berkeley to Washington

To the untrained eye, today's Berkeley is stuck in a thirty-year time warp. Streakers, long-haired hippies, sad-eyed, saffron-robed Hari Krishna bands, junkies, pot-pushers, esoteric book and health-food stores lead the visitor on a magical mystery tour of yesteryear's revolutionary past, a living museum of a long-gone social experiment. It is all so quaint and reassuring.

But do not be misled. Most of the Sixties revolutionaries have cleaned up their act, and are no longer in the Berkeley backwater.[19] Some have even moved to Washington, into pretty nice digs. The baby-boomers have had babies themselves and are pushing fifty. Their ideas are alive and well, and have made phenomenal progress.

Destructive Generation

David Horowitz and Peter Collier were members of the inner circle. Editors of *Ramparts* magazine, the "official" voice of radical Sixties politics, they were friends with most who were anybody in the radical scene, from Huey Newton and Jerry Rubin to Tom Hayden and Jane Fonda. Having helped foment the rebellion, they now have deep misgivings and worried consciences. The denouncing of racist attitudes and social structures was salutary. Not based on religious or Christian convictions, the mature assessment from these leaders of the rebellion on what they call the "destructive generation" is most telling:

> The stones we threw into the water of our world in those days caused ripples that continue to lap on our shores today — for better and more often for worse.

What was destroyed? Nothing less, I believe, than Western Christendom and civilization.

The "spirit entity" that has been channeling messages through Ken Carey underlines the importance of the Sixties for the coming of the new religion:

> our communications during these closing years of the seventies are reaching past the social fringe of your culture that was contacted during the Sixties. This time, we are reaching deep into the heart of global civilization . . . We are not in much contact yet with government officials, nor with world banks or international financiers. Our first contacts with them will occur during the more powerful transmissions of 1987 to 1989. Those who we are contacting now, nonetheless, are critical enough in the maintenance of your social systems to ensure that the world will make some incredible leaps in consciousness during the next decade . . . . By the time of the eighties revelations, knowledge of our existence will be widespread.[20]

If the spirit-entities and New Agers consider the Sixties counterculture rebellion such an important moment for the coming of the new religion, perhaps Christians should pause and listen. The Sixties' rejection of authority, rejection of biblical sexual morals, and the search for a new spirituality are not artifacts of a failed revolution. They are the tools in the destruction of Western civilization.

The destruction has been refined and enshrined in legislation. New Ager Marilyn Ferguson makes the surprising claim: the New Age has not gone mainstream; rather, mainstream is going New Age.[21] A recent book calls the New Age the "Now Age." Mainstream culture, even those claiming to be "fiscally conservative," has willingly adopted the new religious worldview. The revolution has succeeded far beyond the dreams of the long-haired revolutionaries of yesteryear. While we all thought the revolution had failed, its leaders undertook what someone has called "the long march through the institutions." "Tenured radicals"[22] now rule those institutions. A repentant hippie has recently said: "Those who loved the '60s own the '90s."[23] Their destructive ideas have blossomed everywhere in the nineties — in the halls of political, religious and academic power, and especially in the media. The following Sixties molotov cocktail of the mind constitutes the contours of the pagan civilization of the third millennium:

♦ Rejection of Authority: Western Civ Has Got To Go

The New Left radicals of the Sixties wanted to "bring the system down." History will show that they did just that, by taking it over. Rejection of landlords, university senates, police and the federal government has been transformed in the nineties into the rejection of Western civilization *in toto*. Radical students today chant, "Hey ho, wha d'ya know? Western Civ has got to go." They silence dead white male authors such as Plato, Aristotle, Shakespeare, Wordsworth and Jonathan Edwards and bring in general chorus of contemporary intellectuals (including many orthodox Christians) calling for the dismantling of "patriarchy."[24]

Betty Friedan's *The Feminist Mystique* (1963) began the attack on patriarchy through the notion of the autonomous woman. The Sixties plaint of the lonely housewife has become the deafening battle cry of a formidable feminist phalanx that sweeps away the very structure of the biblical civilization upon which the West has been built. Destroying fatherly authority and the responsible, representative role of men dismantles the traditional family unit. There is no use calling for the defense of the traditional family if you do not see this. The document "Project for the Republican Future" notes that the Supreme Court's rulings on abortion, which eliminate the decision-making responsibility of fathers, have "affected a fundamental alteration in the meaning of the American democratic experiment — that of the radically autonomous individual and the coercive state . . . in which the community of husband and wife is no longer of constitutional or legal account."[25] This mortal, though muted, attack on the pillars of our society goes unnoticed by most.

The rejection of patriarchy is but one example of the power of the *deconstructionist movement* that began in the Sixties. Reacting in part against "modernity" (the proud Enlightenment belief that all of mankind's problems could be solved by autonomous human reason, freed from God's revelation), deconstruction destroys all before it. Jesus told of a house swept clean of one demon, into which rush seven more. A world cleansed of rationalistic, atheistic humanism awaits its new tenants.

Deconstruction sees *all* rational discourse, all attempts to explain the world, as the naked use of power.[26] Claims to non-existent absolute truth are only impositions of the ideology of those in power upon those who have no power. "Truth" becomes ideological harassment of minority victims. The Equal Employment Opportunity Commission wants to eliminate religion from the workplace so that no one may be "harassed" by religious ideas at work. The time is coming and now is when the playing of "Silent Night" in shopping malls at the Christmas season will be illegal—like the word "Christmas" itself, even Bing Crosby singing "White Christmas"! In his children's story, *The Lion, the Witch, and the Wardrobe*, C. S. Lewis created a frozen world under the power of the white witch. One of her curses doomed Narnia to everlasting winter with no Christmas. Little did he realize how prophetic his words would be. A world without Christmas mutely proclaims the end of Western civilization as we have known it and the beginning of the silent night of the human soul.

◆ Rejection of Biblical Sexual Norms and Morals: "Smash Monogamy"

Jerry Rubin said in the Sixties, as a bare-chested revolutionary: "We've combined youth, music, sex, drugs and rebellion with treason — that's a hard combination to beat"![27] The balding, be-suited, entrepreneur Rubin has lost his youth, his revolutionary zeal,[28] and, unfortunately, his life (in a traffic accident in Los Angeles), but the contemporary expansion of music, sex and drugs goes beyond anything Rubin imagined. Sexual liberation in the Sixties was "anything goes" *heterosexual* love.[29] Another of first lady Hillary Clinton's spiritual gurus, Michael Lerner, was the leader of the Berkeley *Students for a Democratic Society*. On his first wedding cake he had inscribed: "Smash Monogamy."[30] The manifesto succeeded not only for Lerner, who has weathered a number of marriages, but all over America. Divorce rates are among the highest in the world, and co-habitation is at an all-time high. Today's sexual revolution goes beyond extra-marital, pre-marital, and multiple-partner heterosexual activity. "Anything goes" has become the mass-media promotion not only of boundless immoral heterosexuality[31] but also of sado-masochism, bi-sexuality, homosexuality and pornography.[32] According to the logic of the system, pedophilia[33] and bestiality cannot be far behind.

A biblical text thousands of years old captures the Sixties' sliding morality. Leviticus twenty-three lists prohibitions in the following order: adultery, the sacrificial killing of children, homosexuality and bestiality. Such abominations were the root cause of the destruction of the ancient pagan nations.[34] Can this nation avoid a similar fate? Gary Bauer, reacting to the government policy for the promotion of condoms in pornographic television ads, said: "For the first time in our nation's history, a generation of young Americans is being told by government leaders that, if they will just use condoms, promiscuity is perfectly safe and, in fact, no big deal."[35] The Sixties' revolutionaries who now head many government agencies have made free love into official government policy.

◆ Search for a New Spirituality: Magical Mystery Tour

The Sixties counter-culture revolution was a spiritual movement.[36] Woodstock, a spiritual happening, was the drug trip search for the Garden of Eden.[37] Richard Alpert's soul journey exemplifies the spiritual maturation of the Sixties. Professor of psychology at Harvard, and colleague of Timothy Leary, Alpert broke with Freudian reductionism and with the help of LSD discovered that there was being beyond the *id*. The chemically-inspired mind/soul-expansion of consciousness that gave him unity with the universe sent him on a religious quest to India where he practiced Hinduism for many years. He returned as Ram Dass, a westernized Hindu guru, and now does well-paid lecture tours in the States, replete with hip humor, a male lover, and a spirit guide named Emmanuel. His midriff corpulence brings to mind the fattened Buddha rather than bony Eastern holy men on the streets of Calcutta. Ram Dass now supports the "politics of meaning" popular in Washington and, as a practitioner of New Age Hindu spirituality, claims to have finally rediscovered his Judaism.[38] The "rainbow" trajectory of Ram Dass is reflected in the musings of a "death of God" theologian at the beginning of the seventies:

> It may be that this need to recall an old symbol system [polytheism] for new purposes may be behind the recent interest in the occult, in magic, in extraterrestrial life, in Hindu India and Buddhist Japan, in multidaemoned China, in sorcery, in new forms of multiple family life, in communes, in the "new religions," and many other alternative life-styles and meaning systems which have been hitherto foreign.[39]

The revolutionaries said it. We just didn't believe them. The Beatles went East while the gurus came West. Chemically-inspired highs of acidheads and predictions of polytheists have diversified into the New Age multi-cultural spiritual highs of the nineties. Just check your New Age advertiser: Hindu "chakra" meditation, yoga, witchcraft, channeling, astral travel, visualization, kundalini sex, native American animism, plus all the gods and goddesses you can handle. The movement has not lost its quest for spirituality. It has diversified and gone mainline, just as the Hindu mystic, Swami Vivekananda prophesied at the first *Parliament of the World's Religions* in Chicago in 1893. His dream was the creation of "a society of Western Science and Socialism and Indian spirituality."[40] The 1993 Parliament in Chicago realized Vivekananda's dream and tasted of global strength.

The Indicators of Social Destruction

The "destructive generation" has done its work. It has torn down Western Christian civilization, especially the family. Social indicators prove that our consciousness has changed. Victims of the radical social experimentation of the Sixties fill self-help groups. Having promised freedom, peace and love, the revolution delivered only the freedom of a de-railed train and the peace of a beached fish. Scott Peck, a Sixties psychologist, was amused to find that when he asked a five-hundred member audience how many had been or were currently in therapy, "practically every one in the auditorium raised their hands."[41] The "therapeutic age" spares no expense or counsel to achieve personal emotional comfort. Yet devotees of the "destructive generation" have gone through one, two, even three divorces in the search for personal freedom. Their children, lacking strong family structures, have rejected what discipline the parents tried to mete out and turned to peers and drugs for solace.

The statistics speak. America leads the "civilized" world in father absence from the home and in its permissive laws regulating abortion and divorce.[42] Barbara Dafoe Whitehead, in the *Atlantic Monthly* (1993), called the last twenty five years "a vast experiment in family life."[43] She could have said a vast "destruction" of family life.[44] Today, only one quarter of American households is composed of married parents with children.[45] One in every four children in the U.S. is born to an unwed mother. In 1960 243,000 children lived in single parent homes. In 1993 the figure climbed to 6.3 million, provoking a demographic expert to describe the trend as "astonishing." Nearly two thirds of all black children live with a single parents.[46] From 1970 to 1993 the number of unmarried adults nearly doubled and the number of divorcees tripled.[47]

Education at all levels is in disarray, but none more so than "higher" education. According to Arthur Levine, president of the Teachers College at Columbia University and an expert on the history of college curricula: "We are in the midst of one of the broadest debates we have ever had on what knowledge ought to be common to all people."[48] Echoing this, the president of the National Association of Scholars, Stephen Balch, believes that "the nation is in danger of losing the common frame of reference that for many generations has sustained our liberal, democratic society."[49]

What can stop the American culture from implosion? George Gilder predicts that the American culture at large will follow the pattern already established in the black urban communities.[50] The deconstruction of the American "Judeo-Christian" family creates a voracious vacuum quickly filled by "alternate family styles." Because these structures seem better than none, the public accepts them without examining the worldview of *pagan spirituality* that spawned them.

Destruction of the "Christian" Culture

The Sixties movement did not rebel against religion. It rebelled against the *Christian* religion.[51] The dust of history has settled enough to see that the counter-culture movement of the Sixties *countered* Western Judeo-Christian culture, seeking not secularization but a new kind of religion, a radically different spirituality.

Baby Boomers are accurately called "a generation of seekers."[52] Only four percent of baby boomers are atheists or agnostics. The rest follow some kind of religion.[53] People speak sadly of "declining moral standards." Standards have changed because *the religious consciousness of the nation has changed.* The Sixties' noble search for expanded consciousness and its tolerance for alternate spiritualities went East to discover mysticism and returned to spawn a relativistic religious hybrid, Western spiritual monism.[54] This new pagan monism joins the Eastern religious idea that all is one and one is all, to Western technology, democratic self-determination and the ideal of autonomous egalitarianism. The whole is clothed in "Christian" dress for general Western consumption. The mix creates a potent elixir that fires the minds and hearts of social transformers at the brink of a new millennium.

The Second Coming of the Sixties: Regeneration for the "Me Generation"

So the Sixties came of age in the nineties. In her book, *Do You Believe in Magic? The Second Coming of the 60s Generation*, published in 1987, sociologist Annie Gottlieb posits that the rage of the Sixties has been channeled into a new expression of spirituality. No longer hooked on the self (the "Me generation"), it has developed a social conscience, "the politics of love," or "the politics of virtue or meaning." Rooted in the Sixties revolution, the new consciousness flowers in liberation theology, the women's liberation movement, the gay and lesbian quest for social and religious recognition, multiculturalism, and political correctness. Gottlieb analyzes the Sixties' "second coming" as a new agenda for the spiritual and religious transformation, not only of the self, but of the world.[55]

The real enemy is no longer anti-religious atheistic humanism but a revived pagan religion. The problem is not *no* God but *too many*, not a lack of spirituality but spiritual syncretism. Few who decry the dissolution of society see the religious threat of the new spirituality. Hidden under its free-flowing robes of tolerance lies the skeleton of *pagan monism*.

CHAPTER 2

THE CREED OF THE
RELIGIOUS LEFT

Do not forget that the fundamental contrast has always been, is still, and always will be until the end: Christianity and Paganism, the idols or the living God.
   - Abraham Kuyper, *The Stone Lectures*, Princeton Seminary, 1898

The Heart of Aquarian Spirituality:
The Five Points of Monism

The disparate themes of our pro-choice culture have a central core. Its vaunted diversity hides profound ideological coherence: religious paganism, the worship of the earth and of the goddess behind it. The apostle Paul would describe this religion as worship of the creature rather than the Creator.[1] However, "paganism" is still imprecise, suggesting the sum of unrelated, non-Christian religions. It is vitally important to see beyond the external diversity and subtle distinctions to the inner coherence of paganism which is known as MONISM.

The Sixties counter-culture revolution popularized in Western Christendom the spirituality of the East. Spiritual "highs" through drugs and Eastern meditation revealed the real revolution: Eastern, pagan monism penetrated the Judeo-Christian "theistic" world.

"Ism" words frighten the average reader, but we had better understand this one. "Mono" means "one." In a monopoly, one company captures the market. Monism as a philosophy of life seeks to capture the church in our day. Its tentacles, some secular and some "Christian"/liberal, surround a sleepy Zion. They have drawn in most movements, claiming to deliver peace and prosperity for a renewed planet. Monism's symbol is the circle: its goal is to encircle the globe.

The following five elements summarize monism in its contemporary expression.[2] It is essential to grasp them, in order to understand what is happening in our society:

1. All is One and One is All:

This is the essence of monism. The universe is a mass of undifferentiated, related energy. God is not *outside* the universe; God *is* the universe. Christianity's Creator/creature distinction is eradicated. The big "O" of Monism is a circle — everything, including God, is within the circle. You cannot contain a watch-maker in his watch, but this is what monism does to God. The ancient symbol of the circle has reappeared — in witchcraft (whose ceremony begins by "casting a sacred circle"), in Hinduism, in goddess worship — even the symbol of the *Parliament of the World's Religions* was a circle.[3]

This circular, all-is-one notion underlies New Age/Taoist physics, "deep ecology," the worship of Mother Earth and ultimately the use of female imagery for God. *Restoring the Goddess to Judaism and Christianity*, the title of a recent politically correct publication, is a blatant attempt to re-introduce paganism into biblical faith. The "mother" is none other than encircling, bewitching Mother Earth:

> She [is] . . . everywhere and encompasses everything: . . . She is everything and everybody and its opposite. . . . She shows for me that there is no disunity between something and its opposite. A totality includes all aspects. Linear and dualistic divisions do not exist.[4]

Break the spell. It is impossible to "restore" paganism to the Bible, for it was never there. But paganism clothed in the emotive, seductive colors of tolerance and human rights, gradually changes perceptions of God. Its success would spell the end of Christianity, because the ultimate source of the new gospel is paganism.

In the movie *Star Wars*, Obiwan Kenobi, the Jedi warrior, explains to young Luke Skywalker in monistic prose worthy of any pagan priest/ ess, ancient or modern:

> The Force is an energy field created by all living things: it surrounds us, penetrates us, it binds the galaxy together . . . it is all-powerful [and] controls everything.

When Luke abandons himself to his intuitions, he is able, in harmony with the Force, to pilot a flying machine of unimaginable complexity in a pin-point bombing of the headquarters of the Evil Empire. Skeptical? Monism promises no less incredible results to its adherents.

2. Humanity is One:

If all is one, humanity is an expression of divine oneness. Humans are congealed cosmic energy who create their own reality. Belief that the human is divine, and thus essentially good, helps explain the burgeoning quest for personal spiritual discovery, to the detriment of doctrine and truth.[5] Mysticism has replaced true spirituality.[6] Companies in the West, seeing commercial value in such optimism, are using these ideas to produce better sales personnel. Madison Avenue and the gurus could be an unstoppable, unholy alliance feeding the machine of political correctness. As an expression of divinity, each self is a source of truth. Tolerance and relativity are necessary corollaries, since everybody's truth is different. This monistic ideology defines the "values clarification" programs in the public schools; there is no such thing as right as over against wrong. Children must express their sexuality as they abandon themselves to their intuitions, untrammelled by moral considerations, but protected by condoms. The individual is the final judge, and intuition is the path to oneself, to human freedom and to harmony with "the Force."

3. Religions are One:

In this great expanse of energy, divinity and truth, no religion can claim exclusive truth. Because orthodox Christianity commits this unpardonable sin, it is the major obstacle to the religious and social harmony of the planet. Religions must blend into a global, unified syncretism. A *homogenized* one-world religion is not politically correct but it is not really necessary. Just below the surface of religious diversity of the world's religions, as a matter of fact, the various creeds are interchangeable, and spiritual experiences are in communion the same occult reality.

The "Parliament" of the World's Religions in Chicago in 1993 was a pre-programmed happening of monistic spirituality. Conferees were to discover behind their external differences a shared human experience of the divine within. Monistic syncretism will be the inspiration for many more such gatherings and programs planned for the years ahead, especially the Parliament of the year 2000.[7]

4. One Problem:

If all is one, the great problem is the splintering of reality into opposing camps; making distinctions between good and evil, right and wrong, truth and error, God and Satan, human and animal, male and female, homosexual and heterosexual, pagan and Christian, heresy and orthodoxy, reason and irrationality. Monists argue that such distinctions, typical of Western Christian culture, have numbed human beings into a spiritual and metaphysical amnesia in which they are no longer aware of belonging to the whole.[8] Evil is not tragic moral rebellion against the transcendent Creator. It is mere forgetfulness. The monistic circle must be unbroken or the spell will be. A mystical experience of the whole is essential.

5. One Means of Escape:

Spiritual understanding through intuition and meditation is the only way to salvation. Such insight comes through a non-rational, mystical experience of seeing oneself as a the center of a circle that has no boundaries.[9] From the center of its own limitless universe the self necessarily reigns supreme! The experience is engendered in the fast track through drugs or, in the safer lane, through time-honored (Hindu) meditation. Rightly practiced, such meditation enables the mind/soul to be disconnected from the limitations of the body. In the experience of this knowledge (gnosis) of the self as connected to the whole and thus divine, there occurs the liberating paradigm shift through which redemption of the self and the planet becomes possible. The experience, though antithetical to the Creator's designs, and therefore ultimately noxious, nevertheless produces a profound sense of release and liberation, a bogus "virtual redemption." In the triumph of mind over matter, as the mind empties itself of all thought, human beings "realize" their divinity. Needless to say, salvation through the redemptive, objective death of Christ on behalf of sinners has no function here. One is one's own savior, thank you.

This Eastern monism with a Western spin directly contradicts Christian theism and the civilization it has engendered. There is no neutral ground.

Monism and Theism: A Clash of Worldviews

Anyone with even a superficial knowledge of Christianity senses that these five points of religious monism are radically antithetical to orthodox Christianity (theism). While using terms like God and the divine, this new spirituality is a form of atheism because it denies the true God who created the heavens and the earth. Orthodox Christian theologians are not the only ones to understand the life-and-death nature of the conflict. Leaders of the new spirituality realize it, too. Though tolerance is the ultimate virtue, one theological position is not tolerated.

The *Parliament of the World's Religions* of 1993 scheduled no reasoned discussion of these two theological options. It refused to recognize the conflict: such recognition would only slow the world-wide monistic/syncretistic revival. Faint echoes of the debate were banalized into "conflict-resolution" exercises by teams of professional "dialogue facilitators." Historic theism was absent, invoked only as the source of the planet's problems.[10]

In its global pretensions, this Parliament of peace represents a more intolerant totalitarian view of religious freedom than its favorite whipping boy, Fundamentalism. Refusal to recognize the legitimacy of theism systematically characterizes the new liberal international gatherings and networks. In Chicago, theists and other outsiders were asked to leave whenever the *practice* of pagan spirituality began. Inclusiveness was extended to the orthodox Christian voice only as it was represented in a black choir, invited to sing gospel songs that nobody understood.

Theists are non-persons or heretics. Opponents do not use the word "theism." They rely on the loaded word "Fundamentalism." A widely-recognized spokesman for the new spirituality, Deepak Chopra, describes the present as a period of "some of the worse turbulence in the world." His next phrase contains the predictable dismissal: "There has been a resurgence of religious Fundamentalism, violence, terrorism, bigotry, racism, ethnocentrism and prejudice." He further adds: "I do not even attempt to convince fundamentalists."[11] Theists are included with violent extremists and racists, and are branded as mindless bigots, impossible to convince. In this latter affirmation, Chopra is unwittingly correct: monists and theists always end in a stand-off because their positions are mutually exclusive. In the present rhetoric, however, only the theists get the blame.

The Confusion Gap

The clash of worldviews has been called "culture wars" but the war goes much deeper than cultural preferences. The present clash of irreconcilable worldviews, of monism and theism, creates total confusion and profound animosity. Who knows what the future will bring? One can only imagine what kind of spiritual hurricanes are lurking off our cultural coasts. Interestingly, James Davidson Hunter, who wrote the best-selling *Culture Wars*, recently published a further book whose title is most telling: *Before the Shooting Begins*.[12] Signs of cultural disarray and debilitating confusion are as ubiquitous and as obvious as McDonald's golden arches in downtown USA. Martin Marty, respected commentator on religious trends in the West wrote in 1981:

> many observers envision that the twenty-first century, far from being merely secular, may be hyperreligious. . . . potent human organization may no longer follow the lines of nations but the outlines of religions until great tribes, well-armed, will clash.[13]

A Presidential Mix

Like many baby-boomers, Clinton and Gore combine aspects of both traditional Christianity and more modern spirituality.
- Michael D'Antonio, L.A.Times, November 29, 1992

The most significant and dangerous confusion is religious in nature: the mixing of "traditional Christianity" and "modern spirituality." The combination, like a pizza special with all the toppings, is dynamite. The pizza burns the roof of your mouth, but the religious combination blows the roof off Western civilization. Much of America, whether Democrat or Republican, left or right, is now in the hands of ideologues of the religious Left who practice what D'Antonio calls the "more modern spirituality."

Confusion Reigns — Storms on the Horizon: Some Notable Trouble Spots

Weather conditions in this religious climate? Easy — a one hundred percent chance of confusion. Jesus hailed the Pharisees as expert meteorologists, unable to read the theological signs of their time. In our day, spiritual confusion and moral schizophrenia reign. How about a remedial course in reading the signs of the times?

♦ Five Gospels:

One of the first tangible results of recent New Testament scholarship of the liberal left,[14] *The Five Gospels*[15] sets the Gnostic *Gospel of Thomas* alongside the four Gospels of the church's historic canon. Monism and theism are served up together, creating confusion in the book store. A *new Bible*, politically correct, and neo-Gnostic may follow, creating confusion in the pews.

♦ Jesus Has a Twin:

Beside Jesus the Son of God walks a human, monistic Jesus akin to Buddha, Gandhi and other spiritual leaders, a prophet inhabited by "Christ consciousness," who does not believe he came to die for the sins of the world. *A new Christ* is preached inside and outside the church.

♦ The *God Within* Demands Equal Time in Church:

Lazaris, popular New Age guru, speaks of "God, Goddess, The All That Is."[16] Taking pro-choice thinking to the gates of heaven, a politically correct *new theology* encompasses all extremes, from the "god" of Christian theism, to the "goddess" of ancient paganism, and even to the faceless impersonal "all that is" of Eastern religions. Flagging faith revives as radical *syncretists* re-imagine the biblical God as a pagan deity and offer milk and honey to Sophia (Wisdom) in a eucharistic "Lady's Supper."

♦ Sunday Celebrations:

In the opposite direction, *new pagan churches* (Unity, Unification and Religious Science)[17] offer Sunday celebrations led by "reverends" (male and female), Sunday schools, nurseries, youth ministry and teen groups, prayer meetings, inspirational hymn singing, and special music from attractive vocal artists who would surely, if there were any, win Dove awards, New Age division! In a new twist these "churches" stage "Easter Pageants," which include "Good Friday" and "Easter Sunday" services, choirs singing Handel's *Hallelujah Chorus,* and meditations on the "mystical Christ." Everything is picture-perfect, except that there is no sin, no Gospel, no Cross, no space-time resurrection, no Christ of Scripture, no God of the Bible — and so, no redemption.

♦ Spiritual Supplements:

Orthodox Christians supplement the Bible and prayer with visualization, yoga meditation, I Ching (pagan Chinese divination), Tarot cards and New Age channeling. The First Congregational Church of a midwestern town offers a seminar for spiritual growth entitled "Sacred Eyes," featuring Robert Keck, an "expert" in the "transformational trip" of mind-spirit synergy. A *new spirituality* blends theistic piety and monistic meditation. The Scriptures are at best one option among many.

◆ **Equal Time for Egalitarianism:**

Role-confusion, sexual identity crisis, divorce, and the breakdown of the family are a social epidemic.[18] In 1992, the surgeon general declared sodomy a dangerous practice; in 1993 the following surgeon general spoke of "healthy homosexual sex";[19] "healthy" homosexuals seek the right to ordination in the church, and "heterosexism" (the belief that male-female sexuality is required by God) is denounced by Christian theologians as a grievous sin. An Episcopal seminary allows homosexual couples in its campus housing, including the Professor of New Testament and her lover, but disallows cohabiting heterosexual students. Says a dissenting cleric: "The inability of our church to address the question (of sexual ethics) clearly . . . leads to a lot of confusion among lay people."[20] Is anyone *not* confused? A *new sexuality* tries to have it all but may lose both body and soul.

◆ **Abortion: Murder or Health Care?**

Abortions and births are performed in the same hospital by the same doctors, sometimes on pre-born babies of the same age.[21] Recent legal decisions make the killing of a fetus from gun or knife attacks on pregnant women a punishable crime, but make exceptions for abortion procedures.[22] Such legal niceties are hardly good news to the unborn child. Another example of legal "newspeak": In my small town of Escondido, CA, a twenty-two-year-old unwed mother, Tiffany Nicole Sandeffer was given fifteen-years-to-life for killing her newborn baby and pitching his body into a trash can.[23] When doctors do the same it is called "health care." But the result is another dead baby in a trash can.

◆ **Misdemeanor or Felony?**

Employees of an abortion clinic picket for higher wages — misdemeanor. Citizens picket to rescue babies from death — federal felony with fines of up to $250,000 and imprisonment from six months to three years (with the new Freedom of Access to Clinics Bill).

Is anyone not in the "confusion gap?" Contradictory views of reality are joined in the name of tolerance; of the implacable progress of the democratic process; of freedom of choice. But, like oil and water, they cannot blend. The attempted blend creates a bewildering world, dislodging Christianity as the touchstone of morals and truth. The tolerant, inclusive "newspeak" does not please every one. The press speaks of "visceral opposition . . . unprecedented in tone and intensity." Simple people sense that behind the confusing rhetoric, they are losing something of major proportions.[24]

Kiss Chaos: A Positive Spin on The "Confusion Gap"

For some, confusion is part of the plan. Dr. Peter Russell, (an expert in Transcendental Meditation and a consultant for 'the development of the learning process and creativity' for such multinational corporations as IBM, Shell, BP, Barclay's Bank, D.E.C.), is a New Age channeler. Speaking through him, the spirit entities reveal the immediate future of the earth:

> There is a new vibrational pattern descending upon your planet. . . .
> You are being offered an opportunity to enter a new reality. . . . Soon it
> will be the only reality to be seen. . . . Two worlds of consciousness
> will begin to form ever more distinctly: the world of Love and Life,
> and the world of fear and death. There will continue to be some over-
> lap of these worlds for several years to come, some going back and
> forth for certain individuals, but as the century draws to a close, the
> polarization will continue to intensify. The moment of birth will also
> be the moment of Last Judgment, the moment of final separation.[25]

This is heady wine for corporate global leaders thirsty for significance. The Charles Manson family, justifying the Sharon Tate mass-murders, wrote in the blood of their victims on the refrigerator door "Helter-Skelter," a term taken from a Beatles' song, describing the social destruction that would precede the new era of peace and love.[26] Marilyn Ferguson sees the "Confusion Gap" as a positive sign. That families are falling apart, that education is in disarray, that many, especially the young, are plagued by gender confusion — these are all good things, for *destruction must precede revolutionary reconstruction.*

The world is not falling apart. It is *reconstituting* itself. Ferguson appeals to modern science which claims that "large perturbations of energy cause living systems to fall apart, then fall together again in a more elegant order." This is then used to support the claims of the spiritual proponents of social confusion that experiments eventually bring about a better world, even if no one knows for sure where things are leading.[27] So the Whole Earth Festival at the University of California, Davis, in May 1996 adopted as its theme: *Kiss Chaos.*

Few realize that the real game is religious warfare between truth and falsehood, with deep consequences for the spiritual and moral survival of the planet. Reality has been redefined: the "world of Love and Life" is the new religious monism. The "world of fear and death" is Christian theism. Because few are aware of the struggle, the program goes on unopposed, taught to world business leaders, military per-

sonnel, and school children; aided by the buzz-words that ring
everybody's bells — freedom, justice, democratic rights, and diversity.

The Same Old Alternatives:
Christianity and Paganism

This juxtaposition of antithetical worlds is not "business as usual."
We live in a most uncommon time. Opposition to recent changes in
Western society is not mere sentimental idealization of yesteryear, or
the fear of change.[28] We are not faced with differences between mini-
skirts and maxiskirts, wide ties or narrow. Ours is a choice of civilization. This is cleverly masked by political rhetoric. "When our memo-
ries exceed our dreams," said President Clinton to a University of
California, Los Angeles convocation in 1994, "we have begun to grow
old, and it is the destiny of America to be forever young."[29] Monism
is as old as the hills, and "youthful America" is naively setting the
clock back thousands of years. Monism and theism have always been
the only two ways of relating to God and the world, and thus the only
two bases of any human civilization. It is not a question of turning
back the clock to the rosy world of the fifties. It is the question of
whether we opt for a Christian or pagan society.

Our society struggles at the brink of a new age, characterized by an
unusual mixing of fundamentally antithetical views regarding the world
and God. In the confusion of world views, monism and theism lock in
a battle to the death. Which will emerge victorious to affect the future
of the next generations? Though ultimate victory belongs to the Creator, the church has never been promised every battle. Professor
Wilken of the University of Virginia recently observed, with excep-
tional insight:

> The ferocity of the current assault on the legacy of Christian culture .
> . . has brought a new clarity of vision. The alternatives are set before
> us with unusual starkness: either there will be a genuine renewal of
> Christian culture — there is no serious alternative — or we will be
> enveloped by the darkness of paganism in which the worship of the
> true God is abandoned and forgotten. The sources of the cultural
> crisis, it turns out, are theological.[30]

Opposition is "in-your-face," as the sticker on a truck — "Jesus is lard"
— indicates. At least such open antagonism identifies the enemy. When
pagan ideas masquerade as *Christian* values, the assault is more insidi-

ous and more deadly, for it is difficult to see that the velvet glove conceals an iron fist. Earth-centered monism has slipped into the pew beside transcendent Christian theism.

The Greatest Threat Ever to the Christian Church?

Does the average Christian know what is going on in our ostensibly civilized society? Pagan ideology, sometimes of the most radical and anti-Christian nature, is taught in university departments of religion, theological seminaries, mainline church agencies, feminist networks and wicca covens across the land. It adopts the name of Christianity, but will render our world unrecognizable. The political events begun in 1992 are the consequence of an ideological revolution promoted since the Sixties in our halls of learning,[31] in our living rooms and "home entertainment centers,"[32] and in our schools via the social engineers of the NEA and Planned Parenthood.[33]

If you doubt the success of this revolution, note the following statistic: in 1994, seventy-one percent of Americans and forty percent of those calling themselves "evangelicals" no longer believed in absolute truth.[34] Since the Sixties, consciousness has changed.

The present hour is crucial. "The church faces a crisis of identity possibly unmatched since the second century. . . . We are back on Mount Carmel."[35] The threat has monumental implications for believers and especially for their children. What is the church doing to prepare our children for survival in the Aquarian nightmare?

Writing in 1973 about the counter-culture revolution of the Sixties, Os Guinness remarked: "The swing to the East has come at a time when Christianity is weak at just those points where it would need to be strong to withstand the East. Without this strength, the Eastern religions will be to Christianity a new and dangerous gnosticism."[36] This insightful prophesy has become a woeful reality.

CHAPTER 3

CHRISTIAN LIBERALISM: CRISIS AND CONVERSION

In polytheism man's free-thinking . . . has a proto-type . . . the power to create for himself.
  - Nietzsche[1]

Theological Liberalism in Crisis

The "Religious Left" has emerged like a phoenix from the ashes of liberalism. Old liberals are tired.[2] They are tired of orthodoxy as "televangelists" exploit it on radio and television for the aggrandizement of their personal empires. They are weary of orthodoxy's suspicion of exciting trends in society. But they are also tired of the old critical liberalism, so concerned with "scientific" solutions to the Bible's supernaturalism. Like political Marxism, liberalism in the church has given few answers to spiritual needs[3] and has not produced a gospel capable of meeting the global expectations of a unified planet.[4] Liberalism needs a new lease on life.

Mainline's Decline

For thirty years, the news, like British weather, has not been good. Sociological studies of the Methodists, Presbyterians, Congregationalists and Episcopalians pronounce gloom and doom. After a period of growth in the fifties, mainline denominations began to shrink by the end of the sixties. The burgeoning liberalism of the theological seminaries spread to the churches. A 1993 study notes that by 1990 the loss of members had reached staggering proportions — between one fifth and one third[5] — and the three most liberal denominations declined the most.[6] Mainline churches have cut their staff[7] and moved their central offices to less imposing addresses in the heartland.

A recent poll of baby-boomers who were confirmed in the mainline church in the Sixties shows that seventy-five per cent left church at age twenty-one, half of them never to return. Sixty-eight percent of those who did (middle-aged parents who traditionally wield power in the church) do not believe that a person can be saved only through Jesus Christ.[8] The orthodoxy of their children will be even less robust.

The drop-outs considered themselves religious, but felt that the mainline church offered them conjectures, not commitment; a social agenda of "peace and justice," but no spiritual power. The mainline church "lost the will or the ability to teach the Christian faith . . . in such a way as to command . . . allegiance,"[9] thereby also losing the battle with competing secular or non-Christian religious systems.

The study ends on a depressing note. "Perhaps some now unforeseen cultural shift will one day bring millions of baby boom dropouts back to the mainline churches. *But nothing we discovered suggests the likelihood of such a shift* [emphasis mine]." Is New Age liberal spirituality too big to be seen?[10]

Radical Skepticism

Liberals are the most radical critics of liberal modernism. Confidence in the power of human reason to solve human problems has evaporated in a century infamous for its bloody inhumanity. The collapse of secular humanism has forced a repeal of its four spiritual laws: biological evolutionism (found to have more holes than Swiss cheese and the ozone layer combined); existentialism (among whose fruits are Nazism and the Cambodian genocide of Pol Pot); Freudianism (which has produced more mental illness than it ever cured); and Marxism (a massively embarrassing social and economic failure that only survives, moribund, in China and Cuba).

Chafing under middle-class ethics and politics, radical scholars pushed modernity to its logical extreme. If truth is relative for the most essential questions of religious knowledge, as liberalism held, why is it not relative for all knowledge? This radical position is known as postmodern deconstructionism.

Explanations of reality, say the deconstructionists, have no connection with the way things really are, but only serve to justify the *status quo* of those in power. Truth is not true. It is social power. It is what the winners use to write history and structure society. French philosopher Michel Foucault sought to justify his homosexuality by showing that heterosexuality was but a social construct. Radical feminist thinkers have sought to undermine Western civilization, labeling it a scam used only to justify patriarchy.

Deconstruction means that those who control the organs of power also control what others do with their own organs. A blatant example of practical deconstructionism recently came across my desk: When Professor John Paul DeCecco of San Francisco State University was asked by a journalist whether anonymous, wordless sex between two males in the so-called "tearoom trade" was abnormal, he replied: (Yes) . . . when you're talking about social norms. . . . But who the h—— is bothering with that anymore?" DeCecco is editor of the *Journal of Homosexuality* and sits on the editorial board of *Paidika: The Journal of Paedophilia.*[11] Deconstruction of biblical ethics for the planet proceeds apace.

A New Day for Orthodoxy?

Thomas Oden had done it all. Member of the United World Federalist Association, (which promotes world government), he was an ardent protagonist of the ecumenical movement, the NAACP and pacifism. A theoretical Marxist, he supported the ACLU and liberalized abortion. His search for meaning took him into Transactional Analysis, Gestalt therapy, psychoanalysis, behaviorism, and T-Groups. Finally he dabbled in parapsychology, pyramids, tarot cards and astrology. At the end of this colorful activism, he denounced modernism's intoxication with the "new." Oden's frenzy ended when he spectacularly returned to Christian orthodoxy. His book, *After Modernity . . . What?* (1990) answers his own question. "By now many of us are experiencing a gnawing disenchantment with the enchantments of modernity."[12] Oden predicts that the liberal intellectual elite will return to orthodoxy, but Oden seems a notable exception rather than a groundhog announcing an orthodox Spring.

Conversion

The collapse of secular humanism is not necessarily good news for orthodox Christianity or society in general.[13] Like a quick-change artist, liberalism now appears cloaked in the mantle of pagan spiritu-

ality. The misunderstood doctrine of separation of church and state has
paralyzed Christianity, the religion most closely associated with
America's history and culture. The call for more religion in the public
square[14] may favor a state-supported religious syncretism rather than
a new day of Christian freedom.

Liberals find deconstructionist philosophy a useful tool for shat-
tering the Western Christian worldview, but the beast must not be
allowed to turn on its handlers. It can be used to support sexual liberation and to undermine Judeo-Christian values, or employed to
dislodge the classic forms of Bible interpretation. But no one can survive long in the same cage with radical skepticism. Brilliant ecofeminist
authoress, Charlene Spretnak says you *can* have it both ways:

> I agree with the deconstructive-postmodern project to stimulate aware-
> ness of processes by which conceptualizations are culturally con-
> structed [she is thinking especially of patriarchy] . . . but I do not
> agree with their leap to conclude that there is *nothing but* cultural con-
> struction in human experience.[15]

Deconstruction has done its negative work. Now the pagans will reconstruct!

A Madman's Polytheism:
Blueprint For a Liberated Future

Some readers remember the "Death of God" theology of the Sixties.
Twenty-five years after the Holocaust, certain radical scholars announced
that the evolved humanity of the twentieth century could do without
the God of the Bible. But as nature abhors a vacuum, mankind abhors
atheism. So some of these theologians moved forward to the past of
polytheism. Atheist "theologian" Friedrich Nietzsche (1844-1990) became a prophet of this new age of human freedom. Son of a Lutheran
pastor, Nietzsche believed that true human evolution would lead to the
creation of a "superman" who would throw off Christianity, the faith of
weaklings, and adopt a "moral" code of total freedom for "strong," autonomous individuals. Nietzsche despised Christian humility, meekness
and self-sacrifice, calling for the "transvaluation of values,"[16] that is, for
turning moral values on their head, making evil good and good evil.
The best form of theism was not *mono*theism but *poly*theism — a personal god for everybody, and a multiple choice pantheon for each state
of mind.[17] His influence on the later German notion of the pagan Aryan
"super race" is a matter of debate,[18] but his words ring with uncanny

programmatic foresight for our own time of pro-choice ethics and religious pluralism:

> For the individual to set up his *own* ideal and derive from it his laws, his pleasures and his rights. . . . it was in the marvelous art and capacity for creating Gods — in polytheism — that this impulse was permitted to discharge itself . . . . Monotheism . . . . the belief in a normal God, beside whom there are only false, spurious Gods . . . has perhaps been the greatest danger of mankind in the past.[19]

Though Nietzsche died demented in the arms of his doting sister,[20] one proponent of the death-of-God theology (now a major influence in religious higher education in America) said in 1974 of the above citation: "There is a bright, new future lurking in these lines, still waiting to be understood."[21] The future lay in the rebirth of polytheism, that is, the rebirth of the gods and goddesses.

The "bright, new future" would also come, according to one of the leaders in the modern study of religions, the Rumanian Mircea Eliade (1907-1986), from the contemporary meeting of East and West. Eliade believed that through this "the West will arrive at a deeper and broader knowledge of what it means to be human," and that this will bring about "transformations [of] human consciousness" to a new "global consciousness."[22]

A New Day for Liberalism: the Revival of Paganism

While orthodox theologians fought Kant, von Harnack and Bultmann on the cold German front of skeptical rationalism, the opposition cross-dressed into warm, spiritual, irrational mysticism. The future may belong to "marginals" such as Nietzsche, Mircea Eliade, Rudolf Otto, C. G. Jung and Joseph Campbell. The brush fire has jumped the interstate and orthodoxy faces the threat of *mystical pagan polytheism* on its own side of the theistic/atheistic divide.

The Goddess and Other Deities

The bumper sticker "Honk if you love Jesus" has been replaced in California by "The goddess is back: magic is afoot." In 1970, the Leadership Conference of Women Religious (nuns) of the Roman Catholic Church in America called for "autonomy and self-realization" rather than "corporate identity and self-sacrifice."[23] Who could have imagined autonomous nietzschean nuns?

Charlene Spretnak entitled her book: *States of Grace: The Recovery of Meaning in the Postmodern Age.* How can a feminist deconstructionist philosopher speak of "grace" and the "recovery of meaning?" Are we on the verge of religious revival? Spretnak claims to recover meaning in spite of an intellectual context that mercilessly pours contempt on such a claim. How? By a "paradigm shift," consisting of:

> a radical reorientation that . . . is rooted in ecological sanity . . . an ecofeminist orientation [that feeds on] . . . the long-lost earth-based spirituality . . . of Mother Earth and other manifestations of the Goddess . . . the Dharma [of] Buddh[ism], the renewal movement within Judaism, . . . Native American spirituality . . . New Age spirituality.[24]

For those raised on biblical orthodoxy, this is truly amazing grace. *Meaning* derives from a neo-pagan earth spirituality that finds God within — a lot of human effort and not much grace. In this new *spirituality* contemporary liberals recover meaning.[25] Spretnak takes as an example for the modern world the ancient Greek author, Heraclitus (6th-5th century B.C.). In "an anachronistic burst of primal organicism," Heraclitus reacted against the rationalists of his day, embraced the spirituality of monism and, paying "homage to the old ways" of earlier Greek "superstition," deposited a copy of his book, *On Nature*, in the temple of the goddess Artemis in Ephesus.[26] Heraclitus the rationalist, became Heraclitus the goddess worshiper. Old liberals had little time for spirituality. The new have converted by rediscovering "traditional" religion in a oneness with the All.[27] A witch I met in 1993 has a doctorate in jurisprudence. Grace is no longer a divine gift, but "organic" human potential. There is a crush at the door of the pagan temples of the goddess.

I listened attentively as a Hindu swami with long black hair and a long yellow robe, gave an hour-long, rambling lecture in an accent that made me savor the wonderful curries I had enjoyed in the Taj Mahal in Manchester, England's Indian quarter. A featured speaker at the *Parliament of the World's Religions* (Chicago, 1993), he sought to demonstrate "rationally" that the doctrines of Christianity were logically non-verifiable — that you could neither prove heaven, nor the existence of the transcendent Christian God who lives there. At the end of the lecture I asked him just what was verifiable in the religious domain, and with a typical Indian twinkle in his dark eyes he said, "The spiritual experience of the divine within." On this the world will be reconstructed.

Eastern monistic spirituality attacks the foundations of our Western culture and in particular, rational discourse. If the source of meaning lies within the divine self, choice and opinion are the highest values.

This is how the NEA teaches our children how to read history.[28] This is how we interpret texts.[29] Writing in the *New York Times* of January 28, 1994, Michiko Kakutani deplored the disappearance of reasoned exchange and the rise of subjectivity. "The old notions of 'truth' and 'knowledge' are in danger of being replaced by the new ones of 'opinion,' 'perception,' and 'credibility.'" Having absorbed deconstructionist thinking without realizing it, many in our modern society reject the Judeo-Christian world and life view, objective truth and revelation. Stanley Fish of Duke University and a leader of deconstructionism believes that "since all principles are preferences, they are nothing but masks for the will to power."[30]

If truth, both intellectual and moral, is merely raw power to dominate and control, then intellectual exchange is not appropriate. Ironically, as truth is laid aside in favor of personal experience, insult, accusation, and hierarchically-imposed political correctness flourish. The two-thousand year Christian tradition that offered our country a foundation of genuine exchange within the structure of mutual submission to a Creator, is now dismissed as a monotheistic, patriarchal will to power. Its adherents are mocked as extremists, the lunatic fringe endangering the planet. In this atmosphere of tolerance which avoids true intellectual exchange and rejects objective truth as extremism, the spirit of inclusivistic monistic paganism thrives like a new baby in a warm incubator. The new baby is growing by the minute.

Life-line for the Mainline

Liberalism will live again, not just because orthodoxy does not seem to be posing a particular threat but because a "spiritual" revival is taking place in the liberal ranks. Hope is on the way. Mainline biblical scholars are finding ancient heretical Gnostic texts theologically re-invigorating. Contemporary skeptics, church drop-outs, and confused church members are getting religion from a similar source, namely New Age spirituality.[31] Presbyterian Church (USA) minister, Don Shriver, having given over the presidency of Union Seminary to a Unitarian, might find this infusion of new spiritual blood appropriate. In a public forum on "The Church: From Yesterday to Tomorrow" held at the Interchurch Center in New York in 1993, Shriver suggested that one way to keep the "church of tomorrow alive" would be to "develop partner relationships" with Eastern religions.[32] If this is Presbyterianism, John Calvin was a buddhist!

The "unforeseen cultural shift" is actually shaking the church's foundations. Already in 1980, Carl A. Raschke, professor of Religious Studies at the University of Denver, saw tell-tale cracks. In his prophetic book, *The Interruption of Eternity: Modern Gnosticism and the Origins of the New Religious Consciousness*, he argued that Westerners are becoming Gnostics. He singles out mainline churches that are regaining spirituality through the revival of Gnosticism without returning to Christian orthodoxy.[33] That's a deal. Old-time *religion* without old-time *theology and old-time morals.*

The "New Age" Goes to Church

Lynn Willeford, contributing editor of the *New Age Journal*, went back. She was raised in a "dignified Congregational church on the town green . . . where no one seemed to connect . . . (where) we spoke up to God and the minister spoke down to us . . . but was careful never to ask too much of us."[34] In a long article in the *New Age Journal*, Willeford recounts how she has gone back to church after thirty years, and rediscovered "Christianity" in a "freedom and justice" United Methodist church. "At times," she says, "it feels like my chest has been filled with a golden light." Never once is Jesus Christ as Savior mentioned as the source of her new-found spirituality. The following comment shows how far her experience strays from orthodox Christianity:

> A friend who follows some Eastern practices says I'm illuminating my heart chakra. I think I'm tapping into the Source, but whatever the name, I'm glad to be back.

Meanwhile, the *New Age Journal* no less also plans to be back — in the "Christian" mainstream, adding a new-look form of Christianity to its potpourri of recommended spiritual techniques. A recent cover portrays a naked woman whose lower body is superimposed on that of a wolf. The title reads: "The Wild Woman." How can such a magazine also endorse Christianity?[35] Either the editors were converted, or their version of Christianity is not the one most people know.

New Age Spirituality Revives Moribund Calvinism

Some time ago a Dutch couple spent the night in our home. On tour with a Christian choir from Holland, they lustily sang the old hymns with contagious conviction. Over hot chocolate, after the concert, Rudi told us his story. Members of the liberal Dutch Reformed

Church, he and his wife had been burned by social gospel and radical causes. Their children had long since left the faith, something they too might have done with a little more courage. But their faith had recently revived. Their local Reformed church introduced them to a group studying *A Course in Miracles*, an extremely popular New Age counterfeit of Christianity. Rudi beamed as he spoke. "Since studying the *Course*," he exuded, "I have been walking on air."

The air is getting thicker, and anecdotes such as these suggest a significant trend in the mainline.[36] Thanks to New Age infiltration, social gospel liberalism is acquiring a dimension it has long lacked — *spirituality*. Famished baby boomers left the Church in search of the potent spirituality offered by drugs and Eastern religions. Such New Age spirituality is now christianized, "mainlined."

New Wine For Old Wine Skins: A Message of Hope From Sociologists, Seers and Spirit Guides

Confirmed by the following disparate sources, the above anecdotes should be taken with utmost seriousness:

♦ **The Sociologist:**
W. C. Roof, Professor of Sociology at the University of California, Santa Barbara, moves the discussion beyond anecdotes and hunches. His studies unveil a "new spirituality," wedded to a new social conscience, which transforms and reshapes those progressive churches "open to this new spiritual vision." He predicts the formation of networks, the *rediscovery* of community. Roof's final word describes the "innermost being" of the flower-power people as fundamentally religious. "Religion," he argues, "was never the problem, only social forms of religion that stifle the human spirit."[37] Apparently, the particularly stifling form was orthodox Christian faith (theism), whose disappearance would presumably not bother Roof, protestant though he may be.

♦ **The Seer:**
The analysis of the sociologist recalls the musings of Marilyn Ferguson, New Age popularizer of Helen Shucman's *A Course in Miracles*. Certain that she is a true Christian, she writes:

My definition of Christianity has expanded over the years. After I became involved in meditation, for example, I experienced *the vision of*

Christ more vividly than I ever had through sermons and dogma. You would be surprised, I think, to know how much of the New Age Movement centers on Christ Consciousness. Many Christian churches are seeing that direct spiritual experience offers a revitalization for modern Christianity.[38]

Her description of what is happening in "many Christian churches" is not frivolous; spirits are at work.

♦ **The Spirit Guide:**

Ken Carey, the author of *Starseed: The Third Millennium: Living in the Posthistoric World* (1991), makes a similar statement.[39] Actually, "author" is the wrong word. As noted above, Ken Carey is but a "channel" for a "spirit being in the eternal fields of light," who, along with other "entities," dictated messages concerning humanity's origins and future state. As the spirit-being possessed him, Carey felt himself "experiencing a consciousness radically different from anything (he) had ever encountered before," as if something enormous was looking through his eyes. The spirit beings reveal that Satan is not evil, that truth "does not lend itself to absolutes . . . . [except, of course, this absolute statement they/he are making about truth!] (for) the world has seen enough dogmatism,"[40] and that the essence of the Fall is not sin but self-doubt concerning one's divinity.[41] What the spirit entities reveal about religion is most instructive, fitting perfectly with the contemporary theological agenda. The forthcoming planetary transformation will include various churches, great and small, and so the spirits exhort:

> Associate only with congregations whose atmosphere encourages love, whose atmosphere helps to dissolve the sense of separation among people, and between people and their God, congregations whose members welcome all without judgment, recognizing the eternal spirit of each one . . .

A "new baptism . . . clarifies human understanding in the living waters of truth." To receive it "you must release all that you know and all that you believe (including) the illusions of your history-bound cognitive [that is, rational] systems."[42]

Appropriate churches are those that have rejected biblical ethics, Scriptural demands for holiness, and the Christian doctrine of redemption in a space/time incarnation of the eternal Son. This is abundantly clear in the spirits' polemic against "many denominations . . . entirely concept-oriented, dogmatic institutions." They warn true, spiritual believers to avoid locking themselves into a "structure of their understanding," and "begin trusting in the truth I have created in you, the truth that you yourself are." Like the call of modern liberal theologians to experience the breadth of theological truth in all religions, the spirit guides encourage believers to "enjoy the rich diversity of truth's multiple expressions."[43]

This religion is made for Aquarian baby-boomers, heavily into self-discovery and self-expression. When sociologists, seers, and spirit guides agree, we can suspect that something of great import for society is afoot. When Presbyterians are affected, you *know* something is afoot.

New Age Spirituality:
An Up-Beat Assessment For Presbyterians

Presbyterians come from the dour tradition of no-nonsense Scottish piety and English Cromwellian politics. But even Presbyterians are getting "the spirit." In 1993 Duncan Ferguson, Director of the Committee on Higher Education of the Presbyterian Church (U.S.A.), edited a book, *New Age Spirituality: An Assessment*.[44] Meant to guide mainline Presbyterians in evaluating this religious phenomenon, the book contains no significant theological evaluation from a traditional Presbyterian position.[45] It is mainly an up-beat endorsement of New Age belief and practice. One contributor is David Spangler, a major figure in New Age circles, who shocked many Christians by his description of the coming of Christ as "Luciferic initiation."[46] In his contribution, he endorses the New Age redefinition of God. Moderate contributors depict the New Age as an opportunity for Christian renewal.[47]

Duncan Ferguson, the Presbyterian editor, gives the final chapter of exhortation to Matthew Fox. This is asking a fox to give a lecture to chickens on the great spiritual values of life outside the chicken coop! Matthew Fox, recently excommunicated from his Dominican order (surprising enough in our age of tolerance) collaborates with Miriam Starhawk, feminist pagan witch; Luisah Teish, Yoruba voodoo priestess; and Senator Tom Hayden, Sixties violent revolutionary, in his Institute in Culture and Creation Spirituality at Holy Names College, Oakland, California. There he teaches a paganized, pantheistic, syncretistic Christianity at the opposite extreme from all Presbyterian standards and confessions. Needless to say, Fox, though coyly and politically distancing himself from certain frivolous expressions of New Age exotica,[48] calls upon mainline believers to see the New Age spirituality as "an important movement along the way of the in-depth transformation . . . (of) our species . . . (a part of) the work of the Spirit calling us to a New Pentecost."[49]

Though presented in pious, semi-Christian language, the spirituality of Fox's transformed species — pan-sexual promiscuity allied with the empowerment of animistic nature rites — is all that the Bible denounces as paganism. This is the new spiritual fare now offered to Presbyterians, who certainly would not want to be caught eating the toxic food of yesterday's orthodoxy.

Treating the Mortal Sickness of Orthodox Christianity

Just as the demented Nietzsche's "Übermensch" (superman) promoted the abolition of Christianity and its moral values, Matthew Fox now dismisses orthodox Christianity as mental illness. Though more subtle than Nietzsche, Fox is just as radical. Nietzsche knew only one form of Christianity — orthodoxy. Fox identifies two. One, "pessimistic, very male and dualistic," emphasizes original sin. The other, which is "holistic and cosmological and includes women's wisdom," emphasizes original blessing and is creation-affirming, full of hope. For the pessimistic kind, Fox does not hesitate to use the "f" word — "fundamentalism."[50] From this Christianity, which is an enemy to life on this planet, one needs to be "healed."[51] The secular press has already pegged orthodox Christians as bigots living on the lunatic fringe. But from a so-called Christian theologian, we learn that biblical Christianity is a mortal disease! The ecological disasters, competitive economics and academics, and repressive sexual norms of "heteropatriarchy"[52] are now presented as the rotting fruit of jaded Christian Fundamentalism. Christianity, argues Fox, will have to change radically or, via the new theories of interpretation, say the very opposite of what it clearly affirms.[53] According to Fox, if there is no change, Christianity will not survive in the third millennium. A new religious paradigm is needed to solve the planet's problems and create a new age of human liberation. Once again the future of human progress comes to the rescue.[54]

New Age spirituality and eschatology dazzle the liberal mind: a global utopia of liberated human beings in a planetary community, pulsating to the rhythms of the Earth — a strong drug for those hooked on future-shock. This seduction shimmers in Smart and Konstantine, who in 1991 reaffirm liberalism's commitment to theological novelty. In their book, Christian Systematic Theology in a World-Context, the authors enthuse: "The notion of the Divine as somehow lying in the future expresses a vital theme in Jewish and Christian thought and feeling. It is as if the future attracts us forward, drawing us on by its holy magnetism."[55] This is the essence of the recent discovery of religious meaning. The brilliant physicist, Stephen Hawking, is also impelled by a religious vision. Seeking to find out why we and the universe exist, he says: "If we found the answer to that, it would be the ultimate triumph of the human reason — for then we would know the mind of God."[56]

In the days to come the enemy of true faith will no longer be the unbelieving skepticism of rationalistic liberalism and atheistic materialism. It is with the dazzling promises of utopian liberalism and its new-look spirituality that the Church will contend, and which we now must analyze in more detail. In the next chapter we ask: "Where is revived liberalism going?"

CHAPTER 4

CHRISTIAN LIBERALISM:
AFTER CONVERSION, MISSION

Postchristian (1975 ed.) adj.: occurring after definitive departure from
christianity in all its religious and secular forms and simultaneously with entry
into New Time/Space
- Mary Daly[1]

The New Liberalism:
Pagan Christianity For the Third Millennium

Cracks in Western Civilization

America has never been more divided. Societal shifts suggest
that the culture is imploding. Even during the Civil War, Confeder-
ate and Unionist generals and foot-soldiers participated in the same
prayer and Bible study groups. They differed in regional loyalties or on
the place of slavery, but not about worldview. Even those who never
read the Bible probably held a begrudging jealousy for those who did.
"Culture Wars"[2] may be an apt description of their time, but it does not
do justice to ours. Today's conflicts are closer to *religious warfare — a
war of two worlds.*[3] Imagine solving social problems with a Bible study
in a culture where the Bible has been banned from public recognition
and discourse.

New Agers speak of the "Christian interlude."[4] For them, Western
civilization dominated by Christian values will be superseded in the
third millennium by the neo-pagan religious world of the Age of

Aquarius.[5] The recent dechristianization of the West lends credence to this reading of history. New Age spirituality is not a fading fad from the freaky "left coast." It is the exotic tip of a religious iceberg — the syncretistic religion of the new liberalism — whose chilling progress may remodel life on this planet. Music, medicine, business, politics, sexuality, ecology and psychology; all areas of existence are affected by this utopian ideology.

Pink Ice Cream

This new ideology is not confined to the ivory tower or the church pew. The medical corps of the U.S. military promotes "spiritual" healing techniques with little opposition, while Fortune 500 companies employ New Age teachers to motivate their sales personnel. Recently I received a flyer proposing a new telephone company, Working Assets, that offers a pint of Ben and Jerry's ice cream, competitive rates, and a network of liberal activists. The service includes "Action Alerts" on liberal social issues, and pre-written "Citizen Letters" to be sent to political and corporate leaders. The deal includes free telephone calls to politicians every Monday. On the Board are Pamela J. Maraldo of Planned Parenthood, Marian Wright Edelman (friend of Hillary Clinton) of Children's Defense Fund, David Brower of Earth Island Institute, Ben Cohen of Ben and Jerry's Homemade,[6] Tim Smith of the Interfaith Center for Corporate Responsibility and Peri Jude Radecic, executive director of the National Gay and Lesbian Task Force. What the attractive brochure does not say is that Radecic is both executive director of the National Gay and Lesbian Task Force (NGLTF) and an advocate and practitioner of violent "sadomasochistic" (S/M) "leather-fetish" homosexual sex[7] — (the reader might wonder what the defense of children and violent lesbian sex have in common). This notwithstanding, the radical agenda and orientation of Working Assets gets the endorsement of Ralph Nader and Gloria Steinem.

Since 1993, the ideology behind such changes continues its political and social consolidation and normalization as numerous radicals take key administrative and judicial positions[8] in the most powerful country in the world. As the above example shows, the liberal networking has diversified beyond academia and public service to infiltrate not only government, but the corridors of corporate and commercial power.[9] The cutesy claim — "The Phone Bill That Saves You Money While It Helps You Change The World" — should be taken with utmost seriousness. The "Religious Left" means business when it proposes business with meaning.[10]

This "New Age" spirituality is not a cult. Cults remain marginal. World and life views transform everything. Christian colleges and seminaries tend to discuss the New Age as the last chapter in a course on "the cults." But in proper perspective, the New Age is not a cult. Nor is it a heresy, which stresses one aspect of the truth to the exclusion of all others. New Age liberalism is *apostasy*. "Apo-stasis" means literally "a standing away from." The new liberalism stands away from biblical Christianity and the Judeo-Christian worldview, perhaps even more than the old liberalism. This apostasy is not a modification of Christianity but its obliteration. The hazy specter of "New Age" liberalism takes form before our eyes, recognizable as the very antithesis of biblical Christianity. The sleepy church must awake and defend itself. Its enemy is busy defining it out of existence.

Aquarian Ecclesiology: A Church of Religious Syncretism

> Although the paths to the summit may differ, from the top of the mountain one sees the same moon.[11]

This Japanese proverb neatly express the agenda of much of contemporary theological liberalism. Classical liberalism denied the truth claims of Christian orthodoxy. Today's liberalism simply relativizes Christianity as one religious option among many so that it can participate in the coming unification of the planet and of religion, advancing mankind along its evolutionary path.

According to the "Christian" theologian Knitter, Professor of Theology at Xavier University, Cincinnati, this stage of religious evolution is upon us.

> The world's religions are evolving out of the *microphase* of religious history in which the various traditions grew and consolidated in relative isolation from each other. The direction today is towards a *macrophase* in which each religion will be able to grow and understand itself only through interrelating with other religions.[12]

"Christianity" forges ahead, leading the world into the Third Millennium, moving from "the Age of Monologue," through the Age of Dialogue," which is its essence, into the Age of "Interrelation" and syncretistic assimilation. According to Knitter, only open-ended "dialogical" Christianity will survive, and in so doing will determine the shape of all the world's religions.[13]

The recent book, *Christian Systematic Theology In a World Context* by Ninian Smart and Steven Konstantine, should be read against this background. In the section entitled "Towards a World Theology," their statement of purpose is a jewel of syncretistic convergence: [14]

> our presentation of a *darsana* is more than the presentation of an intellectual construction. It is the putting forward of a *Tao*, a form of *bhakti* and *jnana* or "knowledge," a life clothed in sacramental *li*, a stimulus to *dhyana* and *karuna*, and invitation to eschew *shirk*, and to be called by the power of the *avatara*.[15]

This might be Aquarian liberalism. It is not what the dust-jacket produced by the Lutheran publisher, Fortress Press, would have us believe, namely, a "fresh understanding of Christianity."

Syncretistic Fellowship in Chicago

Knitter was in Chicago for the Parliament of the World's Religions — along with 6000 delegates, 250 religious leaders and 120 religions and sects — helping to promote unity through spiritual communion. It was not a Parliament. Parliaments are representative bodies that debate, propose competing and contradictory ideas, and vote. Not here. It was not representative, for historic Christianity was absent. The Chicago event was a religious festival, a consciousness-raising happening of shared pagan spirituality. Delegates were obliged to *practice* unity — in syncretistic "interfaith celebrations" that the apostle Paul would doubtless have called "fellowship with demons." Singing "Leaning on the Everlasting Arms," I suddenly stopped. The "everlasting arms of Jesus," had been unceremoniously amputated. The crowd now sang the unforgettable lines, "O, what fellowship, O, what joy divine, I can feel the friendship all around . . . " Talking about the Chicago weather, or the hard chairs in the cavernous hall, people around me were friendly, but their common bond was syncretistic convergence. Buddhist monks chanted, the high-priestess to Venus gave a ponderous pagan blessing. Delegates danced round the hall to the beat of drums led by an American Indian shaman. Chicago demonstrated that liberal Christians, Hindus, Buddhists, worshipers of Isis and witches of the Covenant of the Goddess *do* have comparable earth-based spiritual experiences. Human friendship had become the fellowship of humanistic, pagan spirituality.

Global Religious Vision

The syncretism evident in Chicago is reflected in the texts of the new liberal vision. It is part of the theory. Huston Smith, an expert on world religions, (whose influence on the new Jesus of the *Jesus Seminar* will be examined in chapter 6), in his latest book, *Forgotten Truth* (1994) shows "how the great religious traditions of the world converge . . . . One finds remarkable unity underlying the surface differences . . . . It is as if an invisible geometry has everywhere been working to shape them into a single truth."[16]   This is a significant statement by a syncretist, for it supports the Bible's affirmation that there are finally but two religious possibilities: pagan idols or the living God. Tertullian (160-225) might have been in Chicago, rather than referring to the exclusionary "ecumenical" spirit of Gnosticism. How modern his comment now sounds:

> They maintain (ecclesiastical) harmony with all, making no distinction. As a matter of fact, it (harmony) exists among them although they hold different doctrines as long as they wage common warfare against one thing, the truth (orthodoxy).[17]

Following this logic, the "creation theologian" Matthew Fox, argues that the renewal of the church must include the elimination of orthodoxy and the incorporation of the mystical practices of all the major religions, notably the spirit worship and initiatory rituals of Native American religion — hey, what could be more American?[18]   He calls not merely for dialogue, but for "deep ecumenism," spiritual/mystical union.[19]   This includes sweat lodges, nocturnal dances, moon rituals, pow-wow dances, the Sun dance, pipe ceremonies, and vision quests of native American religion. According to Fox, "Christians" should therefore seek "mystical solidarity" with all the world's religions.[20] Little wonder Fox's new-look "Christian" theology gets a thumbs-up sign from a pagan witch. Caitlín Matthews, priestess of the Fellowship of Isis, the Egyptian goddess of witchcraft, finds in Fox's "creation spirituality" a perfectly valid expression of her own pagan practice.[21]

Theologian Katherine Zappone accepts all kinds of empowering experiences, from liberation theology to witchcraft. "In journeying with other feminists," (who were highly conspicuous at the syncretistic Parliament of the World's Religions), she observes, "I have found that the sacred stories of goddess religions affect my imagination in ways the story of Jesus never will."[22] More power to Zappone. Too bad for Jesus!

New Age Theology

Radical theologians and bureaucrats of the World Council of Churches no longer monopolize syncretistic spirituality. The "New Age in Christian Theology" is now "an emerging consensus . . . among an increasing number of theologians within every major branch of the Christian church."[23] One of the leading mainline Protestant theologians, Jürgen Moltmann, and his wife, Elizabeth Moltmann-Wendel, in two recent articles in the Princeton Theological Seminary journal, *Theology Today*, spell out their vision for Christianity. For Elizabeth Moltmann, we are "on the open road" to a post-patriarchal, just society of "a new sexuality and an erotic existence."[24] For Jürgen Moltmann, stolid German Lutheran liberal, dizzied by the fanciful flights of his liberated wife, the question is whether we, as Christians, are prepared for "an interreligious community."[25] He explains: "Out of our different religions, a 'religion of the earth' will emerge that will teach us the spirituality of the earth." According to Moltmann, This interreligious earth religion "will save the earth."[26] As a Christian theologian, he has forgotten to ask whether, in the process, mankind would lose its own soul.

The Princeton Seminary "think-tank" agrees with Moltmann's definition of salvation. Scholars there are studying "the connection of the issues of today with faith and to discern afresh the full scope of God's work in the world."[27] Translation: "faith" is the faith of all religions, not the Christian faith; the "scope of God's work" is the syncretistic movement in the world's religions.

It is difficult to think of "ecclesiology" in this broad sense. The Christian faith has always identified Christ's church as a distinct body of believers — believers in a specific, revealed truth, personified by Jesus Christ, who lived and died in history to put an end to sin. Naturally, monistic ecclesiology refuses such restraints. This soft "Christian" syncretism ties its future to similar movements in the world's religions as well as to political and social movements such as the Earth Summit,[28] and to agencies within the United Nations. Planetary polytheism controls the imagination of those committed to a peaceful, global community. In the short term, the temptation is irresistible, its success virtually assured.

These "mainline" radicals are not effete, elitist intellectuals or funky West Coast religionists on the margins of society. They are serious thinkers with powerful backers. They are dreaming but also planning for a new future. If their fantasies become the future, Christians will find themselves in a waking nightmare.

Aquarian Eschatology:
A Planetary Revolution

The eschatology of New Age liberalism is up-beat. Matthew Fox announces the "Coming of the Cosmic Christ." But do not be taken in. This is not *Jesus* Christ.[29] This is the spiritual principle, the "over-soul" uniting all religions. The subtitle is revealing: "The Healing of Mother Earth and the Birth of a Global Renaissance." In other words, ecology leads us to this new religion of union with all creatures.

The idea of the rebirth of humanity in a new age of utopian progress appears in many places. A liberal, Presbyterian theologian seeks to answer the challenge of this historic moment with a book *Towards a New Age in Christian Theology*.[30] What this "New Age" means is later explained. The redemptive work of Jesus includes reincarnation![31] This is certainly a new age for Presbyterians. So, too, for the Methodists. A United Methodist theologian at Emory University in Atlanta offers a "bold hypothesis" — that we are experiencing a "paradigm shift in cultural consciousness" which will solve the problems in our present living patterns.[32]

Sister Madonna Kolbenschlag, a Roman Catholic nun and popular speaker at "Christian" feminist conferences describes "an evolutionary process that is moving humanity, and the 'God-who-is-coming-to-be,' toward transformation in a 'New Faith.'" In the "Third Age of the Spirit" the church will wither under the direct illumination of "a creative Spiritual Presence that comes from within . . . as well as from beyond."[33] Says another radical thinker: "A new God is being born in our hearts, to teach us to level the heavens and exalt the earth and create a new world."[34] At the same time, the "old" God, Creator of heaven and earth, withers under this blistering attack from pagan eschatology, and is cast away like a used paper napkin.

The Future According to the New Age Gurus

This new-look "Christian" eschatology is closer to secular New Age utopianism than to a Scriptural view of the future. Theological liberals hastily disavow any connection with Shirley MacLaine or other get-rich-quick gurus. But ideological parallels are so close that the difference is often only one of style and vocabulary. The following examples of how hard-core New Agers see the future should suffice.

Marilyn Ferguson, famous New Age authoress of the best-selling *The Aquarian Conspiracy*, declaring that the mainstream had gone New Age, points to the popularity of notions such as spaceship Earth, Gaia, planetary tribe, partnership, community and holism. These widely diffused concepts, she claims, "have potential to shape a planetary civilization."[35]

Chris Griscom, one-time guru of Shirley MacLaine, in prose the literary equivalent of wispy New Age music, describes the coming religious and spiritual transformation with bewildering optimism. She exhorts her followers:

> Let us attune our frequencies . . . to mimic the pulsating formulas of ecstasy. This frequency, with its unlimited divine potential, can create an evolutionary mutation of our physical, emotional, and mental bodies, so that we become ecstatic light bodies of consciousness.[36]

New hope in the power of human spiritual evolution drives many into planet-wide projects. Go with the flow of history, says a New Age publication:

> Functioning in a context of love, trust and safety, small teams of people around the world join with one another for the betterment of all. Eventually, a sufficient, unified field is built, which "jumps" the entire system to a new level of consciousness. . . . When we have co-created heaven on earth, we will live in the moment, listen with our hearts, and respect and enjoy the diversity of all cultures.[37]

The expectation of a human creation of heaven on earth unites theological liberals and New Agers. In predicting the future of warfare, Ben Bova, a writer in *Omni* magazine, believes that after the bloodiest century in history [the twentieth], "the peoples of the world are slowly but steadily making their way to that new era [in which] . . . 'nation shall not lift up sword against nation, neither shall they learn war any more.'"[38] While understanding the deep desire for cosmic peace that is found in the human heart, one must not fail to see the hubris of such a utopian program. The Bible's vision is very different. Just as flesh and blood did not create the original heavens and the earth, so flesh and blood cannot inherit the kingdom of God and create the new heavens and the new earth. Both creations are God's work.

Just before he died in 1987, the mystical philosopher Joseph Campbell was asked by television commentator Bill Moyers if he still believed in what he had earlier written, that "we are at this moment participating in one of the very greatest leaps of the human spirit to a knowledge not only of outside nature but also of our own deep inward mystery." His answer was: "The greatest ever."[39] Campbell's response is not the fruit of scholarly analysis by a respected professor and serious public television commentator. It is religious prophecy.

The question is: who inspired prophet Campbell, and will his prophecy be false? Such prophecy seems more fitting coming from the mouth of off-the-wall New Age channelers. Take Lazaris, whose weekend seminars cost three hundred dollars per person. Lazaris reveals that in the nineties we will witness the end of history — in the sense that human beings will no longer refer to the traditions and precedents of the past. Rather, man's dreams and fantasies concerning the future will determine his present.

This is the American dream gone bananas. The last Western frontier becomes the imagination, and there are enough mainstream, wild-eyed optimists ready to believe it, that the idea becomes dangerous. If the future belongs to fantasy, then perhaps Hitler's fantasy of a thousand-year *Reich* was not a bad idea after all. However, "the end of history" notwithstanding, if you stand on the roof and declare yourself a bird, when they scrape you off the side-walk, they will *not* take you to a vet!

New Ager John White in the introduction to the 1979 International Cooperation Council Directory said:

> There is an evolutionary advance taking place in the world today as a new and higher form of humanity takes control of the planet . . . *homo noeticus* [the new rational/spiritual human being][40] is the name I give to the emerging form of humanity.[41]

Judging by the success (!) of *homo novo* (the new man) of the Aryan super race or of Leninist Marxism, why should *homo noeticus* fare any better? Such skepticism underestimates the mythical mechanism of evolution. Mechanistic-biological evolution, though still perpetrated on thousands of unsuspecting visitors to our museums, has lost scientific ground. But mythico-spiritual evolution offers vitality to the dried remains of evolutionary science. "We are now experiencing that exciting moment when our new meaning, our new story is taking shape," declare the mystical monistic scientists busily rewriting the story. They call for "a new mystique" that brings science and religion together in an understanding of the earth as a unified whole. The cosmos, they argue, was not created in the past by a God outside of creation, but is a self-sustaining organism, ever recreating itself to new levels of wholeness and integration.[42] Religion like this can overcome even the stony hearts of erstwhile Marxist Soviet atheists. The final, spiritual evolution of mankind will depend on a renewal and unification of the world's religious institutions.

The Future of the Global, Syncretistic "Church"

The gurus bring the church into the picture. Already in 1981 channeler John Randolf Price predicted the arrival of a new spirituality.

> The Great Awakening is taking place. In the cities and towns across America, hardly a week goes by without a symposium, seminar or workshop on spiritual healing, extrasensory perception . . . new age living, the power within, creative imagination, the dynamics of positive thinking, mind control, awareness training, higher sense perception, the art of meditation, new dimensions of consciousness, holistic medicine, yoga. . . . This is not by chance. According to one Advanced Soul, "Through the silent hidden work of the Masters, men and women throughout the world are beginning to intuitively understand the Truth. There is a vibration, call it the Master Vibration, that is flowing through the consciousness of mankind, turning each individual toward the Light within, and it is only a matter of time before the Dawning."[43]

In her highly influential book written earlier this century, *Discipleship in the New Age,* Alice Bailey, considered one of the leading New Age 'foremothers,' wrote about the start of an experimental effort by the 'Hierarchy' [the Ascended Masters of the spirit world] to mobilize 'Centers of Light.' To her students, she wrote:

> If it is successful and if the spiritual momentum set up by all of you is adequate to the effort made, and if you can carry on with persistence . . . it may be possible to bring the experimental stage to an end; the Hierarchy can then recognize (as effectively established upon earth) certain *focal points of energy which can constitute magnetic centers or rallying points for the new religion,* the new medicine, the new psychology and education and the new politics [emphasis added].[44]

Bear in mind that these words were first published around the end of the Second World War!

The spirit entity speaking through the medium Ken Carey had no trouble getting a contract with Harper Collins. The reading public now knows the details of the immediate future:

> As you reorient toward the new way of being in the world, you will be drawn to centers where the vibrational atmosphere is more conducive to a healthy state of function. These centers will represent the focal points around which the organs of Planetary Being will form. They will be, in a sense, islands of the future in a sea of the past. Within their vibrational field, the New Age will blossom and spread organically to cover the Earth. These [centers] will be the first beachheads secured by the approaching forces, the points of entry through which

the healing energies of transformation will be channeled. All of these centers will work together to prepare the human species for its collective awakening. . . . Many such places exist at this time. Many more will arise during the remaining decades of this transitional period. By the time the next generation reaches maturity [around the year 2000], there will be a widespread network of these islands."[45]

Stupefying technological advances have produced a small, interconnected planet. Our generation is the first to see live moving pictures in full color of planet earth. Jim Irwin, one of the first astronauts to walk on the moon, describes the perspective he had, seeing earth from space:

From the moon, the earth looked just like a marble, the most beautiful marble you can imagine. The earth is uncommonly lovely. . . . . I know that others will not have the opportunity to visit the moon . . . I went for everybody. . . . It was a human effort, and all human beings can feel proud that another human being made a trip to the moon and came back to earth.[46]

Global Perspective

With that image engraved on our subconscious, it has become obvious that our problems — the relatedness of the world's economies, nuclear proliferation and environmental disasters that respect no boundaries — demand global solutions. With such a new "planetized" awareness, conditions have never been more favorable for an ideology (monism) that affirms the interrelatedness of all things. The planetary circle fits the mystical, monistic circle like a hand in a glove.

But watch out for gloved hands that control planets. Our planet may be too small for both monists and theists. Because of our unique place in the history of the planet, leaders in politics, business, academics, communications, and the liberal hierarchies in many churches may find irresistible the temptation of this totalizing monistic ideology. We recall the words of Marilyn Ferguson: "As consciousness changes, the world changes." If our world has changed radically in the last generation, it is not merely because Hollywood has pumped its agenda into every living room in the land. Hollywood itself is a product of the new consciousness that dominates our culture. The "Religious Left" of revived liberalism has its hands on many of the levers of social control and its eyes on the world.

We see this happening, but can we stop it? Many are caught up in the movement, intrigued by one aspect of the agenda, but lack the perspective of spiritual astronauts. Will we see the "full earth," uncommonly lovely in the hand of its Creator? Or will we see a "new earth," blackened into the oblivion of monistic space? Can we step far enough out of our culture to see the coherence of these various social and religious movements, and so to step back in with some answers to the question, "Where are we going?" We might have to step back as far as the early centuries of the church, but the insights gained are well worth the trip.

CHAPTER 5

THE DEEP ROOTS OF
THE NEW SPIRITUALITY

Some years ago while trekking the wilds of the Soul Journey Jungle, certain explorers stumbled upon the high-flying double-minded Gnostic. Though they considered their discovery to be the dawn of a New Age, research soon revealed that this was merely an ape of ancient origin.
  - *Wildlife in the Kingdom Come*[1]

Liberalism: Carrier of the Pagan Virus
into the Body of the Church

Why should orthodox Christians be concerned about "Christian" liberalism? Has such concern always and only been a dry debate between theologians, while true religion gets on with converting the world?

Well, liberalism has "got religion." Gone is the skeptical liberal reinterpretation of the Gospel in terms of social involvement or Marxist theory. New liberalism has discovered a *spirituality* that will save the planet and fulfill the goals of an aspiring humanity. The liberal vision of an inclusive egalitarian culture of the future — "America as it was meant to be!" — conceives of a new world where the distinctions between the sexes, between right and wrong, between true and false are blurred, where Satan is but the creation of wild-eyed fundamentalists, where tolerance for all — except orthodox Christianity — is the highest good. This is not dry theory. The new liberals teach our children in schools and universities, influence the media by claiming to speak for the Church and for the best interests of the planet, and take positions of political leadership in our *very religious* country. And now they have spiritual power to back them up.

Theological liberalism, commendable for its attempt to express the faith in language that contemporaries understand, ultimately fails because it abandons the essence of that faith, and in so doing introduces the deadly virus of paganism. Throughout history liberalism has rejected orthodoxy without daring to leave the familiar warmth of mother Church. Cut off from the life-blood of Christian belief, liberals construct an intellectual version of Christianity that bears little resemblance to the original. Such a faith, adopted by the average Christian in the pew, produces withered fruit. Just as soul-less Marxism created both material and spiritual famine among the Russian people, so liberalism has failed to feed Christians. Human beings, including theological liberals, need spiritual reality. Today's liberals find their spirituality not in orthodoxy but in revived paganism. But "there is nothing new under the sun." Modern liberals only imitate their long-lost cousins, the Gnostics. To gain understanding of the present religious chaos, we need the perspective of history.

Christian Liberalism and Ancient Gnosticism: Long-Lost Cousins

Just when radical scholars are finding in the Gnostic texts a valid expression of original Christianity, our world is awash in "new age" spirituality. The liberal rehabilitation of these texts supports the thesis that the "new spirituality" adopted by "Christian" liberalism is Gnostic heresy in new dress. In some profound sense, Gnosticism was the earliest expression of "Christian" liberalism, though liberals avoid such parallels.[2] Discovery of the Gnostic texts in 1945 produced a dramatic interest in Gnosticism, which led in turn to a recognition of the parallels between Gnosticism and modern times.[3] "Despite the vast cultural differences between North American Protestantism and ancient Gnosticism," says Philip Lee, "the parallels between the two . . . can no longer be ignored."[4]

A Short Sketch of Gnosticism

Christians should read church history, at least the history of Gnosticism, for it has a thoroughly modern message. Just as our culture offers a choice of secular or Christian liberalism, so the second century allowed both secular and Christian Gnosticism. A long and complex development of the political, social and religious mega-trends of the pre-Christian Mediterranean world molded ancient Gnosticism. This pagan spirituality began when East met West in the fourth century B.C. Alexander the Great took Greek (Western) culture to the Eastern ends of his far-flung empire. In that meeting, the rational culture of Greece was significantly modified by the great religions of the East (Hinduism, Manicheism, Zoroastrianism, Babylonian astrology, the Egyptian goddess worship of Isis, and Judaism, whether orthodox, mystical or apostate).[5] The blending of these great traditions produced the intellectual and religious syncretism of the so-called Hellenistic age (4th century B.C. – 4th century A.D.). This is the thinking alluded to in New Testament books such as 1 Corinthians, Colossians, 1 and 2 Timothy and the Johannine epistles.[6]

Gnosticism was no abstract philosophy. Flesh and blood human beings adopted it because it promised to change their social condition. Just as today, the New Age rejects both orthodox Christianity and secular humanism as tired, old, and inappropriate for the challenges of the third millennium, Gnosticism criticized both "official" state paganism and "orthodox" Christianity. A recent, more sociological analysis of ancient Gnosticism describes "the rootless and the weary who had been cut adrift and were searching for a new life." Gnostic ideas found fertile soil in a newly mobile merchant and military community. Freed slaves, adepts of the transposable Mystery Religions, and devotees of a form of feminism in the leisured classes all grasped at a spirituality that offered hope for a new understanding of individual freedom.[7]

The Importance of Gnosis

Prior to its "Christian" expression, Gnosticism was incubating in the Mystery Religions which in the ancient world represented the revival of spiritual paganism for the spiritually hungry.[8] The Mystery Religions were secret societies which, through devotion to the god and often the goddess, offered *gnosis* or spiritual illumination.[9] Though *gnosis* in Greek means knowledge of all kinds, in this context it means experience of occult powers through secret and mysterious initiation ceremonies, and of the divine self as the possessor of those powers.

Knowledge of the self as divine is the essential pillar of Gnosticism, however elaborate and "Christian" the outer dress. Gnosticism became a full-blown, appealing, religious system in the second century A.D. when certain so-called Christian thinkers (Marcion, Basilides, Valentinus *et al*) re-interpreted their faith to make it more palatable. They did what liberals have always done — reinterpret the faith by the pagan philoso-

phy of the day,[10] claiming such an amalgam to be the truest form of
Christianity. Unconvinced, the Church Fathers saw in Gnosticism a
Christianized form of paganism.

This sell-out of authentic Christianity marked the high-point of
Gnosticism's development both intellectually and numerically. Perhaps
a Christian veneer gave theological sophistication to the pagan Gnostic
liberation movement. Certainly the pagan lie of the self as divine (the
original diabolical temptation) reaches its highest point of believability
when dressed in Christian terminology. The unrelenting denunciation
of Christian Gnosticism by the Church Fathers shows that its appeal
during the early centuries of the Church threatened the very existence
of orthodox Christianity. Some of the finest theologians of the Christian Church devoted their lives to denouncing this heresy and to ex-
punging its pernicious effects from Christian doctrine and practice. The
Christian faith is under similar attack today, from outside the church,
but also from within.

Gnosticism: Early "Liberal" Spirituality

Spirit Wars rage in our day. Repeating the struggle between orthodoxy and heresy that marked the early centuries of the church's history,
the "Religious Left" attacks Christian orthodoxy today. In the second
century the Gospel sustained prolonged frontal attack and subtle infiltration. But the Apostolic Faith survived, victorious. This will always
be the case because "Jesus Christ [is] the same yesterday, today and
forever" (Heb 13:8). The Gospel does not change over time, and it will
triumph. But the liberal temptation to deform it does not change much
either, hence the striking similarities between ancient Gnosticism and
modern liberalism.[11] The Roman Catholic journalist and authoress
Donna Steichen observed that the "liberal consensus is a gnostic agnos-
ticism."[12] The comparison becomes more striking as modern liberalism
sloughs off the mantle of "scientific" atheism, and dabbles in "New Age"
spirituality.

The following parallels offer formal points of contact between an
ancient heresy and its modern counterpart. They constitute the back-
drop against which the detailed analysis of specific doctrines will be
made, in PART TWO:

♦ **The Liberal Spirit:**
The foundations of modern liberalism are the supremacy of human
reason and the right to follow "truth" wherever it may be found. Scrip-

ture is not the norm for truth, but must be subjected to human reason. Today's liberalism treats the Scripture as it would any ancient writing. The same "spirit" is present in ancient Gnosticism. A sympathetic popularizer of Gnostic writings, Elaine Pagels, describes the essence of the Gnostic mind-set:

> They argued that only one's own experience offers the ultimate criterion for truth, taking precedence over all secondhand testimony and all tradition.[13]

"Many liberal Protestants," notes Philip Lee, "seem confidently to accept the notion that because the New Testament authors were unenlightened in regard to modern science, technology and psychology, their understanding of life must have been vastly inferior to our own. They also assume that because of the great intellectual breakthroughs of recent times, intelligent Christians are faced with contradictions concerning the Scripture which have never had to be faced before."[14] This situation is not new, as Lee shows in his citation of the Church Father Irenaeus (130-200 A.D.):

> They [the Gnostics] consider themselves "mature," so that no one can be compared with them in the greatness of their *gnosis* [knowledge], not even if you mention Peter or Paul or any of the other apostles. . . . They imagine that they themselves have discovered more than the apostles, and that the apostles preached the gospel still under the influence of Jewish opinions, but that they themselves are wiser and more intelligent than the apostles.[15]

◆ **Radical Freedom:**
Where human reason sits enthroned, unbounded freedom becomes the law of the land. Freedom to reign over the created order constitutes the primary goal, the highest good. The pillar of radical freedom supports both modern liberal and ancient Gnostic thought. Pagels describes the Gnostic version of this "truth":

> Through . . . initiation . . . the candidate learns to reject the creator's [the God of the Bible] authority. . . . Achieving gnosis involves coming to recognize the true source of divine power . . . the depth of all being. . . . Whoever comes to this gnosis . . . is ready to receive the sacrament of redemption, i.e., release. . . . In this ritual he addresses the demiurge [the Creator], declaring his independence, serving notice that he no longer belongs to the demiurge's sphere of authority and judgment.[16]

One of the Gnostic self-designations, reported by the church father Hippolytus (170-236 A.D.)[17] is "the undominated generation,"[18] by which, adds Hippolytus, "they declare themselves independent of any authority, human or divine. . . ." Initiation into the deep knowledge of Gnosticism shakes the human fist at the Creator, deliberately throwing off the structures inherent in the created order.

"This conviction — that whoever explores human experience simultaneously discovers divine reality — . . . marks Gnosticism as a distinctly religious movement."[19] Pagels, in this observation, is profoundly correct. But this conviction also distinguishes Gnosticism from Christianity, which does not identify all human experience as divine reality. Human moral rebellion against God is treated with utmost seriousness, as is the nefarious work of "the god of this age" (2 Cor 4:4 cp Jn 12:31). As in much New Age thinking, sin is conspicuous by its absence from Gnostic texts.[20] It is equally absent in the thinking of modern day Gnostic/liberal sympathizers. For Elaine Pagels herself,[21] Satan is the creation of late orthodox Judaism and early orthodox Christianity in order to "deminize" their opponents. Satan has no theological or metaphysical existence.

◆ Syncretistic Diversity:

Liberalism often changes intellectual fads and schools of thought. Since everything is in flux, and human experience is the ultimate norm, diversity ensues. But diversity alone leads to chaos. There are three hundred million gods in India, and as many experiences as there are human beings. For liberals, diversity grows out of human spirituality and a bond exists between the "gods." The variety of religions and experiences gives voice to shared human experience. Syncretism results. As a modern scholar observes, "One of the most frequent charges brought against liberalism — one which might raise the question of a gnosticizing tendency in that movement — concerns its syncretism. No doubt, liberalism is syncretistic in the sense that it is open to all sorts of data, regardless of the source."[22]

The orthodox Church stoically guarded the faith, stressing episcopal continuity, common creeds and universal councils. The Gnostics went on a binge of individualistic creativity. By the first century A.D. the gods and goddesses of the Eastern cults (Isis and Osiris, Mithras, Cybele, etc.) had joined those of classical Western Greek mythology and those of the Roman pantheon, producing a syncretism as wide and diverse as any the world has known. Gnosticism was both a product of this religious ferment and its active customer.

According to the Church Fathers, Gnostic belief is a conscious distillation of pagan prototypes reflecting the bewildering diversity that marked the culture. This external variety, according to Kurt Rudolf, is "not accidental but . . . belongs to its very nature."[23] Irenaeus also testifies to this unusual diversity within the Valentinian school of Gnosticism at Rome in the second century.

> Every day every one of them invents something new, and none of them is considered perfect unless he is productive in this way.[24]

Epiphanius (315-403 A.D.) denounces Gnosticism's proliferation of exotically-named sects and guru/leaders:

> (the leaders) of Gnosis, falsely so-called, have begun their evil growth upon the world, namely the so-called Gnostics and Phibionites and the followers of Epiphanes, and the Stratiotici and Levitici and Borborians and the rest. For each of these (leaders) has contrived his own sect to suit his own passions and has devised thousands of ways of evil.[25]

Hans Jonas also notes this syncretistic character:

> The gnostic systems compounded everything — oriental mythologies, astrological doctrines, Iranian theology, elements of Jewish tradition, whether biblical, rabbinical, or occult, Christian salvation-eschatology, Platonic terms and concepts. Syncretism attained in this period its greatest efficacy.[26]

Cultural and religious diversity is as high on the contemporary liberal agenda, as it apparently was on the agenda of Gnosticism!

♦ **Secular Liberation as a Theological Agenda:**
Liberal theology often mimics movements in the society. James Robinson's positive interpretation of the counter-culture movements of the Sixties[27] (there were some positive elements[28]) is but one recent example.[29] The diversity of Gnosticism reflected a socio-religious search for new forms and free expression. Doubtless reacting against the hierarchical nature of the Judeo-Christian worldview, Gnosticism also tore into the elitism of the Greek classical world, in which only heroes penetrated the barrier between gods and men. For the ancients, to imitate semi-divine "heroes" was to commit the sin of "hubris," or arrogant pride. Some scholars contend that before Gnosticism was Christianized, it was a social liberation movement, promising freedom to all.[30]

At the birth of Christianity, people cut adrift and searching for new life began to carve a new spiritual and social identity in a changing, cosmopolitan world that "encouraged travel and trade, but undermined family ties, bonds of friendship and social relationships to the point of destruction."[31] James Robinson characterized the Gnostics as the "dropouts" of Roman imperial society,[32] comparing them to the "counterculture movements coming from the 60s."[33] This new spiritual identity appeared in "a religious world in ferment."[34] "Christian" Gnosticism was probably an attempt by dissatisfied Christians to re-interpret their faith in accordance with the dominant liberation movements of the day. What could be more liberal? — and more "Christian"?

◆ **Pagan Philosophy and Practice as a Source for Theology:**
The *new man* of Hellenistic society found many advantages to assimilating pagan philosophy and the Christian faith. The resultant religious "gospel" became attractive both to pagans and to dissatisfied believers. There was only one down side. As Gnosticism gained theological sophistication, Christianity was disfigured beyond recognition. Hippolytus relates that "Christian" Gnostics actually frequented the ceremonies of pagan mystery cults to understand what the pagans taught about "the universal mystery."[35] The orthodox church had to fight for its life.

History repeats itself in the contemporary movements of liberation, the rejection of traditional morality, modern radical sexuality, the New Age promise of spiritual rebirth and mastery, the flood of eastern spiritual techniques into the West, the dabbling in witchcraft and goddess worship, and in the growing invasion of the spirit of this age into the church. The most radically "progressive" theological liberalism justifies pagan belief and practice as the way forward for Christianity. "Christian" theologians today, like the Gnostic teachers of old, urge the Church to seek "the universal mystery" in pagan religions.

Roman Catholic theologian Paul Knitter, often associated with the World Council of Churches, wants "a new kind of theologian with a new type of consciousness — a multi-dimensional, cross-cultural consciousness."[36] Knitter elucidates: "Theologians must 'pass over' to the experience . . . that nurtures the creeds and codes and cults of other religions." What the Gnostic Naasenes called "the universal mystery," Knitter would call "cross-cultural consciousness," and others call "the Cosmic Christ." In whatever innocuous costume it appears at our door, we can be sure it carries a trick, not a treat, for it is nothing other than pagan spirituality. Saint Paul would call it "fellowship with demons."[37]

Modern liberal theologians often demonstrate outstanding intellectual gifts. Schleiermacher, von Harnack, Tillich and Bultmann, to name a few, command the highest respect on the level of creative and intellectual ability. So did Valentinus, a brilliant Gnostic thinker. Tertullian (160-225) said of him: "As to talent and eloquence, he (Valentinus) was an able man."[38] Apparently Valentinus almost became Pope.[39] In one of the great intellectual capitals of the ancient world, Alexandria, the Gnostic teacher Basilides had the reputation of being a skilled Bible scholar.[40] Liberals need unusual intelligence to make the obvious in Scripture obscure and the obscure obvious! How else could one transform Christian theism into pagan monism? The Church Father, Jerome (342-420), observed, with a touch of humor and faint praise:

> No one can bring a heresy into being unless he is possessed, by nature, of an outstanding intellect and has gifts provided by God. Such a person was Valentinus.[41]

At first, these parallels seem to share only a similarity of "spirit." Structural similarities, however striking, between two movements separated by 1700 years may not be conclusive. What do leading liberals say? Their oblique comments are revealing. Take, for example, the estimation of Marcion, one of the early Gnostics.

The "First Protestant" or the "First-Born of Satan"?

It takes a liberal to spot one. In A.D. 150, Marcion, a "theologian" from Pontus in Asia Minor was excommunicated from the Church in Rome.[42] He dismissed God the Creator, the Old Testament, the Mosaic law and three of the Gospels. From the few epistles of Paul that he accepted he expunged Old Testament quotations, and worshiped the "alien God" behind the God of Scripture. Because of this rejection of orthodoxy, Adolf von Harnack, the great nineteenth-century German liberal, hailed Marcion as "the first Protestant"! — by "Protestant" Harnack meant "liberal."[43]

Helmut Koester, a New Testament scholar teaching at Harvard Divinity School, calls Marcion "a textual critic, philologian and reformer."[44] Glowing appreciations like this could make you think that Marcion was the early Church's equivalent of Martin Luther.[45]

What a difference 1700 years can make. The Church Fathers expressed another opinion. Tertullian (160-225) called Marcion

the Pontic mouse who has nibbled away the Gospels . . . abolished
marriage, and . . . torn God almighty to bits with [his] blasphemies.[46]

Polycarp (69-155 A.D), who knew the apostle John, called Marcion "the
first-born of Satan."[47]

Only *contradictory understandings* of the Christian faith can explain
such divergent evaluations of Marcion. Orthodox Christianity maintains the antithesis separating all expressions of paganism, including
"Christian" paganism, from biblical truth. Liberalism has always mud-
died the waters. Today liberals claim that ancient Gnosticism is an alternate, authentic expression of early Christianity.[48] Is this estimation plau-
sible? The early Church Fathers said no. Modern liberalism says yes.

What would a modern Gnostic, with no pretensions to Christianity
either orthodox or liberal, say? Duncan Greenlees is just such a Gnostic, an adept of the theosophical/occult tradition. His independent evaluation of Gnosticism is most interesting:

> Gnosticism is a system of direct experiential knowledge of God . . .
> the Soul and the universe; therefore it has no fixed dogmas or creed. . . .
> In the early centuries of this era, amid a growing Christianity, it took
> on the form of the Christian faith, while rejecting most of its specific
> beliefs. Its wording is therefore largely Christian, while *its spirit is
> that of the latest paganism of the West* [emphasis mine].[49]

Here is no claim that Gnosticism is a valid, alternate form of Christianity. Modern Gnostics and ancient Church Fathers agree: Christianity
and Gnosticism are different religions, though they may use common
terminology. One religion is pagan humanism, the other divinely revealed truth.

Christianity and Liberalism:
Still Two Different Religions in 1923

1923 was a gala year for Presbyterian golfers. All golfers know that
in 1923 Bobby Jones won the first of his grand slam tournaments, introducing the famous "Calamity Jane" putter that had been made in Presbyterian Scotland at the beginning of the century. All Presbyterians
should know that in the same year, J. Gresham Machen, then Professor
of New Testament at Princeton Seminary, published *Christianity and Liberalism*. Machen made the same allegation regarding liberalism that the

Church Fathers had made concerning Gnosticism; that it was not Christianity, but a subtly disguised form of paganism. According to Machen:

> the great redemptive religion which has always been known as Christianity is battling against a totally diverse type of religious belief, . . . the movement designated as "liberalism.". . . But manifold as are the forms in which the movement appears, the root of the movement is one; the many varieties of modern liberal religion are rooted in naturalism — that is, in the denial of any entrance of the creative power of God.[50]

By naturalism, Machen meant paganism. Machen tried to be both firm and fair, rightly distinguishing between liberalism as a system and liberals as individuals. His example still inspires:

> whether or not liberals are Christians, it is at any rate perfectly clear that liberalism is not Christianity. . . . liberalism, whether it be true or false, is no mere "heresy" — no mere divergence at isolated points from Christian teaching. On the contrary it proceeds from a totally different root, and it constitutes, in essentials, a unitary system of its own. That does not mean that all liberals hold all parts of the system, or that Christians who have been affected by liberal teaching at one point have been affected at all points. There is sometimes a salutary lack of logic which prevents the whole of a man's faith being destroyed when he has given up a part. . . . it [liberalism] differs from Christianity in its view of God, of man, of the seat of authority and of the way of salvation. And it differs from Christianity not only in theology but in the whole of life. . . . Christianity is being attacked from within by a movement which is anti-Christian to the core.[51]

Two decades earlier, from the other side of the Reformation divide, Pope Pius X made all priests and seminary professors swear an anti-modernist oath, declaring liberalism to be "the synthesis of all the heresies."[52] Machen and Pope Pius X make unusual bedfellows. Adamantly out of tune with the spirit of *our* times, they share a common perspective on liberalism. The evaluation that old style liberalism overturned every Christian doctrine supports the present contention that overt, pagan "New Age" liberalism is a radical and open apostasy from the Christian faith.

The Modern Heresy: Heresy-Hunting

For most scholars and many priests in the Roman Catholic Church, Pope Pius' oath became a pious sentiment, an artifact for the Vatican museum. Machen's allegations won few friends in the Presbyterian Church he had faithfully served: he was defrocked for unacceptable behavior. Machen had committed the unpardonable sin of calling a spade a spade, and heresy heresy.

Such an accusation may soon qualify not only as heresy but as a "hate crime" that disturbs the peace of a society high on tolerance, choice and love. Feminist scholars at the RE-Imagining Conference accuse their critics, concerned for the orthodoxy of the church's confession, of "hostility," "violence" and "harassment."[53] Bishop Earl G. Hunt of the United Methodist Church warns that one symptom of the church's weakness is that its leaders "have declared ours to be a post-heresy age."[54] James Robinson, director of the translation project of the Nag Hammadi texts, reserves vitriol, not for the Gnostic distortions of the Gospel, but for the Church Fathers who denounced the Gnostics as heretics. Eight times in his twenty-five page introductory article to the Nag Hammadi texts he rails against the Church Fathers, describing their polemical defense of orthodoxy against Gnosticism as the "myopic view of heresy hunters."[55]

One might expect such heated language from neo-pagan "Christians," "re-imagining" their way into positions of power in churches they refuse to leave,[56] but why from the cool corridors of academia? Robinson loses his "cool" because naming a person or teaching heretical has become the modern heresy.[57] The former moderator of the Presbyterian Church U.S.A, David Lee Dobler, considers even the use of words like "pagan" and "heretic" by concerned conservatives in his denomination much more worrisome than the actual practice of heretical pagan rituals by appointed officials of his church's bureaucracy.[58] A British churchman has sized up this situation:

> It is Satan's sincerest wish that we should never make a negative judgment about those who set out to destroy the Church and its foundations, or who spread deadly heresy and false doctrine. Correspondingly, the real reason that human non-judgmentalism in any form is becoming so fashionable in this age is that it makes the concept of a judging, avenging God seem ridiculous, anachronistic and implausible.[59]

No Heresy — No Truth

There are limits to the modification of Christian doctrine — or of anything ("a" is still not "non-a," logicians will maintain) — before it is so disfigured that it becomes its own antithesis.

Steve Brown, a popular radio preacher, tells of the Jewish boy who asks his dad for a Honda as a bar mitzvah present. The father asks his orthodox rabbi what a Honda is, but he doesn't know. They both asked the conservative rabbi, who doesn't know either. All three then ask the liberal/reformed rabbi, who proudly informs them that a Honda is a motor-cycle, a wonderful gift for the man's son. But as they leave, the liberal rabbi asks, "Excuse me." May I ask *you* a question? What's a bar mitzvah?

The extremes of Judaism, indicated by this humorous story, illustrate our point about heresy. Philip Lee, hardly a right-wing fundamentalist, remarks: "At some given point, a teaching, an idea or an action which claims to be Christian is so utterly different from the 'faith which was once for all delivered to the saints' (Jude 3) that it becomes the opposite of Christianity."[60]

The formal, historical similarities between an ancient heresy and modern "Christian" liberalism suggest that such liberalism is not an authentic version of Christianity but its antithesis. The case becomes persuasive as we examine more specific doctrinal beliefs. But before developing a more detailed comparison, it is important to note that liberalism has recently changed profoundly, bringing it even more in line with the ancient heresy of Gnosticism.

The arid humanism of theoretical liberalism has "got religion" in the age of Aquarius. Fired by religious passion, the theology that prizes tolerance has raised the level of violent language against those it cannot tolerate. Trust has shifted from Enlightenment rationalism to spirituality and power. Pagan mysteries associated with ancient Gnosticism find fertile soil in the sophisticated, intellectual elite of the Western world — formidable modern opponents of orthodoxy in our time.

Elaine Pagels exemplifies the "new liberal Christian" elite. A successful scholar and best-selling author, with a Ph.D. from Harvard and a professorship at Princeton, she embodies the rigor of rationalistic liberalism that has dominated academia. At the same time, she does not hide her fascination with the Gnostics, whom her work has rehabilitated as forgotten heroes of the class war between the (evil) orthodox patriarchal oppressors and the (good) egalitarian victims. Her book on Satan seeks to prove that the devil is the invention of Judeo-Christian literature for the demonization of all those not buying the system, in particu-

lar, heretics. Such black and white thinking, she argues, has had a nefarious effect on the last two thousand years of Western history. "What
began as a minority sect's rhetorical strategy, became a majority religion's
moral, and even psychological, justification for persecution . . . of all
opponents real or imagined."[61]

Orthodox Christians become suspect in Pagels' mind, while the oppressed Gnostics become *sympathiques*. In her 1979 study, *The Gnostic
Gospels*, Pagels demonstrates an attraction to the Gnostic heresy, while
affirming her attachment to Christianity. Historical objectivity is not
absent from this study. Recently, though, her attraction has matured into
admiration. In the interview/story in *The New Yorker*, she talks of meeting the head of a Gnostic church in Palo Alto, CA: "I was quite en-
chanted by her and delighted by her . . . this is serious stuff."[62] During
an Easter, 1996 interview on *National Public Radio* she admitted to a
fascination with the Gnostic texts, especially *Thunder Perfect Mind*. This
text praises a female personification of the divine, identified as Isis, the
Egyptian Goddess of Witchcraft and Magic. *Thunder* says in typical, all-
inclusive prose: "I am the prostitute and the holy one, . . . the wife and
the virgin, . . . knowledge and ignorance, . . . bride and bridegroom, . . .
shame and shamelessness."[63] Pagels toys with this idolatry while attending an Episcopal church. In a similar way, first lady Hillary Clinton
sees no contradiction between dabbling in New Age channeling and her
"devout" Methodist faith.

These vignettes illustrate the thesis of PART ONE. Liberalism has
had a face-lift. Once associated with a-religious rationalism and social
gospel activism, the new Religious Left has discovered spirituality, not
the spirituality of the Bible but that of paganism. Elaine Pagels and Hillary
Clinton personify a momentous cultural shift: from "modern" to
"postmodern," from rational to irrational, from Christian to pagan, from
social gospel Christianity to occultic spirituality. Such change is now
elevated to law. The majority justices of the present Supreme Court have
drunk deep at the well of pagan religion. Justice Ruth Bader Ginsberg,
previously on the board of the American Civil Liberties Union (ACLU),
declared at her confirmation hearing that courts should sometimes be
"interim legislatures."[64]

The interim has been lasting a long time. The Supreme Court decision in *Planned Parenthood v. Casey* (1992) grants to every citizen "the
right to define one's own concept of existence, of meaning, of the universe, and of the mystery of human life."[65] Apparently democratic, *Casey*
is a "recipe for chaos,"[66] a "private franchise" for all citizens "over matters of life and death,"[67] a wide-open door for "homosexual sodomy,
polygamy, incest and suicide."[68] *Casey* constitutes the legal and social

rehabilitation in Christian America of pagan polytheism. In the eloquent words of one incisive social commentator, "half awake, babbling clichés about rights, America is walking into a nightmare."[69]

As we move into PART TWO, we raise the following questions: What is the essence of this new democratic theory and of the spirituality that lies behind it? Beyond *Culture Wars* there are *Spirit Wars*: behind the pro-choice social agenda and the "politics of meaning" there is the defining component that comes from the *Religious* Left. Will this rediscovery of the religious dimension herald a new day for faith and the expansion of Christianity? Or will the revival of this new spirituality rather usher in ominous days of apostasy such that, were it possible, even the elect would be deceived?[70]

Behind the seductive calls for tolerance and the bewitching promise of universal peace, the Spirit Wars have broken out in earnest, and on various levels. First, the promotion of all-inclusive Gnosticism in church and society undermines the longstanding Christian presuppositions of the American culture. Second, denial of the very existence of spiritual warfare is itself a major offensive in the war. Finally, efforts to suppress the truth that there is conflict between God and Satan shows how far the forces of "tolerance" will go.

A Peek into the Future

The Sixties revolution happened on the university campuses before entering today's mainstream. Campus conflicts in the nineties grant a vision of what the future holds for our children and grandchildren. At the May 1996 *Whole Earth Festival* at UC Davis, a handful of Christian students distributed literature in an overwhelmingly New Age, university-sponsored event. They were stopped by the *"Karma Patrol."* Their offense? Spreading "bad karma" by distributing Christian leaflets. To be forewarned is to be forearmed.

A Peek into the Past

In this new agenda there is deception, whether intended or not. The elements of ancient Gnosticism, presently proposed as a new lease on life for an ageing planet, tend to emphasize the most moderate, least shocking parts of this hoary heresy. However, Gnosticism was a coherent system, and behind its seductive calls to spirituality, human freedom, fascinating diversity, inclusiveness and imagination lay an unimaginably revolutionary agenda whose ultimate aim and inevitable result was to cast the God of the Bible into Hell. Is this also the ultimate intention of the contemporary Karma patrols?

PART TWO

TWO
ANATOMY OF
AN APOSTASY

Part One traced the recent history of the New Spirituality and described the general monistic structure of its thought. Part Two deals with specific key points of doctrine concerning the Bible, Bible study, the nature and person of God, as well as the important issues of sexuality and spirituality. The coherence as well as the great age of this extremely disparate movement becomes even clearer as these points of doctrine are compared with similar teaching in ancient Gnosticism. When Christians understand the coherence of error, they can better identify the battle lines in order to mount a compelling and creditable defense of the Faith.

CHAPTER 6

THE NEW BIBLE

A polytheistic theology, because it makes contact with the immediacy of life
out of the depths, is itself a religion with no scripture, but with many stories.
  - David Miller[1]

We (the Nixon administration) would never have thought of rewriting the
Bible. I found in one visit (with President Clinton) that he is bright and well-
informed and so I assume he knows better. We're in real trouble when not even
the Bible is safe from politically correct revisionism.
  - Charles Colson[2]

A New Bible For the New Spirituality

For two thousand years the Bible has been the most widely distributed and read book in the world. No other book comes close. To
change the civilization that was built by the Bible, *you must change the
Bible*. As we move into a new millennium, many dream of heaven on
earth, produced by an expected macro-jump in spiritual evolution. They
happily pronounce obsolete the fuel that powered Christendom. There
are cleaner energy sources. Pisces is a fish out of water. Aquarius dawns
on the shores of a new age.

The Age of Aquarius needs an Aquarian Bible, for the Bible we know
is the handbook of a dying civilization. Dissatisfied with the Bible of
old, a new ideology of social liberation clamors for a new Holy Scripture. Moderates agree with radicals that the Bible is "the founding document of patriarchal culture."[3] If patriarchy is the great evil that must be
eradicated, the future of its founding document hardly looks promising.

Tired of the Old: Need For the New

A leading New Testament scholar has recently said:

> The "orthodox" Bible today represents only a portion of the inspired books of the early Christian era and, at best, a partial explanation of Christ's teachings.[4]

Here is the handwriting unambiguously on the wall. The new liberalism intends to change the Bible.

A New Age writer, defending abortion, speaks of "the bureaucratic priestly . . . patriarchal truth squad (who will) . . . go to any lengths to discourage independent thought, proclaim(ing) the heresy of certain 'lost' gospels and certify(ing) the infallible truth of their own translation of biblical documents."[5]

Nowhere do bold attacks on the Bible surface with such moral fervor as in the unholy alliance of feminism and radical biblical scholarship. Liberals have always chafed under the orthodox canon of Scripture, but have only rarely called for canonical revision. Feminist liberals, believing they have found high moral ground, do not hesitate to go all the way. And so Rosemary Radford Ruether, who elects to remain within the church, states without nuance or apology:

> Feminist theology must create a new textual base, a new canon. . . . Feminist theology cannot be done from the existing base of the Christian Bible.[6]

Other feminists find the biblical texts "impossible" to read, and feel the "need to write new ones."[7]

The Satanic Verses

Ruether's *Women-Church* exemplifies this approach. On the one hand, parts of the Bible are seen as demonic. A "Ritual of Exorcism of Patriarchal Texts," to the cry, "Out, demons, out," eradicates or exorcises from feminist consciousness Leviticus 12:1-5 (purification after childbirth); Exodus 19:1, 7-9, 14-15. Judges 19 (The Levite and his concubine); Ephesians 5:21-23 (the submission of a wife to her husband); 1 Timothy 2:11-15 (a woman saved through childbirth); and 1 Peter 2:1, mostly texts that express the biblical view of sexual role differentiation. At the end of the reading the liturgist says:

> These texts have lost their power over our lives. We no longer need to apologize for them or try to interpret them as words of truth, but we

cast out their oppressive message as expressions of evil and justifica-
tions of evil.[8]

On the other hand, any text is good that agrees with the new "orthodoxy," and may be incorporated into the demonstration. So Ruether gives
equal time and added weight to Gnostic texts like the *Gospel of Mary* —
which founds the Church not on Peter but on Mary Magdalene — and
cites the apocryphal *Acts of Paul and Thecla* to defend her feminist view:
"We remember Thecla, commissioned by Paul to preach the gospel and
to baptize." For Ruether, the Gnostic texts give evidence of a "simpler,
less hierarchical [original] Christianity," that she finds congenial for
modern Christianity.[9]

As noted above, even a respected historian like Elaine Pagels admits
to being "very attracted by these texts."[10] This is not just intellectual
curiosity. Pagels, though Christian in background and commitment, and
tentative in her opinions, shows "in some cases . . . a clear preference for
a Gnostic interpretation."[11] Just how radical she could be is shown by
her openness to the integration of Gnostic texts into the Christian
canon.[12] Pagels' interest is spiritual. She sees Gnosticism as not having
to do with "belief" but with "dimensions of experience" and "religious
imagination."[13]

The new mystical, self-consciously *non-Christian*, spirituality has a
similar agenda to that of its liberal Christian cousin. Theosophist and
public television personality, Joseph Campbell calls for a new myth, a
new God and new texts:

> The story that we have in the West, so far as it is based on the Bible, is
> based on a view of the universe that belongs to the first millennium
> B.C. It does not accord with our concept either of the universe or of
> the dignity of man. It belongs entirely somewhere else.[14]

Ashamed of the Bible

Some mainline biblical scholars are so ashamed of the Bible they are
not sure they want their children to read it.[15] Others, like the editors of
The New Testament and Psalms: An Inclusive Version (Oxford University
Press, 1995), try to make it safe for children, and other sensitive persons, by eliminating all patriarchal language and any masculine terms
for God or Christ. Claiming to be a work of scholarship, using "new
manuscripts" and "new investigations into the meanings of words,"[16]
this Bible is merely a verbatim reproduction of the *New Revised Standard
Version* with the politically-correct offending phrases reworked. The
imposition on the biblical text of an egalitarian philosophy so foreign to
the Bible produces grotesque English and theological monstrosities. The

editors, who boldly state their commitment to "accelerating changes in English usage towards inclusiveness,"[17] appear to have gone out of their way to improve on the new forms of English they claim are now accepted speech. Phrases such as: "Please contribute to the policeperson's ball," seem positively old fashioned compared to their rendering of John 13:31: "Now the Human One has been glorified, and in that one God has been glorified. If God has been glorified in the Human One, God will also glorify that very one in Godself and will glorify that one at once." Did anyone understand? This egalitarian *newspeak* not only butchers English, it nullifies the Word of God by making it, for the sake of the reigning ideology, incomprehensible. The desire to be sexually inclusive produces a two-headed androgynous divinity that would be more at home in mythologies of ancient Greece than in the Bible. And so the Lord's Prayer begins: "Our Father/Mother in heaven, hallowed be your name." This is surely one of the most impressive attempts not to hallow God's name in the history of Christian thought, for the very heart of the revelation brought by Jesus concerning the Father is disfigured beyond recognition.[18] Generations of children raised in a future egalitarian culture may never know the love of an earthly father because the term will have ceased to exist. Will they recognize the love of the Heavenly Father so graphically described in the Gospel? For the moment they have a whole Bible, however disfigured. More devastating things will yet happen to Holy Scripture.

"Scientific" Undermining of Biblical Orthodoxy

When I began to specialize in New Testament studies some thirty years ago, orthodoxy was everywhere considered the original version of Christianity. To be sure, it was popular for scholars to say that Jesus did not consider himself the Messiah, and that the early church turned this Jewish prophet and the events surrounding his death into the object of faith and the essence of the gospel. But it was the *"Easter faith" of those who wrote the New Testament* that explained the transition. It was the conviction of the *original* disciples, in their experience of the death and the resurrection of Jesus (whatever that meant) that gave rise to the church's gospel.

One generation later New Testament scholars hail the Gnostic heresy, which was denounced by the New Testament and the early church, as the original teaching of Jesus and the propagators of that heresy as the earliest band of disciples after his death. The historical Jesus, they say, was a proto-Gnostic, politically correct, social revolutionary who bears little or no resemblance to the one worshiped as the Christ in the Bible.

Dismantling the Bible

In 1985, as president of the prestigious *Society of Biblical Literature,* James M. Robinson issued a programmatic statement for the twenty-first century. He called upon his fellow Bible scholars to deconstruct their discipline in order to "lay bare [its] . . . biblicistic presuppositions." The Bible would no longer serve as the ultimate source of authority and as the definition of true Christianity.[19] We were warned. Robinson's agenda is picking up momentum not only because the time is right and his message fits the mood of the modern world, but also because James M. Robinson and his colleague Helmut Koester of Harvard Divinity School have done seminal work to bring it about.[20] As a measure of Robinson's importance, Robert Funk of the *Jesus Seminar* calls him "the Secretary of State of the biblical guild . . . (an) academic counterpart . . . (to) Henry Kissenger."[21]

Both Koester and Robinson studied with Rudolf Bultmann, the German scholar who single-handedly convinced New Testament science to look upon ancient Gnosticism and Hellenistic culture as the important source of Christianity, at the expense of the Old Testament and Judaism.[22] Both Koester and Robinson are past presidents of the *Society of Biblical Literature.* Both have been committed to a clearly defined program: the "Dismantling and Reassembling of the Categories of New Testament Scholarship," as one of Robinson's articles is entitled.[23] One category they have successfully dismantled is that of heresy and orthodoxy.[24]

Both separately and together, Koester and Robinson sought to show a radical pluralism in the earliest church, causing Christian theology to develop along various "trajectories."[25] Orthodoxy was one trajectory, but not the only deposit of the true gospel, making the others "heretical."[26] Koester contests that there is not "one gospel" as Paul said, but at least "four."

James Robinson put content to his manifesto. He founded and is Director of the Institute For Antiquity and Christianity at Claremont, CA. It is devoted to the rehabilitation of texts and a theology that the early church denounced as heresy. Within the Institute Robinson launched the Coptic Gnostic Library Project, which translates, publishes, and promotes the Gnostic texts. A great service to the scholarly world, it is also a powerful tool for the neo-Gnostic theological agenda. "Secretary of State" is not an exaggeration. Robinson has been the leading

force behind the *Q Seminar*, (whose importance for the new understanding of Jesus we shall discuss below). He is an active member of the
Jesus Seminar (founded by a colleague, Robert Funk) and director of the
Coptic Magical Texts Project, which rehabilitates heretical Gnostic and
magical "Christianity."

Robinson rails against "myopic heresy hunters" because he believes
the future lies with inclusion. Gnosticism (heresy) and Orthodoxy are
two valid "trajectories" of early Christianity. What was a marginal position just a generation ago, is now touted as majority conviction. Robinson
encourages modern theology to extract values from both trajectories in
order to produce a new formulation of Christianity for today.[27]
Robinson's 1985 manifesto explodes the constraining limits of the orthodox biblical canon.

Helmut Koester, in the epilogue of a collection of essays in his
honor,[28] gives his own prospective for the New Testament field. Early
Christianity, he says, is

> just one of several Hellenistic propaganda religions, competing with
> others who seriously believed in their god and who also imposed moral
> standards on their followers.[29]

He urges scholars to abandon New Testament canon "as part of a special
book that is different from other early Christian writings." Koester issues this call in order to allow the other early Christian voices — "heretics, Marcionites, Gnosticism, Jewish Christians, perhaps also women
— . . . to be heard again."[30] Koester readily admits that this is not value-
free, objective science. The old liberal historical-critical method was, he
grants, "designed as a *hermeneutical tool for the liberation from conservative prejudice and from the power of ecclesiastical and political institutions*
[emphasis mine]."[31] In the same way, future New Testament studies
should have as their goal "political and religious renewal . . . inspired
by the search for equality, freedom and justice" in the "comprehensive
political perspective" of our modern world.[32] For Koester, the egalitarian, all-inclusive worldview of contemporary avant garde thinking becomes *the* criterion of truth.

These two influential scholars apply the program of their mentor,
Rudolf Bultmann, the "demythologization of the New Testament." This
approach dismantles the theistic understanding of the New Testament
in favor of a monistic, paganizing Gnostic one.[33] They are committed to
the destruction of the canon and, consequently, to the undermining of
orthodoxy.

Victims of Canon: Harassed by the Truth

Every one loves a loser, especially if the winners are establishment "fat cats" unfairly tyrannizing the underdog. Today's heretics use sentimentality, political correctness and power politics to defend the downtrodden, theological "canon-fodder."

Liberals deny the possibility of objective truth, depicting truth as merely social power. But this view of truth is like the modern version of the golden rule: those who have the gold rule. Truth is what those in control define it to be; there is no objective truth. In a new form of myopia, suspicion has replaced the noble search for truth.

Elaine Pagels, a student of Koester and colleague of Robinson, reads early church history this way. Gnosticism was suppressed because the bishops won, not because the Christian gospel of orthodox proclamation answered the needs of a reprobate empire, or because it was the true word of God. "It is the winners who write history — their way. No wonder, then," says Pagels, "that the viewpoint of the successful majority has dominated all traditional accounts of the origin of Christianity."[34] "It will be necessary," declares New Testament scholar Elizabeth Schüssler Fiorenza, "to go beyond the limits of the New Testament canon since it is the product of the patristic church, that is, a theological document of the 'historical winners.'"[35]

This same power ideology rules in the *Jesus Seminar*. As one of the members says, in seeking to justify their inclusion of heretical gospels:

> Of course, history is written by the victors, in this case, by the orthodox authors known as the fathers of the church. From an objective historical perspective, however, "heresy" is a label for the rival religious currents that lost; they [the Gnostics] eventually ceased to be politically, socially, or intellectually sustainable alternatives to mainstream Christianity.[36]

The author goes on to call the heretical gospels "losers." "They lost out when the more powerful circles in Christianity imposed their own limits of doctrinal acceptability." Notice how this statement is full of value-laden terms. Heretical texts even receive the coveted status of "victim." The implicit emotional appeal says: "Is it not time to adopt these socially harassed literary orphans and give them a home at last in a church from which they were so unceremoniously and unchristianly dumped so many years ago?" (Besides, they would be so useful for our contemporary new spiritual agenda!)

War of the Canons

Feminist biblical scholarship raises the level on the emotional Rich-
ter scale with a rumble of *patriarchal* power. The ultimate conspiracy
theory, which has fiendish male plotters undermining the family, the
church and the society, works equally well for the history of the canon.
Those who imposed the orthodox canon were Church *Fathers,* whom
one evangelical theologian called "male chauvinists." The will to power
behind the orthodox Bible is the desire for social control through the
patriarchal suppression of women. Women now belong to the category
of "losers." This is why "feminist theology must create . . . a new canon."[37]
Asian feminist theologian Chung Hyun Kyung, a graduate of Union
Theological Seminary in New York, said at a recent "Christian" conference that feminists were free to use the ancient Gnostic texts, originally
rejected as heretical, because the Christian canon was created by men,
and "therefore, women are not obliged to accept a book or 'constitution'
they had no part in framing."[38] Ms. Kyung finished her lecture by encouraging the conference to consider canonizing the Gnostic Gospels,
since in this Gnostic form Asians, who believe that every person has the
light and a the divine spark within them, would finally find the Church's
preaching attractive.

Melanie Morrison, co-founder of CLOUT (Christian Lesbians Out
Together) declared: "I know in my heart that the canon is not closed, it
is open. I know this because the Bible does not reconcile me with the
earth and the Bible does not reconcile me with my sexual self."[39] Has
reconciliation with God and his holy law crossed Melanie Morrison's
mind?

The Coming of Age of American New Testament Scholarship

In November, 1995 at the annual meeting of the Society of Biblical
Literature, victory was declared. Leading New Testament scholars rejoiced that the heretical Gnostic *Gospel of Thomas* had finally made it
into the club, and that now we could disband the club. By club they
meant the New Testament canon of Holy Scripture. They were referring,
in part, to the successful publication of *The Five Gospels* in 1993 [see
below], a volume that places *Thomas* alongside the four canonical Gospels of Matthew, Mark, Luke and John. This year the Society celebrated
the fiftieth anniversary of the finding of the Nag Hammadi library of
Gnostic texts. James Robinson, an ex-orthodox Calvinist and director
of the translation project that has made these texts widely available,
declared the elevation of *Thomas* to the status of the canonical gospels
as "the coming of age of American New Testament scholarship." How
ironic. The great contribution of the sons of Christian America at the

end of the twentieth century is the introduction of pagan heresy into the Church's Scriptures, destroying both the integrity of the canon and the theological coherence of biblical faith.

First Sightings of the New Aquarian Bible

There is a new "liberal" Bible waiting in the wings, hoary with age but oh, so modern. In fact, it has been waiting in the warm, dry sand of Egypt, as if expecting this very moment. Two texts in the recently-discovered Gnostic collection refer to being kept in a mountain for the end times. Perhaps the entire collection was placed in a large jar and hidden[40] for the same purpose. But for one reason or another, this Gnostic Bible came forth again in 1945. It is now being promoted in the church by those who belong to the "incorruptible holy race" of the new Aquarian spirituality. How long will it take for this Gnostic Bible to supplant the Bible of orthodox Christianity?

At least some people today give this fact an eschatological twist. Caitlín Matthews, theologian of the goddess Sophia and pagan priestess of Isis, sees the impetus in our time for the celebration of Sophia coming from the interest in the Nag Hammadi texts. Indeed, for this deeply religious and intelligent neo-pagan, the discovery of these texts "at the start of the New Age itself cannot be insignificant."[41]

Return of the Nag Hammadi:
A New Bible In Old Clay Pots

As he smashed the clay pot, Mohammed Ali finally made it to the big time. Finding old paper in an earthenware jar is not obvious big time. However, this Egyptian Arab camel driver, with the same name as the international boxing star, had unwittingly stepped front and center onto the stage of religious history. In 1945 Ali was in Nag Hammadi, Egypt, three hundred miles south of Cairo, poking around in the *sebakh*, the rich soil left when the Nile periodically overflows its banks. In his earthenware jar was the first of a fifty-two text library of ancient Gnostic scriptures. They describe a coherent, heretical account of Christian doctrine, offering a seductive picture of Jesus to warm any New Age guru's heart.[42] Thanks to Mohammed Ali, the Nag Hammadi writings have returned on the eve of the Age of Aquarius, to threaten the Church again, and perhaps shake it to its roots.

This is eschatology with a malevolent twist. The irony is enormous. Precisely when New Age spirituality has emerged as the most dynamic religious force in the Western world, the first-hand documents of its long-lost spiritual cousin, Gnosticism,[43] have come to light. The object of a well-orchestrated program of scholarly rehabilitation, they have recently been made available in English for all to read. These texts fascinate liberals and New Agers alike — including contemporary New Age prophets. Shirley MacLaine sees the irony. "[Ancient] Christian Gnostics," she states enigmatically, "operated with New Age knowledge."[44] So does New Age spokesman, Theodore Roszak, who describes New Age spirituality as "the reclamation and renewal of the old Gnosis."[45] There is even more irony. Roszak probably did not count on the help of prestigious New Testament scholars studying ancient texts from antiquity.

The battle of the Bibles is upon us. The attack on the Christian Bible comes from many sources, but the most pernicious comes from "Christian" *Bible scholars*. Today the attack is mounted on two fronts: the first is the rehabilitation of Gnostic texts; the second is the "discovery" of the lost Gospel, "Q."

Scholarly Rehabilitation of the Gnostic Texts

The *Gnostic Empire is striking back* in the hallowed halls of New Testament science. The neo-Gnostic revival is to the ancient Gnostic texts as a *steak au roquefort* is to a mellow sauterne; as Moslems to the Qur'an; or Christians to the Bible. How this rendez-vous occurs remains to be seen, but it is only a matter of time. The music plays, the table is laid. The thesis of this book, that the new liberalism is a renewed form of ancient Gnosticism, receives sturdy confirmation when we observe the contemporary liberal crusade to rehabilitate these heretical texts. They are presently employed to justify women's ordination,[46] the goddess character of the Holy Spirit, the moral appropriateness of abortion,[47] the feminist re-interpretation of culture,[48] and much more.[49] Contemporary liberalism is not merely citing Gnostic texts as useful background material. It is promoting them to canonical status.

The Complete Gospels

The Bible is incomplete, we are told. We need more texts to complete it — and radical New Testament scholarship is glad to be of service. Robert Funk, founder of the *Jesus Seminar*, and one of the editors of *Hermeneia*, also recently set up *The Weststar Institute* "devoted to reducing biblical and religious illiteracy in America." Weststar includes the *Jesus Seminar*, a bi-monthly journal, *The Fourth R*, and Polebridge Press. The quest for religious literacy [the fourth R] in America dismantles the Bible as the church has known it. Polebridge Press has published *The Complete Gospels* (1992) edited by Robert J. Miller.[50] This volume began as a new translation of the Bible, known as the *Scholars Version*. But since the translators attempted to avoid any overlay of orthodox theology, they refused the limitations of the orthodox canon as well. The implicit message of the title is that the canonical gospels are incomplete, and those who do not think so are biblically illiterate. The canonical gospels are "completed" by apocryphal gospels such as the *Infancy Gospel of James* and the *Infancy Gospel of Thomas*, (a text long dismissed even by liberal critical scholars as popular folk literature of little theological interest). Also included in this complete canon are a number of Gnostic gospels: the *Gospel of Thomas*, the *Apocryphon of James*, the *Dialogue of the Savior*, and the *Gospel of Mary*, all of which, Miller admits, witness to "the blending of Christianity and Gnosticism." We are asked to accept as "the religious convictions of sincere Christians" what the early church fought as diabolical heresy. There is no ambiguity here. The new definition of biblical literacy revives the Gnostic heresy, and "scientifically" slips it into an emerging new Bible — all done in the name of academic objectivity and all-inclusive tolerance!

The Five Gospels

You thought there were only *four* Gospels. Rub your eyes and look again. "Progressive" scholars, with unprecedented feats of academic legerdemain, have slipped Gnostic texts into the Canon, most notably in Polebridge Press's *The Five Gospels*.[51] This volume uses a double-pronged attack on the orthodox Bible.

First, it determines the authentic words of Jesus using the critical criteria of classic liberals. Mimicking the popular Bibles that print Jesus' words in red, this publication colors only those sayings considered authentic by the *Jesus Seminar* (pitifully few). Black indicates unauthentic sayings. The Gospel of John has no red, one pink, two grays, and all the rest are black. The Seminar thus creates a canon within the canon, rendering much of what the church has considered canonical as secondary accretion, at best.

Second, a heretical text, the *Gospel of Thomas*, is included alongside the four canonical gospels. Sprinkled with far more red and pink than the Gospel of John, it fares very well. *The Five Gospels* surreptitiously "canonizes" the Gnostic *Gospel of Thomas* by including it with Mark,

Matthew, Luke, and John as an (the most?) authentic source for the historical Jesus.[52]

Honey or Gall?

Today's radical Bible scholars attempt what their ancient cousins failed to achieve. In the second century, Irenaeus, defending the four canonical gospels as "four pillars breathing out immortality on every side and vivifying our flesh" (*Against Heresies* 3:11:8), compares them to the four winds, the four zones of the world, and the four faces of the cherubim (Ez. 1:4). Though his comparisons might not impress modern readers, his intention was to oppose the Gnostic proliferation of gospels, insisting on only four true gospels upon which the church was founded — no others need apply.

Line sixty-seven of the second century canonical list, *The Muratorian Canon* specifically refuses to include the writings of the Gnostic teacher Valentinus, a book of psalms from the proto-Gnostic Marcion, and the writings of Montanus. "Gall," the ancient author maintained, "cannot be mixed with honey."

So, placing Thomas among the Bible's gospels is not the triumphant progress of science over prejudice and reason over blind faith, but is rather a contemporary example of the old Gnostic attempt to inject into the honey of the gospels the gall of heresy. Today, as in the second century, two opposing versions of the Gospel, two contradictory pictures of Jesus clash, and readers get to choose whatever turns them on. Into the canonical record has crept the bitter-sweet, proto-Gnostic "Jesus," who came not to die for our sins but to reveal that we are all christs.[53]

If modern Gnostics succeed, it may not be long before a complete New Testament, with black leather binding and Indian paper, will include the *Gospel of Thomas* and exclude 1 and 2 Timothy and Titus, or at least, a selection of "satanic verses." An inclusive Bible that excludes what is politically incorrect is surely already in some publisher's files awaiting the propitious moment for publication. Robert Funk's "fourth R" may well turn out to be the R of religious revolution.

Fair Play?

Though nowadays the addition of Gnostic scriptures to the Christian canon is called for in the name of diversity and fair play, fairness is rather to be found in keeping them apart, for their internal coherence makes them mutually exclusive theologically. Even Bentley Layton, Professor of Ancient Christian History at Yale University, and translator of many Gnostic texts, and favorable to their message, recognizes that the

Gnostic texts share "a coherent symbol system" that explains the texts themselves, the world and its origin, and other people.[54] With regard to coherence, someone has said that what one does with the first three chapters of Genesis determines everything else that one will say about theology. The Gnostic writings are systematically suspicious of Genesis 1-3, denigrating not only the creation, but God the Creator who stands behind the Genesis text. Such suspicion permeates all that the Gnostic revealers and teachers say. The Christian Bible takes the very opposite approach. The whole Bible honors and glorifies God, the good and gracious Creator and Redeemer of heaven and earth.

These two coherent systems are fundamentally opposed. What one calls evil the other calls good, what one calls truth the other calls error. In the real world God created, one of them is false and one of them is true. But they cannot both be right. Only one can function as canon. It is, of course, the devil's work to spin a gray web of confusion from the black and white threads of truth and falsehood. In his world there is no canon.

Q: A Source of Unexpected Liberal Riches

How can a heretical Gnostic text like the *Gospel of Thomas* stand proudly beside the four canonical Gospels, the "four pillars, breathing out immortality on every side and vivifying our flesh," as the redoubtable foe of Gnosticism, Irenaeus, called them?[55] Imagine the stinging review that he would have written of *The Five Gospels*, since he knew Gnosticism first-hand and considered it "an abyss of madness and blasphemy against Christ."[56] Modern reviewers will be tolerant, not least because of the scholarship that such a volume claims. Part of that scholarship is the employment of Q.

James Robinson counters Iranaeus and orthodox Christians by elevating a hypothetical document, Q, as "surely the most important text we have." What makes Q more important than Matthew, Mark, Luke or John, or the great epistles of Paul?

Q, from the German word *quelle*, meaning "source," is the name scholars have given to the material common to Matthew and Luke. First suggested by Johann Gottfried Eichhorn in 1794,[57] Q has served as the most widely accepted theory about the sources used by Matthew and Luke. Known as the "Two Source Theory" this argument suggests that Matthew and Luke had both Mark and Q before them when they composed their own gospels. Matthew had additional material, "M," while

Luke's unique material is known as "L." For a long time Q was considered a miscellaneous collection of sayings.

Recently interest has shifted from Q as a possible collection of sayings used by Matthew and Luke to Q as an independent document, offering its own theology and a window on the earliest Jesus movement.[58] Certain critical circles refer to Q by chapter and verse (for example, Q 9:57)[59] This is something akin to classifying the imaginary bones of a pre-historic man whose only trace in history was the ruins of his house. Q is studied as an independent document at the annual meeting of the Society of Biblical Literature. Some recent titles — *The First Gospel,*[60] *The Lost Gospel,*[61] and *Q Thomas Reader,* (both hailed on the back cover as "The Earliest Sayings Gospels")[62] — have also sought to bestow on Q the wonderful gift of objective existence.

Q has two significant functions in radical New Testament studies: the first is to rehabilitate the *Gospel of Thomas*; the second is to grant access to the radical "Christian" community in which Q is supposedly born.

Q and Thomas: A Dynamic Duo

Thomas, as a collection of 114 sayings with no interest in the story of Jesus' life, is so clearly Gnostic and so different from other gospel forms that it is difficult to place it early in Christian history.[63] Enter Q, on cue.

If Q did exist, it is the earliest written document.[64] If it can be identified with the common material of Matthew and Luke, it too is made up almost entirely of sayings, has hardly any narrative and contains no accounts of, nor reflections on, the death and resurrection of Jesus. *Et voilà* a literary and theological soul mate/twin for Thomas. Q draws Thomas to the historical Jesus as a magnet attracts iron filings. According to Robinson, the hypothetical document Q shows that the *Gospel of Thomas* is among the earliest collections of Jesus' sayings.[65] "[*Thomas*]," says New Testament scholar Stevan Davies, "appears to be roughly as valuable a primary source for the teaching of Jesus as Q."[66] Thomas and Q share the same literary genre — a collection of sayings — and the same theology — Jesus as a wise teacher, not a savior from sin. Robert Funk, in an interview on National Public Radio, conceded that the red and pink sections of *The Five Gospels* [that is, the sayings considered the most authentic] derive in the main from Q and Thomas.[67] Modern scholarship purports to deliver us a new, scientifically-based picture of Jesus.

If the image is the message, the implicit message of the *Jesus Seminar* is bound to please the boomer and buster generations — this is "pro-choice" historical research, truth by the ballot box, as white-coated specialists dispassionately lob colored balls into a jar, in a non-confessional "seminar" of experts,[68] free of ecclesiastical establishments and imposed dogmas, forced by the objective evidence of science to come up with new texts and a new Jesus for a new time.

Says one of the spokesmen for the *Jesus Seminar*: "[our work] is not answerable to any church. . . . Our purpose is simply to let the gospels speak, as much as possible, on their own terms."[69] The only problem with the image is that it is false. There is as much theological commitment here as in any openly religious group.[70] Moreover, the "science" on which the image is based leaves a lot to be desired.

Q is absolutely essential to this new Bible. Once Q exists, the Gnostic *Thomas* can be (somewhat) plausibly drawn into the orbit of the earliest community following the death of Jesus.[71] Without Q, the whole reconstruction falls to the ground like a house of cards.

Q Is What You Believe It To Be

Some of the best minds have sought to make the Q hypothesis stick. At the end of the nineteenth century, the famous German liberal, Adolf von Harnack, warned that work on the sources of the canonical Gospels was like that of a "scavenger's labors in which one is choked with dust."[72] The dust has not settled. In 1980 another German specialist on the subject observed:

> The critical analysis of the sources of the Gospels is justifiably regarded as one of the most difficult research problems in the history of ideas . . . one can truly say that no other enterprise in the history of ideas has been subjected to anywhere near the same degree of scholarly scrutiny.[73]

In spite of all that effort, many well-respected scholars have dissented from the standard view, even of Q as an existing source.[74] A British New Testament scholar, John Wenham, lecturer at Bristol University and warden of Latimer House, Oxford, gives the interesting testimony:

> In 1979 I found myself in the *Synoptic Problem Seminar* of the *Society for New Testament Studies* whose members were in disagreement over every aspect of the subject. When this international group disbanded in 1992 they had sadly to confess that after twelve years' work they had not reached a common mind on a single issue.[75]

Wenham's judgment in 1992 is that the Q hypothesis, since "no one knows for certain whether a Q-document ever existed," is still held as a working hypothesis "but with decreasing confidence."[76] James Robinson, in the same lecture in which he claims that Q is the most important Christian text we have, admits to the ongoing debate about the Synoptic Problem.[77] William Farmer, an old-style liberal, takes him to task:

> contra Robinson, would it not be more reasonable to conclude that if the ongoing debate about the Synoptic Problem raises questions about whether "Q" ever existed, which it certainly is doing, should not theologians like Robinson acknowledge the hypothetical character of their reconstruction, and admit that their projects depend upon a premise that may be false, a premise which an increasing number of competent scholars are prepared to say probably is false?[78]

Is it not the height of speculation for scholars to build further hypotheses upon a hypothesis that still awaits generally accepted scholarly confirmation, especially when the very nature of the Christian faith is at stake? Already in 1955 A.M.Farrer argued there was no need for Q if Luke used Matthew. Everything that was common was the result of Luke incorporating Matthew into his gospel.[79] The simplicity of this argument has convinced more than one contemporary scholar,[80] one of whom described Farrer's article as a "firecracker."[81] Farrer's argument still sparkles, awaiting a satisfactory refutation.[82] Modern support, not refutation is on the way. As Q scholars perfect their critical edition of the text of Q, a new publication by an equally gifted team of scholars puts the whole existence of Q once more into serious question — a state of affairs that William Farmer describes as "exquisitely ironic."[83] *Beyond the Q Impasse — Luke's Use of Matthew*[84] re-examines the old argument that Luke used Matthew and claims to have found "never-before-seen objective data, proving that the author of the Gospel of Luke systematically and respectfully used sequences of material from the canonical Gospel of Matthew in writing his own Gospel."[85] Apparently the Gnostic colossus of Christian origins has embarrassingly large feet of clay!

Anyone For New Age Rugby?

In 1989, Earle E. Ellis reviewed a book on Q by John Kloppenborg, one of the prime movers in Q studies. Ellis asks what any self-respecting expert should:

> Is it wise to pursue such a thesis [about the development of Q] with no recognition and apparently no awareness of the current widespread questioning and rejection of the Q hypothesis? . . . this book preaches

to the converted . . . but it is not designed to address the questions of those who doubt that any definable Q-document ever existed outside scholarly imagination.[86]

Old objections to the so-called scientific case for Q linger stubbornly. Many scholars are dubious of the emperor's new clothes. Ignoring objections is hardly good science. But that does not faze the present proponents of the hypothesis. The mission impossible must go on. The brouhaha over *The Five Gospels* led one conservative British scholar to liken the contemporary situation to a game of rugby in which there are five teams, ten balls and everybody thinks he is winning.[87] Some estimates of the "new science" are less kind. Jacob Neusner, a Jewish professor of religious studies at the University of Florida calls the *Jesus Seminar* "either the greatest scholarly hoax since the Piltdown Man or the utter bankruptcy of New Testament studies — I hope the former."[88]

If the science is not convincing, what ideology propels the movement? Is it a noble, neutral search for truth, a desire to educate and to remove the darkness of religious illiteracy, as its spokesmen stoutly claim? Or is it driven by a deep opposition to Christian orthodoxy, an ideology that serves the new look religion of the Age of Aquarius?

No Agenda . . . But Who Owns Jesus?

The scholarly program has theological fallout. William Farmer saw it coming in 1986, when he observed:

> There will be far-reaching consequences when "Q" is parlayed with gnostic sources like the Gospel of Thomas into fanciful reconstructions where it is implied that there was a primitive apostolic community for which the death and resurrection of Jesus Christ was (contrary to the New Testament) of little or no importance.

Farmer senses the explosive character of the "scholarly" agenda, though he does not spell out the details. Of course, the devil is in the details. Since its inception in the 1980's, the "theology of Q," with its picture of Jesus and the earliest community, has produced a growing body of literature.[89] The new radical Q scholarship agrees with *Thomas*, in three significant areas:

♦ **The Person of Jesus**
Jesus did not proclaim himself as the Messiah and the Son of God, the divine savior who was to die for the sins of the world;[90]

◆ **The Work of Jesus**

The Jesus of Q [the hypothetical document supposedly embedded in Matthew and Luke — see below] is but a teacher of wisdom,[91] a sort of proto-Gnostic guru;

◆ **The Nature of the Church**

The "Q people" (hypothetically reconstructed from the hypothetical document Q) did not focus "on the person of Jesus or his life and destiny. [Rather] they were engrossed with the social program that was called for by his teachings,"[92] including radical poverty, the life-style of the wandering beggar,[93] an attitude of political subversion,[94] and needless to say, an egalitarian, anti-patriarchal feminism.[95]

Speaking of the "Q community," Burton Mack goes on to make the most radical of statements:

> The remarkable thing about the people of Q is that they were not Christians. They did not think of Jesus as a messiah or the Christ; . . . They did not regard his death as a . . . saving event; . . . they did not imagine that he had been raised from the dead; . . . they did not gather to worship in his name. . . . *The people of Q were Jesus people, not Christians* [emphasis mine].[96]

Publicity for Burton L. Mack's volume, *The Lost Gospel: The Book of Q and Christian Origins* trumpets that *The Book of Q* "Pre-dat[es] the New Testament by generations," that the New Testament "presents a fictionalized life of Jesus," and that Jesus' disciples "did not think of him as the Son of God . . . but . . . as a wise, anti-establishment. . . counter-culture . . . teacher."[97]

The question is: Who owns Jesus? The ancient Gnostics and the *Jesus Seminar* or the New Testament and historic orthodoxy?

No Agenda . . . Except a New Pagan Christianity

Some in the Q movement may naively believe themselves "neutral" scholars, pursuing truth wherever it leads,[98] but most of the *Jesus Seminar* scholars have a religious commitment to some form of liberalism and some have no Christian commitment at all. Another god than the God of Scripture seems to be using their science to promote his pernicious agenda. Q scholarship and the new Bible it proposes provide theological foundations for the New Age gospel of egalitarian feminism, sexual androgyny in all its perverse forms, the unity of all religions, the denial of sin, the rejection of the atonement, in a word, the extreme paganization of the Christian faith. The noble principle — "Beware of finding a Jesus entirely congenial to you" — which supposedly guided the *Jesus Seminar*, did not stop these scholars from avoiding what they call "this fatal pitfall . . . (of) creat(ing) Jesus in our own image."[99] Their emerging Jesus would be at home in the pro-choice, politically correct ideology espoused by the post-modern elite of our contemporary culture.

Meeting Jesus Again for the First Time

This very modern, pro-choice Jesus makes one wonder just how "scientific" is the "Jesus" of the Jesus Seminar? If the religious commitment of one of its most notable members is anything to go on, not very. Marcus Borg, author of the recent book on Jesus, *Meeting Jesus Again for the First Time*, is a deeply religious man.[100] Raised an evangelical Lutheran, he now has discovered a new view of the Spirit and of Jesus. The Jesus he met again for the first time is not the Jesus of scriptural orthodoxy. "Like Socrates," says Borg, "Jesus was a teacher of a subversive wisdom. Like the Buddha, he had an Enlightenment experience. Like a shaman, he was a healer. Like Gandhi, he protested against a purity system."[101] Borg is not merely comparing Jesus with elements in the lives of other holy men. Borg is recognizing the validity of other religious traditions. For Borg's new view of the spirit is "rooted in the pantheism of Huston Smith."[102] So we need to ask not merely who is Jesus? We need to ask who is Huston Smith?

Huston Smith is a well-known expert in comparative religions. Deeply committed to monistic spirituality, he associates with New Age and Theosophical thinkers[103] and has published with the Theosophical Publishing House of Wheaton, Illinois.[104] Readers will recall that the Theosophical Society was founded towards the end of the nineteenth century by the spiritualist Helena Blavatsky, and later propagated by Annie Besant. Both women are now considered foremothers of the New Age. An authority on the history of the occult calls the Theosophical Society "the very pillar of the late nineteenth century revival of the occult." [105] Huston Smith is the author cited above who believes that there is "an invisible geometry . . . working to shape (the great religious traditions of the world) into a single truth." Needless to say, this syncretistic view of the spirit when employed by Borg will only consider believable a Jesus-guru who can blend into other religious systems. It will reject as unacceptable and thus unauthentic the exclusive claims of the Jesus of orthodox confessions. In his personal testimony Borg states quite honestly: "I do not believe that Christianity is the only way of salvation, or that the Bible is the revealed will of God, or that Jesus was the unique Son of God." Christianity is only one of many "mediators of the sacred." [106]

One certainly has to respect Borg's belief system, but it is just that —
belief. One *Seminar* member declares it more and more difficult to imagine a Jesus who reflected on his own death (see below, chapter 10).
Perhaps this is due to a change in the belief-system of many modern
Bible scholars, rather than a change in the facts. Now that the shimmering mirage of science has dissipated, the *Jesus Seminar* drags before us a
revived pantheistic spirituality, a Gnostic Jesus. How many of the sev-
enty-three members adopt a similar spirituality behind their claim to
cold dispassionate scholarship? The Fourth R turns out to be the R of
religious monism.

Not surprisingly, it is the "Christian" pagan syncretists who exult
at the publication of *The Five Gospels.* The radical feminist Episcopal
Bishop, John Shelby, who favors homosexuality and denies the bodily
resurrection, hails the book as "a probing, penetrating, and deeply spiritual journey into the hearts of the gospels, . . . and might well become
the means whereby the secularized post-Christian world discovers its
own deepest roots."[107] Another translation of "Jesus' most familiar
words," based on the same kind of scholarship,[108] receives the telling
imprimatur of Matthew Fox, the "Creation Spirituality" theologian who
endorses homosexuality, witchcraft and American Indian animism.
"Reader beware," warns Fox, "though this book is brief, it contains the
seeds of a revolution."

What do the radicals Fox and Spong know that most Christians do
not know? Interestingly, another Creation Spirituality theologian says
of *The Complete Gospels*: "Reading through this book I felt at times like
a child on Christmas morning."[109] Of course, if this view prevails, there
will be no Christmas! Why does the Hindu Vedanta Society of America
accept these Gnostic texts and endorse the radical New Testament scholarship that rehabilitates them?[110] Because the beliefs of Jesus according
to the *Gospel of Thomas* are a virtual carbon copy of the "Creation Spirituality" of Matthew Fox, of western Hindu paganism and New Age mysticism in all its forms.[111] The Jesus of the *Gospel of Thomas* rejects the
notion of sin in Gen 2:5 to 3:24, holding only the optimistic view of
mankind expressed in Gen 1:1 to 2:4. This "authentic" Jesus of left-
wing New Testament scholarship speaks not like the Jesus of the New
Testament canon but just like a New Age channeler. A New Testament
specialist concludes: "Those seeking the place where Jesus is ought *not*
to seek Jesus himself, but will find what they seek within themselves."[112]
This is pure Hinduism. Shirley MacLaine could not have said it better.
Perhaps she should be invited to join the *Jesus Seminar* for yet one more
neutral opinion!

Feminist rhetoric also avails itself of this new scholarship. Notably absent in the seminar devoted to Jesus at the *RE-Imagining Conference* in 1993, attended by some five hundred participants, was the orthodox, New Testament image of Jesus. The proceedings began with songs to the goddess Sophia, and presenter Dolores S. Williams, a "womanist" (a black woman feminist) theology professor at Union Theological Seminary in New York City stated bluntly: "I do not think we need a theory of the atonement at all." A leader of the seminar, Kwok Pui-Lan, asked: "Who is this funny God that would sacrifice a lamb?" She went on to explain, in terms that recalled the *Gospel of Thomas*, that the Chinese do not believe in a God outside the creation, and that the Confucianist tradition emphasized the propensity for good in mankind.[113]

The Complete Bible

The *Jesus Seminar* scholars are intentionally producing a new Bible which augments and completes the Bible we already have. Their *Scholars' Bible* gives us texts such as the *Infancy Gospels of James* and *Thomas* which even liberal scholars in the past dismissed as pious legends and popular fiction, not worthy to be considered, for a moment, as part of authentic, early Christianity.[114]

The new Bible, that adds and takes away from Holy Scripture, spreads pagan monism in the Christian church. Where will this lead?

A New Bible For a Global Religion

The new Bible and the "Q community" may be short-lived creations. But they will have deconstructed the Bible by relativizing the uniqueness of its claims[115] and by setting heretical writings alongside canonical ones. Q, Thomas, and other heretical texts, and eventually 1 Cor 13, will survive in a heady atmosphere, that of the next-generation all-world-religions Bible, already in process of production. We do well to recall here the prediction made in 1974 about the coming new polytheistic religion which, "because it makes contact with the immediacy of life out of the depths, *is itself a religion with no scripture, but with many stories.*"[116]

The production of a world Bible began with enthusiastic prompting by Robert Muller, New Age leader and assistant deputy secretary-general of the UN. In 1989 the United Nations launched the *International Sacred Literature Trust*. The purpose of this Trust is to make the world's sacred writings more accessible in the common language of English. This project is now headed by the *Inter-Religious Federation for World*

Peace, a front organization of the Unification Church.[117] At an *IRFWP "Symposium on World Scriptures,"* organized at the *Parliament of the World's Religions* in September, 1993, a number of well-known scholars, including Dr. Ursula King, a member of the Board of Advisors of IRFWP and Professor of Theology and Religious Studies at Bristol University, U.K., gave lectures on this exciting program. In her lecture King announced that the International Sacred Literature Trust had agreed upon a publishing venture with Harper Collins, and concluded that this series of ancient sacred traditions would "become a contemporary resource for shaping our future as a global community."[118]

A New, All-Faiths Bible

The new Bible will likely look something like the texts read at one of the plenary sessions of the *Parliament of the World's Religions,* "Voices of Spirit and Tradition." Texts from Hindu and Buddhist Scriptures were read along with selections from the Coran and the Sufi masters, an American Indian animistic chant, and a poem by a womanist claiming that humanity needs new revelations. The death-of-God theologian and polytheist, David Miller, Professor of Religion at Syracuse University and member of the Joseph Campbell Institute called for the end of dogmas and doctrines that limit unity and for the discovery of a world soul through weaning and emptying. Miller read from Meister Eckhardt, a medieval mystic who prayed: "I pray God, free me of God." A representative of the "School of Spiritual Psychology" read from the Gnostic text, *Pistis Sophia,* which revered the goddess and denounced the "lion-faced" prideful Creator God of the Old Testament. There was one reading from the Bible, a text where God and Christ are absent. A New Age liberal Benedictine monk declared that as a representative of the Christian tradition, he was faced with an impossible choice. Unable to choose a passage that mentioned God, for fear of offending all the women present, or a passage mentioning Jesus Christ, since that would be too divisive, he solved his dilemma by reading from First Corinthians 13 as a text about love that speaks to the heart of every religion whose deep concern is to help humans become truly human in deep communion with plants and animals. I could not help noticing that this statement was enthusiastically received by all the witches on the platform.

In 1984, the year George Orwell made famous in his novel describing the ultimate form of totalitarianism, Harper Publishing brought us *The Other Bible,* a collection of "inspired" writings from the ancient Judeo-Christian world, including many Gnostic texts and material from the mystical Jewish Kabbala, that did not make it into the Christian canon. Its editor, Willis Barnstone, Professor of Comparative Religions at Indiana State University, makes the following statement as he introduces the collection. "Had events been otherwise and certain of these [non-canonical] texts been incorporated in our Bible, our understanding of religious thought would have been radically altered. Today, free of doctrinal strictures, we can read the 'greater bible' of the Judeo-Christian world."[119] The implication is that these books did not make it into the canon as the result of arbitrary dogmatism. But the accusation does not stick. Most of the material in *The Other Bible* (with the exception of the Dead Sea Scrolls) defends a monistic, anti-Christian worldview in fundamental contradiction to the Christian gospel. A case in point. The contents of Gnostic *Apocryphon of John* are described in this publication as having to do with "Sophia, Mother of the monstrous Creator, Ialdabaoth, Jahweh." For a Christian this is unspeakable blasphemy since the New Testament presents God as the Father of our Lord Jesus Christ and the maker of heaven and earth. You go for *The Other Bible* and you adopt a non-Christian world and life view. You cannot have both Bibles just as you cannot serve two masters. But that of course is the point. Harper San Francisco also brings us *The World's Wisdom: Sacred texts of the World's Religions*,[120] calling it "Virtually a World Bible for an age of intercultural understanding." Penguin Books offers The Portable World Bible which includes selections from the "bibles" of the major world religions — the Upanishads and the Bhagavad-Gita of Hinduism, the Lotus of the True Law and The Tibetan Doctrine from Buddhism, The Gatas from Zoroastrianism, the Koran from Islam, the Li Ki and the Book of Filial Piety from Confucianism, the Tao-Te King from Taoism, and "substantial selections from the Old and New Testaments" from Judaism and Christianity.[121]

The World Scriptures — a gender and religion inclusive interfaith planetary Bible — is part of the brave new world of the Age of Aquarius awaiting us in the Third Millennium. Though not yet [to my knowledge] available in church pew editions, for use in "Christian" interfaith liturgies, the time is surely not far off when the World Bible is a standard part of mainline Christianity. How important it is that Christians understand what is going on now, as liberals tinker with their Bible and seek to undermine the very objective basis of the Christian faith. How important that we preserve the Bible from such blatant attacks and continue to make it available for all to read, understand and obey.

CHAPTER 7

THE ANCIENT GNOSTIC BIBLE

There was revealed in their hearts the living book of the living.
  - *Gospel of Truth*

The Use and Misuse of the Scriptures

Strictly speaking, the Gnostics did not have a Bible.[1] A Bible only makes sense in a theistic universe in which the transcendent God, distinct from his creation, reveals himself in space and time, for the sake of redemption through the means of special revelation. Since the Gnostics redeemed themselves, and were in touch with their divine selves, they had no need of revelation. God's intervention to save and to reveal were superfluous to those who possessed inner knowledge of their divinity. Spiritual gurus suggested wisdom from their own quest for personal transformation.

But Gnostics used Scripture when it suited them. They related to the Bible in three ways:

♦ they quoted (and misquoted) the Christian Bible;

♦ they produced bogus "scriptures";

♦ they used mystical sources for creating Gnostic wisdom from which they created a "canon" that looked nothing like the canon of the Church.

The Old Testament

One of the earliest Gnostics, Marcion, so detested the God of Creation and Law that he expunged the Old Testament from his "Christian" canon. The texts preached by the Apostles, the "Scripture" of the Early Church, were dismissed by second century Gnostics as the disagreeable musings of an inferior God. Later Gnostics, like Valentinus, were more ingenious. As the chapter on Gnostic Bible study will show, the full-blown Gnostic systems commandeered the Old Testament for Gnostic purposes by turning the sacred text on its head. The Church Father, Tertullian (160-225 A.D), captures the subtleties of this later approach when he compares Marcion and Valentinus:

> One man perverts Scripture with his hand, another with his exegesis. If Valentinus seems to have used the whole Bible, he laid violent hands upon the truth with just as much cunning as Marcion. Marcion openly and nakedly used the knife, not the pen, massacring Scripture to suit his own material. Valentinus spared the text, since he did not invent Scriptures to suit his matter, but matter to suit the Scriptures. Yet he took more away, and added more, by taking away the proper meanings of particular words, and by adding fantastic arguments.[2]

Generally, Gnostics disregarded the Old Testament. While numerous Nag Hammadi texts focus on Genesis 1-3, the rest of the Old Testament is virtually absent. The reason is simple. Gnosticism is a revolution of independence from the Creator God revealed in the Bible. Once the Creator is dethroned, the rest falls of its own weight. The Gnostics had no interest in the *history* of redemption, which is the unifying theme of the Old Testament. History has no status in a monistic world. Since the Old Testament Creator defines Himself as the Redeemer of Israel, He is of no interest whatsoever. Delivering the Law to his people sealed Jahweh's fate.

The New Testament

What befell the Old Testament also befell the New. It is interesting to compare the Gnostics with another ancient religious sect, the people of Qumran. The Dead Sea Scrolls of the Qumran Community were discovered just three years after the Nag Hammadi library. They contain some commentaries on and full copies or fragments of every book in the Old Testament except Esther.[3] Though a marginal group in ancient Judaism, the Qumran community was clearly committed to the Old Testament Bible, even if their interpretations were at times idiosyncratic.

By contrast, the Nag Hammadi Library, the only extant collection of texts of this marginal "Christian" movement witnesses to a profound disdain for the scriptures of its tradition. There is not one copy of a New Testament book. By their allusions to well-known phrases, Gnostic writings show familiarity with the apostolic writings. But they seemed deliberately to suppress the New Testament writings themselves. The Gnostics show apathy to Jesus as a person, and see no importance in his deeds, especially in his death and resurrection. The apostolic, eye-witness teaching on the person and ministry of Jesus is wrapped in Gnostic interpretation or changed to divert the original sense. An excellent case in point is the *Gospel of Thomas*.

Thomas and the Gospels

Scholarship associated with the *Jesus Seminar*[4] regularly claims *Thomas* to be one of the earliest, if not the earliest written gospel. But an earlier generation of specialists affirmed the contrary. Kurt Rudolf, whose work, *Gnosis*, was first published in 1977, sees in *Thomas* the typical Gnostic approach to other people's scripture, when he says:

> The *Gospel of Thomas* presents the ancient material of the sayings and parables of Jesus in a Gnostic interpretation and adds new material of the same sort . . . the Gnostic men of letters were frequently leaders in the production of such "gospels."[5]

Rudolf further observes that Gnosticism

> frequently draws its material from the most varied existing tradition, attaches itself to it, and at the same time sets it in a new frame. . . . the Gnostic view of the world . . . attaches itself . . . to old religious imagery, almost as a parasite prospers on the soil of host religions, it can also be described as parasitic. To this extent Gnosticism strictly speaking has no tradition of its own but only a borrowed one. Its mythology is a tradition consciously created from alien material.[6]

A wonderful example of this Gnostic method is saying twenty-one:

> Mary said to Jesus, "What are your disciples like?" He said, "They are similar to children who have settled in a field which is not theirs. When the lords of the field come, they will say, 'Give our field back to us.' (The children will) disrobe before them in order to return their field and to give it back to them. Consequently I say, if the house owner is aware that a robber is coming, he will begin to keep guard before he comes and will not allow him to break into his house of his domain to seize all his goods. You then, be on your guard against the world. Equip yourselves with great fortitude lest the thieves find a way to get to you, for the distress you anticipate will take place. May there be in your midst a man of wisdom. When the crop ripened, he came promptly, sickle in hand, and reaped it. He who has ears to hear, let him hear."

Such a saying bears no hint of an individual author's creativity or literary artifice. This is clearly not the Gnostic author's purpose. Rather, numerous biblical allusions are combined with some Gnostic phrases in a collage of ideas that blunts the original scriptural intention and promotes obscure Gnostic teaching.[7] Scripture is not functioning here with canonical authority but as a mine of sayings and images to be used for other purposes and another agenda, while projecting a veneer of Christian truth. This is not serious exegesis. It appears distinctly like the self-serving, picking and choosing self, denounced by the church father Irenaeus (130-200 A.D.). Here is his contemporary eye-witness report:

> They try to adapt to their own sayings in a manner worthy of credence, either the Lord's parables, or the prophets' sayings, or the apostles' words, so that their fabrication might not appear to be without witness. They disregard the order and the connection of the Scriptures and, as much as in them lies, they disjoint the members of the truth. They transfer passages and rearrange them; and making one thing out of another, they deceive many by the badly composed fantasy of the Lord's words they adapt.[8]

This same Gnostic spirit is very much alive today. Rosemary Radford Ruether, while remaining in the church and teaching at Garret-Evangelical Theological Seminary, Evanston, Illinois, in *Womanguides* recommends the use of any text, including Platonic, Gnostic, or sectarian, that make references to the divine female.[9] Personal agenda removes the canonical authority from Scripture and places it alongside any documents that further the theological program in question.

Another Gnostic specialist underlines the difference between Gnostic "Gospels" and the Gospels of the Bible. With regard to the Gnostic *Gospel of Truth*, its editor says:

> "In spite of the title, this work is not a gospel of the same sort as the New Testament gospels: it does not focus upon the words and deed of the historical Jesus. Yet the *Gospel of Truth* is 'gospel' in the sense of 'good news' about Jesus, about the eternal and divine Son, the word who reveals the Father and passes on knowledge, particularly self-knowledge . . . through this . . . the Gnostics . . . realize that they themselves are essentially sons of the Father."[10]

This is hardly good news if the truth about us is that we have all sinned and fallen short of the glory of God.[11]

The Gnostics used biblical texts, discarded others and imported material from any religious tradition to express the "good news" of their own divine nature. Theistic Old and New Testament Scriptures are brought under the yoke of that essential idea of Gnosticism. But since the Scriptures are theistic not monistic, they gave little support to the Gnostic program. Inevitably, the Gnostics were obliged to write their own texts and produce their own "Bible."

The Production of Gnostic Scriptures

Gnostics claimed secret revelation that was kept from the church in general and revealed to the truly spiritual. Paying scant attention to what Jesus did and said on earth, they emphasized the teaching of the "living" or resurrected Jesus who brought secret knowledge to his initiates after his time on earth. The apocryphal *Acts of Peter* describes Peter entering a church where the congregation is reading from the Gospel scroll. Peter rolls up the scroll, and explains that only the deeper knowledge brings true gnosis: Jesus only appeared to take on flesh.[12]

This is the claim of the *Gospel of Thomas*, which begins: "These are the secret sayings which the living Jesus spoke and which Didymos Judas Thomas wrote down . . . Whoever finds the interpretation of these sayings will not experience death." Thomas receives knowledge that goes beyond what is in the canonical Gospels, giving him the authority to reconfigure the Gospel. The Gnostic gnosis defines the principle of the reconfiguration. Irenaeus recounts the vision of Marcus the magician who sees

the Supreme Tetrad descended from invisible, unnameable places in the Pleroma in female form to reveal to him something never before revealed to God or man, who he really was and how he came into being.[13]

This knowledge lies beyond Scripture, and gives to Scripture its true meaning.

Apocalypse Now

The New Testament contains one book entitled an *apocalypse*, and uses the term on many occasions. Behind the term is a verb which means "openly reveal, make known, disclose."[14] This word characterizes the Gospel message of the New Testament as the revelation of God in the Old Testament, now fully and openly revealed in Jesus Christ and the writings of the apostolic witness. Gnosticism emphasizes the "*apocryphon.*" Behind this noun stands a verb meaning "hide from sight, keep hidden, conceal."[15] This term characterizes the Gnostic view of Scripture: secret revelation to be kept away from prying eyes, and revealed only to the inner circle. No New Testament book is called an "apocryphon." The Nag Hammadi collection contains two, the *Apocryphon of James* and the *Apocryphon of John. James* claims to be special, secret revelation, kept even from the Twelve, and thus superior to orthodoxy. James writes to a disciple and minister, a certain [...]thos:

> But because you are a servant of the salvation of the saints, strive diligently and take care not to relate this writing to many — this very one, which the Savior did not desire to tell even to all of us; his twelve disciples. But blessed will they become, namely, those who will be saved through the faith of this word (logos).

> And I also sent another *Apocryphon* to you ten months ago, which was revealed to me by the Savior. As the case may be, I consider that one revealed to me, James.[16]

At the conclusion of the *Apocryphon of John*, Jesus says to John:

> And I have I said [sic] you everything
> that you shall write it down
> and give it secretly to your brethren in the spirit, for this is the mystery of the generation which does not waiver.[17]

The difference between this heretical "Johannine" apocryphon and the canonical Gospel of John is most notable. At the conclusion of the canonical Gospel of John, the apostle declares: "Jesus did many other miraculous signs in the presence of his disciples, which are not recorded in this book. But these are written that you may believe that Jesus is the Christ, the son of the living God, and that believing you may have life in his name."[18] The emphasis is on the astonishing deeds of Jesus, and the gospel is written to be spread in broad daylight, as Jesus prophesied: "But I, when I am lifted up from the earth, will draw all men to myself."[19] Where the Bible reveals, Gnosticism conceals.

It is true that there are five apocalypses in the recently-discovered Gnostic texts, the *Apocalypse of Paul*, the *First Apocalypse of James*, the *Second Apocalypse of James*, the *Apocalypse of Adam* and the *Apocalypse of Peter*. When the term *apocalypse* (revelation) is used, however, it is in the sense of *secret* revelation for those in the inner circle. The *Apoca-*

lypse of Paul is a classic statement of the ascent of the initiated one into deeper and deeper realms of gnosis. It goes beyond 2 Corinthians 12 and reveals what Paul in the New Testament said was unlawful to reveal, even to believers. "Paul" ascends through the third to the fourth, fifth, six and at the seventh is stopped by "an old man [....] light [and] [whose clothing] was white, [His throne], which is in the seventh heaven, [was] [seven] times brighter than the sun." When the Spirit tells "Paul" to move on, "The old man answered me and said, 'How will you be able to escape from me? Look around and see the principalities and the authorities.' Then he spoke, namely the spirit, and said, 'Give him [the] token from your hand, and [he will] open for you. And then I gave him the token. He (the old man, that is, Jahweh) turned his face down towards his creation." Then "Paul" goes to the Ogdoad, that is, the eighth mystical realm, then to the ninth and eventually the tenth heaven, where he is greeted by his fellow spirits.[20] This is secret knowledge of the mystical ascent, a classic type of pagan spirituality.

The *First Apocalypse of James*, says the editor, contains "the secret teachings of the Lord to James."[21] In the *Second Apocalypse of James*, "James" is "the escort guiding the Gnostic through the heavenly door."[22] The *Apocalypse of Adam* ends with the phrase: "This is the secret knowledge (*gnosis*) of Adam which he gave to Seth, which is the sacred baptism of the ones who know the everlasting knowledge (*gnosis*)."[23] The *Apocalypse of Peter* is the account of a revelation seen by Peter and interpreted by Jesus for an oppressed faithful remnant of Gnostics who are "summoned to knowledge."[24]

In Gnosticism, even the "Gospels" are not to be preached on the rooftops, as in the New Testament.[25] The *Gospel of Thomas* describes its content as "the secret sayings" of the living Jesus.[26] *The Gospel of Truth* speaks of esoteric knowledge in a most [deliberately?] confusing way:

> This is the knowledge of the living book that he made manifest at the end to the Aeons . . . Every letter is an entire [thought], like a finished book, because they are written in unity, by the Father, for the Aeons, so that they may know the Father through his letters.[27]

These secret revelations claim divine origin. The *Gospel of the Egyptians* claims to be "the God-written, holy, secret book . . . of the great invisible Spirit."[28] *Zostrianos* makes the same claim: "Zostrianos: Words of truth of Zostrianos. God of Truth. Words of Zoroast[er].[29] *Trimorphic Protennoia* ends with the phrase "A sacred scripture written by the Father with perfect knowledge."[30] Though claiming divine inspiration, these books have another, different source.

The Ultimate Source of the Gnostic Bible

The source of the Gnostic Bible is not the transcendent God outside the universe he created. Gnostic "truth comes from within the circle of existence and from within the human heart. Says the *Gospel of Truth* about "the little children," that is, the Gnostic believers, "there was revealed in their hearts the living book of the living — the one written in the thought and mind of the Father."[31] Knowledge of the unknown God is found within oneself. But is there anything else out there that might determine what the human heart knows? The editor of the Nag Hammadi text *Zostrianos,* argues that Zostrianos is directly related to Zoroaster, the founder of Persian Zoroastrian system and of "all sorts of philosophical, speculative and magical systems."[32] *Zostrianos* presents, says the modern editor, "a series of revelations made by exalted beings regarding the nature of the heavenly realm."[33]

One is reminded of the source of contemporary New Age revelations, the spirit entities, who speak through channels such as Ken Carey (*Starseed: The Third Millennium*), and Helen Shucman (*A Course in Miracles*). Others in the movement are claiming similar inspiration. Fritjof Capra, who teaches physics at UC Berkeley speaks of "outside powers" so strong that "sometimes, while writing the *Tao of Physics,* I felt that it was being written through me, rather than by me. The subsequent events have confirmed these feelings."[34] David Miller, the "death-of-God" theologian and Professor of Religion at Syracuse University speaks in almost "evangelical" terms of the process by which the gods and goddesses "in their reality and potency. . . . entered my life."[35] He describes bizarre occurrences during his lectures on Greek religion when these pagan deities would "take on a life of their own in the classroom." He would add details of his own to the Greek myths — as "the stories carried on with (or perhaps without) me — only to discover later, in further research, that these details were already in the ancient texts.[36]

Claims to mystical "inspiration" are made by evangelical writers who have strayed far from biblical orthodoxy into neo-Gnosticism. Madeleine L'Engle maintains that she does not write her books. Rather they are written through her.[37] Virginia Mollenkott, who acknowledges being greatly helped by the New Age text *A Course in Miracles* thanks "the angels who hover near and the Depth that has called to my depth throughout this writing." In working to undermine the evil heteropatriarchal society that obstructs the advent of a new day of human liberation — "God's 'kindom,' emphatically different from

God's kingdom."[38] Mollenkott claims to have been "told," and she quotes the divine message:

> it is your nature to work for the social change that is already in the process of happening. . . . a great shift of consciousness is occurring in the world, and you are a part of that shift. . . . it is essential for you to cooperate by being one of my activist channels into the world. . . . it is a special blessing to play your position willingly, because then your heart is able to feel the tenderness . . . of my angels and Spirit Guides.[39]

Christians are told to test the spirits.[40] Gnostic knowledge found within is occult knowledge. Its source is not only the human heart, as many so naively think, but also the forces of evil amassed against the truth of God as revealed in Scripture. It claims to be divine prophecy, but it is false prophecy from the Father of lies.

The Gnostics effectively silenced the Bible in their communities by not recognizing its existence or power. The same is happening in our day, when two canons vie for ultimate authority. As yet the Bible still occupies first place in pulpits and hearts across the land. But more and more an alternate "bible" is subtly introduced for the tolerant consideration of believers, so that one is forced to wonder if the day will ever come, as it did in the time of Gnosticism, when the Scriptures were eclipsed in many places by the esoteric writings of the heretics.

But this apostate movement, both in its ancient and modern forms, held and holds still another ace. If you cannot totally eliminate the Bible, you can so disfigure it by questionable interpretation and elimination of passages that irk, so that the Bible is turned to serve falsehood rather than truth. How to interpret the Bible has become another crucial theater of the *Spirit Wars*.

CHAPTER 8

A NEW METHOD OF BIBLE STUDY

The scripture is the church's book. I think the church can do with its scripture what it wants to do with its scripture.

- Burton Throckmorton, member of the National Council of Churches revision committee for the RSV Bible[1]

Reading the Bible with Power:
The Dream of an Empty Bible

Whisked through the clouds, Sherry Ruth Anderson, a Jewish feminist,[2] is transported in a dream to a temple defended by a ferocious guardian with bulging eyes and surrounded by snarling black dogs. With uncharacteristic bravery she enters; the fearsome guards disappear as if made of fog. An old man, Melchizedek, with long robes and white beard leads her to the cabinet containing the holy Torah. He allows her to take the scroll, reserved for men, and cradle it like a baby.

"This is a very special Torah," says [Melchizedek]. Pulling out his dagger, he breaks the seal and rolls open the scrolls. They are blank. "The Torah is empty," he says, "because what you need to know now is not written in any book. You already contain that knowledge. It is to be unfolded from within you. . . . Without speaking Melchizedek . . . places the [Torah] inside my body, from my shoulders to my knees."

The room fills with long-bearded patriarchs — including Moses, David, Solomon, Abraham, Isaac and Jacob — dressed in black coats and trousers, dancing in celebration of the emergence of spiritually responsible women. "But who will be our [women's] teachers?" she asks, and the answer comes: "You will be teachers for each other. You will come together in circles and speak your truth to each other." Finally the patriarchs give her their blessing, saying: "We have initiated you. . . . But we no longer know the way. Our ways do not work any more. You women must find a new way."

"Well, burn my bush," says a fictional feminist character, as she dismisses God and invokes the goddess. Woman, says a radical feminist, will be the new Moses for the new order.[3]

Many leading women — and what feminists call "women identified men" — are discovering feeling and experience as the true source of divine revelation. Recounts a Roman Catholic woman who left the church in the fall of 1980,

> Last fall I experienced a ten-week consciousness raising seminar for women sponsored by the National Organization for Women. . . . I began to see the impossible situation of women existing in a society ruled by men and male gods. And the real issue is the overwhelming denial of power to women. . . . I feel it's time to begin to celebrate ourselves, our own spirituality; to learn to do things for our own reasons and to measure ourselves by our own standards . . . to realize our own inner creative force, which, I think, is our true image of God.[4]

"What happens right here, right now, is revelation," says spokeswoman Rosemary Radford Ruether. "Women's experience is a legitimate context for the continual self-communication of the divine in the human community."[5] That view makes prophets out of feminists and opens a "new way of reading old texts."[6]

In the postmodern world, the primacy of experience is not unique to feminism. New Agers in general believe that experiencing themselves as divine constitutes saving knowledge (*gnosis*).[7] David Wells shows how evangelicalism follows society's intoxication with experience.[8] Some Christians read the Bible that way. "Whatever it says to me," regardless of the writer's intent, must be the Spirit's meaning. The reader's emotional needs dictate the meaning of the passage.[9] "Whatever it says to me" is reaching new levels of absurdity.

To affirm that feminism leads the way is not an expression of male prejudice. Feminists, male and female, proudly claim as much. Says a New Testament scholar in the movement: "the program of feminist biblical exegesis. . . . [is] one of the most important aspects of current biblical scholarship."[10] Others trumpet that feminism has brought a "revolution in religious thought."

Such revolutionary and heart-felt convictions, when turned on the Bible, make it unrecognizable. Only an "empty Torah" has room for its world-changing agenda.

The Deconstruction of Bible Study

The most important event in our lifetime is not the bulldozing of the Berlin Wall or the fall of communism in Eastern Europe and Russia. This event cannot be captured on TV news footage, for it is an idea, "deconstruction." Deconstruction was originally the product of hermeneutics, which is the theory of interpretation, associated with Jacques Derrida, a French philosopher and literary theorist. Literary deconstruction doubts that any literary theory can truly describe written communication. By extension, it questions any explanation of anything. No general descriptions of why things are the way they are (called "metanarratives") are acceptable, since they are "totalizing discourses" that impose someone's or some group's ideas on the rest of us.[11] Deconstruction "is a worldview that denies all worldviews." Stanley Fish of Duke University, the leading deconstructionist in America, says: "Since all principles are preferences, they are nothing but masks for the will to power. . . . someone is always going to be restricted next, and it is your job to make sure that that someone is not you."[12]

David Wells measures the devastating effect of this intellectual movement:

> In literature, a whole generation of deconstructionists. . . . now make their living by denying that words have any meaning at all. Words mean only whatever we wish them to mean.[13]

The disturbing development in deconstructionism is the identification of truth as power. If there is no absolute truth (which most people in the West now accept as "true"), then all truth claims are mere power plays. So everyone gets to play, but the game is deadly serious. In short order the Marxist belief that political power comes out of the nozzle of a gun again becomes a real possibility for the global society of the age of Aquarius.

The On-Going Saga of Charles and Di

You know the world has changed when the British royal family changes. Earlier monarchs of the House of Windsor were far from angels. But Charles is the first modern royal and heir to the throne to admit, without remorse and on prime time telly, that he is an adulterer. The future king can justify sexual pluralism — having more than one woman — because, like most of his western contemporaries, he has bought the new "truth" of religious pluralism (having more than one truth). For His Royal Highness, there are many ways to God, and possibly many gods. Since 1521 the British monarch has borne the title "Defender of the Faith." When Charles becomes king he intends to drop the definite article and be known as "Defender of Faith" since, as he explains, with an exquisite sense of modern-day tolerance, all religions "contain common elements of truth."[14] Charles will be the first deconstructed king (if by then that title is not politically incorrect) on the British throne.

The Dethroning of God

The new view of truth as power tries to saw the legs off the throne of the universe. Employing their principle for Bible study, Fewell and Gunn, Methodist and Presbyterian Bible scholars, argue that every one has their own truth and a right to empowerment. Everything else (especially one-sided revelation), must be treated with suspicion. They further argue that "gender relations, at least as constructed in . . . patriarchy, are power relations." This false totalizing discourse of patriarchy produces "the binary world of heterosexuality."[15]

In their technical language these scholars affirm that the Bible, which masquerades as "truth" is really an exercise of male social control." it needs to be deconstructed, along with its "binary world" (the belief in right and wrong, good and evil). Our Methodist and Presbyterian scholars have entered the strange new world of pagan monism. The immediate result is the deconstruction of the Bible as truth and of God the Father Almighty, Maker of Heaven and Earth, as distinct from his creation, the only true expression of divinity.

"Deconstructed" evangelical, Virginia Mollenkott, speaks of "the one really foolish assumption . . . that anyone could possibly arrive at a situationless, culture-free, objective interpretation of any text, let alone a text as complex as the Bible."[16] What happened to the sufficiency and perspicuity of Scripture?

From Author via Text to Reader:
A Free Fall into "Pro-Choice" Hermeneutics

Deconstructionism and the loss of the sense of absolute truth has clearly affected the way people read the Scriptures, or for that matter, any piece of writing. Interpretation has become much more complicated, to the detriment of the Bible and to the advantage of the Bible interpreter. The following three stages trace this slide from confidence in the text to confidence in the reader.

The Author

Traditional Bible study has always tried to discover what the author of a passage meant to say, otherwise known as "authorial intent." If you know Paul was in prison, might that not help in understanding some of his letters written from prison? Using the "worst case scenario" method,[17] some have recently argued that authors may be the worst judge of their writing,[18] and therefore justify eliminating "authorial intent" in the interpretation of texts.

The Text

Those who minimize the author's intention tend to adopt an approach known as "literary theory."[19] This approach believes that a literary work is self-sufficient and has no need of outside information about the author's meaning and the history in which the text was written. Understanding depends on the underlying structure of the narrative. The text has a life of its own, independent of the author. To discover meaning, the reader must expose the deep structures of the text itself. Recently the emphasis has moved from the text to the reader's decisive contribution to the meaning of a text.

The Reader

Most readers of the Bible go there for a deeper knowledge of the will and mind of God. Not modern literary theorists. Due to their relativistic approach to truth, interpretation is a matter of personal taste.[20] They argue that since the author's intention cannot be known, and the structural approach is too mechanical, the meaning of a text is always obscure. If readers are to derive meaning it is because *they bring their own questions*, and in interaction with the text *create their own ever-renewed meaning*. This has become known as "reader-response theory." As one can imagine, it is enthusiastically taken up by readers with an agenda, e.g., liberation theologies of all stripes, which take experience as divine revelation. This method has become a major force in our experience-saturated world. "Hardly any sphere of the interpretative process has escaped major restructuring and rethinking since the decade of the sixties."[21]

While these new methods contain valuable insights,[22] the extremist employment of "reader response" methodology in particular, blunts the two-edged sword of God's Word, and allows advocates of all kinds of agendas, including the homosexual, to maintain the appearance of knowing Scripture while actually ignoring it and the power of God.

"Reader response" Bible study is part of the sweeping change in Western intellectual history over the past generation. The old rationalistic method has given rise to a new definition of what constitutes responsible scholarship. Here are some of the ingredients of the new method of Bible study.

The New Bible Study: All Methods are Fair

Today's Bible sits on the family table, trussed-up like a Christmas turkey, from which everyone carves his choice piece of meat; white for some, dark for others, a wing or leg to suit your fancy. Hendrik Hart, a Christian Reformed theologian defends homosexual marriage to his conservative denomination. While admitting that no biblical texts favor homosexual behavior, he urges the church to step out: "Most churches can now make use of legitimate and accepted hermeneutical approaches to the Bible that would enable them to consider that these texts do not directly apply to our modern situation."[23]

With these new liberating methods, Scripture cannot touch us even if it wanted to. Some, not ready to ditch the Bible, content themselves with "radical transformation."[24] "New rules," says a feminist theorist, "will require feminist interpreters to assume that Scripture is *not* 'the word of God'. . . is *not* a container of revelation" and to "correct as we read . . . in the way one might say to a friend, 'I know that is what you said, but I know that's not what you meant.'"[25] Notice how radical this judgment is. Scripture is not even a container of revelation. You cannot find jewels within the rubble. Everything must be re-interpreted by feminist interpreters who know what the Bible really wants to say, but is incapable of articulating. The Bible needs lots of help, and lots of help now exists.

Eclecticism — Pick and Choose

Often known as the "scissors and paste" method, this has been a classic liberal method of Bible study. What fits liberal theory stays, what doesn't goes. Old-style liberals tried to remain within Scripture as long as they could, but today's reconstructed liberals make no such pretense. Ruether states without embarrassment:

> religious feminists . . . seek to reclaim aspects of the biblical tradition . . . but . . . recognize the need both to go back behind biblical religion and to transcend it. . . . looking backward to options in biblical and prebiblical faith."[26]

She recommends the use of any text, whether pagan Greek or heretical Gnostic.[27] The Scriptural texts that do not fit, she deletes. Ephesians 6 stays, for it supports her interpretation of patriarchy as an expression of the evil principalities and powers against which liberationists must wrestle,[28] whereas Ephesians 5:21-23 must go. (This text and other "satanic verses," as mentioned in chapter 6, are publicly "exorcised.") Clearly, this is a new way of reading the Bible. It has been called by feminists "a hermeneutic of suspicion."

Suspicion

Elizabeth Schlüssler Fiorenza, a leading theorist of feminist interpretation, proposes a "hermeneutic of suspicion" capable of unraveling the patriarchal politics inscribed in the biblical text. Since the Bible is written in androcentric, grammatically masculine language, feminist interpretation must develop a "hermeneutic of critical evaluation for proclamation" that is able to assess theologically whether scriptural texts function to inculcate patriarchal values (the reader is left to imagine what she would do with those), or whether they must be read against their linguistic "androcentric grain" in order to set free their liberating vision for today and for the future. Such a feminist hermeneutics of liberation reconceptualizes the understanding of Scripture as nourishing bread rather than as unchanging sacred word engraved in stone.[29]

According to the modern myth of feminism, there exists an oppressive, pervasive patriarchal conspiracy[30] which demands vigilance, indeed radical suspicion.[31] Even the most civilizing and noble of all books merits scrutiny. According to this theory, the men of the Bible were just as scheming and power-hungry as all the rest and sought to suppress an original goddess worship and the attendant liberation of women that early pre-biblical cultures knew. Rage and anger, empowerment and suspicion are the new "Christian" values to be turned upon the very source of Christianity, the Holy Scriptures. Indeed, the Bible is turned upon itself, as the "Exodus" myth is used to exit from the Bible's authority.

"Exodus" Liberation Interpretation

Such "suspicious" picking and choosing is motivated by a new understanding of truth and justice, found by the human heart within experience and a personal conviction of what is liberating. By calling this interpretative method "Exodus hermeneutics"[32] an aura of biblical thinking is projected. In fact, one is slowly but surely exiting from the Bible itself. Just as Israel came out of Egyptian bondage, so liberation interpreters believe they are freeing the Bible's essential liberative message from its oppressive patriarchal husk.

Some may not realize how radical this program is. Exodus from patriarchy and suspicion of its oppressive power are proposed by Fewell and Gunn, both mainline Protestant Bible teachers and parents, who love their children enough to ask if they really want them reading such a reactionary book as the Bible.[33] Radical suspicion, convinced that texts are written for social control, asks whose interest the text will serve. For the biblical text, suspicion falls on the ultimate Male, God. The biblical God is therefore seen as a construct of the oppressive patriarchy in control when the texts were composed. These radical scholars argue rightly, I believe, that "neither Christianity nor Judaism has yet come to terms with the real challenge of feminist thought." Gender inclusive translations "only mask the extent of the problem." The real problem, they maintain, is idolatry, worshiping the Bible's male construct of God. One can sense the shock that consistent application of the new method produces. "We do not know," they say, "where our own reading takes us. The problems feminist criticism raises for traditional notions of revelation and biblical authority are immense."[34] Their honest reading through the lens of feminist suspicion takes them and their children right out of Christianity into paganism. The void beckons, and imagination is called in to fill the bill.

Imagination

If the Bible is full of androcentric texts, to save it for use in the church, feminists male and female, in this theological movement feel compelled to re-imagine feminine presence in the Bible, thereby placing women as well as men into the center of early Christian history.

> Such a feminist critical method could be likened to the work of a detective insofar as it does not rely solely on historical "facts" nor invents its evidence, but is engaged in an imaginative reconstruction of historical reality.[35]

Fiorenza, who holds the position of Professor of New Testament Studies and Theology at the University of Notre Dame, suggests female authorship for early Christian writings. She does this not because of solid evidence or new facts, but to challenge the androcentric dogmatism that ascribes apostolic authorship only to men. "The issue has become now, not whether or not such suggestions are *true*, but which of the various possibilities is most useful to the feminist case."[36] Fiorenza concludes that "the suggestion of female authorship . . . has great imaginative-theological value because it opens up the possibility of attributing the authority of apostolic writings to women and of claiming theological authority for women." To "relativize the impact of androcentric texts and their unarticulated patriarchal mind-sets" on her students, Fiorenza encourages them to write "apocryphal" texts from the perspective of leading women in early Christianity.

Much of this imagining is born within the warming structures of community spirituality as well as the white-hot cauldron of group rage.

Community

Deconstruction leaves the intellectual landscape as barren as a desert after a nuclear explosion. No truth means no significance, and no significant action. If there is no truth then what is left? There is the individual and his "truth," but from the point of view of power, the individual is insignificant. Truth must arise from communities.

Stanley Fish, the well-known American deconstructionist, explains the importance of communities. "The self does not exist apart from the communal or conventional categories of thought that enable its operations (of thinking, seeing, reading)."[37] But we may wonder how communities survive the skepticism of the deconstructionist worldview. As someone has said: "Those who attack the objectivity of meaning go about their lives assuming that this [meaning] is in fact possible."[38] A glorious example is the statement by Marjorie Suchocki, Vice President for Academic Affairs of the School of Theology at Claremont, in defense of multiculturalism in academia:

> Notions of absolutes and universals have given way to recognition that what we call knowledge is conditioned by its social/cultural location . . . education that implicitly or explicitly promotes the hegemony of one mode of thought and being as if it were universally valid is flawed.[39]

Our arbiter of the intellect denies absolutes, but in so doing makes an absolute statement about the way things should be. Her statement, in making an implicit claim to universality, shows its own hopeless flaws.

Living with such absurdity may be easier in communities because they give a semblance of "objectivity," if that is anybody's concern anymore.

There is enormous arbitrariness here. You join a community and accept its story as true and empowering for you, if it fits your life style and sense of justice. The Bible is used, not to establish the Christian community, but to give various communities a claim on the Christian faith and family whenever it happens to fit. "A new critical hermeneutics," says feminist Fiorenza, "does not center on the text but on the people whose story with God is remembered in the texts of the Bible."[40]

Such reasoning denies the Bible any objective power. There is no general truth, only "truth" for me and my community. In this "postmodern" situation debate and intellectual exchange have become a rarity. If academia does not yet quite resemble the L.A. gang scene, intellectual warfare between "communities" already typifies American campuses.[41]

Advocacy

If truth is a form of naked power, it is little wonder that our time has discovered a new form of Bible interpretation known as "advocacy exegesis."[42] In particular, communities make better advocates than individuals. Though numbers do not mean that something is true, there is strength in numbers.

Rosemary Ruether states the case for advocacy baldly: "women's studies do not pretend to an ethical neutrality. This stance is actually a ruling class ideology. Neutrality hides a commitment to the status quo. All liberation scholarship is advocacy scholarship."[43] Name-calling and disruptive demonstrations characterize even the church's business. This academic belligerence leaves the old-style liberals breathless. Walter Brueggemann, Professor of Old Testament, Columbia Theological Seminary, Decatur, GA, recognizes a "new definition of what constitutes responsible scholarship." His article title, "On Writing a Commentary. . . An Emergency," betrays his disarray. He notes that "advocacy exegesis" gives primacy to the situation of the interpreter over what the text once meant. Realizing the excesses of rationalism, Brueggemann feels the pull of spiritual involvement offered in advocacy exegesis, yet he sighs with regret at the loss of objectivity.[44] Brueggemann should not worry. A new constructive vision will rebuild the world.

A New Unity

Behind the wide diversity of readings, and in spite of the rejection of totalizing discourses (especially the Christian one), there is a new, unifying — totalizing! — ideology. It is so diverse it can live within a deconstructed world, but so totalitarian that it leaves room for no one but monists. The "hegemony of one mode of thought and being as if it were universally valid," so feared by modern intellectuals, has not disappeared. It has merely changed form. The original Christian theistic claim to truth is now made by pagan monism. Pagan totalitarianism is coming, if one is to believe Harvey Cox: "we must shape and reconceive our rites and myths in order that they unite and enlarge us (humanity). . . . We must now take the initiative, not just to predict the future . . . but to shape it." This is the last phrase in his book, appropriately entitled *Many Mansions*.[45] In this new vision of human unity the New Babel becomes heaven on earth.

As individuals or community members, human beings need to speak meaningfully. Truth, in the new paradigm, does not come from rational discourse based on revelation from the divine Creator who is distinct from the universe he created. Truth comes rather from human "experience" — the experience of a new "reconstructed" pagan unity of all things, found within the human soul, not in sacred books. With this new, unifying ideology, the new Bible study method has no need of the Bible. Attachment to the Bible is window-dressing, a strategic ploy to remain within the church and eventually to take it over.

The well-known expert in comparative religions, Rumanian Mircea Eliade, himself greatly fascinated by Hinduism, saw in all religions great unifying symbols for humanity. His life's work was the attempt to define these universal symbols because "Symbols universalize. They cohere. They express the unity of mankind. And all local/provincial phenomena find their true and more complete meaning in the larger global meaning of symbols."[46] Though he died during the 1980s, he sensed the coming of what he called "the new humanism," to be constructed via the encounter with other worlds of meaning, in particular the encounter of the East with the West. He saw this as the occasion for (spiritual) knowledge to increase. It was he who coined the phrase "creative hermeneutics." What he meant by it was a willingness on the part of people to engage with the spiritual world of the 'other,' even if that might imply being 'converted' to the 'other's' views."[47]

Behind the "communities of interpretation," a monistic unity appears that gives direction to exegesis in a deconstructed world that has lost its way. "Reader response" is to monism as authorial intent is to theism. Let me explain. If truth is to be found within, then the reader holds the keys. If truth is revealed from the God without, then it is the inspired author and his inspired text which hold the keys of the kingdom of heaven. Right now, "reader response," like monism in all its forms, is on the cutting edge. Its cutting edge is playing havoc with the text of Scripture. Take a look at what radical "reader response" exegesis has done to Genesis 1-3, the foundation pillar of the Christian world and life view — and for that reason was, incidentally, the object of constant re-interpretation by the Gnostics.

Genesis 1-3: A Feminist View of the Garden

Eve was framed.
        - Mary Daly[48]

The response of the contemporary feminist reader to Genesis 1-3 is one of anger, unbelief and suspicion, a reading "against the grain," an imaginative reading that puts woman in the center and drives man and the male biblical God out of the garden. Everything is suspect because:

> The myth of the Father God ensured a world of dominance and dependence . . . Patriarchy, embedded in the creation story of Genesis, is the universal religion. What explains the persistence of the myth? What explains its selection? There were other myths available at the time. . . . But the Genesis myth marked the establishment of monotheism and the legitimation of patriarchy as the way of nature — as God's will![49]

How can liberal Christians, committed to radical liberation, continue to use Scripture, which is so committed to an ideology opposed to their agenda? By turning the Genesis account on its head.

Many "Christian" scholars go this far.[50] This "new" reader-response exegesis changes the cast of the original drama. God, Adam, Eve and the Serpent mysteriously change places and a new hierarchy emerges — the Serpent, Eve, Adam and God. Here is the new interpretation by radical Bible scholars (largely in their own words). Seeing is believing.

God
The procedure is announced.

> The notion that the figure God in the biblical text is actually God . . . [is] a form of idolatry. . . . Unless the character of God is subjected to

the same kind of critical scrutiny as all the other characters, we are not really reading the text.[51]

"God as male is part and parcel of this story" and the story is about male oppression that produces "anger and irreverence." Thus in the Decalogue, God is depicted as "a jealous god who forbids any relationship with any other god . . . [the] perspective [of this metaphor] is the husband's. The deity is the model of the jealous husband."[52]

In Gen 1-3 God is "a curious figure. . . . [who] has a strong penchant for order. . . . and a strong bias for the binary."[53] "This creator God is plainly not . . . omniscient" [because he discovers that things are good].[54]

God is the source of evil, because the evil desire for dominance and totalitarian power is first and foremost his. In this, he is not the sophisticated God of the monists.

> Where JHWH, the judge of all the earth, might fit on the grid of innocence and evil is no less problematic a question than it is in respect to Abraham, the family sacrificer. Put another way, theology built on binary terms is found wanting.[55]

In placing the tree, God is a tempter who tantalizes the first couple: "Trust me! . . . Stay ignorant — or seek [knowledge] at your own risk."[56] God's control of the garden is less than complete. His placing the tree might suggest that God is "anxious, even insecure" and "jealous of his power. . . . [57] we . . . need . . . to recognize God's vulnerability and culpability. . . . god is not capable of simply fixing up the mess."[58]

This picture of God is reminiscent of a leading feminist's description of God in Numbers 11-12. Having overcome old religious feelings that caused her to "overrate the character of Yahweh," in the freedom of the new exegesis, she can call God "desperate" and "distressed." The people's questioning of His judgment is taken by Jahweh "as personal affront. All he can do is take out his frustration on their bodies, the all-too-common response of a distressed parent."[59] In the curses following the Fall, Jahweh "does not inspire our gratitude" since he functions as an "ideological agent" for the creation of the male/female identities which are the source of oppression.[60] God is duplicitous, for he is immortal and knows good and evil, but denies this to man.[61]

One of the above scholars[62] argues that from a structural analysis, Jahweh should be seen in the role of the villain who steals the man from the earth to till his garden. The villain allows one flaw in his plan — the tree that will give man knowledge. The serpent and the woman succeed in thwarting the villain's plan by getting the man to eat the fruit, which restores the tiller to the real earth. God is careless, only remembering the Tree of Life at the last moment as an afterthought.[63]

The above scholars certainly do not "overrate" the God of the Bible. Clearly, like the Gnostics, they are in touch with a higher god than the God revealed in Scripture.

Adam

In the new tradition, Adam gets short shrift. He is a pale reflection of God — like God, a blame-shifter, who, in the fine tradition of Ahab, simply sulks when he cannot get Naboth's vineyard.[64] The earth-creature, Adam, is the original "clod."[65] Adam is a profoundly passive character throughout the story.[66] "If the woman be intelligent, sensitive and ingenious, the man is passive, brutish and inept."[67] "The Woman gives him the fruit and he eats it as if he were a baby."[68]

Eve

Elizabeth Cady Stanton, the first modern feminist interpreter of the Bible, stated in 1895: "the reader must be impressed with the courage, the dignity and the lofty ambition of the woman" in whom was aroused "that intense thirst for knowledge."[69] "Eve is unable to know the difference between good and evil. How then can she be blamed for her actions?"[70] She only does what comes naturally. She reaches for sustenance, beauty and wisdom, and in doing so, is blamed forever by the male text and the male commentators.[71] Eve, indeed, was framed! "Though Eve's behavior is condemned by God and berated by centuries of readers, she emerges as a character with initiative and courage. . . . she is a child testing her boundaries, weighing her options, making her choices. She makes her decision independent of those who claim authority over her."[72]

Like God, the woman is an explorer. "She seeks, reasonably, to be in a position to make a choice." [73] "Eve's decision is . . . the first act of human independence."[74] She shares God's image of free will.[75] "Eve does not 'sin'; she chooses reality over her naive paradisiacal existence. Her choice marks the emergence of human character."[76] In this, Eve anticipates Lot's wife (whose looking back is "a choice to be human,"[77]) as well as Jezebel who is seen as "a woman of strength . . . acting independently. . . . As the quintessential foreign woman of power she is for the patriarchal Subject the quintessential Other, to be feared and blamed."[78]

The woman is associated with knowledge. "At the deepest level of the text . . . the human transformation in which the woman took powerful initiative was positive rather than negative (and) that complex human world is to be preferred over any male ideal."[79] What has been called sheer disobedience is, from another perspective, emancipation from blind command.[80] Eve gains wisdom i.e., "the acceptance of the human condition, including death, and the continuity of history it allows," showing that "Eve is open to reality and ready to adopt it." [81]

The woman and the serpent "heroically oppose Yahweh the villain."[82] The woman "is no easy prey for a seducing demon, as later tradition represents her, but a conscious actor choosing knowledge. Together with the snake, she is a bringer of culture."[83]

"Paul's" arguments in 1 Tim 2:11-14 are most obviously wrong — in particular, man and woman were created at the same time, a son and a daughter of the androgynous earth-creature, Ha Adam, and in this sense Eve was created first.[84]

The Serpent

The serpent is not evil, but is the other face of God, the tempter, who proposes both good and evil. This profound fact the God of Genesis refuses to recognize.[85] With regard to truth, the serpent and Jahweh share the same position. Both are sly, withholding information. Both in collaboration trick the humans. The serpent seems to be God's helper.[86] He asks intelligent questions, and he could have asked others to embarrass God.[87]

The serpent is the spokesman of the tree of the knowledge of good and evil.[88] "The serpent is an agent of regeneration. . . . and assists in the delivery of the human race. He contains also the possibility of imaginative integration, for in the garden his is the voice of hope and ambition."[89] The snake does not lie, and has the "capacity to transform situations and overturn the status quo."[90]

This new-style "exegesis" is popping up everywhere lately, in more or less radical forms.[91] One of note comes from the scholarly British publication, the *Journal For the Study of the New Testament*, published at the University of Sheffield and known for its conservative, even "evangelical" leanings. Its present editor, Francis Watson, from London University, publishes an article in which he finds the biblical text (new and old) hopelessly patriarchal and hierarchical. Watson considers quite unconvincing (no doubt correctly) all attempts to save these texts by recovering between the lines a sort of pristine egalitarianism. He leaves the reader with what he judges the "more appropriate strategy" — "resistance." Such resistance, according to Watson, would take the form of a "counter-reading," reading the text "defiantly 'against the grain.'" In practice, this would involve seeing:

the serpent as liberator, Eve as heroine in her courageous quest for wisdom and the Lord God as a jealous tyrant concerned only with the preservation of his own prerogatives. *Such a reading was, of course, adopted within Gnosticism.*[92]

This conscious adoption of ancient Gnostic exegesis in a respected scholarly journal of classic Christian roots at the end of the twentieth century, may make the most skeptical concede that *the Gnostic empire is striking back.*

This theological reversal is the end result of the singular commitment to gender-liberation ideology. Everything else can be jettisoned — traditional family values, biblical canonical authority, the wisdom and goodness of God the Creator, and the very definition of the source of evil — and especially the plain sense of the text.

Bible Study for the End of Civilization

Recently John Richard Neuhaus, respected commentator of the state of religion in America has said:

> The teaching of the Bible in theological schools is in the grip of gnosticism, the belief that it is necessary to appeal away from the plain sense of Scripture to a higher knowledge that lies above or behind the text. The aim of biblical studies is to put the students "in the know" so that they will be privy to an esoteric knowledge that even most intelligent and educated folks cannot get from their reading of the Scriptures in Hebrew, Greek or English."[93]

The new version of Genesis is living proof of this statement, as well as a chilling example of how the new Bible study has quite simply shaken itself free of the Bible. The "higher knowledge" behind this reversal of Genesis is not another interesting hypothesis to enliven our tired traditionalism. In its destruction of Genesis 1-3, which makes the devil God and God the devil, this "knowledge" is the most radical expression of Christian apostasy. It lays the axe to the roots of Western civilization. Orthodox believers, especially those tempted by certain aspects of the new agenda, must take stock of the enormity of the revolution. The God of the Bible is now rejected as a symbol of evil oppression in favor of an unknown god whose wisdom the Serpent speaks. The new Bible study seems to lead ineluctably not to readers' "innocent" questions but to the Seducer's age-old lies.

There is nothing new in that, as ancient Gnosticism shows.

CHAPTER 9

GNOSTIC BIBLE STUDY

They try to adapt to their own sayings in a manner worthy of credence, either the Lord's parables, or the prophets' sayings, or the apostles' words . . . They disregard the order and the connection of the Scriptures . . . They transfer passages and rearrange them.[1]
  - Irenaeus

The Text is Anything You Want it to Be

Readers shocked by the manipulation of Genesis described in the previous chapter may take solace in knowing that the new look version is as old as the hills. Its wild implausibility may have contributed to its fifteen hundred year disappearance. No betting man would have given odds for its resurrection by intelligent scholars at the end of the twentieth century. But the new "reader response" view of Adam and Eve is only a modern rehash of the heretical interpretation invented by Gnostics in the second and third centuries A.D.[2]

Ancient Textual Arm-Wrestling with Jahweh

According to the Gnostic *Hypostasis of the Archons*, the struggle of the true spiritual Gnostic is not with flesh and blood but with "the authorities of the universe and the spirits of wickedness (Ephesians 6:12)." All Christians could agree with this citation from the Apostle Paul. Most Christians, though, would be shocked to learn that the chief of these evil authorities is the God of the Old Testament, the Creator of Heaven and Earth, who in ignorance and arrogance claims, "It is I who am God; there is none [apart from me]."[3]

These Rulers or *Archons* (the Biblical Lord God and his angelic host) are from "Below" whereas the Spirit is from "Above," from the "Entirety." They create a man of "soil from the earth" and place him in their Garden, depriving him of the fruit of "the tree of recognizing good and evil." Unbeknownst to the Rulers, however, the "Spirit from Above" enters the man. The Rulers cause a great sleep to fall upon him. This is the sleep of spiritual ignorance, of which all mankind suffers until illuminated with knowledge. During the sleep, they open his side, and out comes "the spirit-endowed Woman." She awakens Adam to spiritual life again, and Adam praises her: "It is you who have given me life; you will be called 'Mother of the Living.' — For it is she who is my mother. It is she who is the Physician."[4]

The "Female Spiritual Principle," the heavenly Eve, enters the snake, called the "Teacher,"[5] and teaches Adam and Eve the true way of salvation. The Snake is Teacher, "the one who is wiser than all of them."[6] This is a recurring theme in Gnostic literature.[7] The serpent is the redeemer. The God of Scripture is the evil usurper. "But of what kind is this God?" asked the exasperated author of the *Testimony of Truth*.[8]

> First [he] begrudged Adam that he should eat from the tree of knowledge. And, second, he asked, "Where are you, Adam?" And God does not possess foreknowledge, that is, at the beginning he did not know this? And later he said, "Let us banish him from this place lest he eat of the tree of life and live for eternity." He has truly shown that he is a jealous envier.

Hippolytus reports that Justinus, one of the Gnostic leaders of the second century, identified the tree of the knowledge of good and evil with Naas [the Serpent], "'For so,' says (Justinus), 'one ought to interpret the words of Moses [for] Moses said these things disguisedly, from the fact that all do not attain to the truth.'"[9]

On the Origin of the World, another text of the Nag Hammadi library, has a similar inverted interpretation of Genesis. The author of this text claims to reveal what existed "prior to Chaos."[10] This is perhaps a reference to "chaos" referred to in Genesis 1:1, "and the earth was without form and void." As with all Gnostic systems that speculate about the time before creation, this one spins a complicated tale of divine emanations from the ultimate "Father of the All." At one point in the process Sophia, whom "the Hebrews call . . . Eve of Life, i.e. the teacher of life" gives birth to an androgynous being whom the authorities called "the beast" but who in reality is the "lord" and "the Teacher" for "he was found to be wiser than all of them."[11]

"Then the one who is wiser than all of them, this one who is called 'the beast' came," and revealed the truth about the tree of knowledge, that it was actually good, and that "god" had prohibited them from eating its fruit out of jealousy. When "Eve was certain concerning the word of the teacher . . . their minds opened. For when they ate, the light of knowledge (gnosis) illuminated them." Having gained this gnosis, Adam and Eve despise "god." "When they saw their makers (God the Creator and his angels), they loathed them since they were beastly forms. They understood very much."[12] In a further statement of loathing the text goes on to describe God as impotent since the only thing he can do is curse the teacher (serpent), as well as curse everything they created. Of the Creator God it is said: "There is no blessing for them. Good is not able to come from evil."[13] Here is *total reversal*. Good has become evil, and evil has become good.

Gnostic Method

How could the Gnostics get away with this kind of exegesis, present everywhere in their writing?[14] In much the same way that modern Bible scholars turn the obvious meaning to their personal and communal agendas. Without the technical apparatus and sophisticated intellectual jargon of their modern cousins, the Gnostics created a similar justification for their "reader response" approach to Holy Scripture. The contemporary explosion in the production of interpretative techniques should not surprise us. Whenever "Christian" theology looks to pagan polytheism for inspiration — as it is doing now and as it did then — it discovers a titillating variety of reading techniques, without which the Scriptures of the one, true God would be strictly unusable.

Imagination
The Christian Gnostic "revival," like its contemporary counterpart, laid great store on imagination. Like other monists and pantheists, they believed that God is "the unknown God," totally distinct and untouched by creation, yet confounded with every part of it. The Gnostics concluded that there is no direct, special communication from such a God. So where is truth found? They looked to the spark of the divine within. Imagination, part of the divine spark, helps in the discovery of ever-renewing and expanding truth. In Gnostic texts, others who have looked within share their experience of gnosis. Even authoritative Scripture is useful to the extent that it serves the monistic understanding of life.

If truth is fundamentally personal, depending upon individual experiences of inner divine illumination, it follows that experience is to be preferred over rational discourse. It will be imagination freed from reason. So the *Apocryphon of James* 4:19-20 exhorts Gnostic believers: "be filled with the Spirit but be lacking in reason." The *First Apocalypse of James* 27:1-5 states: "until you fling away from yourself blind understanding, this chain of flesh which surrounds you. And then you will attain The One Who Exists. And no longer will you be James, instead you yourself are The One Who Exists." This anti-rational bent reappears in new age spirituality: "the conditions necessary for new faith, hope and love . . . [are that] you have to be flexible, open, have high energy and be non-linear or intuitive."[15] The very spiritual feminist witch, Mary Daly, excoriates the contemporary use of (male) reason for trying to snuff out intuitive contact with the spirits:

> This removal from the philosophical enterprise of intuitive/imaginative reasoning about angels (which some identify as "Elemental Spirits") is associated with the bore-ocratization of philosophy. It is connected . . . with the "philosophical" discrediting and erasure of "final causality". . . (viz.,) spirit-force.[16]

The great "come-back" story of our age is the return of "the spirits." The ancient world was full of them, as Plutarch, a first century Greek historian notes. He described the Greco-Roman culture of the Mediterranean as "a goblet seething with myths."[17] The "Christian" Gnostic teachers were only following the culture. Gnostic expert, Giovanni Filoramo speaks of the Gnostic "mythological revival."[18] With no particular reflection on the present situation, he notes that after a period of rationalism and the critique of *the old Greek myths* — *muthos* by Plato and Aristotle using *logos* (reason), myth is rediscovered and given new meaning. Gnosticism is no longer interested in the stories of the gods *per se*, but only as they relate to human experience.[19] A new person-centered spirituality was born. Parallels with the present time are fascinating. As we come to the end of the twentieth century after the so-called Enlightenment or Age of Reason, people are rediscovering gods, goddesses, myths and spirituality, sometimes under the guise of a revitalized Christianity.

So it was in the ancient world. The Gnostics claimed a new understanding of the myths. Gnostic gospels seem to have been written this way. The "living Jesus" reveals timeless wisdom not tied to any historical moment, thus giving prophetic insight and imagination free course. Observes Irenaeus: "they adduce an untold multitude of apocryphal and spurious writings, which they have composed."[20] "No limits," says a modern commentator, "were set to free representation and theological speculation."[21]

Here are two of many possible examples recorded by the Church Father, Hippolytus:

♦ **Valentinus**
believed the "Creator (acted) from fear: (and) that is what Scripture affirms: `The fear of the Lord is the beginning of wisdom.' For this is the beginning of the affections of Sophia."[22]

♦ **Marcus,**
using the mystical number system of Pythagorus, finds "each of the particulars of Scripture to accord with the aforesaid numbers." They thus attempt, says Hippolytus, to "criminate Moses and the Prophets, alleging that these speak allegorically of the measures of the Aeons."[23]

Eclecticism: Picking and Choosing At Will

What they did not write themselves they "borrowed" from other sources, thereby picking and choosing at will. Gnosticism, observes Rudolf, "frequently draws its material from the most varied existing traditions, attaches itself to it, and at the same time sets it in a new frame . . . the Gnostic view of the world . . . attaches itself . . . to old religious imagery, almost as a parasite prospers on the soil of "host religions, it can also be described as parasitic. To this extent Gnosticism strictly speaking has no tradition of its own," continues Rudolf, "but only a borrowed one. Its mythology is a tradition consciously created from alien material."[24]

If truth is to be found within, it can be found anywhere, so long as it agrees with the subjective experience of gnosis. "Christianity," says Rudolf, "tended to drive towards doctrinal unity while Gnostic thinkers apparently preferred their independent ways. They seemed to seek and incorporate into their systems any bit of "truth" or "knowledge" they found, regardless of the source."[25]

A case in point is the Gnostic treatment of the Gospel material, especially as expressed in the Gnostic *Gospel of Thomas*, as discussed above. There is no interest in real history. The Gnostic gospels were only vehicles to express their thoughts, picking what might be superficially appropriate and adding it to their system, leaving the rest as so much husk.

Tertullian rejects the Gnostics' constant illegitimate search for truth:

Away with the person who is seeking where he never finds; for he seeks where nothing can be found. Away with him who is always knocking; because it will never be opened to him, for he knocks where there is no one to open. Away with the one who is always asking, because he will never be heard, for he asks of one who does not hear.[26]

Ancient Reader Response Hermeneutics

Rudolf calls the Gnostic exegetical method a

> masterful practice . . . of extracting as much as possible . . . (via) the interpretative method of allegory and symbolism . . . a statement of the text was given a deeper meaning, or even several, in order to claim it for one's own doctrine or to display its inner richness. This method of exegesis is in Gnosis a chief means of producing one's own ideas under the cloak of the older literature — above all the sacred and canonical.[27]

This same scholar, who in his own theology is not entirely opposed to Gnostic thinking, nevertheless speaks of "contortionist tricks" and "protest exegesis."[28]

Regarding their approach to Genesis, Filoramo the Italian Gnostic scholar notes that the "Gnostic editors manipulate the sacred text in order to make it suit their purpose . . . by retouching, adding a phrase or choosing a different translation."[29] The Church Father, Clement of Alexandria (150-215 A.D.) gives an example of reader response exegesis. He mentions Epiphanes, son of Carpocrates, who believed in the common sharing of all things including wives and husbands, and who argued that the Mosaic injunction not to desire the goods or wife of one's neighbor "turned what was [originally] communal into private property."[30] Again, renaeus is forthright in his denunciation of their method: "They do violence to the good words [of Scripture] in adapting them to their wicked fabrications." He also decries their clever distortion of texts. In "allegories [which] have been spoken and can be made to mean many things, what is ambiguous they cleverly and deceitfully adapt to their fabrication by an unusual explanation." Finally, enaeus notes, to suit their own theological questions and answers, "they divide the prophecies into various classes: one portion they hold was spoken by the Mother, another by the offspring, and still another by Demiurge."[31]

Community Interpretation

The Gnostics developed communities rallying around teachers and agendas. Epiphanius (315-403 A.D.) complains: "the leaders of Gnosis falsely so-called have begun their evil growth upon the world, namely the so-called gnostics. . . . For each of these (leaders) has contrived his own sect to suit his own passions and has devised thousands of ways of evil."[32] Each sect had its own angle on the "truth" and produced endless variations. The modern historian, Elaine Pagels,[33] herself a theological liberal, grants that the Gnostics show something of the liberal spirit of modern day pluralism, i.e., the tolerance for all kinds of religious expression. Long ago Tertullian observed that the tolerance only went so far: "they do not care how differently they treat topics," so long as they . . . approach "the city of the sole truth," that is, the Gnostic version of the monistic circle. Orthodoxy was nevertheless rejected toxic error. Their "truth" was "approaches." Pagels notes that this commitment to truth is not the same as that of the Orthodox. "Gnostics tended to regard all doctrines, speculations, and myths — their own as well as others — as only *approaches* to the truth."[34]

For the Gnostics truth was found only in community: no one can know truth in any absolute sense, but each community must find its own. As in modern multiculturalism, the ancient Gnostics were *absolutely* sure that there was no absolute truth.

With this notion of private or communal truth goes the idea of initiation and secrecy. Revelation is secret, reserved for the initiated. Irenaeus notes the communal consciousness of Gnostic groups, which functioned as secret societies. As always, everyone had his price.

> they [are] unwilling to teach these things to all in public but only to those who are able to pay a large sum for such mysteries! . . . they are abstruse and portentous and profound mysteries, acquired with much toil by lovers of falsehood.[35]

Hermeneutics of Gnostic Suspicion

A number of modern-day experts agree that Gnostic Bible interpretation is an exercise in subterfuge and self-serving re-interpretation. Says one:

> If the starting point of gnostic myth is the exegesis of the Book of Genesis, it is not an innocent exegesis. On the contrary, this exegesis reverses, constantly and systematically, the received and accepted interpretations of the Bible. "Inverse exegesis" may be singled out as the main hermeneutical principle of the gnostics.[36]

In this inverse exegesis, "the content of the Bible is not taken at face value but in the light of previous information that contributes to the escalation of a 'hermeneutic of suspicion.' . . . of which gnostics seem to be the earliest systematic representatives." [37] Though the text is about original innocence, there is no innocence in the interpretations the Gnostics forced upon it.

One path that this "inverse exegesis" takes is that "anything that the Bible calls good is taken to be evil, and vice versa." In the *Paraphrase of Shem,* the Sodomites are the righteous members of the immovable race of Seth which is why they incur the wrath of the Demiurge.[38] These Sethians naturally claimed that their accounts of creation are the true Bible and that the biblical accounts are false, deceptive distortions.[39]

On the Origin of the World demonstrates how the story of the rib of Adam is a manifest falsehood:

> But we will not speak of this to Adam, for (s)he is not from among us. Let us instead put a deep sleep upon him and let us rehearse to him in his sleep that she came into being from his rib, so that his wife may submit, and he may be master over her.[40]

Similarly, the *Apocryphon of John* exhibits radical suspicion of the Genesis account:

> and he caused sleep to come upon Adam. And I said to the Savior, "What is sleep?" And he said, "It is not as Moses wrote and you heard." Then the Epinoia of light concealed herself in him (Adam) and the leader of the archons desired to bring her out of his rib. But the Epinoia of light is unreachable. While the darkness pursued her, it was unable to catch her, and he brought forth a portion of his power from himself. And he made another creation in the form of a woman, according to the likeness of Epinoia, which was revealed to him. And he put the portion of the power he had taken from the power of the man into the womanly creation, and not, as according to Moses, "his rib."[41]

Four times in this short text the author exhibits his profound suspicion of the biblical account by repeating the refrain "not as Moses said." At the same time his far-fetched interpretation must be right because it fits with his Gnostic theory.

A. F. J. Klijn, the Dutch scholar and authority on Gnosticism, says, "Finally we have to conclude . . . that the Jewish elements [the use of Genesis] were thoroughly reinterpreted or inverted in Gnosticism. . . . [and that] Gnosticism had a thorough disdain for its sources which it only used for its own aims."[42]

Gnostic Exodus from Jahweh

Modern radical scholars at the end of the twentieth century seek to lead readers in an exodus from patriarchy and from the great Patriarch, the God of Scripture. Ancient Gnostic teachers invited believers to leave their slavery/submission to the great Archon, the biblical God, Creator of Heaven and Earth. The *First Apocalypse of James* surveys the mighty works of creation and, with a little help from ancient astrology, enumerates seventy-two heavens. But the author reassures the Gnostic believer that in spite of this massive display of power, the Creator is inferior to the true God, to Him Who Is. Indeed since all Gnostics become "He Who Is," they too are superior to the Maker of the Heavens and the Earth.[43] Similarly, in the Gnostic text the *Dialogue of the Savior*, Judas says to Jesus: "Behold, the Archons dwell in heaven; surely, then, it is they who will rule over us." But Jesus replies: "You will rule over them."[44]

So the whole system of creation, impressive though it is, comes tumbling down in the Gnostic mega-interpretation of reality and of Scripture. Modern Bible interpreters argue that the worship of the God of the Bible is idolatry since Jahweh is but an intellectual construct of male oppression, and the true God is beyond all human words. Gnostics saw the God of Scripture as a usurper to be spurned and the true God as the unknown God who was only known in the divine spark within the human soul. The former "god" belongs to the realm of darkness which is also creation, matter, the body, the planets, and fate — a prison from which there is no escape. The latter, true God, the "unknown God" beyond all that is visible or sensible, who incorporates a "fullness" (pleroma) of heavenly beings, inhabits the realm of light. Ancient Gnostic Bible teachers were willing to "deconstruct" the Bible's fundamental teaching about God in order to beat a path of freedom to the unknown God beyond the Bible. Theirs certainly was liberation exegesis, but the exodus from the God of Scripture led not to the promised land but to diabolical slavery.

Ultimate Unity: Pagan Monism
Behind the great diversity of ancient Gnosticism lay a coherent ideology, profoundly opposed to Christian theism, but able to embrace most other religious options. Since the true God was unknown, except through the human heart, all interpretative paths that passed through the experience of "spiritual knowledge" led to God. Though it is common to describe Gnosticism as dualistic, rejecting the flesh and embracing the spirit, recognized expert, Kurt Rudolf, describes the movement as a "dualism on a monistic background."[45] Monism, old and new, welcomes all paths that lead to the "ultimate mystery" — all except one, the plain sense of Scripture, and the God of the Bible.

Conclusion

In the second century, Irenaeus, who devoted his life to reading, evaluating and finally denouncing Gnostic teaching as heretical, saw that an essential element of their pernicious teaching, which aided in the seduction of ordinary Christians, involved their twisting of Scripture to suit their own ends. He called their Bible study method a "misuse of Scripture" producing "distort(ed) exegesis." The procedure was, for him, patently obvious: "After having entirely fabricated their own system, they gather together sayings and names from scattered places and transfer them, as we have already said, from their natural meaning to an unnatural one."[46]

In Bible interpretation too, history repeats itself. From sexuality and morals to Bible study methods, the "unnatural" once again claims to be "natural." A fabricated system of liberation, backed by new myths and "self-evident" truths, has descended on the biblical text, skewing its obvious and natural sense.

The parchments of Gnosticism lie unrolled before us on our strategy tables. These plans have been used before, and the Church Fathers have shown us effective defense tactics. Their vigilance against heresy both warns and arms us in our own defense of the Faith. Christians today will remain ignorant of the past to their own and their children's peril. Church history teaches us what the Scriptures have declared: defense includes offense. If we do not denounce and reject "Gnostic" Bible study techniques, the church's foundations will crumble.

CHAPTER 10

A NEW GOD FOR A NEW WORLD ORDER

God is "not transcendence — that orgy of self-alienation beloved of the fathers — but immanence, god working out god's self in everything."[1]
- Rita Nakashima Brock

God Vs. Goddess

Not even a four letter word, "God" is still the most dynamite of notions. It stands for ultimate power and supreme truth. The stakes of the present debate concerning the nature and person of God could not be higher. Whoever defines God plays the role of the great Archon for the human society of tomorrow. Far from being secular and humanistic, the future will be, according to many expert observers, "hyperreligious."[2] The "new world order" is not satisfied with international trade agreements, arms reduction and innovative planetary politics. Such an order must develop a global ethic, a syncretistic religion with a new god on the throne. Every civilization has had its god. The utopian Age of Aquarius will crown an Aquarian god. "The emergence of a new cultural paradigm,"[3] calls for a new world view.[4] Madeleine L'Engle judges that the new worldview needs a new god "who's big enough for the atomic age" since the God of Christ's time "has deteriorated."[5]

Joseph Campbell, TV's guru of the new spirituality, makes a similar bid for a new myth, a new god:

The story that we have in the West, so far as it is based on the Bible, is based on a view of the universe that belongs to the first millennium B.C. It does not accord with our concept either of the universe or of the dignity of man.[6]

Journalist and Southern Baptist minister Bill Moyers enthusiastically agreed. Since their series of interviews were a major success on Public Television (where was the separation of church and state?), one can only imagine the influence they have had on contemporary America's way of thinking about God. Leading feminist theologian, Carol Christ, declares:

we are living in a revolutionary time when new religious symbols are being formed by a process of syncretism and creativity. . . . the work that feminists are doing to transform the image of God has profound . . . consequences for social life.[7]

So if you are really looking for a new god with transformative power,[8] you certainly need to meet Sophia.

Meet Sophia

Sophia is the new god for the new world, the new myth for the Age of Aquarius. In a strange and disorienting twist in feminine seductive power, it is "Sophia, . . . the Logos, . . . Christ Herself," according to "evangelical" Virginia Mollenkott, who will make all things new and all things possible. She will give birth to the "New Humanity."[9] Without her, the planet will implode and the glorious human story will never make its final rendez-vous of destiny with evolution. Sister Madonna Kolbenschlag, the influential ex-nun and militant feminist in the Roman Catholic church, sees in the goddess movement a "stage, necessary for some, in an evolutionary process that is moving humanity — and the 'God-who-is-coming-to-be' — toward transformation in a 'New Faith.'"[10]

Sophia: The Divine Homecoming Queen of Minneapolis

Many met Sophia for the first time in the Lutheran homelands of Minneapolis, Minnesota in the fall of 1993.[11] She was the guest of honor at the *RE-Imagining Conference* organized by mainline Protestant Christian feminists. In the first session participants repeated the litany: "it is time to . . . dream wildly . . . about who we intend to be in the future through the power and guidance of the spirit of wisdom whom we name Sophia."[12] Like a theme chorus at a *Youth For Christ* rally, the following line was constantly repeated: "Now Sophia, dream the vision, share the wisdom dwelling deep within."[13] Program literature declared: "Sophia's voice has been silenced too long.[14] Let her speak and bless us throughout these days." Though organizers claimed Sophia to be the personified Wisdom (*sophia* in Greek) of Proverbs 8, her teaching in Minneapolis was at best the teaching of Dame Folly, and at worst the rank paganism associated with ancient goddess worship.[15] Various definitions of Sophia sprouted: "Sophia is the divine energy in women being unlocked by the goddess rituals." "Sophia is the wisdom within me." The program definition said it all: "Sophia is the place in you where the entire universe resides."[16]

Conference speakers filled in the blanks. Aruna Gnanadason, an Indian feminist from the Church of South India, and a Director of the WCC Sub-unit on Women in the Church and Society in Geneva, explained that her red dot was a protest against those who saw the forehead as a place for the sign of the cross. For her, it was the sign of "the divine in each other." Naturally, all the participants drew a red dot on their foreheads.[17] Rita Nakashima Brock, associate professor at Hamline University in St. Paul, MN, declared, in terms reminiscent of ancient heretical Gnosticism:

> Although . . . he [Jahweh] refers to himself in the plural form . . . (he) remind(s) us inadvertently, of *the goddess and the earth from which he came* [emphasis mine].[18]

Elizabeth Bettenhausen, coordinator of the Study/Action Program at the Women's Theological Center in Boston, MA, and a member of the Evangelical Lutheran Church in America, declared: "We have to [re]imagine the doctrine of creation." Rejecting the biblical view of the creation of the earth, she made the astonishing statement: "Women, not God, are the true creators."[19]

This Sophia is the very antithesis of Wisdom in the Bible, for it denies the very legitimacy of God's creative handiwork. On the contrary, Proverbs shows Wisdom "at his side" as God made the Heavens and the Earth. As the New Testament reveals, the Wisdom at God's side was Christ, the eternal Son and Wisdom of God, by whom and through whom all things were created.[20] Use of this text is a pretext to import alien notions into the Christian church, and make a mockery of God the Creator. There is no relationship between personified Wisdom in Holy Scripture and the debutante divinity of Minneapolis. Who is Sophia? Why was the massive head of a beast without name paraded four times a day through the conference hall in Minneapolis?

The real agenda of the conference answers this question: "Be speculative, there is no 'answer.' We can't imagine what God is like. Being together in our own images is the ultimate." One astute observer noted that imprecision was part of the program:

> Sophia is the answer to the prayers of a multi-cultural, therapeutic world. . . . [She] serves 'reformers' of this ilk as an invaluable *tabula rasa*. Their adherents' ignorance of Sophia — far from being an obstacle — is essential to the project of fashioning a new religion while retaining tenuous and self-interested links to the Christian faith.[21]

The link is tenuous indeed. But Christian believers need to meet and recognize Sophia, the god of the brave new Aquarian world our children will inherit.

Sophia: Goddess of Ancient Paganism

One of the brilliant theoreticians of the "re-imagining" feminist movement, Rosemary Radford Ruether, stated already in 1983: "A new God is being born in our hearts."[22] This is a strange place for a god to get started, but Ruether seems to know her subject. Such an unusual birth is occurring because of a new power, "our power to name ourselves . . . and God."[23] Her *Women-Church* serves as a model for many of the movers and shakers in Sophia's retinue. This "church's" creed makes no mention of the God of Scripture or of Christ.[24] Ruether sees spiritual awakening as "a new rapprochement" between Christianity and paganism.[25] In a *Rite of Healing From Rape*, the worshipers in *Women-Church* use their power to name the new pagano-Christian deity: "The Mother-Spirit of Original Blessing surrounds you, upholds you on all sides, flows round about you, caresses you, loves you, and wills you to be whole."[26]

Sophia: Pagan Darling

Caitlín Matthews, is an ordained priestess in the ancient Egyptian cult for the worship of the Goddess, Isis, Queen of the Witches. You cannot get much more pagan than that. In 1992 she published a book in praise of her goddess entitled *Sophia, Goddess of Wisdom*.[27] This neopagan notes that "Sophia appears in nearly every culture and society," and that "the connections between Isis and Sophia are very significant and show us Sophia's strongest links to the ancient Goddess tradition." [28] In other words, there is much to connect Sophia with Isis, the Egyptian Goddess of magic and witchcraft. Isis, "the Goddess of a Thousand Names in the Completeness of Her Majesty"[29] has one name in particular — Sophia.

Conference participants in Minneapolis, invoked the following blessing over the elements of milk and honey in their blasphemous simulacre of the Lord's Supper: "Our maker, Sophia, we are women in your spirit."[30] Sophia is not an abstract feminist principle. As Creator, she has the attributes of deity. The "innocent" Sophia theme, developed by imaginative and creative "Christian" women in Minneapolis is pagan goddess religion, as many gladly admit.

Sophia: All-American Girl

Goddess spirituality in America at the end of the twentieth century? Twenty years ago, the very idea would have been preposterous. Today it is a powerful reality in the lives of many feminist movers and shakers. The recent re-edition of *The Politics of Women's Spirituality* (1982)[31] shows how power and goddess spirituality have come together in our day. Forty-five feminist thinkers, including Charlene Spretnak, Gloria Steinem, Mary Daly and Naomi Goldenberg make an impassioned plea for the rediscovery of women's spirituality through the goddess. Some of the articles deserve particular note, especially the following: "The Great Goddess: Who Was She?," "The Origins of Music: Women's Goddess Worship," "Witchcraft as Goddess Religion," "Why Women Need the Goddess: Phenomenological, Psychological, and Political Reflections." These and many others are written by extremely intelligent Western women at the end of our very sophisticated twentieth century. We are acquainted with Christian spirituality and with the non-spirituality of Western intellectuals toying with atheistic humanism and Marxist philosophy. These contemporary thinkers espouse spirituality, but a spirituality that jumps the millennia to find sustenance in the long-lost traditions of pagan goddess worship. Such thinking is no longer the speculation of a lunatic fringe. Many of the women mentioned are leaders in contemporary society and in mainline churches. Moreover, the presence of the word "politics" indicates a movement not content with secret societies and private fantasies. We are already seeing the first signs of this renewed paganism in legislation, gender issues, the media and in education. The *spiritual* power of the goddess threatens to take *political* power as we enter the Age of Aquarius.

The spirit entity, Lazaris, speaking through an ex-insurance salesman from California, confirms the place of the goddess in modern America:

> Though She never left, the Goddess is returning to you . . . and She brings a Light. . . . Yours is the Great Work: Receiving and then bringing Her Light into a seemingly darkening world. She is returning to you and She brings gifts and treasures that are bountiful and without limit. . . . As She returns, you can come to know the Goddess and you can know God. And . . . you can come to know who you are.[32]

The introduction of Sophia into "Christian" worship is actually, as a recent book title suggests, the "Restoring [of] the Goddess to Judaism and Christianity."[33] The goddess being restored is that divinity found "at the intersection of Christianity and paganism," the Gnostic female divinity Sophia, revealed in one Gnostic text as "Thunder Perfect Mind."

> Thunder Perfect Mind . . . appears to be everywhere and encompasses everything: . . . She is everything and everybody and its opposite. She is female and within her there is a the whole range of female life from birth to death, from the mundane woman in the world to the divine Wisdom of Heaven. She shows for me that there is no disunity between something and its opposite. A totality includes all aspects. Linear and dualistic divisions do not exist. . . . Asherah and Ashteroth were called whore, abomination and death, by those who hated them. Hochma [Hebrew for Sophia], their sister and descendant, was called the tree of life (Proverbs) before she was divested of her female form. I see in the "Thunder" the vision of a goddess human and divine who speaks again. Her words are taken over by the newer male-oriented religions. "I am the first and the last" is a description of God and of Christ (Rev. 21:6; 22:13); it not only recalls "Thunder" but also Egyptian Isis.[34]

Here Sophia is clearly identified with the form of pagan monism that joins all opposites in the pagan Mother goddess of Egypt, Isis, patron goddess of the witches. "Today women are rediscovering Isis," says radical feminist Alexander-Berghorn. She goes on:

> The re-awakening of Isis as a source of inspiration for contemporary women is exemplified by the healing ministry of Selena Fox, co-founder and High Priestess of Circle Sanctuary near Madison, Wisconsin. Every month at New Moon, Selena holds a spiritual Healing Circle cen-

tered around an Isis Healing Altar . . . each of us can personally experience the healing presence of the Goddess within us. All women are Isis and Isis is all women.[35]

There is more to Sophia than meets the eye. Sophia is either the wisdom of God or the wisdom of idols. Jesus said, "wisdom [sophia] is proved right by her actions."[36] The actions of Sophia as the new goddess for the Age of Aquarius reveal her pagan heart. Humanity closes the door on the Age of the Fish, Pisces. With an impatient shake, it sheds Christian values in society, patriarchy, and the male God of Holy Scripture. With hope it looks down a corridor of light into the new Age of Aquarius, the age of the goddess, feminine intuition and monism. Sophia is the Goddess of the Age of Aquarius. The future belongs to Sophia.

Sophia: Queen of the Witches

Witchcraft is the wave of the future. In the rethinking of witchcraft "the feminist religion of the future is presently being formed."[37] This programmatic statement comes from Miriam Starhawk, a leading theorist of goddess worship and witchcraft, a wiccan priestess/licensed minister of the Covenant of the Goddess, and a teacher at Matthew Fox's Institute for Culture and Creation Spirituality at Holy Names College in Oakland, CA. She finds in witchcraft a perfect foil to the "divisive absolutism" of the Judeo-Christian heritage, and an excellent bridge to the notion of balanced polarities in many Eastern religions. This yin and yang balance undermines the idea that something could be "wrong." Everything is useful. Apparent antipathies pull and push for ascendance, producing renewal. The explicitly Eastern spirituality suggests to Starhawk the development of a "new world view."

> The longing for expanded consciousness has taken many of us on a spiritual "journey to the East," and Hindu, Taoist, and Buddhist concepts are infusing Western culture with new understandings. The East-West dialogue has become a major influence on *the evolution of a new world view*. Eastern religions offer a radically different approach to spirituality than Judeo-Christian traditions. They are experiential rather than intellectual; they offer exercises, practices, and meditations, rather than catechisms. The image of god is not the anthropomorphic, bearded God-Father in the sky — but the abstract, unknowable ground of consciousness itself, the void, the Tao, the flow. Their goal is not to *know* God, but to *be* God. In many ways, their philosophies are very close to that of witchcraft.[38]

Starhawk brings together in witchcraft all the concerns of the New Age Movement — a new world religion for a new world order, ecology and science based on goddess/Mother Nature spirituality, consciousness transformation through "magical" techniques — and adds a zest of feminist eschatology — ultimate salvation through the woman. For many feminists, the liberation of women is the key to a new age of freedom. With the liberation of women will come the end of poverty, racial and sexual discrimination and the particularly male activity of war.[39]

"Out of the Broom Closet"

The above title appeared on the front page spread of my local paper. The favorable article about the return of witchcraft supports the attempt to find a "church" building where "parents can bring their children to learn about [Wicca's] ancient heritage."[40] Homosexuals are not the only ones coming out of the closet. Our multicultural time tolerates almost anything. Witches were granted official status at the Parliament of the World's Religions in Chicago in 1993; academics are rewriting their history, especially the history of the famous witch hunts as "ethnic cleansing . . . of independent women in Reformation Europe";[41] Virginia Mollenkott includes witchcraft as a valid expression of today's quest for authentic spirituality;[42] a leading Catholic feminist, Sister Madonna Kolbenschlag in her book, *Kiss Sleeping Beauty Goodbye*, approves of witchcraft;[43] as does Madeleine L'Engle;[44] "Christian" feminist theologian Rosemary Radford Ruether promotes rituals in her Women-Church such as a Halloween ceremony in remembrance of the persecution of witches.[45]

Christianity with its distinction between God and the creation, right and wrong, man and women, is joyfully abandoned as the essence of an outmoded worldview that produced "inquisitions, witch-hunts, pogroms, executions, censorship and concentration camps." In the Brave New World of this apocalyptic vision, "the Goddess is ourselves *and* the world." All distinctions are eliminated and everything goes as "our culture as a whole. . . evolve(s) toward life."[46]

> Mother Goddess is reawakening and we can begin to recover our primal birthright, the sheer intoxicating joy of being alive. We can open our eyes and see that there is nothing to be saved from . . . no God outside the world to be feared and obeyed.[47]

Anticipating what transpired in Minneapolis in 1993, Starhawk said in 1979: "Today women are creating new myths, singing a new liturgy, painting our own icons, and drawing strength from the new-old symbols of the Goddess, of the 'legitimacy and beneficence of female power.'"[48] Just before the *RE-Imagining Conference*, Christian theologian, Mary Elizabeth Moore of the Claremont School of Theology and Claremont Graduate School stated that many women found Starhawk's work "compatible with, or at least, adaptable to, Christian teaching."[49]

Through feminism and the religion of the goddess, witchcraft is "adapted" to Christianity. We can no longer dismiss witchcraft as the lunatic radical fringe of far-out feminism.[50] Even if it denies connection with Satanism,[51] witchcraft is at the very least a virulent form of occult paganism, standing at the opposite pole from Christian theism.

What is a Witch?

Zsuzsanna E. Budapest, a "feminist" witch whose mother was a medium and practicing witch in Budapest, Hungary, provides a very simple and clear description of a witch: "A witch is a woman or a man who considers the earth a living, breathing, conscious being — part of the family of the vast universe — to be regarded and respected as God herself. To be a witch you have to see yourself as part of God, who is present in, not separate from us and all living beings."[52] It would certainly appear that there is very little to distinguish between modern-day witches and other spiritually-attuned New Age people such as shamans, mediums and channelers. At the very least, they all claim to plug into the spiritual power of the earth, and turn away from the biblical God, distinct from the earth he created. Roman Catholic journalist Donna Steichen documents, with chilling accuracy, how witchcraft has masterminded a progressive takeover of a substantial portion of the Catholic Church in the United States. She shows how witchcraft has swept through the convents of America and decimated many orders. Her studied judgment is disturbing: "Most of the old Catholic culture has been devoured by spiritual termites, leaving behind a structure that looks solid to the eye but crumbles at a touch."[53]

Isis, the "great prototype of all goddesses"[54] called "the Mighty in Magic," the queen of the witches, was one of the chief antagonists of Christianity during the first three centuries of the Christian era. As we shall show below,[55] Isis already appeared as Sophia in the heretical Christianity of ancient Gnosticism. Modern Christianity, if it is to be true to its forebears in the faith, will have to resist this same occult, nature magic of witchcraft that centers on the Goddess.

Sophia: Quick Change Artist

Have you ever met a polytheist, someone who believes in the existence of many (*poly*) gods (*theoi*)? You probably think of exotic places
like Polynesia where everyone wears grass skirts and not much else and
people dance to the haunting beat of native tom toms. But David Miller
is a bespectacled "suit," the epitome of middle-class urbane America.
He is the Watson-Ledden Professor of Religion at Syracuse University
and recent candidate for the presidency of the American Academy of
Religion, the prestigious professional society of Religion teachers in North
America, that meets jointly every year with the Society of Biblical Literature. David Miller is, nevertheless, a polytheist.

Sophia: Born from the Ashes of God

using the titles Goddess and God the Mother is probably the only way
to shatter the hold of [the] idolatrous male God on the psyche.
   - Nelle Morton[56]

Before becoming a polytheist, Miller was part of the "death of God"
movement of the Sixties. Radical theologians led by William Hamilton
and Thomas Altizer declared God dead. Come of age, man no longer
needed an external divinity. When the movement fizzled, Altizer ended
up teaching American literature to undergraduates at a state university.
One more outrageous radical thesis, no more clever than a newspaper
headline had passed away. Or so it seemed.
   Princess Elizabeth of England flew home from Australia hastily when
her Father, George VI passed away in 1952. As she stepped onto the
tarmac in London, an official greeted her with the phrase I heard then as
a young boy: "The King is dead; long live the Queen." Just a decade
after George VI went to meet his maker, William Hamilton might have
said: "God is dead, long live the Goddess." He actually said: "The revolution does not look like monotheism, Christian or post-Christian. What
it looks like is polytheism."[57] Hamilton's analysis has proved accurate,
in spite of Nixon, Reagan, Bush and the emerging Religious Right.
   In 1974 David Miller recognized that "the announcement of the death
of God was the obituary of a useless single-minded and one-dimensional
norm of a civilization that has been predominantly monotheistic, not
only in its religion, but also in its politics, its history, its social order, its
ethics, and its psychology. When released from the tyrannical imperialism of monotheism by the death of God, man has the opportunity of

discovering new dimensions hidden in the depths of reality's history."[58] At the funeral of the God of the Bible, Miller announced "the rebirth of the Gods and Goddesses." Such an experience, the experience of paganism, he found to be "liberating." He found freedom in the "multiple patterns of polytheism [which] allow room to move meaningfully through a pluralistic universe. They free one to affirm the radical plurality of the self, an affirmation that one has seldom been able to manage because of the guilt surrounding monotheism's insidious implication that we have to "get it all together."[59]

As he solemnly proclaimed the death of God, Miller proudly declared: "The Gods and Goddesses of Greece are our heritage. Sooner or later it is they who will reappear."[60] Polytheistic paganism does not hinder one's career, especially when it includes a feminist angle. David Miller now wields considerable influence both in the American Academy of Religion and, ironically, as a member of the publications board, in the *Society of Biblical Literature*, a prestigious professional *Society of Bible Teachers*.

The goddesses have returned. Secular feminism has developed a psychology of women based on Greek goddess archetypes. Our local community college offers an evening course for eight to thirteen year-old girls designed to help them develop identity through the study of six Greek goddesses. Radical "Christian" feminists are not far behind. Their rediscovery of Sophia dates from the "death of God" movement in the Sixties. But is it legitimate to associate Sophia with polytheism?

Sophia: Legion

Sophia is the gateway to polytheism for those still imprisoned by biblical monotheism. At the *RE-Imagining Conference* Chung Hyun Kyung, assistant professor in theology, Ewha Women's University, Seoul, Korea, spoke of three goddesses — Kali (Hindu), Quani (Buddhist) and Enna (animist) whom she integrates with Christianity to produce a "change of perspective" and the "fusion of different horizons."[61] Virginia Mollenkott agreed.[62] So the fusion of goddesses leads to the fusion of religions, which is to be expected since all pagan religions begin with man, not God. The acceptance of polytheism throws the net wide.

Lois M. Wilson, chancellor at Lakehead University, Thunder Bay, Canada is also an ordained minister in the United Church of Canada and a past president of the World Council of Churches and of the Canadian Council of Churches. Of the passage in the Acts of the Apostles, "I shall pour out my spirit on all humanity," she said in Minneapolis, "Did he mean neo pagans, did she mean the wiccans, the Sikhs, the Muslims, the Hindus, the men and the women?"[63] One ritual at the *RE-Imagining Conference* included a liturgical song, listing names for God, from different religious traditions:

> divine ancestor, Mother God, Father God, Elohim, Adonai, Spirit, Ruach, mystery, lover, eternal goodness, alpha and omega, fire of love, living presence, she who is eternal, she who will be, Sophia, Earth Mother, spirit woman, she who is, ninjan, cosmic maxim, weaver God, transforming laughter, womb of creation, higher power, yin and yang, unknown God, unnameable God, holy one of blessing.[64]

The witches and goddess worshipers say the same. Starhawk speaks of "the Goddess [who] has infinite aspects and thousands of names."[65] Witches Sjoo and Mor describe "the Great goddess of All Living [who] gave birth to herself and the entire cosmos — she is the world egg, containing the yin and the yang . . . [she is] Kali [the Hindu goddess of life and death] dancing the universe into being and then to destruction and death."[66] David Miller prophesied it: "A polytheistic theology will be a feminine theology, but in the manner of all the Goddesses — the thousands of daughters of Oceanus and Tethys, to name only a few. By being many, these Goddesses avoid a monotheistically chauvinistic view of the feminine."[67]

Today there exists in many churches a modified polytheism, first suggested by one of the great feminist foremothers, Elizabeth Cady Stanton, master-mind behind *The Women's Bible* of 1895. Cady Stanton saw in the plural of Genesis 1, not a hint of the Christian Trinity, but rather a trinity of Heavenly Father, Mother and Son.[68] She continues: "The first step in the elevation of women . . . is the cultivation . . . by the rising generation . . . of an ideal Heavenly Mother, to whom their prayers should be addressed." Such an understanding of God, she claimed (rightly), is "witnessed to in the holy books of all religions."[69] Today that vision is taken up by "Christian" feminists such as Virginia Mollenkott. "We had better learn," says Mollenkott, "to "bring *many* names" by which to address this God who is our strong Mother as well as our tender Father, a "young, growing God" as well as an "old, aching God," a "great, living God" who is "never fully known" even though She is "closer yet than breathing."[70]

This solution seems less drastic than the eradication of God the Father and the adoption of goddess polytheism. It seeks to 'balance' our idea of God by such liturgical formulae as 'in the name of the Father and the Mother, the Son and the Spirit.' But enormous difficulties soon arise. Such formulations force Christians to one of two solutions:

♦ enlarge the Trinity by the addition of the Mother Goddess. But to remain a Christian we cannot enlarge the Trinity. The apparently innocuous search for many names leads to the inclusion of names of pagan gods and to the elimination of the names (Father, Lord, King) by which the one true God has revealed himself;

♦ produce a Trinitarian God, one of whose persons becomes an androgynous "parent," "God the Mother/Father,"[71] a being who bears no resemblance to anything we know in created reality. By such a notion the personhood of God is subtly dissolved into non-personal symbols, which finally leads to the impersonal All of Eastern monism. This is clear in Cady Stanton. Her deep understanding of God is "our ideal first cause, the 'Spirit of all Good,'" witnessed to in "the holy books of all religions."[72]

Sophia: Feminine Symbol of the Monistic All

Sophia endorsed monism in Minneapolis. Said Mollenkott, a leading speaker at the conference:

> everything that lives is holy . . . the one divine presence . . . in everybody. . . . the monism I'm talking about assumes that god is so all-inclusive that she is involved in every cell of those who are thoughts in her mind. . . . like Jesus, we and the source are one.[73]

To think of God in the specific sense of Scripture as the transcendent God who may never be identified with the substance of the creation He has made is now dismissed as the "mythical-literal" faith of "elementary school."[74] "Christian" believers must move to the "Universalizing stage" of oneness with the divine,[75] and understand the world as "God's body."[76]

These notions about God bring together odd bed-fellows. The Theosophical Society of the late nineteenth century, a precursor of the New Age Movement, was a minuscule elitist minority dedicated to eradicating Christianity and to promoting both the occult and a Western form of Hindu mysticism. The society's vision has made enormous strides. In 1994, Theosophy was adopted as a recognized section of the annual meeting of the American Academy of Religion. The Theosophical Society pronounced valid the contemporary mystical notions of unification and convergence as well as any other ideas about God found in all the world's religions — all but one, Biblical/Christian monotheism. As the Society's brochure states:

Esoteric Philosophy [read proto-New Age thinking] reconciles all nations, strips every one of its outward human garments, and shows the
root of each to be identical with that of every other great religion. It
proves the necessity of a Divine Absolute Principle in Nature. It denies Deity no more than it does the sun. Esoteric Philosophy has never
rejected God in Nature, nor Deity as the absolute and abstract *End*. It
only refuses to accept any of the gods of the so-called monotheistic
religions, gods created by man in his own image and likeness, a blasphemous and sorry caricature of the Ever Unknowable.[77]

The "Divine Absolute Principle" of monism is finally so diffuse and
ultimately so indefinable, that "god" loses all specific identity. The highest title monism can give to this god is that of "the Deity, *who is beyond
all our knowing.*"[78] That contemporary "Christian" thinkers adopt such
a "God," proves how successful is the project to eliminate the revealed
monotheistic God of Scripture.[79]

Towards the end of the heyday of the cultural revolution of the Sixties, cultural analyst Os Guinness predicted the probability that Hinduism would seek by a "fraternal embrace" especially directed to mainline
liberalism, to "strangle" Christianity. Guinness argued that Eastern tolerance, which has been widely adopted as an unquestioned "democratic" value in our day, is actually the "kiss of death." Hinduism embraced
Buddhism by declaring that Buddha was a further revelation of Krishna.
Some Hindu gurus have similarly spoken of the "Blessed Lord Jesus
Christ" as an expression of Hinduism. Guinness predicted: "Probably
the same approach will be made openly to Christian theology in the
next few years. Liberalism is already showing signs of response before
the overtures are made."[80] Guinness was right.

Sophia: Every Woman

"Hey, we are God." Such is one writer's estimation of the result of
Shirley Maclaine's TV mini-series "Out On A Limb."[81] Her book states
the message clearly.

God lies within, and therefore we are each part of God. Since there is
no separateness, we are each Godlike, and God is in each of us. . . .
We are literally made up of God energy, therefore we can create whatever we want in life because we are each co-creating with the energy
of God — the energy that makes the universe itself.[82]

Recently MacLaine claimed that the mainstream had gone "new age." How right she is. Says Virginia Mollenkott: "when Shirley MacLaine teaches people to chant "I am God," she is correct."[83]

There is one final surprise. The RE-Imagining Conference has already taught us that God is unknowable, and that Humanity is God: "We can't imagine what God is like. *Being together in our own images is the ultimate.*"[84]   The perverse sexuality at the conference underlines the nature of its theology. According to the Apostle Paul, when mankind worships the creature rather than the Creator and exchanges the truth of God for an (imaginative) lie God gives them over to sexual impurity.[85]

But the ultimate blasphemy might surprise even some at the conference. The end point of the reduction of God, as ancient Gnosticism eloquently shows, is not the identification of God as an impersonal, unknowable Force nor even the elevation of Man as God. The ultimate blasphemy is to make Satan God. For behind the Force and divinized humanity is the ultimate personal source of evil, the Devil.

Sophia: Satan

Is this life imitating art or art imitating life? Radical religious feminist theater interprets in vivid green the true nature of Sophia. In this view, the serpent was actually Lilith, a female spirit, who, according to the stage directions of this feminist drama "in green body make-up or leotard, slithers into view round a tree." With "serpentine" movements "she slithers round the tree again, and reappears immediately with a red apple in her hand, which she offers to Eve," and utters the classic words: "Well, Eve?"[86]

The Jewish feminist, Alix Pirani, whose book attempts to restore the Goddess into Judaism and Christianity, explains who Lilith is. Though the term appears but once in the Bible and means "night creature,"[87] modern religious feminists, following a few speculations by medieval rabbis,[88] have resurrected the myth. Pirani herself claims that Lilith appears to her in her study,[89] and that she is a manifestation of the goddess.[90] In particular, modern feminism identifies Lilith with the Serpent of Genesis.[91]

> Lilith appeared to her [Eve] in the shape of a serpent in the garden of Eden and tempted her to defy God by biting into the apple of the tree of knowledge of good and evil[92] . . . . Saturn is also Satan and the fallen angel Lucifer, who descends to earth in the guise of the immortal light-

ning serpent Sata. When God denied Adam and Eve the fruit of the
tree of knowledge in order to keep them ignorant, it was Lucifer, in
the form of the serpent Lilith, who offered them the "light" of consciousness.

Pirani does not miss the relationship with Gnosticism, which she approves.[93] So this "ancient Goddess who appeared in the form of the
Serpent is now insistently demanding the restoration of her rightful
position — that of the Great Mother Goddess who is bestower of life as
well as being a powerful Queen of the Otherworld. Otherwise we shall
continue to suffer the consequences: the curse of Lilith."[94] Needless to
say, the curse of Lilith is the Christian faith.

Who is Sophia? Sophia is Lilith, the feminine expression of Satan.
The head of the beast paraded in Minneapolis did have a name. Its name
was Sophia.

Sophia: Future of the Planet

The many faces of Sophia represent the continuum of pagan thinking within the present society and much of the Christian church. Not
everyone espouses the whole philosophy. Some may not see the ramifications. But Sophia's ratings are improving. She is an attractive alternative to the God of Scripture, for she fits the aspirations of the Age of
Aquarius. She is the new star in the pantheon of the gods, the divine
Tinkerbell upon whom the hopes and wishes of the modern world ride.
In her person she expresses the "manifold wisdom" of the pagan agenda:

The New Evolution:[95]

As the creator spirit, Sophia gives voice to the utopian belief that the
next stage of evolution will be human and spiritual. This is the intoxicating eschatology of human self-redemption. In this age of theological
re-imagination, humanity is on the verge of an evolutionary leap to a
new consciousness where all problems are solved. Sophia is a perfect
symbol of the future that humanity will create;

The New Popularity of Process Theology:[96]

As the rising star of the new polytheism, Sophia is the God-who-is-
coming-to-be. Popular in many departments of religion and theological
seminaries, Process Theology is a theological form of spiritual evolution. It holds that God is evolving with his creation, so that all creative

experience which produces movement and process is also helping in the maturing of God;

The Rejection of Patriarchy:[97]

Patriarchy is judged to be the greatest of all evils, and the God of Scripture is the God of law, of war, of rationality, of hierarchy, and of male violence.[98] Such a God is a mere projection of male power thrown up on the screen of human myths. Sophia, the goddess, is the soft, enveloping divinity of love, inclusiveness and intuition;

The New View of Democracy:

Sophia is the perfect symbol of the tolerant, inclusive, pro-choice society of tomorrow, able to welcome all forms of religion,[99] all expressions of sexuality and all ethical choices. Her monistic embrace encircles the good and the evil in a higher synthesis that will be good for everyone — well, almost everyone;

The New Global Religious Vision:

Emerging democracy will be global, with a common religious center. The many-faceted goddess, Sophia, is able to join the many faiths and nations of the world in a new monistic unity;[100]

The New Ecology:

One of the faces of Sophia is Gaia, Mother Earth, the divine spirit that animates the natural world. Sophia/Gaia relieves the anxiety surrounding the demise of the ecological system. Sophia both needs our help and will lead us out of all man-made and male-god-made catastrophes to a nuclear-free world of zero-population. It is not always known, though, that Sophia has another face. James Lovelock, creator of the Gaia hypothesis according to which the earth is a goddess, warns that "Gaia is not a tolerant Mother. . . . she is ruthless in the destruction of whoever transgresses" her rule. They "will be eliminated without pity."[101] In this ruthlessness, one is reminded of the bloodied Hindu goddess Kali, another face of Sophia.

The New View of Authority:

Sophia represents, in spite of her violence, the longing for a softer, more personalized religion, which does away with notions such as role, hierarchy and authority[102] and replaces them with inner motivation and egalitarian structures;[103]

The New Psychology:

Many now believe that polytheism best fits multiple personalities and "mutually exclusive aspects of the self."[104] The new society of personal freedom, pluralism and diversity has its psychological counterpart in the many options of the self, which enables people to keep their options open without being pronounced sick. Virginia Mollenkott, in a chapter dealing with the "Wisdom of God Herself" makes the interesting statement that "one of my identities is that of an evangelical lesbian feminist."[105] With her new monistic goddess spirituality, Virginia Mollenkott has a much looser connection with Virginia Mollenkott. "I am a sinless Self travelling through eternity and temporarily having human experiences in a body known as Virginia Ramey Mollenkott;[106]

The New Pro-choice Ethics:[107]

Since the new world that Sophia spins is circular, there is no absolute truth and no ultimate right or wrong. The yin joins the yang, bringing together opposites to extend personal choice and satisfaction.[108] Sophia's world prohibits nothing. Under Sophia's banner, numerous elements can be joined. In *Gay and Gaia*, Daniel Spencer, professor of Philosophy and Religion, seeks to normalize homosexuality by showing that ethics, ecology and the erotic come together in the new world synthesis. This is earthy wisdom worthy of the new Sophia;[109]

The New Understanding of Jesus:

The new answer, given by many contemporary Bible scholars in the context of the rehabilitation of ancient Gnostic heresy, is: Jesus is "Sophia's most trusted envoy,"[110] "Miriam's Child," "Sophia's Prophet,"[111] "Very Goddess and Very Man,"[112] "*an* epiphany of God, *a* "disclosure". . . of God," but "there have been many figures in every culture who experience the 'other world'" [emphasis mine].[113] Jesus is interesting — he was a prophet, "a charismatic healer, unconventional sage, and founder of an alternative community. . . . he is clearly one of the most remarkable figures who ever lived"[114] — but he *is not* unique. A confidence trick worthy of Houdini whisks Jesus Christ away from the historic confessions of the Faith and recreates him as a mystical guru founder of a sect of doctrinal and sexual deviance. Our Lord is no longer the unique and only God and Savior whose death on the cross deals once for all with sin. His ultimate work is that of cohort. Like the dying and rising Osiris, forever dependent on his Lady Isis, Jesus Christ is now revealed in these last times as "Sophia's most trusted envoy," the Last Adam forever subservient to the eschatological Eve.

The New Spirituality:

Sophia offers to an experience-oriented world the immediacy of pagan spirituality, but the offering is so enormous, it deserves its own chapter.

These are just some of the reasons why the future of the "new" god on the block looks bright. Can anything stop the thunderous return of Sophia?

CHAPTER 11

THE GOD OF
ANCIENT GNOSTICISM

I am the prostitute and the venerable one.
I am the wife and the virgin . . .
I am the one whose likeness is great in Egypt.
  - *Thunder, Perfect Mind*

Sophia in Historical Perspective

Minneapolis 1993 was not the first sighting of Sophia in Christian circles. She made an early appearance in the heretical Gnostic writings of the early centuries of the Church's history. Mainline women in Minneapolis imagined they were creating new images of the divine *ex nihilo* (out of nothing). But Gnostic musings of fifteen hundred years ago give their vain imaginations, in the unforgettable phrase of Yogi Berra, a surprising aura of *"déjà vu all over again!"*

Sophia appeared among the Gnostics as a fresh young goddess with fascinating new ideas that got her in trouble but brought redemption.[1] For those tired of the male God of the Bible, she promised liberation and radical freedom. Her wisdom surpassed the biblical wisdom of Proverbs, for under her mysterious and alluring mantle lay hidden both the pearls of Lady Wisdom and the dark secrets of Dame Folly. This Gnostic prayer to Sophia would have been welcomed in Minneapolis: "May She who is before all things, the incomprehensible and indescribable Grace, fill you within, and increase in you her own knowledge."[2]

Sophia in Gnosticism

Sophia is God's First Thought. She becomes "fallen" wisdom[3] because through her inquisitiveness, [like that of Eve], the physical world eventually comes into being. Ialdabaoth (Jahweh), her aborted fetus, born from her desire to know, creates the physical world. Because she realizes her mistake, Sophia "misses no occasion to cheat the Rulers, [namely God and his angels] in order to help [humankind]."[4] Her mission of self-redemption is two-fold: to expose the truly evil nature of the biblical God, and to point mankind to the true God behind the Creator and the visible oppressive world He foolishly created.

Sophia is bad news and good news. There is a negative and a positive side to Sophia's function according to Gnostic theory. Negatively, her revelation "deconstructs" the Creator of Heaven and earth and all his works, thus clearing the way for her positive function, that of revealing the true, unknown God from whom she emanates. These two functions must be seen in order to appreciate just how extreme is the "Christian" Gnostic attack against orthodoxy. While the feminine Sophia evokes notions of tenderness and creativity, her true work is a violent death blow to the Christian God. This is why we need to know these ancient texts, for they can tell us something about our own future.

Sophia Overthrows God

Recognized specialists of Gnosticism have consistently emphasized the truly radical nature of the Gnostic system. Kurt Rudolf notes, for instance, that the *Gospel of Philip* produces a "fundamental re-evaluation of things and names — the names of this world belong to error, introduced by the archons."[5] According to Rudolf, the Gnostic conception of God is "thoroughly revolutionary."[6] Hans Jonas, the great German expert of Gnosticism argued, in the 1950s, that the syncretistic tendency in Gnostic circles was not "directionless" but had a distinct purpose — to collect and use "any material that can set the scene in a world other than this world," that is, in a world other than the world of the created order made by the Creator of Heaven and Earth.[7]

Recent feminist thinkers have discovered the revolutionary character of Gnosticism as it applies to gender and patriarchal civilization. Says one, "Gnosticism is becoming a powerful influence in feminist research into the overthrow of the male in the divine."[8] An egalitarian, non-patriarchal vision constitutes the agenda of cutting-edge theology, sociology, and global politics in the West. Gnosticism and anti-patriarchal feminism are a match made in heaven since divine Sophia's mission was [and apparently still is] the overthrow of Jahweh. Sophia's key role in the overthrow of patriarchy has not always been acknowledged in the analysis of this second and third century heresy. But present preoccupation with gender liberation makes the nature of her mission fairly jump off the ancient pages. Sophia's overthrow of God is accomplished in the following ways:

Sophia Proves Jahweh a Fool

Like a blustering earthly macho brute who thinks that because he is male he knows everything, the heavenly prototype of all patriarchal oppression, Jahweh, foolishly thinks he is the creator of all things. He is mistaken. Sophia is the Creator.[9] According to Ptolemy, a Gnostic theologian of the second century, she is the true origin of creation:

> They say that the Demiurge [the Creator] believed that he had created all this himself, but in fact he had made them because Achamoth [another name for Sophia] had prompted him.[10]

As the Goddess of Wisdom, Sophia is all-wise, simply brimming with intellectual vigor, whereas the classic Gnostic name for the male God of Scripture is Samael, the "blind one." Sophia is the "Mother of the Universe."[11] Spiritual illumination is to be desired, whereas Jahweh's work of creation through the process of childbirth, is to be jettisoned as uncouth and animalistic. So the living Jesus of the *Gospel of Thomas* declares: "My mother [gave me falsehood], but [My] true [Mother] gave me life."[12] While Sophia instructs in wisdom, Ialdabaoth (Jahweh) is in a fog of confusion. Says one Gnostic text: "[Yaldabaoth] appeared out of the waters, in the likeness of a lion and gynandrous [a mixture of female and male], possessing great authority in himself, but not knowing where he had come into being." The only authority he has is the "authority of matter,"[13] which, of course, for Gnostics, was the one authority which did not matter! Even human beings know more than this divine fool. Adam tells Seth, "And we are like the great eternal angels, for we were greater than the god who made us and the powers who were with him."[14] *The Apocryphon of John* speaks of man's wisdom as making him "greater than those who had made him, and made him stronger than that of the first archon [Jahweh]."[15] So Paul's statement in 1 Corinthians 2:9 is turned against Paul's God. To the Gnostic believer is promised what no "angel-eye" has seen and what no "archon-ear" has heard.[16] (Archon, "ruler," is a derogatory title for the God of the Bible). The Gnostic believer sees and hears more than the God of Scripture. *Sola Scriptura* was not a Gnostic watch-word.

As souls at death return to their divine origin, met by the Archons (Jahweh and his angels) who seek to bring them under their power, the Gnostic Jesus reminds them that the power they must evoke is the power of Sophia, "mistress of [souls]." By this power Gnostic believers will put Jahweh and his hosts to flight.[17]

To summarize, the God of Scripture, most often known as Ialdabaoth, an apparent play on Jahweh and Sabaoth, which perhaps means "Son of Shame,"[18] is presented variously as "ignorant, arrogant,[19] conceited, disdainful, stupid, mad,[20] assassin . . . a lionlike freak who will exert his ludicrous talents at the expense of humankind . . . a perfect object for gnostic hatred and contempt."[21] With such a despicable male god as this who could not be charmed by the alluring wisdom of sophisticated Sophia?[22]

♦ Jahweh Confused about His Gender

The Gnostic critique implies the foolishness of imagining God in purely masculine terms. It is the same critique we hear today, even among "progressive" conservatives. The Gnostic attempted to dislodge the God of Scripture by positing gender confusion in God. Today inclusive programs in many Christian churches change hymns, liturgies and even the biblical text in order to conform to a "gender-inclusive" divine image.

The *Apocryphon of John* proposes a new revelation of divinity that is as inclusive as any modern jewel of political correctness: The divine reality reveals itself to John through Barbelo [Sophia] as alternately a youth, an old man and a servant, and then as the Father, the Mother and the Son.[23] Similarly, in the *Gospel of the Egyptians*, we read: there are three powers that come from the ultimate, unknowable God; the Father, the Mother and the Son.[24] Sophia shows in her multiple nature the transformation of gender, exposing the binary, limited character of the male Jahweh. Such a reduction of God to exclusively male metaphors deserves derision, and here it is:

♦ Jahweh the Joke

The male God of the Bible and biblical patriarchal history deserve mockery and scornful laughter. Everything in the Old Testament is a "laughingstock" from Adam to the Chief Archon. Creation and biblical theology are rejected *en bloc*. The whole thing is a big joke.

For Greek speakers, the name "Demiurge" for Jahweh was a form of mockery. In Plato and Aristotle a demiurge is an artisan/craftsman who merely follows the ideas of others (the artist) but is incapable himself of true creativity. Thus when the Demiurge presented himself as Lord of Creation, his folly and pride were obvious to all who knew Greek.[25]

The mockery becomes much less subtle. According to the *Second Treatise of the Great Seth*, the Creator of the world is mocked because he makes the statement: "I am God and there is no other beside me."[26] Seth, the Christ-figure in this version of Gnosticism, with laughter, calls this "empty glory." When God asks, "Who is man?"[27] all the angels cannot conceal their mirth at the smallness of the knowledge of such a God.

♦   **Orthodoxy: Good for a Laugh**

This mockery extends from the creator through the creation to the entire history of redemption and onto the cross. *The Apocalypse of John* mocks the entire sabbatic structure of creation by identifying the seven days of creation with seven perverse powers. Like the faces of the gruesome animals, God's biblical names are derisively distorted: "The first, Athoth, who is sheep-faced. The second, Eloaiou, who is donkey-faced. The third, Astaphaios, who is [hyena]-faced. The fourth, Iao, who is serpent-faced with seven heads. The fifth is Sabaoth, who is dragon-faced. The sixth is Adonin, who is ape-faced. The Seventh is Sabbede, who has a luminous fire-face. This is the hebdomad (the 'sevenness') of the week."[28] According to the *Great Seth*, Adam is a laughingstock since he was created by this foolish creator; Abraham, Isaac and Jacob were a laughingstock since they were named by this same God; David was a laughingstock since he was a friend of this God; Solomon was a laughingstock, since, with the vanity of the Creator, he took himself to be Christ; the twelve prophets were laughingstocks since they were actually false prophets appointed by the Creator; Moses is a laughingstock because he was the friend of this imposter God.[29] Finally, the true Christ/Seth laughs at the ignorance of those who thought he (Christ) had died on the cross. It was another, not Christ who was nailed to the cross, who drank the bitter herbs, and on whom the crown of thorns was placed. While all this was going on Seth, looking down, was rejoicing and laughing at their ignorance.[30]

The biblical revelation of creation, fall and redemption is here overturned as worthy only of laughter and derision — as it is in much postmodern liberal theology. Laughter and mockery are back. At the *RE-Imagining Conference*, the audience erupted in laughter and applause when a speaker pointed out that neither God the Father nor Jesus Christ had been mentioned in their worship.

Behind the laughter Sophia stands, smiling.

Jahweh is a Demon

It is no laughing matter. When the laughing stops the hissing begins. There is no neutral ground. God the creator, the crucified Jesus and all those who foolishly follow them must be denounced as diabolical.

The ancient Gnostic texts explain that Sophia, in order to undo the evil activity of her aborted fetus, Ialdabaoth (Jahweh), sends the [good] serpent to "seduce Adam and Eve into breaking Ialdabaoth's command."[31] In this reversal exegesis, the serpent has become not just wise but good. God has become both a fool and the personification of the Devil. In a number of ways, God is shown as the Devil:

God's Work of Creation Is Diabolical

The *Apocryphon of John* paints a very different picture of Eden than the one found on the first pages of the Bible:

> And they, namely, the archons, took him,
> and put him in paradise, and bade him,
> "Eat, for this is delight," for their delight is bitter
> and their beauty is perverted.
> But their delight is a lie and their trees are ungodliness
> and their fruit is a fatal toxin and their oath is death.
> And they put the tree of their life in the middle of Paradise.
> But I will teach you all which is the secret of their life,
> which is the counsel which they took together,
> that is the image of their spirit.
> It's root is bitter and its branches are death,
> hatred is its shadow and deception is in its leaves,
> and its flower is the unguent of evil
> and its fruit is death and lust is its seed.
> And it yields its fruit in the darkness.
> The ones who taste of it, their dwelling place is in Hades
> and their place of rest is darkness.[32]

God's Associates Include the Devil

Ialdabaoth, the "first archon" begat authorities for himself. Some of these authorities bear the various biblical names of God such as Adonaiou and Sabaoth, but one is Belias "who is over the abyss of Hades."[33]

Another ancient Gnostic text, the *Gospel of the Egyptians*, makes the same association: Sakla, (a derogatory name for Jahweh, which in He-

brew means "mad") joins with the demon Nebruel and produces assist-
ing spirits, two of which are named Adonaios and Sabaoth.[34]

God Looks Like the Devil

The God of the Bible, Ialdabaoth, is portrayed as a lion-headed
creature born from confusion who is called Ariel (from the Hebrew
term "ari" meaning "lion"). This arrogant wild animal form, called Saklas,
"the mad one," appears as "a lionfaced serpent with glittering eyes of
fire."[35]

God Is the Devil

Finally in bald, unimaginable blasphemy, God is the Devil. The
Gnostic "reversal exegesis" practiced on the "satanic verses" of Genesis
is now turned on Paul's Epistle to the Ephesians. The God of Old Testament Scripture, whom Paul identifies as the God of Israel and the Father of our Lord Jesus Christ[36] is identified with the principalities and
powers and with the Devil who throws the flaming darts. In *Trimorphic
Protennoia* God the creator appears without nuance as the great Demon
who rules over the lowest part of the underworld, that is, Hell. The text
calls him "Yaltabaoth," (Yahweh and Sabaoth), and lest there be any
doubt as to whom is meant, he is called the "Archigenitor," (the Chief
Creator) the one who falsely boasted saying "I am God and . . . there is
no other beside me."[37]

In similar blasphemous manner, the *Apocalypse of Peter* includes
the crucified Jesus, Elohim and the cross with the demons:

> And he [the Savior] said to me [Peter], "Strengthen yourself, for it is
> you to whom these mysteries have been given, to perceive them through
> revelation, that this one whom they crucified is the firstborn, and the
> abode of demons, and the stony vessel (?) in which they live, of Elohim,
> of the cross which exists under the Law.[38]

Sophia casts Jahweh into Hell

Jahweh gets what any devil deserves — Hell. The laughter has
long since ceased. Things are deathly serious. Pushing reversal interpretation to its incredible but logical conclusion, in about as auda-
cious a show of "against the grain" exegesis as one can find, Sophia
casts the God of Scripture into the destructive fires of Hell.

The Italian specialist G.Filoramo recognizes that Gnosticism presses
its system to a logical conclusion: the archons and the Demiurgos are

defeated and destroyed in a universal conflagration.[39] There is hardly
need of scholarly support. The texts are crystal-clear. *The Hypostasis of
the Archons* affirms the sad end of Jahweh in no uncertain terms.
Ialdabaoth, for his blind arrogance in thinking that he is the one true
God is reprimanded by the feminine goddess, Zoe, daughter of Pistis
Sophia. "She breathed upon his face, and her breath became an angel of
fire and that very angel shackled Ialdabaoth and threw him down into
Tartaros [Hell], under the abyss."[40]

According to *On the Origin of the World*, at the end of the world,
Sophia will chase the chaotic divine beings whom she had made, together with the First Father into the pit where they will devour one
another. Finally the First Father (Jahweh), when he has destroyed them,
will destroy himself.[41]

Such is the radical destructive work of Sophia — to bring an end to
God. This should be seriously noted. This is the underbelly of an ancient apostasy now being promoted, often by means of its less shocking
elements as a valid, alternative expression of early Christianity and as
the new form of Christianity for the third millennium.

Sophia Reveals the True
Unknowable God of Pagan Monism

What is left when Jahweh is banished to Hell? Having
"deconstructed" the tired old God of orthodoxy, Sophia takes up her
"positive" role as revealer of the "true" God. As in the dream of the
empty Bible that needs re-writing, we now have eerily empty heavens
that need an occupant. Swept clean, the cosmos awaits new inhabitants.
The God whom Sophia reveals is the unknown and unknowable God of
pagan monism "who" bears a striking resemblance to the new god of
Aquarian spirituality.

Getting to Know the Unknown God

God in the Gnostic system is the "unknown God" beyond all that is
visible or sensible, who incorporates a "fullness" (pleroma) of heavenly
beings.[42] According to the Church Fathers, Gnostic theologians delighted
in describing the indescribable. The proto-Gnostic Marcion (150 A.D.)
called his preaching the "gospel of the alien God." Basilides (second
century) spoke of "the primal non-existent God." Valentinus (second

century), perhaps the greatest Gnostic theologian, states with eloquence this pillar of Gnostic thinking:

> there is in invisible and ineffable heights a pre-existent perfect aeon whom they call Pre-beginning, forefather and Primal Ground, that is inconceivable and invisible, eternal and uncreated and that existed in great peace and stillness in unending spaces (aeons).[43]

The recently-found texts bear out the Church fathers' witness to Gnostic teaching — God is everything and nothing:

> He is [not] in completion, nor in blessedness,
> nor in godliness, but he is far above this.
> He is not corporeal [nor] is he incorporeal.
> He is neither large [nor] is he small.
> [There is no] way to say,
> 'What is his quantity?' or 'What [is his quality?'],
> for no one is able [know him].[44]

The *Gospel of the Egyptians* describes him as:

> the great unseen [spirit the] Father, the name of whom can not be spoken, [it is he who has come] forth from the highest place of [the completion, the] light of the light of the [aeons of light], the light of the [stillness of the] forethought <and> the father of the stillness, the [light] of the word and the truth, the light [of the] [uncorrupted] the limitless light, [the] brilliance, from the aeons of light of the unrepealable, indistinguishable, ageless, unproclaimable, the aeon of aeons, self-producing, the stranger, the truly authentic aeon.[45]

Like the Protestant scholars Fewell and Gunn, cited above, who claim that the God of the Bible is a human male construct not be taken as the real God, so the Gnostics argued that the true God is beyond all representation, biblical or otherwise. Like Fewell and Gunn, the Gnostics, to judge from the following quote from *Allogenes*, would doubtless have said that worship of the God of the Old Testament was idolatry. In prose reminiscent of Buddhist nihilism, we read:

> He is neither god-like, nor is he a blessed one nor is he a perfected one, but it (this triad) is an entity of his of which nothing can be know, not that which is distinctive to him, but another is he, who is superior to being a blessed one and being god-like or a perfected one. He is not perfect, instead is another, superior thing. . . . Nor is he anything that is which one is able to know. But he is another thing of

himself that is superior which on does not have the ability to know. . . .
Since he is limitless and impotent and nonexistent.[46]

For the Gnostic, to describe God is proof of inferior spiritual perception. Thus, Jahweh is already shown to be inferior because he is
known. The gracious condescension of the Lord of glory in revealing
himself to creation is thrown back into God's face. In The *Teaching of
Silvanus* the comparison is drawn between the inferior God, the Creator, who is easy to know, and the true God who is impossible to com-
prehend.[47] The very character of the Scriptural God as the God who
comes to his people and makes himself known is a cause for derision in
the Gnostic system.

This ultimate spiritual principle is not a trinity of divine persons
but a lone, impersonal cause referred to as "The Father of the Totalities,"[48] or the "All."[49] We have come full circle. At the end of the twentieth century, the new spirituality now refers to God in inclusive, politically correct fashion as "the God/Goddess/All That Is." In this grab-bag
terminology, everything is included — except a divinity of individual
personhood

Gnosticism: Dualist or Monist?

It is often said that Gnosticism is dualist.[50] At one level this is right.
If Gnosticism rejects matter and embraces spirit, which it does, how can
it have an overarching system that includes everything in a monistic
embrace? There are reasons for thinking that Gnosticism is, in an ultimate sense, monist. Like other forms of pantheism, it sees God everywhere, even in matter. While theism separates God from his creation,
Gnosticism denies to God any specific identity. God is so diffuse that he
is nowhere.[51]

While there is an anti-cosmic emphasis, the essential Gnostic opposition to the world is opposition to God the Creator and his created
order. The Christian view of God and creation cedes to a pagan monistic
God who is everywhere but unknowable. The so-called *Gospel of Mary*
hints of this pagan pantheism when it predicts that all things "exist in
and with one another," and "will be resolved again into their own roots."[52]
This is not anti-cosmic. It is anti-creational, rejecting things the way
they are now. The living Jesus in the *Gospel of Thomas* expresses a similar monistic sentiment:

Jesus said, "I, myself, am the light above all. I, myself, am the all. The all came forth from me and the all extended to me. Cleave a piece of wood, I am there. Lift up the stone and there I will be found."[53]

These texts whisk matter from the God of Scripture and give it to the monistic God behind all things. Indeed in one text (and many others imply it) matter comes not from Jahweh but from his mother Sophia: "He made the heavens without knowing the heaven; he formed man without knowing him; he brought the earth to light without knowing it. And in every case, they say, he was ignorant of the ideas of the things he made, and even of his own mother, and imagined that he alone was all things."[54]

Even Jahweh's one claim to infamy, the creation of the world, is not his to claim, and is brought into the domain of the divine emanations as the work of Sophia. Even the physical world does not finally belong to Ialdabaoth but is employed by the true and ultimate God as a vehicle whereby he might be known.

The Gnostic Sophia: Epitome of a Monistic Pagan Deity

Ultimate divine power is often described in the male imagery of the unknowable Father. Gnostics claim that the knowable, revealing, teaching divine power is female.[55] (The equivalent on earth is Eve teaching Adam as a wise Instructor). God is so unknown and removed that one must speak of non-being existence. The dynamic force that brings one face to face with the unknown is female. Sophia is the divine element that spans both the physical and the spiritual worlds and joins the opposites of earthly existence into a mystical unity. *Trimorphic Protennoia* describes "three descents of the Gnostic heavenly redeemer Protennoia, who is actually Sophia. She is the First Thought of the Father. . . . She dwells at all levels of the universe."[56] Notice how Sophia takes the place of the Eternal Son in the divine Trinity. Sophia's revelation is pantheistic monism. She is everywhere, declaring:

I am revealed out of the immeasurable and the unspeakable. I am beyond comprehension, I live in the incomprehensible. I stir in all creation. I myself am the life of my Conception that exists in every power and stirs in every eternal movement and in Lights unseen and in the Archons and Angels and Demons and in every soul which exists in [Tatatros] and in every soul made of matter. I exist in those who came to be in existence.[57]

A Mystical Weather Forecast: Thunder Everywhere

Thunder, Perfect Mind, a mysterious name for Sophia, reveals that while we can never know the source of all unity (God), all is united in Sophia's cosmic embrace.[58] Sophia is the perfect expression of pagan spirituality. She deconstructs rational categories in a monistic joining of the opposites:

> For the first and the last am I.
> I am the adored and the despised one.
> I am the prostitute and the venerable one.
> I am the wife and the virgin.
> I am the mother and the daughter. . . .
> I myself am the stillness that is beyond understanding
> and the conception whose thoughts are numerous.
> I am the voice, the sound of which is myriad
> and the word (logos), whose appearance is manifold. . . .
> I am shame and fearlessness.
> I am without shame; I am ashamed. . . .
> I am without mind and I am wise. . . .
> For I myself am the Greek's wisdom and the barbarians knowledge.
> I myself am the judgment of the Greeks and the barbarians.
> I am the one whose likeness is great in Egypt. . . .
> I am the one who is called life and whom you call death.
> I am the one who is called law and whom you have called lawless. . . .
> I, I myself am godless, and
> it is I whose God is manifold. . . .
> I am the immutable essence and the one who has no immutable
> essence. . . .
> I am the joining and the dissolution. . . .
> I, I myself am without sin and
> the root of sin originates from me. . . .
> It is I who is called truth and lawlessness. . . .

This text, according to the original editor of the document, has no distinctively Gnostic themes.[59] But contemporary feminists know better. The text bears some resemblance to the personification of Wisdom in Proverbs 8, but the difference in content is radical. In Proverbs Dames Wisdom and Folly are set in opposition. Here wisdom and folly belong to the same divine principle. This female revealer resembles not biblical wisdom but the Hindu goddess Kali[60] or the Egyptian Isis. Little wonder Thunder/Sophia is gratefully welcomed into modern religious feminists' pantheon:[61]

Another female divinity who calls to women and assures us of our divinity and our power is the otherwise un-named Thunder Perfect Mind. She appears to be everywhere and encompasses everything: . . . She is everything and everybody and its opposite. She is female and within her there is a the whole range of female life from birth to death, from the mundane woman in the world to the divine Wisdom of Heaven. . . . I see in the "Thunder" the vision of a goddess human and divine who speaks again. . . . [in the manner of] Egyptian Isis.

Sophia Hails From Egypt

This feminist author puts her finger on the pagan origin of Sophia as an expression of the Egyptian Goddess, Isis. Of course, the text itself clearly makes this connection when Thunder/Sophia declares: "[I] am the one whose image is great in Egypt." The connection is appropriate since Isis was the Egyptian Goddess of Wisdom.[62] It is said of Isis that she is "the still point of the turning world"[63] who proclaims: "I am Nature, the Universal Mother . . . single manifestation of all gods and goddesses am I."[64] Like Thunder/Sophia, Isis joins everything within her all-inclusive embrace. I cite again the description of her wisdom by an Isis scholar:

Curiously, . . . the Egyptians [when characterizing Isis by her wisdom] called her "great in magical power." [For them] real wisdom consisted of insight into the mystery of life and death. . . . Thus wisdom was to the Egyptians equivalent to the capacity of exerting magical power.[65]

This is also affirmed in more technical language by Caitlín Matthews, the modern priestess of Isis and specialist of the history of Sophia. "The Greek-Egyptian experience (after Alexander the Great's conquest of Egypt) is truly a catalyst in this study of Wisdom, for the strong character of Isis the Goddess became the Sophianic touchstone of . . . Gnosticism."[66] Here you have it stated unambiguously by a pagan priestess that Gnosticism serves most admirably as a bridge for paganism to infiltrate Christianity.

Initiation into the mysteries of Isis and the ecstatic secret experiences in her temples gave adherents a foretaste of transformation into immortality.[67] Isis was thus the giver of magical, occult knowledge and wisdom through which, like Sophia, she revealed the distant, unknown Egyptian God behind all things, Re.[68] Isis "RE-Imagined" God for her adepts!

That "Christian" Gnostics borrow from paganism is here patently obvious — as therefore should be the pagan nature of present-day speculation about Sophia. The Sophia who made a brief appearance in Minneapolis did not fly in from Jerusalem nor can traces of her identity be found in the Bible. She came from pagan Egypt via "Christian" Gnosticism and her passport bore her real name–Isis.

Protennoia, which means "First Thought," another manifestation of Sophia in the ancient Gnostic texts, reveals in the starkest terminology the joining of the opposites in a non-rational unity so essential to pagan thinking both ancient and modern:

> I am gynandrous [I am Mother, I am] Father since [I] [have coitus] with myself. I [have coitus] with myself [and the ones who love] me [and] I am the one through whom the All [endures]. I am the womb [that gives form] to the All by birthing the Light that [shines in] glory.[69]

The text goes to explain that the above revelation and the androgynous or gynandrous joining of all duality is the ultimate mystery, a mystery called "the Sound of the Mother," hidden from the "Aeons and the Archigenitor, granted to the Sons of the Thought."[70] In other words, Sophia brings a new revelation of divinity that goes beyond anything the ignorant God of Scripture could imagine. It is the "sound" of the monistic mystical experience of connection with all things in the hearts of those who know.

Through the gender confusion Sophia brings, she deconstructs the God of the Bible. But her ultimate role is to point beyond the feminine gender to the androgynous state of true monism. For, as one Gnostic specialist rightly notes, in Gnosticism "the ultimate image of salvation is neither male nor female but the restored unity of an androgynous Mother-Father, who has passed through diversity."[71] This historical fact, noted by a Gnostic specialist, is all the more interesting in the light of the contemporary promotion of inclusive versions of the Lord's Prayer which address God as "Our Father/Mother in heaven,[72] as well as radical egalitarian interpretations of Galatians 3:28.

The Heart of Gnosticism is the Heart of Paganism: Man is God

Sophia brings to light the essence of this diabolical revelation — there is no God other than Man. As Gnostic expert Filoramo notes, "God is, in fact, Anthropos, Man/Human, or rather the archetypal Androgyne." In Gnosticism, he adds, "the human has now become the predicate of the divine. The manifestation of God to himself: this is the heart of Gnostic myth"[73] It is also the heart of the original lie of the Devil: "You will be as God."[74]

The second century Church Father, Irenaeus, saw the dreadful consequence of Gnostic teaching. He reports that the Sethian Gnostics called God Man:

> Ialdabaoth, becoming arrogant in spirit, boasted himself over all those who were below him, and explained, "I am father, and God, and above me there is no one." His mother, hearing him speak thus, cried out against him: "Do not lie, Ialdabaoth; for the father of all, the primal anthropos, is above you; and so is Anthropos, the son of Anthropos.[75]

This version of primal history declares Man to be God. On earth, Seth's antitype, Jesus, reveals that when James reaches Him Who Is "you will no longer be James; rather *you are the One Who Exists*."[76] Such is surely the most pernicious form of humanism, divinized humanism. Today atheistic humanism is on the run. The new enemy is a spiritualized view of Man. He is no longer simply the measure of all things, as rationalism maintained: Man is now also the measure of God, for Man is God. This new spirituality is the final expression of idolatry because it is not just disobedience of "God's laws: it replaces the divine with the human.

In Minneapolis the same transaction took place. The organizers told the participants, as already noted above: "Be speculative . . . there is no 'answer.' We cannot imagine what God is like. *Being together in our own image is the ultimate* [emphasis added]."[77]

Inevitably, once the ontological distinction between the Creator and the creation disappears — which happens in pagan monism — humanity is divinized. All appears to be well, except that human sin has not been eradicated. Alas, history is full of examples that *sinful* gods are extremely dangerous!

The pieces fit. *Philosophical deconstruction* eliminates rational (left brain masculine) thought, leaving intuition and personal taste. *Radical New Testament scholarship* reconstructs Jesus, envoy of Sophia as a blueprint for a compassionate, tolerant, politically correct, multicultural, multisexual, feminist egalitarian society, liberated from notions of sin, guilt and the New Testament theology of the Cross. *Radical religious feminism* worships the goddess Sophia, rejecting all hints of orthodox Christianity. Both scholarship and feminism restore Gnostic teaching on the same theme. At the same time, New Age thinking awaits a global transformation based upon the rediscovery of the feminine, right brain "*yin*" intuition of the Age of Aquarius. It decries rational, male-inspired, "*yang*" "theories of the atonement" of the Age of Pisces. All this is supported by an age-old heresy that gives the movement ancient texts and a semblance of historical veracity. These disparate movements come together to replace the historic confession of the crucified Jesus as the true wisdom of God and the unique means of redemption with the confession of a brand human god (really quite old), who will save us all here and now.

Such a God/Man is the Mouthpiece of Satan

Many naively rid themselves of a patriarchal construct and re-imagine the divine in more user-friendly ways. It is simple to exchange one set of mythological ideas for another. Replace God with Man, and bring heaven to earth in the establishment of a new utopia. But there is a forgotten element in the equation, a third player in the cosmic contest for the soul — the self-effacing, slithering Satan. The human heart is not an autonomous place of spiritual goodness. It is a tablet on which either God or Satan writes.

Sophia did not replace the bumbling Jahweh with a third, optimistic option. Sophia, the goddess of occult wisdom is in every way opposed to the wisdom of God. The new spirituality she offers she has offered before. Its earth-centered wisdom and light-illumination (see chapter 16), brings unsuspecting and spiritually hungry contemporaries into the foyer of Satan's kingdom. Her voice is His. Our world wobbles on the brink of a great delusion. If it ignores the warning the ancient Gnostic apostasy provides, our brave new world will stagger, inebriated, into the euphoria produced by the dazzling false promise of a liberated humanity and androgynous, uninhibited sexuality.

CHAPTER 12

THE NEW SEXUALITY

Times and trends do change and unisex is unquestionably in fashion.
- Justice Antonin Scalia[1]

God and Sex in the Third Millennium

Psst. . . Do you want to invade France? The best time is in August around 2:00 p.m. Those not on vacation are taking a nap. Do you want to capture a civilization? Change perceptions of sexuality. Though few may practice New Age Eastern spirituality with chakras, crystals, astral travel and channeling, everyone is a male or a female. Sexuality keeps a civilization functioning. Insidiously, a new definition of sexuality in tune with New Age liberal monism beckons our world, promising liberation for the oppressed, justice for the deprived and peace on earth.

Sex and religion make a formidable twosome. Sexuality can never be disassociated from the religious quest. By a new sexuality liberalism will transform religion and the planet. "We are doomed as a species and a planet," prophesies a religious feminist, "unless we have a radical change of consciousness."[2] The liberation of sexuality accompanies a change of planetary consciousness and the revival of pagan spirituality on the eve of the "Aquarian" millennium.

The agenda for sexual revolution follows the same logical progression mentioned in earlier chapters: crisis, deconstruction and reconstruction. Take the program for unity of the world's religions. First comes a description of ecological crisis; then a call to dismantle the

Christian view of creation. Finally theological syncretism beckons. In the case of sexuality, the crisis is due to the evils of patriarchy; the deconstruction destroys the Christian view of sex and gender roles; and from the ashes rises a monistic phoenix: the new androgynous ideal.

The Crisis — Patriarchy

Rosemary Radford Ruether's Ruthless Rage-Raising Rhetoric

In "Christian" theologian Ruether's universe, patriarchy has replaced sin.[3] Since this affirmation cannot be established from Genesis 3, these founding texts become the adopted myths of patriarchal religion. According Ruether, patriarchy is the work of the Devil, the Mark of the Beast, the Great Babylon, the evil land of Egyptian slavery from which the church should organize a modern-day exodus, the inward reality of which prostitution is the outward expression. "Rapists are the shock troops of patriarchy, while wife-batterers are the army of occupation." The essence of the contemporary church is liberation from patriarchy[4] — the new culprit to be eliminated in the class struggle for social justice, identified as the enemy in the struggle with the principalities and powers, the idol of masculinity, of father rule, the mechanical idol with flashing eyes and smoking nostrils who spews out blasphemies in the temples of patriarchy and who is about to consume the earth, the great Leviathan of violence and misery whose "evil powers have entered into the deep layers of our unconscious" from which we need to be baptized. As in postmodernism generally, the louder the shouts, the higher the feminist consciousness is raised.[5]

The Great Evil

Pagans might well reject the patriarchal structure of creation[6] (though many do not), but Christians? Extending the evangelical denunciation of patriarchy, Virginia Mollenkott blames "*hetero*patriarchy" for most social ills, including racism and classism. "It is vital for us to understand the ways in which distorted concepts of human sexuality, gender distortions, and misconstructions of our God-language have blocked human freedom and healthy relationships and therefore have stunted any possibility of feeling fully alive. Only after accurate diagnosis of what is ailing us can we hope for an adequate cure." She defines "*heteropatriarchy*" as:

the hierarchial ways of organizing by which everything and everyone is ranked and whatever is male and white tends to get the upper hand. People and things cannot simply be *different* from one another: one way of being, doing, and thinking must always be the norm, everything else being *ab*normal. . . . Patriarchy is a profoundly mistaken social system that has caused misery to millions and could yet cause the destruction of humankind and the planet we share together.[7]

A practicing lesbian, Mollenkott adds: "compulsory heterosexuality is the very backbone that holds patriarchy together."[8] Homosexuality will break that "backbone." "If society is to turn from patriarchy to partnership," we must learn that lesbian, bisexual, and gay issues are not just private bedroom matters of "doing whatever turns you on." They are "wedges driven into the superstructure of the heteropatriarchal system." Mollenkott echoes Kate Millet's pagan vision: "A woman is called lesbian when she functions autonomously. Women's autonomy is what women's liberation is all about."[9]

The revolution is about the personal power to be autonomous of all structures and relationships. It is the power of radical freedom to do what you please. This is a pagan agenda, but in good faith many Christians try to extract good from the revolution by "christianizing" it as today's goal for the Christian faith. The glorious liberty and high calling of homosexuality leads some liberal Christians to denounce the "sin of heterosexism." Two Christian scholars, one a Roman Catholic laywoman, the other a Lutheran minister, challenge the church not only to "accept" homosexuality with Christian tolerance, but to see it as a normative "given." Not only is the Judeo-Christian heterosexual ethic no longer useful; insistence upon it is sin.[10]

On a less radical level, evangelical egalitarian feminism makes a similar move. A systematic theology published by InterVarsity Press, (the publishing arm of a historically orthodox parachurch student organization), expresses a blanket rejection of patriarchy, so typical of radical feminism: "Feminist theology has done a great service to the Christian community by pointing out the evils of androcentrism, patriarchy and misogyny."[11] Misogyny certainly, and perhaps also androcentrism in some forms could be described as evil — but patriarchy, which is at the very basis of Scripture and of Western civilization? Gretchen Gabelein Hull, a board member of the *Council for Biblical Equality*, speaks of the "sin of patriarchy." To Christianize patriarchy is to end it."[12] One cannot reform patriarchy in the light of the Christian revelation of God as Father of our Lord Jesus Christ.[13] One can only eliminate it! Egalitarianism is the first step to autonomous individualism just as the relativization of sexual differences is the first step to gender-confusion. The new liberalism is feminist to the marrow, as was the *Parliament of the World's Religions*.[14] Do evangelicals embrace egalitarian feminism as a theological/exegetical discovery of the glorious liberty of the Gospel? Or are they encouraged by enormous societal, ideological and economic pressures, and a naive faith in the democratic process?[15]

The Jewish feminist, Naomi Goldenberg, is not so naive. She fingers God the Father of the Judeo-Christian Scripture as the architect of the patriarchal society. Like patriarchy, this God will have to go, as the title of her book, *Changing of the Gods*, affirms:

> The new wave of feminism desperately needs to be not only many-faced but cosmic and ultimately religious in its vision. This means reaching outward and inward toward the God beyond and beneath the gods who have stolen our identity.[16]

Goldenberg's words ring with uncanny certainty: "We women are going to bring an end to God."[17] How are they doing?

DECONSTRUCTION:
The Destruction of the Christian View of Sex and Gender Roles in Contemporary Society

Is it fortuitous that liberalism's conversion to monistic spirituality coincides with major changes in sexual practice, gender roles, and family structures? The sexuality of Western civilization has been deconstructed in just one generation. The role of women has changed drastically, representing a mega-shift in the perceptions of human sexuality. Feminism has opened doors to many other changes. Oddly, not many are willing to consider feminism as a driving force of the neopagan ideal,[18] even though radicals do at every occasion.

Revolution and Nothing Less
The Women's Movement, according to its leading theorists, "is not a reformist movement but a revolutionary one."[19] Dissident Roman Catholic priest and professor of sociology, Andrew Greeley prophesied major changes in the Church in the near future. His article, published in a "New Age" magazine, states:

> the power of the Pope definitely will shrink. Today we are now experiencing the last gasp of a dying order, and in twenty years most of it will be gone. . . . Women will remake religion.[20]

Some find this revolution exhilarating, the best thing to happen to women, and especially to housewives, since sliced bread. *Time Magazine*, like Greeley, is full of optimism, wondering if this movement constitutes a "New Reformation."[21] The radicals chuckle at such naivete, disdaining the very idea of "reformation" which implies a return to purity in some lost form. They prefer to see the women's movement as "paradigm shift" of "far-reaching ramifications,"[22] a "new dispensation" or a "new revelation." The arrival of "being" which makes everything before it "nothingness,"[23] is a radical "conversion to a new consciousness."

Some are appalled. A Roman Catholic journalist, Donna Steichen, in her documentation of the progress of feminism in the American Catholic church, entitled *Ungodly Rage*, says in the introduction regarding feminism:

> This book is about darkness. Its pages document one of the most devastating religious epidemics of our, or any other, time.[24]

These authors, both for and against, agree on one thing: feminism is a force of revolutionary power. Its staggering progress in just one generation cannot be dismissed as the normal ticking of the democratic process, the next step in the civilization of the planet. Something else is happening.

A Social Tidal Wave A Mile off the Coast

While sociologists in 1993 did not see any major cultural changes on the religious horizon to alter the face of the mainline churches,[25] a Jewish feminist predicted in the seventies a tsunami of revolutionary change: "When feminists succeed in changing the position of women in Christianity and Judaism, they will shake these religions at their roots."[26] In 1971, when she first met feminists she remembers thinking: Such women will change the world."[27] Naomi Goldenberg's prophecies are unusually perceptive as many feminists now turn to goddess worship and witchcraft. Indeed, Goldenberg herself has since become a witch.[28] Through the use of powerful female images such as the goddess, the gorgon, or the amazon, radical feminists intend to bring about "a major change of consciousness, a new symbolic transformation."[29] Transformation into marketable social engineering is rapid. Advertisements in my local supermarket invite eight to eleven year old girls to learn empowerment through the study of six pagan goddesses. In schools and day care centers, apparently innocuous programs of "gender-equality education" which have cost millions of tax dollars, ensure that the biblical teaching on sexual and role distinctions are erased from the future generation's collective consciousness — with most people's silent approval.

When, in 1996, the Supreme Court, in its ruling on the status of the all-male Virginia Military Institute, decided by a seven to one margin that State-supported single-sex education was unconstitutional, it essentially declared as law of the land the unconstitutionality of gender roles and distinctions. In the one dissenting opinion, Justice Antonin Scalia noted that this decision was, in the final analysis, an attack against the "old-fashioned" concept of "manly honor" embodied in VMI's code of "gentlemanly" behavior. The highest judicial authority in the land had declared "patriarchy" un-American. "I do not know," observes Scalia regretfully, "whether the men of VMI lived by this code. But . . . I do not think any of us, women included, will be better off for its destruction."[30]

The new understanding of sexuality finds fertile soil in the economic and social realities of the post-Sixties West. A University of California sociologist observes that seventy-five percent of boomer women (born since 1946) are in the labor force full or part-time. These figures are related both to financial needs/desires and to new cultural expectations. "Gender equality and career opportunities for women are deeply rooted values for this generation."[31] "This generation" is the generation affected most by the sexual revolution of the Sixties. The economic and cultural realities translate into theological opinion. Eight of ten boomer Catholic women favor the ordination of women. The percentage is even higher for Protestant mainline boomer women. More than half of conservative Protestant boomer women and three-quarters of conservative Protestant boomer men favor women's ordination.

These realities have revolutionized seminaries. According to the painstakingly established documentation of Gale Research Inc., "In 1986 there was an estimated 20,730 female clergy in the United States, an increase of almost 100 percent just since 1977. . . . During the same time, the number of women enrolled in ordination programs in seminaries increased 110 percent."[32] Says Gary L.Ward, author of this report:

> The speed and magnitude of these changes show no sign of reduction or alteration as we move into the 1990s, and there is every indication that more and more denominations will open their holy orders to women. This generation is witnessing shifts which, both literally and figuratively, are changing the face of religion.

The effects are mixed. The reconsideration of the place of the woman in society and the church, and the creative search to employ women's gifts are salutary and beneficial. However, "true spirituality," without a blush now casts aside the biblical revelation of God as Father, creational sexuality and Biblical sexual morality as the ultimate expression of evil oppression. Madeleine L'Engle feels morally entitled to call the God and Father of our Lord Jesus Christ "the paternalistic male chauvinist pig Old Testament God."[33] The new hymnal of the United Church of Christ goes beyond calling God names. It simply removes them. Its General Synod has "cleansed" its hymns of unacceptable patriarchal notions like "Father" and "King."[34] The Father-Son relationship at the very heart of the Gospel is thereby "deconstructed" and the blood of what Goldenberg calls the "slow execution of Jahweh and Christ" is on the hands of a mainline "Christian" denomination. At certain evangelical colleges it is appropriate to call God "Parent" in order to avoid the sexist and oppressive term "Father."

Biblical Bull

It was standing room only. Between five and six hundred Bible scholars, theologians and teachers of religion packed a lecture hall and part of the hallway in a downtown hotel in San Francisco in November, 1992 to hear the latest revelations from post-Christian lesbian feminist witch and professor with tenure in the Department of Theology at the Jesuit Boston College, Mary Daly. In the middle of the joint annual meeting of the American Academy of Religion and the Society of Biblical Literature, in the middle of her account of the great inter-galactic reunion of feminist heroines past and present taking place "on the other side of the moon," Daly suddenly stopped. With deliberation, she looked her attentive audience up and down. Then, raising her arms in the form of prophetic utterance, and in a voice half-way between a cackle and a screech, she blurted out: "What's all this biblical bulls—t?" At the end of her lecture, the "biblical" scholars gave her a thunderous ovation. "Theology" has come a long way, baby — all the way back to the Gnostic rejection of Scripture and the God of Scripture.

If publications, reviews and public endorsements are anything to go by, there are thousands of teachers in University departments of religion and in theological seminaries who have adopted some form of this humanist program of ethical, spiritual and sexual liberation.[35] Liberal theology can run the gamut from the white, straight, male Harvard professor of theology to the lesbian ecofeminist witch who has severed all ties with biblical Christianity. But the twain do meet. Mary Daly who screams blasphemies on virtually every page of her recent books promoting witchcraft and erotic "spiritual" lesbianism receives accolades from Harvey Cox, respected liberal theologian, Victor S. Thomas Professor of Divinity at the Harvard Divinity School. Mary Daly dismisses the Incarnation of the eternal Son as the "symbolic legitimation of the rape of all women and all matter," and describes as "bull... the apostles creed."[36] Cox considers her "a woman who makes a Big Difference" of whom he is a self-styled "fan."[37]

Cox, one of 300 scholars who signed a petition from the American Academy of Religion which helped force Jesuit Boston College to promote Daly to a tenured professorship, even though she had rejected Christianity for paganism, said, "It is hard to imagine where the whole field of religious and theological studies would be today were it not for the contributions she has made." [38]

At one of the leading theological institutions in the country, The Claremont Graduate School, two witches, Naomi Goldenberg and Mary Daly, were featured guest speakers in 1993 in the Women's Studies in Religion Program. This program also co-sponsored a four-day conference on "Women and Goddess Traditions" in May, 1992, which included lectures on "The Goddess and Women's Power: A Hindu Case Study," and "Goddess, Matriarch and Pregnancy: A Long Tradition." Participants included Professor Emily Culpepper of the University of Redlands, an ex-Baptist fundamentalist and now a witch and collaborator with Mary Daly, who finds spiritual strength and solace in the Hindu Goddess, Kali.[39]

At the Harvard Divinity School studies are now dominated by the feminist perspective. In a semi-humorous but well-documented article entitled "What's up at Harvard Divinity School," Jewish social commentator, Don Heder recounts that Buddhist chanting and meditation are now more popular than hymn-singing, and the Christian calendar is passed over in favor of pagan holidays. According to Heder, feminist goddess worship is the interpretative grill through which religion, Christian theology and the Bible are now interpreted.[40]

Witches and Liberal Professors

Witches and liberal professors of theology meet where the air is heavy with burning incense and oriental oils, the music drowsy and the pagan agenda a silent scream — in the hushed atmosphere of your neighborhood New Age bookstore. Opposite the crystals and exotic oils and the ominous black robes with pointed hoods for only $98.00 each, the spiritually inquisitive can find, dust-jacket to dust-jacket, jostling for attention on the same purple-colored shelf, the works of pagan thinkers such as Joseph Campbell, Ken Carey and Ram Dass, as well as those of "Christian" authors Matthew Fox, Elaine Pagels and James Robinson.[41]

While the latter, it is true, have no say in where their titles end up, the keen commercial nose — call it "in-sense" — of no-nonsense New Age bookstore capitalists suggests that, on a larger scale, such a hybrid collection is no accident. The readers must be given what the readers want. The hard reality of supply and demand economics turns out to be a surprisingly objective indicator of deep ideological coherence between these unlikely allies. After all, as they say, the customer is always right!

A growing number believe that women will be instrumental in the realization of a unified humanity and a global religion. But feminism has to do, surely, only with social conditions and democratic rights, not religion! Wrong. Feminists see themselves as called to transform both society and religion. Two examples:

Roman Catholic theologian, Paul Knitter, is a thinker committed to the development of one worldwide religion. He is also the general editor of the series *Faith Meets Faith* whose recent offering is entitled *After Patriarchy: Feminist Transformations of the World Religions.*[42] This book argues that since the "second class status, if not the outward oppression, of women . . . (is) rooted in the theologies . . . of world religions," it is feminism's globalized vision of gender and sexual liberation that will transform all the world's religions. At that point emancipation will be won for all.

Virginia Mollenkott sees in the sexual revolution the religious possibility of a new humanity. "We know that all women and men who will enter a covenant of caring express the nature of Sophia, of the Logos, of the Christ Herself, the New Humanity."[43] Make no mistake about it, feminism's agenda of sexual revolution is a religious agenda, that goes far beyond issues of civil rights — and far beyond feminism.

Gays R Us

The proof of this mega-shift and of its radical implications is the growing acceptance and power of the homosexual community. "We are no longer seeking just a right to privacy and a protection from wrong," says a leading spokesman for the movement. "We have a right . . . to see government and society affirm our lives."[44]

The project is clearly succeeding in modern day America, in spite of the scores of millions of Americans who doubtless oppose it. In 1975 the venerable institution of *Time Magazine* opposed this agenda: "It is one thing to remove legal discrimination against homosexuals. It is another to mandate approval."[45] In 1992 *Time* invites its readers to accept homosexuality the way they accepted black Americans, women voters or the automated-teller machines.[46] The boundaries move every day.

Today one of the major debates is the place of gay groups on *high school* campuses.[47] Recently the Los Angeles Unified School District sponsored an end of year prom for gay students. The cutesy reporting of *The Los Angeles Times* asked readers to believe that there is nothing more natural for the progress of American democracy than a teenage boy making himself a lace dress to wear at the end-of-year dance.

Like feminist ideology, the homosexual program has been written into the law of the land. A few weeks before the VMI decision, the Supreme Court, on May 20, 1996, in striking down Colorado's Amendment 2, ruled that homosexuals are a legally-recognized minority who henceforth may seek all the benefits of a state-protected minority — including same-sex marriage and the general promotion of gay sex as an acceptable, state-recognized life-style. Things are changing. Just ten years earlier, the Court recognized the constitutionality of anti-sodomy laws. Said Tom Minnery of *Focus on the Family*: "We are puzzled that the court has chosen to protect a group of people whose only identifiable trait is a behavior that the court has allowed states to criminalize." Many who believed that democracy (the power of the people) was their great defense against ideological tyranny are equally puzzled. Six unelected justices, in thrall to the new godless definition of reality, have managed to elevate the deconstruction of traditional/creational sexuality into a constitutional necessity.

Is this a foretaste of the liberated future to which we are headed with unbounded enthusiasm? It sounds more like a Fellini movie about the last orgiastic days of a decadent Roman empire. Indeed, like Fellini, Hollywood is ever obliging, having already produced in 1993 the first major motion picture, *Philadelphia*, whose leading character/hero is a gay man. But gays are still not satisfied. They now want Hollywood to give the general public full nudity gay love scenes, for equal time in steamy sex.[48] If the L.A school district can give us gay proms, it will surely only be a matter of time for Hollywood to give us gay sex in full-color in the local theater near you.

In academia, feminism and homosexuality have urged each other to more and more radical positions, as the well-researched and finely-titled article, "Coming Out Ahead: The Homosexual Moment in the Academy," demonstrates.[49] The author reports that "at many colleges, gay/lesbian/bisexual student associations are among the most active . . . on campus, funded by student fees and by institutional funds from the university's Office of Multiculturalism." He notes that at Harvard each dorm has a designated gay tutor; at Columbia University, the chairman of the English department is committed to "hiring, tenuring and working with" gay and lesbian scholars; many universities including

Stanford, Chicago, Iowa and Pitzer College, offer spousal benefits to homosexual partners of faculty members.[50]

The homosexual agenda progresses by suggesting that democracy is the source of morality, and many "straights" are buying the line.

Les/bi/gay and Proud of It

American society reached a watershed in 1993 when twenty-seven practicing gays and lesbians were named to posts in the Clinton administration. For Bruce Lehman, a Clinton appointee at the Commerce Department, this courageous gesture is "the first time in the history of mankind [that] a president has sought to break the taboo on this gentle people."[51] These gentle people have a not-so-gentle agenda. It is clearly stated in the gay platform of the March on Washington in 1993. Their demands included: a gay civil rights bill; homosexual adoptions and the redefinition of the family; gay curricula in the schools; an end to gender dysphoria as a psychiatric disorder; homosexual polygamy; a lowering of the age of sexual consent for children;[52] obligation to force all organizations, including the Boy Scouts, to accept gays; medical insurance for sex-change operations; admission of AIDS-infected immigrants; passage of ERA; legalization of homosexual "marriages."[53] The power and influence on the thinking and practice of mainstream "Christian" America of a group representing not much more than one or two percent of the population defies belief.

Until recently, Western society has borne the name Christendom, implying a Judeo-Christian understanding of male and female. Radical deconstruction favors neo-pagan gender confusion in an androgynous ideal. To succeed, the program must eradicate the last vestiges of Christendom from Western society. Patriarchy and normative heterosexuality must go. The broad liberal agenda behind these societal changes points to an all-inclusive monistic religion. People are profoundly religious.

RECONSTRUCTION
The Ideal:
Neither Male Nor Female But an
Androgynous Superhuman

Homo Noeticus — The New Spiritual Human

Somewhere over the rainbow, just around the corner, in the third millennium, the earth should tilt on its axis, and a convergence of like-

minded believers will bring the final jump in evolutionary progress. A
star will be born. A new humanity will sprout wings, and mankind will
fly to its ultimate destiny of unity with the All. This kind of evolution is
religion not science, as many now recognize. "Religion," says New Ager
and United Nations undersecretary, Robert Muller, and key figure in the
recent *Parliament of the World's Religions*, "[will] cooperate to bring to
unprecedented heights a better understanding of the mysteries of life
and of our place in the universe."[54] This rosy religious future on earth
will come about because, according to Muller, "a new and higher form
of humanity [is taking] control of the planet. . . . homo noeticus is the
name I give to the emerging form of humanity."[55] *Homo noeticus* — the
new rational/spiritual human being. This is the New Age savior. Cloned
by the thousands, as people reach altered states of consciousness through
meditation, this spiritually empowered New Man will save humanity
and the planet.[56]

The skeptical listener smiles in disbelief. Thousands of years of
human history have not produced rebirth. But tomorrow is always a
new day, and the Aquarian revolution *will* be different because mankind
will be different.

The Androgynous Ideal — Anything You Want To Be

The New Man (male and female) of pagan monism is an attractive
chap. As a hybrid of Eastern and Western monism, he is not the emaci-
ated guru on the streets of Calcutta. That would hardly sell on Madison
Ave. He is an optimist who can realize all his dreams and be whatever he
wants to be. He can do "all things," that is, all things within the monistic circle. He is no longer limited by the hard and fast separation of
reality into right and wrong, true and false, male and female. His ultimate goal is union with the all, and on the sexual plane, androgyny.[57]

Sexual Alchemy for the Aquarian New Man

We imagine medieval alchemists as disneyesque magicians who turn
everything to gold, just as Disney has with theme parks (except, of course,
in Paris).[58] Actually, the alchemists were serious theological mystics —
medieval Gnostics, who believed that the goal of life was to join all
the opposites that Christianity held apart. Their search for the so-
called philosopher's stone was the search, not for gold, but for a formula that would join opposites, creating fundamental unity. They were
classical monists.

A professor at a well-respected Catholic university[59] gives the mystical pursuit of the alchemists a sexual twist. Professor Frederica
Halligan perceives in the alchemists' quest for "god" a blue-print for the

planet's future. The alchemists were both would-be scientists and mystics who practiced meditation long before the Indians yogis of the twentieth century made it a multi-million dollar industry in the West. It is most striking that their seven stages of meditation resemble the seven chakras of Hinduism and their modern New Age adaptation. The Hindu concept of sexual energy, called *kundalini*, according to which a serpent of passion is coiled at the base of the spine, to be aroused and summoned up through the body by meditation compares with the Medieval alchemists' notion of *libido*. *Libido*, of course, was the term Freud used for sexual energy.

According to Halligan, the final, seventh stage, which is called *conjunctio*, ("joining") is a "new reality," the final bringing together of all the opposites, producing "gold," i.e., spiritual gold, i.e., "a tremendously deepened sense of the oneness of all. . . . the unification of all the opposites within oneself."[60] Halligan's final definition of the *conjunctio* is clear: "Beyond gender differences now, the mystics of both Eastern and Western traditions describe the bliss of abiding love."[61] Thus hermaphrodites but also lesbians and homosexuals have in some sense reached the goal of *conjuctio*, for in homosexuality males act as females and in lesbianism females act as males.[62]

The proof of this conclusion comes from the radical left itself, both feminist and homosexual. For Mary Daly, the way forward in God's dealings with the human race is through feminist liberation and the creation of a "mysticism of sorority." Her eschatological vision for the future of humanity is summed up in the following passage:

> What is at stake is *a real leap in human evolution*, (italics mine) initiated by women . . . to an intuition of being which . . . is an intuition of human integrity or of androgynous being.[63]

In today's feminism not only self-confessed pagan witches espouse comparable beliefs. One of the leaders of the "Christian" feminist movement, Rosemary Radford Ruether, rejected orthodox Catholicism early in her career for paganism.[64] "A lot of evil had been done in the name of Christ," she wrote, but "no crusades or pogroms had been sent in the name of Ba'al, Isis or Apollo."[65] Rejecting Judaism and Christianity as "linear" religions which see history as moving from past to future, she is attracted by the cyclical character of "the nature and fertility religions, pagan religions." In her spirituality, what is important is celebrating "the cycles of the day and night, the cycles of the seasons, the cycles of our own bodies month by month, our own life cycles. . . . Nature recreates itself through cycles, and that means we have to be as positive about the death side of the cycle as we are about the resurrection side. Rituals can incorporate observances of social oppression, such as a Halloween ceremony in remembrance of the persecution of witches."[66] The pagan monism of Ruether is only less radical by being partly dressed, like ancient Gnosticism, in Christian clothing.[67] The effect is the same. It is not surprising that for Ruether as well, the ideal is androgynous sexuality.[68]

The theory holds that there is no essential difference between the sexes (apart from certain biological features); that there is no basis apart from social conditioning for sexually differentiated roles within society; and that such differentiation ought therefore to be eliminated. This ideal drives the movement of mystical spirituality. Mircea Eliade, a specialist of Comparative Religions and certainly one of the architects of the new spirituality, recalls a representation of Christ in a basilica in San Marco as a beardless youth of incomparable beauty in which was contained the mystery of the androgyne.[69] The illustration on the front cover of Matthew Fox's *The Cosmic Christ* represents "Christ" as a naked adolescent youth of uncertain sex above the title "Holy Wisdom." This Sophia is certainly androgynous, as is Shirley MacLaine's "higher self." MacLaine wonders aloud if "the point of life itself" is to "balance both the masculine and the feminine in ourselves. . . . Then we will have spiritualized the material and materialized the spiritual" to express ourselves "for what we truly are — androgynous, a perfect balance."[70] According to Eliade, the androgynous being sums up the very goal of the mystical, monistic quest: "in mystical love and at death one completely integrates the spirit world: all contraries are collapsed. The distinctions between the sexes are erased: the two merge into an androgynous whole. In short, at the center one knows oneself, is known, and knows the nature of reality.[71]

For most people, androgyny is a mental not a physical state.[72] Very few human beings are born with both male and female organs. The closest most come to androgyny is homosexuality and bi-sexuality, for in homosexuality and bi-sexuality, as we have noted, gay males and lesbian females play both the male and the female role. Support of this idea comes from the noted psychologist Carl Jung who suggested that "homosexuality preserve[d] an archetype of the androgynous original person."[73] Homosexuals are thus the true pagan monists, who have succeeded in translating spiritual theory into physical reality. They are the proto-type of the Aquarian *New Man* of the twenty-first century.

Homosexual Shamans for Spirituality in the New Age

> The story of the occult in world history is also a story of homo-
> sexuality. . . . In pagan cultures, homosexuals often hold an elevated
> position in religion and society. When pagan civilizations ruled the
> world, homosexuality and pederasty were widely practiced and ac-
> cepted.[74]

The move from radical feminism to homosexuality is as rapid as it is
logical. Feminism has deconstructed the creational sexuality of Christian theism. Homosexuality reconstructs it according to the norms of
pagan monism. A long-time "evangelical" feminist, Virginia Mollenkott,
recently announced her homosexuality. Discovering and practicing her
homosexuality was for her a moment of deep self-understanding. "To
live in the gender I preferred: this striking phrase causes me to think
about the native American shamans who were permitted to live and
dress like the other sex without stigma and with a great deal of respect
for their spiritual power."[75] Such a discovery has led Mollenkott to spiritual monism. Her new "sensuous spirituality" includes comparing her
own experience with that of pagan homosexual shamans as well as her
adoption of New Age thinking and practice.[76] This is spiritual monism
because it is founded upon the joining of the opposites of classic pagan
ideology.

It is well-documented that pagan religion has always held a special place for androgyny/homosexuality. Mircea Eliade saw androgyny
in many traditional religions as:

> an archaic and universal formula for the expression of wholeness, the
> co-existence of the contraries, or *coincidentia oppositorum* . . . symboliz-
> [ing]. . . perfection. . . [and] ultimate being.[77]

Sex and religion are clearly an inseparable dynamic duo, but not
just any sex for any religion.[78] Androgyny is expressive of the monistic
vision just as heterosexuality expresses the mystery of theism. The autonomous androgynous individual symbolizes the faceless divine Spirit
who inhabits the undifferentiated All just as heterosexuality reflects both
the unity and personal distinctiveness of the triune Christian God and
the relationship between Christ and his Church.[79] In our day confusion
reigns. A new sexuality, alien to everything the church has known, is
forcing itself onto the Christian religion. Dominican "Christian" theologian Matthew Fox actually says: "In some ways, homosexuality is superior to heterosexuality. There's no better birth control, . . . and there
is cosmological merit in the fact that it is not productive; there's a lot of

merit in rediscovering sexuality as play."[80] Radical Episcopalian Bishop
Spong affirms: "Feminism and homosexuality lie at the heart and soul
of what the Gospel is all about."[81] This new "gospel" is not the announcement of deliverance from sin but an incitation to sin even more.

In the monistic tradition, the same religious claim is made for homosexuality as it is for androgyny. "Lesbian/gay peoples have always
held . . . [a] shamanistic function and ceremonial office . . . in every
society."[82] Homosexuals see themselves as high priests of the coming
new religion.

The reader is invited to step back for a moment and make what at
first glimpse does not look like an obvious connection. What do Bill
Moyers and Huston Smith have to do with occult gay mediums? Smith
is professor at the University of California at Berkeley. Bill Moyers is a
Southern Baptist minister and well-respected Public Broadcasting journalist. Both he and Smith are religious syncretists and believe in "the
intertwining of the opposites which is the key to understanding Confucianism, Taoism and Buddhism."[83] This same spirituality of joining the
opposites, when extended to the sphere of sexuality, is the principle
behind religious homosexual practice.

This is clearly illustrated in American Indian religion where homosexual transvestite males functioned as shamans.[84] Examples abound,
even closer to home. Emily Culpepper, the ecofeminist lesbian witch
with an M.Div. and Th.D. from Harvard Divinity School, was once a
"deep South," "highly involved" evangelical Christian. Even now, while
calling herself an "amazon, pagan, oddwoman, [and] 'Nag-gnostic,'"
Culpepper honestly admits that "Sunday night hymn singing echoes
still in my inner ear." In spite of this interference, she sees gays and
lesbians as "shamans for a future age."[85] What is a shaman? A shaman is
"a charged, potent, awe-inspiring, and even fear-inspiring person who
takes true risks by crossing over into other worlds."[86] A fuller definition leaves little to the imagination: "The power and effectiveness of
shamans — witches, sibyls, Druids — emerges from their ability to com-
municate with the *non-human*: extra-terrestrial and subterranean forces,
and the spirit-world of the dead."[87] *The Encyclopedia of New Age Be-*
liefs[88] documents the deeply spiritual relationship between shamanism
and homosexuality. Shamans are guided by "guardian spirits" which often
take the form of "power animals" or "familiars." This certainly happened in the case of ex-evangelical Emily Culpepper, whose black cat
became for her the incarnation of the bloodthirsty Hindu Goddess Kali.

This incarnation of Kali became my wise companion for eighteen years,
teaching me much (as witches' familiars do), about the mysteries of
living and dying. . . . My cat taught me that the fearful symmetries of

nature . . . included her flashing beauty, her sweet friendliness and playfulness, and her appetite for hunting and killing.[89]

Culpepper's cat taught her how to live "beyond dualism,"[90] that is, to join the opposites in both mind and body. The deep spiritual communion between this woman and her cat proves the affirmations of the experts concerning the shaman. From the "power animal" the shaman "derives his psychic abilities, spiritual assistance. . . . Basically, the power animal becomes the shaman's alter ego." By the same token, the shaman "permanently incarnates these spirits into his own body."[91] In an attempt to join the opposites, not only are sexual differences eliminated but the distinction between human and animal has been virtually lost.

Part of the shaman's initiation is sexual perversion. "Many shamans become androgynous, homosexual or lesbian at the insistence of their spirit guides.[92] Homosexuality appears to be not just a physical condition but a spiritual commitment. A recent book traces the history of gay male spirituality, and argues that "gender-variant men have fulfilled a sacred role throughout the millennia." Contemporary examples given include the homosexual priests of the Yoruba religion in Cuba and "young gay witches in Manhattan."[93] In more familiar but strangely comparable terms, Virginia Mollenkott, calling herself "an evangelical lesbian feminist," speaks for gays and lesbians, when she says, "We are God's Ambassadors."[94] Indeed, Mollenkott claims she "was told" by her "guardian angel, a Spirit Guide, the Holy Spirit or Jesus [she is not sure]: "A great shift is occurring in the world, and you are a part of that shift."[95] Similarly, Judy Westerdorf, a United Methodist clergywoman, triumphantly declared to the delegates at the pagano-"christian" feminist *RE-Imagining Conference* in Minneapolis (1993) that "the Church has always been blessed by gays and lesbians, . . . witches . . . [and] shamans."[96] Some see a brave new world of sexual pluralism where all are free to do their own thing. The androgyne will be the spiritual leader and heterosexuality will be tolerated, as in ancient Greece.[97]

Homophobia

Christians are exhorted to love sinners but flee sin. Though sexual revolutionaries throw the charge of homophobia at anyone who opposes homosexuality, theistic Christians have reason to resist acceptance of homosexuality in Western society. While not all homosexuals are overtly anti-Christian — indeed some claim to be Christian — one may not underestimate the role of homosexual theory in the normalization of paganism in the Christian West.

Friedrich Nietzsche was the nineteenth century philosopher who called for the total overthrow of Christianity, for the transvaluation of values [that is, calling good evil, and evil good], and for the rediscovery of polytheism. Some believe he was a homosexual.[98] The contemporary pagan revival reveres Nietzsche as one of the movement's great patron saints, whose time has now come.[99] If homosexuality is to monism what heterosexuality is to theism, then the transvaluation of sexual values will lead to paganism. Sexuality and spirituality are profoundly related. Harry Britt, gay activist, San Francisco supervisor and ex-Methodist minister, recently admitted as much when he described the struggle for gay liberation as "spiritual warfare."[100]

It is little wonder that a leading voice in the contemporary deconstruction of Western Christendom was the French homosexual, Michel Foucault. Foucault sought to deconstruct the value system of heterosexuality by arguing that truth is only power and that heterosexual values are a power-play of the majority imposed upon the homosexual minority. Reducing truth and morals to power has created a place in the culture wars for homosexuals. Gay-bashing is a heinous crime but so are homosexual bully tactics. Naked power describes the constant, violent persecution of a Protestant pastor, Charles McIlhenny and his family, who for a number of years have opposed the gay power that controls San Francisco's city government (police department, school board, fire department, health department and much of the religious community).[101] The McIlhenny's simple, disturbing testimony, hauntingly entitled, *When the Wicked Seize a City: A Grim Look at the Future and a Warning to the Church*, should alert all to the kind of "ethics" gays in power will eventually use. Any methods are fair to rid modern Western Sodom of this meddlesome priest. "Straight society," says McIlhenny, "is now out of power (in San Francisco) and without influence — living on the fringes of society."[102] He fears that San Francisco is a foretaste of what America will become.

The rejection of traditional values finds a certain expression in "evangelical" authoress, Virginia Mollenkott, who, as an openly practicing lesbian with a new moral code, is now righteously committed to lying and deceiving to bring down the heteropatriarchal culture.[103] In spite of her Christian phrases, she has become a pagan monist, and in the monist circle, where evil is merely the dark side of the force, such "dark" power can be used to promote the new morality. After all, "good" and "evil" are only relatively fixed points on the ever-revolving monistic circle where all is one and one is all.

Feminism:
A Foothold For Paganism in the
Church of the Third Millennium?

In the Gnostic texts found at Nag Hammadi, the dominant theme is asceticism, the refusal of all sexuality (see chapter 13). This has the appearance of Christian holiness, and appealed to Christians living in the dissolute Greco-roman pagan world. Kurt Rudolf argues that it was through asceticism that Gnosticism gained a foothold in the un-suspecting church.[104] One may well wonder if in our day, through the Christian-sounding notions of gender liberation and egalitarian rights for all, neo-Gnostic New Age liberalism is succeeding doing the same in an equally unsuspecting twentieth century church.[105]

Strangely, much of the Christian literature seeking to appraise the New Age and the new paganism, avoids one of its most fundamental themes, namely, the transformation of sexuality and the promotion of woman as the autonomous savior figure of the race.[106] Because the church has bowed to societal pressures and bought into a certain kind of femi-nism, it seems blind to the stakes of this social revolution.[107]

No Agenda

A member of the task force on sexuality for the Evangelical Lutheran Church of America, defending the statement's acceptance of masturba-tion and same-sex "marriage," said, and no doubt quite sincerely: "We are not coming in with an agenda."[108] That most people do not see any agenda is as disturbing as the agenda itself. Many Christian egalitarians believe in good faith that they can avoid contamination by this new religion while using the feminist critique to rid the faith of androcentric abuse and oppressive patriarchy. They want to eliminate the patriarchal husk of Christianity and retain the egalitarian kernel. The radical Jew-ish feminist Naomi Goldenberg is not convinced.

> The feminist movement in Western culture is engaged in the slow execution of Christ and Jahweh. Yet very few of the women and men now working for sexual equality within Christianity and Judaism re-alize the extent of their heresy.[109]

Christian "feminists" are rightly concerned to ask what is the time-less teaching of Scripture on male/female relationships, and how the Christian Gospel transforms male and female sinners. No doubt the tra-ditional Church has many questions to ask itself. I trust Goldenberg is wrong and my feminist brothers and sisters are right. But the danger of throwing the baby out with the bath water is enormous, especially for following generations.[110] This issue must not be decided on the basis of "inner certainty" or "a sense of call" or "the tide of history" or "societal, democratic progress." The Gnostics could claim all that, and history has shown them to be profoundly wrong. The issue can only be decided on solid exegesis of Holy Scripture, and, alas, of that there is a great dearth. Thus, the danger is great that instead of a recovery of biblical sexuality, the result will be sexual and theological confusion, and a failure to see the compromises with paganism in large sectors of the church. Christians must realize that the religious feminist movement carries with it a frontal assault on the normativity of creational heterosexuality and, beyond that, on God Himself as the Creator.[111] Its "liberating" fruit can only be destructive for both men and women.

There is an agenda: the theoretical ideal of the androgynous, sexually unfettered New Man of Aquarian liberalism. In its pristine purity, only the radical fringe followed by the intellectual and cultural elite actually believe and promote it as such. It is rather promoted via the emotive democratic notions of freedom and civil rights and pro-choice liberty. But behind popular debates about the place of women in military academies, about co-ed bathrooms and prisons, and about the determination of the Clinton Administration (through its Justice Department) to eliminate any state-recognized distinctions between men and women, hides a new definition of sexuality that slaps the face of the Creator God of Scripture. As doctrinaire radical feminists scream, "New Women, New Earth,"[112] we witness the stirrings of a revolution that will remake the world.

Perhaps this ideology is a fashionable fad of the effete elite.[113] However, the early church's exposure to the Gnostic heresy is hardly encouraging. As one scholar said of Gnosticism, "this kind of *gnosis* (knowledge) was in the air they breathed and some of it entered their lungs."[114] Anyone from Tokyo will tell you that a few drops of poison can bring a nation to its knees. There is reason to think, as the Evangelical Lutheran situation indicates, that the agenda is already in the mainstream. Perhaps one percent of vocal radicals can infect an entire society and with it large sections of the Christian church.[115]

CHAPTER 13

GNOSTIC SEXUALITY

Feminists . . . engage in dialogue outside [the Judeo-Christian] tradition, and never before allowed by it, [namely] dialogue with heresies . . . dialogue with pre-Christian and pre-biblical religion.
  - Rosemary Radford Ruether[1]

Radical Freedom from the God of the Bible

The image is unforgettable. As the Gnostic believer exits from the sacramental bridal chamber, having undergone the secret initiation of spiritual wedlock, he shakes his fist at the God of Scripture, the Creator and Law-giver, and declares himself free from his authority.[2] He does this to follow "Christ," the one who leads this ultimate rebellion against "the Almighty of chaos," the "Prime Begetter [or Archprogenitor] who is called Yaldabaoth"[3]:

> But I [Christ] came to take them [mankind] from their blindness so that I might educate them all about the God who is above all creation [the ultimate unknowable divine spirit]. Therefore trample their [the archons — the creator God and his angels] graves and humiliate their wicked designs, and break their yoke and cause to arise those who are mine. For I have given you the authority of the Sons of Light over everything to crush their power underfoot.[4]

The Masterless: This title, of a recent book on American history, expresses the author's belief that the story of civilization in the New World has been marked, on the one hand, by the eroding of the power of familial and local institutions and, on the other, by the rise of federal power and the autonomous citizen. Americans are *The Masterless*.[5] Oddly, this was the favorite self-designation of the ancient Gnostics.

This ancient liberation movement shook free from existing structures and traditions, especially the God of Scripture. The note of *autonomous* liberty is fundamental to the Gnostic self-understanding. They prided themselves on being a "kingless generation," beholden to no person, institution or tradition.[6]

Enter sex, as it always does when theology is involved. "Sex . . . is the means by which enslavement to the powers is perpetuated," says Douglas M. Parrot, one of the translators of the Nag Hammadi texts.[7] A program of sexual liberation is therefore an integral part of the Gnostic system. Liberation from enslavement is either the adoption of religious pagan sexuality, especially that expressed in the Mother goddess cults, or in the total rejection of sexuality.

Pagan Sex for a Heresy: Homosexual Priests of the Mother Goddess

Gnostics carried goddess worship and homosexuality into "Christianity."[8] This eloquent distortion of orthodox belief is instructive in our day when the same incredible phenomena are re-occurring.

Hippolytus (170-236 A.D.) reports that the serpent-worshiping, Naasene Gnostics attended celebrations of the mysteries of the Great Mother in order to understand the "universal mystery."[9] Like modern syncretists, the Gnostics believed truth was one, to be found everywhere. Hippolytus denounces as a fundamental error the Naasene attempt to Christianize and spiritualize a pagan perversion of the created order. In his eyes, and he was not alone in the early church,[10] the spiritualizing of such humanistic thinking and practice in no way redeemed this borrowing as a possible Christian option.

An independent witness, the first century Latin poet, Catullus, attended pagan cultic practices of goddess worship like those attended by the Gnostics. He graphically depicts the self-emasculation of Attis, lover of the goddess Cybele,[11] whereby he becomes a "counterfeit woman." The poet portrays the act and its results:

> Attis, . . . exalted by amorous rage, his mind gone, . . . cut off his testicles with a sharp flint.

She (the emasculated Attis) then, aware of her limbs without the
man, While the ground was still spotted with fresh blood . . .
(expressing regret for what he/she has done, says):
There is nothing for me but misery.
What shape is there that I have not had?
A woman now, I have been man, youth and boy;
I was athlete, the wrestler . . .
Shall I be a waiting maid to the gods, the slave of Cybele?
I a Maenad, I a part of myself, I impotent? . . .
I regret now, now, what I have done, I repent of it, now!

Such equivocation stirs the wrath of Cybele:

Cybele, letting her lions off the leash
And urging forward the beast on her left hand,
Said, "Get on, be fierce, see that he is driven mad;
Make him insane enough to return to the forest;
He has the impertinence to want to be out of my power . . .

The poem ends with the following three line stanza:

Great Goddess, Goddess Cybele, Goddess lady of Dindymus,
May all your fury be far from my house.
Incite the others, go. Drive other men mad.[12]

Another form of this cultic spirituality is found in Syria, where Cybele
is called Rhea. According to this version, Rhea castrates Attis, who from
that moment adopted a female life-style, put on women's clothes, and
traveled through the ancient world singing the praises of Rhea.[13] The
Galli or effeminate itinerant priests of Rhea imitated precisely the deeds
of the mythological Attis.[14]

The rites of initiation into the Cybele cult included baptism in the
blood of a slaughtered bull or ram. This took place in a pit or taurobolium.
At the end of the ceremony sometimes certain "powers" of the sacrificial bull, no doubt the animal's genitals, were offered to the Mother of
the gods, again a powerful symbol of male emasculation before the female divinity.[15] The obvious intentions and results of such cultic mythology and practice was the feminization and emasculation of men under
the power of the goddess. One can only imagine what the revival of
goddess worship in our time, in the name of Christianity, could do to
our civilization.

These grotesque and perverted practices of *non-Christian* paganism are not included for sensationalism but because they constitute a
particularly clear example of how paganism was introduced into Chris-

tianity. Hippolytus explains the Naasene procedure. "Because they claimed that 'everything is spiritual,' *the Naasenes did not become Galli physically but rather spiritually*: 'they only perform the functions of those who are castrated' by abstaining from sexual intercourse.[16] The mythological story of the castration of Attis led the Naasenes to conclude that the image of emasculation was a symbol of salvation.[17]

So, concludes Hippolytus, the Naasene Gnostics imitate the Galli, the castrated priests of Cybele. "For they urge most severely and carefully that one should abstain, as those men (the Galli) do, from intercourse with women; their behavior otherwise . . . is like that of the castrated."[18] Hippolytus indicates that Naas was associated with both adultery and homosexuality, since the Serpent was said to have had relations with both Eve and Adam.[19] It is therefore possible that the Naasenes, who worshiped the Serpent, would have practiced some form of deviant sexuality.

Gnosticism and Pagan Homosexuality

In the Nag Hammadi texts, one has to read between the lines for suggestions of homosexuality. The *Paraphrase of Shem* speaks of Sodom as the place of the revelation of the Spirit,[20] and the *Gospel of the Egyptians* traces the origin of the seed of Seth the Revealer to Sodom and Gomorrah.[21] The constant praise of "spiritual" homosexuality [androgyny] as the preferred "sexual" state beyond gender differences, certainly makes the likelihood of homosexual practice amongst some radical Gnostic groups a possibility.

The church father, Epiphanius, who seems to have known radical Gnostic groups better than any one, unambiguously affirms the practice of sodomy in some expressions of Gnosticism.

> These people [the Gnostic Carpocratians] perform everything unspeakable and unlawful, which is not right to mention, and every kind of homosexual act and carnal intercourse with women, with every member of the body.[22]

This accusation he also makes with respect to the Gnostic Nicolaitans[23] and the Borborites.[24]

Hippolytus's account of the Naasene adoption and spiritualization of the sexual perversions of the Cybele/Rhea goddess cult shows to what extent "Christian" Gnosticism was a variant of non-Christian paganism. The leading Gnostic specialists of a generation ago would have agreed.[25] The theological agenda behind this negation of sexuality is the transformation of creation. Through the mysteries of the Great Mother disclosed to the Egyptians and the Phrygians, these so-called Christian Gnostics come to understand "the universal mystery," i.e., what is true in all religions, viz., "the process of change is displayed by the ineffable, unimaginable, inconceivable, formless being transforming creation."[26] Through pagan sexual perversion the Gnostics discover the divine, which is the unknowable, ineffable spiritual Force of monism, not the Creator and Redeemer of Scripture.

Hippolytus' 1800-year-old example illuminates our present situation.[27] Many seek to recuperate pagan goddess spirituality in order to create a "new look" Christianity in step with an "eco-feminist," post-patriarchal society. The God of Scripture is ditched for the divine spirit in all things.

The early Church Fathers saw the profound logic in the deconstructionist theology of Gnosticism with regard to sexuality. So should we. The logic builds:

♦ the rejection of God the Creator and the establishment of human independence;

♦ the denunciation of creational sexuality;

♦ an elaboration of various forms of androgyny.

Rejection of God the Creator: Then Archy Now Patriarchy, Always Autarchy

The Gnostic system achieves human independence by eliminating God the Creator, the so-called world ruler or Archon. The vehemence of this ancient heresy's rejection is comparable to the prevalent feminist rejection of this same Old Testament "patriarchal" God.[28] Indeed, the parallels are eerily striking. The term "patriarchy" is composed of two Greek words — *pater* (father) and *archon* (authority/ruler). For the ancient Gnostic, liberation comes by shaking one's fist at the archon/creator; for the modern feminist, liberation comes from the rejection of the patri-archon. Today the great "evil" of patriarchy is identified as the sinful structure prohibiting humanity's true freedom. Gnosticism identified the archons (God and his angels) as the great obstacle to authentic, unfettered existence of the Gnostic believer, who "stands alone" (*monachos*).[29] This "standing alone" or autonomy (a law to oneself) produces autarchy (rule by the self).

Such autonomous autarchy is an early rejection of the creational structures of patriarchy. The elimination of both God the Father and the dismissal of biological fatherhood and reproduction was as much a powerful polemic against patriarchy as any modern feminist diatribe.

As a counterpoint to this theme of "autarchy" (self-rule) went the theme of "superman" (hyperanthropos).[30] According the *Apocryphon of John*, Adam is superior to the God who created him.[31] Superior to the male Archon, this "creature" knows himself to be a "solitary one," that is, one standing alone, possessing autonomous power, related only to the unknown god within. This fundamental theological autonomy must be understood sexually.

Denunciation of Creational Sex:
Motherhood Ruled Out, Apple Pie Threatened

The *Gospel of Thomas* takes the teaching of Jesus that places all family relationships in *subordination* to the eventual demands of kingdom of God, and makes of it a Gnostic principle for the outright *rejection* of natural family ties.[32] The Gnostic is *monachos*, "standing alone," with regard to family and sexual ties. Many claim that *Thomas* is not a radical expression of Gnosticism, but on this subject, this apocryphal gospel is notably extreme. In saying 105, Jesus teaches: "The one who is acquainted with father and mother will be called the son of a prostitute." In saying 101, the living Jesus denies any value in physical fathers and mothers, and opts for his "spiritual mother."[33]

The Gnostic *Apocryphon of John* teaches that sexual intercourse is evil: "up to today sexual intercourse continued due to the First Archon."[34] The *Book of Thomas the Contender* teaches that intercourse produces beasts, and that the elect must "abandon bestiality."[35] "Woe to you," the text continues, "who love sexual relations with women and defiled intercourse with them."[36] In The *Dialogue of the Savior*, Matthew recalls one of the commands of Jesus: "Annihilate the works which pertain to the woman (that is, childbearing) . . . so that they (the works) may cease."[37] The *Authoritative Teaching* denigrates the body: "the body came from sexual desire, and sexual desire came from . . . matter."[38] The *Paraphrase of Shem* speaks of Nature and her "unclean femininity," Nature's "dark vagina,"[39] and the "intercourse of Darkness" which will be destroyed at the end of time." *Zostrianos* tells the Gnostic believer: "Flee from the insanity and fetters of femaleness, and embrace instead the salvation of maleness."[40]

These citations, from a variety of Gnostic documents, are not expressions of male chauvinism (though doubtless there was some of that) but are denunciations of the created order of heterosexuality and the bearing of children. Though *apparently* deriving from a quite different agenda, the end result has deep concordance with today's rejection of heteropatriarchy, motherhood, the traditional family, and the right to abortion on demand — because they flow from the same spiritual source.

An Elaboration of Androgyny: Spiritual Marriage

Denying creational sexuality, the Gnostics substituted a new kind of sexuality, symbolized by their sacrament of the "Bridal Chamber."[41] In the holy marriage with the new "Christ," the Gnostic believer swears to destroy all that God has made. In particular he swears to join together what God had put asunder and thus to destroy the Creator through his works, in particular, the work of created sexuality.

The *Gospel of Philip* identifies sexual distinction as the cause of death.

> When Eve was still in Adam, death did not come into being. When she was divided from him, death came into being. If he goes in again, attaining his former self, death will not exist any more.[42]

Establishing this completeness is the point of the coming of Christ. "For this purpose, Christ came to reverse the division which was from the beginning and again join the two, and give life to those who died as a result of the division and join them. But the woman is joined to her husband in the wedding chamber. Indeed, those who have joined in the wedding chamber will no longer be divided."[43]

Though on the surface less radical, the *Gospel of Thomas* is similarly driven by the androgynous ideal and the refusal of femininity and motherhood. Doubtless representing the goal of the gospel, the last saying, #114, holds out for the believer the attainment of an androgynous or sexless state.

> Simon Peter said to them: "Mary should depart from us, for women are not worthy of life." Jesus said, "I, myself will draw her, to cause

her to become male, that she may also become a living spirit that is like you males. For each woman who will make herself male will enter the kingdom of heaven."

Saying 114 should be understood in the light of saying twenty-two: "Jesus said to them, 'When you make the two as one, and when you make the inside like the outside, and the outside like the inside, and the above like the below, and when you make the male and female one and the same, so that the male may not be male nor the female be female; . . . then will you enter [the kingdom]." Both these sayings suggest the "neutralization" of sexuality so that the ideal for Gnostics is to become sexless.[44] *Thomas* is *not* a macho attack on women, as Pagels rightly sees.[45] It is a rejection of creational sexuality, a radical refusal of sexual differentiation, as presented in the Genesis account.[46]

When *Thomas* says that females will first become males in order then to become "living spirits," he is speaking about a "backwards" creation, which undoes the original order: from the female rib into the male Adam, back into the 'living spirit.'"[47] Thus Gnostic women become "autonomous males,"[48] and together with males, become "living spirits" beyond sexual differentiation. In this implosion of creation, the two become one by destroying differentiation in a return to unity: the monistic ideal.

The Living Jesus of the *Gospel of Thomas* declares that only the "solitary [*monachos*] will enter the bridal chamber."[49] In other words, only autonomous egalitarian beings can find true spirituality. Just what this Jesus of *Thomas* means is clear in his teaching to Salome. To her he declares himself to be he who "exists from the Whole (or the Undivided)." Salome responds with the confession, "I am your disciple," to which Jesus replies with a statement of pure Gnostic principle: if he (the Gnostic disciple) is [undivided (or destroyed)], he will be filled with light, but if he should become divided, he will be filled with darkness."[50]

Salome has done what *Zostrianos* recommends, as noted above: "Flee from the insanity and the fetters of femaleness, and embrace instead the salvation of maleness."[51] Salome is the ideal disciple, the liberated, autonomous, egalitarian Gnostic, untrammeled by the sexual distinctions of the original creation. "Standing alone" she has moved beyond the bondage of her sex. She has become spiritually androgynous.

Androgyny: Superman/woman:
Neither Male Nor Female, Quite the Contrary

Gnosticism was not simply a movement of sexual freedom. At a deeper level, it was the introduction of monistic, pagan thinking about God into Christian theism. Noted scholar Giovanni Filoramo speaks of the "androgynous god of the Gnostics," who expresses the "concept of *coniunction oppositorum*, or joining of opposites, to embody the conquest of all duality."[52] There are many texts illustrating this Gnostic monism.[53] In the same way, contemporary feminism is not just about sexuality. The new religious feminism seeks to "move beyond God the Father" to an imagery of bisexual androgynous deity by reintroducing the image of god as female to complement the image of God as male."[54] Androgyny has deep religious meaning, and the Gnostic texts ring the changes on this mysterious theme. In *On The Origin Of The World* Sophia (Wisdom) outfoxes Jahweh and his angels by creating a man who would instruct the wretched creatures to despise the god who created them (Jahweh) and thus escape from his clutches. After twelve months she produced an "androgynous man . . . whom the Greeks call Hermaphrodite." He was to be "the Teacher." This "son" of Sophia is called "the beast" by Yahweh and his hordes but he is "wiser than all of them."[55] In other words, Christ, the androgynous son first appeared as the serpent-teacher of Genesis 3.[56]

We have already seen in *Thunder, Perfect Mind* that Sophia herself is an androgynous being who joins male and female together — and everything else as well, including truth and iniquity. This is a perfect expression of monism.[57] Note how *Sophia* joins not just the opposites of sexuality but all the aspects of existence. Androgyny is thus the sexual expression of a deeply religious agenda, that of pagan monism.

Sophia makes an even more sexually explicit statement of androgyny in a text already cited, *Trimorphic Protennoia*.[58]

> I am gynandrous (or androgynous) [I am Mother, I am] Father since [I] [have coitus] with myself. I [have coitus] with myself [and the ones who love] me [and] I am the one through whom the All [endures]. I am the womb [that gives form] to the All by birthing the Light that [shines in] glory.[59]

Androgyny is thus the ideal, as in today's new Aquarian humanity. Having mocked the God who created heterosexuality, the Gnostics propose the opposite as an act of defiance. Sexual rebellion in Gnosticism runs the gamut — from the denial of sexuality and femininity, especially child-bearing and motherhood (as part of the Archon's works and pomps),[60] to heterosexual license,[61] and even, perhaps to homosexuality.[62] The destruction of normative, creational sexuality has as its ultimate goal the joining of the opposites in androgyny, as *The Apocalypse of James* so eloquently puts it: "The perishable has [gone up] to the imperishable and the female element has attained to this male element."[63] This is the return to the supposed original androgynous state of Genesis 1, where God created Man, male and female, an androgynous being.[64]

From Theory to Practice:
The Place of Gnostic Women

Whether in mild or extreme form, Gnostic practice is a logical extension of its theory. If every Gnostic, male or female, is autonomous, and if differentiated sexuality is unspiritual, then a radical egalitarianism is the necessary result. If gender hierarchy and subordination are the accursed work of the evil Archon, they must be eliminated. Epiphanes, an early Gnostic teacher, proposes an extreme egalitarian communism.

> The righteousness of God is a communion with equality, for heaven, equally stretched out on all sides like a circle embraces the whole earth . . . God makes no distinction between . . . male and female . . . he declared righteousness to be fellowship with equality . . . that he (the Jewish lawgiver) said "thou shalt not covet (is) laughable . . . that he said "your neighbor's wife" is even more laughable, since he compels what was common possession to become private property.[65]

The egalitarian view of the sexes and ethics in general, according to Rudolf, brings the Gnostics to an "inversion of values" and the removal of earthly distinctions.[66] Tertullian denounces a much less extreme form of the rejection of distinctions which had practical implications in church life:

> They maintain (ecclesiastical) harmony with all, making no distinction. As a matter of fact, it (harmony) exists among them although they hold different doctrines as long as they wage common warfare against one thing, the truth (orthodoxy). They are all puffed up, all promise "knowledge." Their catechumens are already perfected before they are taught. Even the heretical women . . . make bold to teach,

to dispute, to perform exorcisms, to promise cures, perhaps also to baptize.[67]

Historians note that women frequently occupied leading positions as teachers and prophetesses, or played a leading role in cultic ceremonies.[68] The Gnostic Marcus practiced not only the prophetic ordination of women but had them function also as priests.[69] The authoritative function of teacher is granted to women through the inversion of the Genesis account where Eve is represented as the teacher of Adam.[70] Is this why Saint Paul insists that women should not teach men in the Church?[71] This inverted exegesis is put into practice in the Nag Hammadi *Gospel of Mary*, where Mary instructs Peter and the other apostles with hidden knowledge the Lord revealed only to her.[72] Mary stands up and demands that all praise the Lord's greatness, for he "has prepared us (and) made us into men."[73] Andrew identifies what Mary says as "strange ideas" (17:15), and Peter cannot believe that the Lord would speak privately with a woman (17:19). Levi states that "the Savior knows her very well. That is why he loved her more than us." Peter then begs Mary to tell the words of the Savior, and Mary replies that she will reveal to Peter what was hidden.[74] In this strand of Gnosticism, Christ is building his church not on Peter but on Mary Magdalene.

Both Kurt Rudolf and Elaine Pagels, liberal theologians and recognized experts in the field of Ancient Gnosticism, affirm that the Gnostic *practice* was a consistent application of Gnostic *theory*. "Many gnostic Christians," says Pagels, "correlate their description of God in both masculine and feminine terms with a complimentary description of human nature . . . [and] often take the principle of equality between men and women [based on an androgynous notion of creation] into the social and political structures of their communities."[75] Rudolf argues that dominance of female deities in the Gnostic story translates into female religious power in the Gnostic churches.[76] The same Gnostic theory is back in town. Is there any reason to be surprised that the Gnostic practice is back too?

CHAPTER 14

THE NEW
SPIRITUAL EXPERIENCE

There is no help from within — without the supernatural the natural is a pit of horror.
  - John Updike[1]

In the Beginning Was the Experience:
Embraced by the Light

"Whatever turns you on" aptly expresses modern tolerance of experience, in terms reminiscent of an LSD high. Drugs turned on people's lights in the Sixties, and still do. According to Marilyn Ferguson, researchers can produce mystical experiences, almost at will. After submitting to an "Altered State of Consciousness Inducing Device" (ASCID — apparently the pun is intended), a willing human guinea pig described the trip in glowing terms:

> There was a tremendous slow-motion kind of explosion and upsurge and outgo of energy all around and from the point where the light disappeared. It was incredible. Then the circle grew and grew to infinite proportions within me, and all the sound was white. It was a silent Beethoven symphony throbbing all over the place. . . . I grew huge and transparent, filled and permeated with the light and the fire. And I thought: My God is a God of Love and he lives within me.[2]

Betty Eadie, author of *Embraced by the Light*, now a best seller, even among Christians, describes her "near-death" experience in a strikingly similar way:

> I saw a pin-point of light in the distance, . . . and felt myself traveling . . . at an even greater speed, rushing toward [it]. . . . As I approached it, I noticed the figure of a man [Jesus Christ] standing in it. . . . As I got closer the light became brilliant . . . beyond any description, far more brilliant than the sun. . . . a brilliant, magnificent whiteness that extended out for some distance. I felt his light blending into mine . . . And as our lights merged, . . . I felt an utter explosion of love.[3]

Everybody wants an experience like that. Apparently both New Agers and Christians can have it. Who would opt for *faith* if you could genuinely have *knowledge* like that? The feeling of flying through the clouds in mind-blowing ecstasy, with no hint of fear, in touch with God and one's true self. . . . Sounds like heaven on earth. If you could bottle the formula, market possibilities would go off the charts. People have, of course. "Dream upon a star" has done very well for Disney, even if the flying Tinkerbell of Anaheim is in her sixties. With much more effectiveness, the billion dollar drug trade feeds fantasy-starved trippers with fleeting moments of blissful *bonheur*. The real thing, hawked by gurus, is much better — and (almost) free of charge. It just takes a little work, a lot of spiritual commitment, and $350.00 a weekend.

In the new religion *everything* exists to create this experience, as the feminist wing concedes with characteristic clarity. "Wild women" speak of the discovery of a "spiritual tradition as women," which they find/ create "in new translations, new interpretations, new language . . . new namings of the holy . . . expressed in a vast array of religious forms . . . [and] new images of God."[4] The ideas we have already studied — the new Bible and Bible study method, the new humanity, and the new God — have been created from a new experience. All produce a "new theological paradigm" which both creates and perpetuates the experience.[5] The new paradigm leads to a "paradigm shift," a leap into a new perception of reality for the sake of a "new spiritual experience." In describing ancient pagans, David Wells notes that they "proceeded from the basis of their *experience* to understand the supernatural."[6] So it is with the religious quest of our modern world. The contemporary *experience* of liberation is "revelation" and "truly . . . redemptive."[7] This experience is, in essence, a rediscovery of the spirituality of ancient paganism, as one "gentle, smiling, silver-haired" Roman Catholic sister explained.

The whole word [pagan] is taking on new meaning, [it is] being redeemed . . . It is not the belief we condemned in the past . . . I believe
that was where Jesus was coming from . . . We *are* part of the earth,
and we must work out our evolution into the beings we must become,
in harmony with the earth.[8]

Personal experience is raised to a formal philosophical principle by
theorists of pagan witchcraft: "Subjectivity, we must know, is the only
state of experience in the universe. The only state of being is as the
subject experiencing itself and the world, from within."[9] All the blocks
fit together to undergird this "new" way of encountering the divine,
even if Jesus becomes a pagan. For in our day, as in the heyday of paganism, experience is queen.

The Appeal of the New Religious Experience
Virtual Spiritual Reality

Sister Madonna, a feminist nun, sees the new spirituality as world-
creating:

The sign of ultimate religious experience will surely be . . . its power
to release truly spiritual redemptive energies. . . . In this "truly catholic" New Faith . . . the Church will wither away, made unnecessary by
the direct illumination of "a creative Spiritual Presence that comes
from *within* them as well as from *beyond*.[10]

Sister Madonna first rejects "the spirituality of this 'false god' [God the
Father of the Bible]" who has "created the world we live in. . . ." Spirituality of a different kind will create the world we want to live in."[11]

The self-focused religious experience that will save the world, seen
in the light of its pagan roots, is appalling. Most moderns, ignorant of
this family background, find this spirituality alluring. Those raised on
instant coffee and mashed potatoes, instant entertainment at the push
of a remote control and instant gratification in virtual reality, will find
the ecstatic spirituality of the new religion appealing. What's more, it
offers immediate success for the problems of our stressful world.

Some health care experts foresee the coming of "the Age of Anxiety"
— created, ironically enough, by the "age of therapy." The National Institute of Mental Health (NIMH) estimates that 24 million people suffer
from anxiety disorders and see in newer, more spiritual techniques like
massage and yoga, significant ways of avoiding the "stress monster."[12]
The reduction of stress is power. Power makes winners out of victims,

and is ultimately religious. Instant religious power is a consumer product whose day has hardly begun.

The new spirituality promises apocalypse now, ecstasy now — you can have it all and you can have it now. Deferred pleasure went out of style with Woodstock and Roe versus Wade. In the TV movie *Thorn Birds*, everyone resonates with the justification given to his bishop by the Roman cleric caught with his pants down: "I never felt such ecstasy as I felt with her."

Roof's study of boomers found that only four per cent were atheistic or agnostic. These products of the Sixties revolution do not want a life style with no "transcendent symbol," no "overarching 'sacred canopy,'" to use the sociologist's terminology.[13] The "me-generation" of the Sixties finds regeneration in the new spirituality, which one observer calls "transformed narcissism" by which God and the self become interchangeable. There is "a new emphasis on God — [but] as the "accessible self." "Accessibility must involve alternative ways of experiencing the sacred. . . . [for] we all access God differently."[14] The pro-choice envelope for religion expands to include syncretism and polytheism.

The Loss of Traditional Faith

As a schoolboy, I was hopeless in math and science. I still am, as my family will attest. There is one scientific law that I still remember, however: nature abhors a vacuum. It seems that spirit does, too. The loss of traditional faith and religious experience creates a void that makes the new religious experience especially appealing. The Eastern worldview that has flooded into the West since the Sixties fills the void. It teaches that the created world is an illusion. In its classic expression, Hinduism,

> *Maya* is the power of God, which creates the illusion of a differentiated universe and conceals the divine unity behind appearances, while ignorance creates the seemingly separate self at the individual level.[15]

This is unadulterated monism, to be found equally clearly in modern feminism, witchcraft and in New Age "Christian" and pagan thinking. Its glittering but false promise is to reconnect our fragmented selves to our higher, better selves and to reconnect us all to the fragmented cosmos. This is a heady brew for the spiritually thirsty who have lost connection with traditional faith.

Witches, Nuns, Gurus and Evangelicals

If God is not a reality outside ourselves, the good news is: the only god to know, the only divine will to obey, the only spiritual imperative to heed is found within the human soul. Clear statements of this monistic view abound, from all otherwise disparate sources:

◆ **from modern pagan proponents of witchcraft:**
The truth is that "God" is not in a book — "holy," golden, or otherwise. God is not in a church, a cathedral, a synagogue, a mosque. . . . God is the universe. We are all now living inside the body of God. There is nowhere to go to get there, we are already here. There is nowhere to go to get outside of God; there is just a forgetting of this truth. It is impossible not to be living, right now and always, within God's body. It is only possible to be aware, or unaware, of this fact.[16]

◆ **from two leading feminist Roman Catholic nuns:**
We cannot seek God as an object separate from our world, outside our lived experience, . . . God is experienced not so much as a separate being, but God is sensed as the deepest dimension of our own being. What we find is not God but *ourselves*. . . . The process of self-knowledge is the process of knowing God.[17]   God, who has been imprinted in our minds as a transcendent absolute, must somehow be recovered in an epiphany of immanence, of divine self-revelation.[18]

◆ **from a liberal "Christian" New Ager:**
Since the unconscious is God all along, we may further define the goal of spiritual growth to be the attainment of godhood by the conscious self. It is for the individual to become totally, wholly god.[19]

◆ **from an "evangelical" New Ager:**
The Ultimate, the Sacred, God Herself is everywhere at the core of everything and everyone (including me).[20]

The theoretical structure of the new spirituality is the reduction of God to the human self. Theory is never neutral, and this theory has as its aim the salvation of mankind and the planet.

The Aim of the New Religious Experience

The goal of salvation contains various aspects — utopia, power, knowledge and transformation. To understand the appeal and the workings of this spirituality, one needs to grasp how these aspects function in the system.

Utopia:

The new religious experience is driven by a noble goal, the eradication of oppression and the establishment of a just human society. Who has not imagined an idyllic, rosy future, with no fear, no death, no hell, no crying, no oppression, no rules nor limits, no IRS nor speed limits and no comprehensive health insurance (no one will ever be ill)? But be careful. Pinnochio believed, and turned into a donkey.

John Lennon asked us to imagine an earthly paradise with no heaven and no hell; it is the refrain of the new Western gurus who believe the new world order will come about as more people get turned on to spiritual power.

Power: Masters of Our Own Destiny

Gurus of the new religious experience make no bones about the grab for power: 'Whether or not we become all that we may be is up to us. We have been given every opportunity and facility. But we have also been given mastery of our own destiny.[21]

Morrison calls it right: "'*Mastery of our own destiny.*' Here we have the fountainhead of all Gnostic teaching — the nuts and bolts of the 'Satanic Initiation' which our first parents received in the Garden of Eden."[22] The first sin, which determines all others, is the desire for an independent, autonomous existence beyond the word of God. The taste of illegitimate power is intoxicating. Says Virginia Mollenkott:

> Spirituality refers to our ways of believing, belonging, and responding to the power and presence of Divinity, Holiness, the Higher Power, the All-Inclusive One who connects us spiritually to one another and the whole ecosystem. The experience of connectedness is too empowering and joyous to relinquish for any reason.[23]

Knowledge: You Gotta Serve Somebody

Power is *knowledge.* Knowledge is power. In the end, Oppenheimer, the scientist who invented the atomic bomb, was far more powerful than the American government who got it from his mind and dropped it on Hiroshima. In Eden, Satan offers an alternate knowledge source that tells them what they want to hear. But if God had not "really said," then who speaks wisdom?

The ancient Gnostics had the answer. The Serpent whispers true knowledge which is innate within the human heart. You find it by going within. This ancient formula has a decidedly modern ring. Indeed "going within" is the great discovery of the new age, though our age has been well prepared. The enormously influential psychologist, Carl Jung, claimed that "*the unconscious is the only accessible source of religious experience.*"[24] Jung was a great admirer of the Gnostics, and followed them into the occult. For the radical Gnostics believed that it is not even the self which is the source of true knowledge. If God does not speak wisdom, then the Serpent does. The truth is that when people search within themselves for wisdom, they only find the diabolical lie. As Bob Dylan sang: "You gotta serve somebody. . . . It may be the Devil or it may be the Lord."

This occult knowledge, derived by turning within and thereby turning to the Serpent, is forbidden in Scripture.[25] The renewed interest both in the goddess, often depicted with a serpent and in Hindu *kundalini* meditation, which depicts personal spiritual energy as a serpent coiled at the base of the spine [see below], shows how much the fascination with diabolical knowledge has returned. This is particularly evident in the "rediscovery" of shamanism, the science of contact with spiritual knowledge.

I have on my desk a glossy magazine called *Shaman's Drum: A Journal of Experimental Shamanism.* Its editorial board has eighteen members, fourteen of whom have doctorates. This ancient occult practice is doing well in the sophisticated academic world of "Christian" America. Shamanism facilitates contact with the spirit world, and the spirituality accruing is power. Once the domain of the witch-doctor, shamanistic power is now available to all — at a small fee (major credit cards accepted). New Age guru and channeler, Lazaris, promises a significant return on your investment: "Conjuring Power: Engaging and Enlisting the Elements" is what your dollars buy. As the brochure explains:

> We seek a deeper, more beautiful spirituality. . . . Conjuring power, an ancient tool of the Shamaness and Shaman, an ancient secret of the mystic and the magician, is too frequently a lost art today. It sounds too clandestine, too "occult," or too old for most of us. [But] Lazaris will lift the essence of what it was and show us an incredible new way. A lost art can become a vibrant new tool in our lives and in our modern world where "practice is over."[26]

"Practice is over." The war has begun. Occult power is nothing less than the Serpent's seductive lie. The lie refuses to reveal to people the truth about themselves, and parades, in particular, as knowledge of the goddess, who holds out a glittering promise of personal transformation.

> Shamanism, inspiration, mysteries of drunkenness, vision, madness, ecstasy leading to expansions of consciousness — these are the transformative processes of the Goddess.[27]

Transformation: "No Fear"

This forbidden, occult knowledge is not powerless delusion. Evil is difficult to explain, but no one has difficulty understanding the phrase "the power of evil." The *New Age Encyclopedia* states that

> the New Age Movement can be defined by its primal experience of transformation. . . . Having experienced a personal transformation, New Agers project the possibility of the transformation not just of a number of additional individuals, but of the culture and of humanity itself. . . . (it) has (also) become a movement to heal the earth.[28]

"Christian" feminist Rosemary Radford Ruether recalls her "great excitement" when a course on comparative religion gave her a "new orientation" toward religion as a "metaphor for inner transformation" rather than as a body of revealed truth.[29] Christianity offers transformation, but *this* transformation is not Christian. It was "comparative religions," that is, paganism, that transformed Ruether. "You gotta serve somebody!"

NO FEAR!! scream the decals from tee-shirts and pick-ups. No fear of life, but especially no fear of death. In the union with the Higher Self and the spirit world, death, the ultimate "stress monster" is relativized. As the father in *Lion King* tells the young cub and future king, as well as millions of young Americans, death holds no fear because we are one with the evolutionary, life-giving process.

God lied. "You will not die." Here is the Serpent's promise of eternal life. "Eat and your eyes will be opened."[30] Occult knowledge is transformation into immortality. In this version, death is not the "sting" of the "last enemy."[31] There is no Hell. Death is not eternal separation from God. It is the "final state of growth . . . the awakening of the True Self to a higher reality." So says Elisabeth Kübler-Ross, with the help of her spirit-guide, Salem.[32] Many books on near-death experiences, including Christian versions,[33] describe death as a wonderful experience of peace, joy and light. We no longer need Lennon helping us imagine no Hell. Near-death experiences prove that there is only love and light.

We don't have to wait for death. Immortality is available now, in ecstatic moments of pure spirit. Says Elizabeth Clare Prophet, a "Christian New Age" teacher in Montana,

> You can pray, you can meditate, you can contact God. The God of very gods is within you. You can make contact if you will it so . . . Jesus is the open door to the individual Christ consciousness — the kingdom of God that is, even now, within you.[34]

Because *self*-transformation includes the transformation of human-ity and the planet, spiritual narcissism becomes altruism. Meditation on the self is selfless. It not only eliminates stress but saves the earth. Such is the promise and function of the new spirituality, but how is it prac-ticed?

The Practice of the New Spirituality

Like most human experiences, (with the exception of the dentist's chair), the new spirituality is both communal and individual. Usually the community initiates individuals into the secret methods which they then use for personal spiritual advancement. Just as true spirituality affirms both the "communion of the saints" in the church, and a per-sonal devotion to the Lord, so false spirituality has its "churches" and "quiet times."

Isis Visits Chicago

I managed to find a seat in the back left corner of the room, a long way from the door, and began to wonder whether my courage had ex-ceeded my wisdom. As an observer at the *Parliament of the World's Reli-gions*, I judged it important to observe as much as I could, so here I was in a seance/presentation of the Fellowship of Isis, a modern revival of the Egyptian cult to the goddess Isis. A frail but intense priestess from England, with pale skin — perhaps from countless drenchings of dreary British rain — now resplendent in white, began to recount the myth of Isis and her consort Osiris, as recorded in the ancient text *The Golden Ass*. Suddenly she was caught up in an ecstatic trance and spoke, in powerful wailing tones, a revelation in the name of Isis. Everyone then joined hands (I remained transfixed in my corner, trying to look incon-spicuous) in the circle of life, inhaling and exhaling deeply. It was then the turn of a young black American immediately in front of me to enter a trance-like state and utter his soul-devotion to the goddess. All eyes turned on him (and many on me!). Fortunately he was followed by a Japanese priest of Isis doing the same on the other side of the room. I pinched myself, remembering that we were in the luxurious Palmer House in downtown Chicago in 1993. I managed to slip out before the seance passed from the "first chamber," open to the world, into the "sec-ond chamber" for initiated Isians only.

An elaborate process, initiation includes the creation of new stories and rituals, and the acceptance of polytheism, and leads to a consciousness-raising experience that can only be called a "conversion."

♦ **New Stories:**

Even the modern pagan experience requires stories or myths to create a context in which spiritual initiation takes place. A number of the examples given below come from radical religious feminism. This is so for a number of reasons: feminism provides an encounter with the new spirituality; feminism is an especially powerful vehicle for the introduction of paganism into the church because of its belief in the equality of males and females; New Age prophets declare the Age of Aquarius to be the age of feminist intuition/experience, so it is not surprising that women are leading the crusade to create new images. Indeed the radical feminist claims special knowledge; her 'feminist consciousness' is a sort of *gnosis*, enabling her for the first time to give a true account of the relations of men and women;[35] feminists themselves gladly claim the leadership of the new religion;

♦ **Women Spinning New Stories**

Like few others, feminists recognize the importance of new myths, and are devoting great energy to create them. Women are "renaming," "re-imagining" the world from the feminist perspective. God, the "male" Father is "exorcised" in favor of the goddess. The language is strong, and so is the program. "Radical transformation" brings Scripture into line with feminist attitudes, and gives women a voice. Women are encouraged to write apocryphal Bible stories with women as heroines — that's right, just make them up![36] Genesis is re-interpreted to elevate Eve as the heroine, and the Serpent is celebrated as the true instructor in wisdom (see chapter 8). Creation includes the mysterious Lilith, known in Scripture as a "night hag" but now re-interpreted as Eve's higher self, who comes to her in the Serpent and liberates her from the control of Adam and God.[37] The program notes of a recent "Christian" feminist conference invites conferees to create a new symbolic world:

> TOGETHER — combining ancient text and modern dreams . . . dance, drama and ritual, we shall draw aside a curtain woven by patriarchal consciousness to reveal within each of us the Goddesses and the Wild Woman.
> TOGETHER we shall reckon with Her dark side and honor Her bright side. Related to one another, we shall draw Her energy into our souls and celebrate Her return to our lives.[38]

The products of such "Christian" re-imagining are often expressions of radical paganism. The following is a typical example, a prayer in poetic form to the unknown goddess, suggested as material for the renewal of Christian feminist worship:

> Lady, the unknown goddess, we have prayed long enough only to Yahweh the thunder god. Now we should pray to you again, goddess of a thousand names and faces, Ceres, Venus, Demeter, Isis, Dianna Queen of Heaven, or by whatever name you would be known.[39]

This poetic ritual, invoking many goddesses, was not composed "primarily for women who have moved beyond the structures of the Christian Church," says Anglican minister, William Oddie. It is published in a book which aims to create "materials for prayer, meditation and worship drawn from women's experiences of the holy to provide ways to *enrich the Christian tradition*." This material is offered, by women of impeccable (Christian) "establishment" credentials, as "an excellent resource for any congregation wishing to undertake the difficult task of changing the image of God in its liturgy."[40]

Rosemary Radford Ruether gives the now classic feminist line: "These new stories do not necessarily repudiate the old stories, but they may well enable us to reconceptualize them."[41] Presbyterian and Methodist feminists said the same when they worshiped the goddess Sophia in Minneapolis in 1993. A new book on experimental feminist worship, from the same radical perspective as that of the *RE-Imagining Conference*, claims only to be "revitalizing traditional liturgical expressions."[42] But as this poem makes so abundantly clear, such re-imagining was not enriching Christian conceptuality. Like most expressions of this new spirituality, it was an exercise in unadulterated pagan polytheism. When you join monism and theism, monism wins every time, for the God of heaven and earth will not share his glory with another.

The electronic gaudiness of the Las Vegas "Strip" and its larger-than-life casinos disorient the mind. In its unbelievably glitzy, fairy-tale atmosphere of constant fun and continuous daylight, people lose their bearings. Squandering hard-earned cash against impossible odds at the betting tables becomes strangely feasible.

Such is the function of the new stories. The new religion seeks to make its constructions perfectly believable, and everything before it a bad dream. This is the first phase of consciousness alteration. Step into the shimmering house of the gods, and you will be drawn into occult initiation, happy to let go the hard-earned cash of revealed truth and the rich experience of creational wisdom.[43]

◆ **Syncretistic Paganism**

There they stood at the opening ceremony — the gray-haired, distinguished Protestant professor of theology from a mainline seminary in his black doctoral robe with blue epaulets; the Roman Cardinal, resplendent in archepiscopal purple; the Buddhist monk with shaved head and saffron tunic; the high-priestess of the Fellowship of Isis in a white robe and a tall thin hat; the bearded Hindu guru robed in hues of orange and brown; the Jainist sister wearing a cloth mask to avoid swallowing a fly — a colorful sight of global religious diversity. An American Baptist clergywoman called for the forming of a circle, an interfaith Seminary project was announced, another women leading the discussion introduced herself as a "Jewish Hindu witch with Bahai Quaker leanings."

The principle that brought 6000 delegates from 150 religions to the *Parliament of the World's Religions* in 1993 was that the spirituality of all religions is the same. Ultimately, this is true. All pagan religions worship the creature rather than the Creator. Theologians in the World Council of Churches now declare the age of dialogue to be over and the time for mutual participation in pagan religion to be the order of the day.[44] It is ironic that "Christians" who have rejected the spirituality of orthodoxy, finally turn for spirituality to paganism. Rosemary Radford Ruether adopts Fox's pagan creation spirituality, the higher self, psychic healing, chakra mediation and hatha yoga exercises.[45] Virginia Mollenkott, who has dabbled in pagan and New Age practices suggests that people who are unsatisfied with orthodox spirituality consider "joining an alternate spirituality group, a witches coven, a Course in Miracles study group, or a twelve-step group."[46] Syncretistic spirituality is in the air. Observers of the Sixties' spiritual quest saw it coming:

> interest in the occult, in magic, in extraterrestrial life, in Hindu India and Buddhist Japan, in multidaemoned China, in sorcery, in new forms of multiple family life, in communes, in the 'new religions,' and many other alternative life-styles and meaning-systems which have been hitherto foreign.[47]

They may not have understood its underlying pagan coherence, just now surfacing. Feminists who seek to make creative additions to the Christian tradition find themselves up to their ears in pagan practices. Virginia Mollenkott "imagined" worship as "inter-religious," without abandoning "Christ" since the "term has proved to be acceptable to people from many other religious traditions."[48] But in syncretism the Christ of Scripture is history!

♦ **New Rituals**

New stories and openness to the spirituality of other religions produces new rituals. Miriam Starhawk, who teaches with the ex-Dominican, now Episcopalian Matthew Fox, is a goddess-worshiping pagan witch. Her book, *Spiral Dance* contains an account of *wiccan* ritual, defined as four procedures: 1) relaxation, 2) concentration, 3) visualization, and 4) projection or manifestation.[49] These stages are the goals of wiccan rituals, designed for creating altered states of mind and for practicing magic. Witches cast a "sacred circle" to create a "sacred space" or "portable temple" for the proceedings. Then they "go within" or "center the energy," in order to inform the "forces of the universe" that they are being called. This is followed by "raising energy," drawing it up from the earth through "guided meditation," dance or shouting. Later, the "energy" is "directed" through a "cone of power" to the object of "magick."[50] Such pagan witchcraft is an important aspect of much of contemporary radical religious feminism.

We shall observe in the next chapter that the ancient Gnostics frequented the mystery cults to share in the pagan rituals and discover the pagan experience of spirituality. We observe the same phenomenon today. A stark example comes from the Presbyterian publishing house, Westminster/John Knox. In a book entitled *Women at Worship* (1993) two Christian theologians, Marjorie Procter-Smith, Associate Professor of Worship in the Perkins School of Theology at Southern Methodist University, and Janet R. Walton, Associate Professor of Worship at Union Theological Seminary in New York offer "glimpses of the changing scene of women at worship" who are claiming "ritual authority."[51] They propose to the church and to women in particular, selections from radical Jewish and Christian liturgies as well as pagan and African animistic rituals "for the learning of a new ritual language."[52] The old Gnostic "Christians," participating in pagan cults for deeper spiritual lessons is clearly not just a past memory.

The article by Wendy Hunter Roberts, a "Pagan (Unitarian) Universalist," entitled: "In Her Name: Towards a Feminist Theology of Pagan Ritual," catches the reader's attention. The ritual takes place at night at Samhain, the classic wiccan celebration of the winter solstice, and begins with the casting of the sacred circle and the invocation of the god and the goddess via the chant:

Magic, magic everywhere, in the earth and in the air,
How to hold the magic here?
How to raise it up and bring it down?

Then a priest "invokes the Goddess . . . in the priestess," and the priestess "evokes the Lord of the Underworld into a priest,"[53] followed by welcoming of the "beloved dead" — Martin Luther King, Jr., Gandhi, Crooked Fox Woman, Elizabeth Cady Stanton (Creator of the *Women's Bible*, 1895), Margaret Sanger (founder of Planned Parenthood), and other worthies. Roberts notes that only the core initiates are permitted to enter "the holy of holies," for the symbol system is "sexually explicit" and "honors darkness and death," "birth and light," and "good and evil."

In the time of prayer, Roberts "call[s] out for protection of the Goddess's people from the wrath of right-wing fundamentalists and their God,"[54] but she recalls that while, in the past, "the patriarchal hordes" destroyed the temples and defamed the Goddess, there is great hope in the present. "Now we are returning."[55]

These pagans are returning within the church as well, as the appearance of this article from a mainline denominational publisher testifies. For many "Christian" feminists, a christianized form of witchcraft characterizes their new rituals, as Donna Steichen has demonstrated for the Roman Catholic Church. She shows how the nuns are now into crystal reading, dream work, tarot cards, and other New Age techniques for their spiritual quest.[56]

These techniques can be read between the lines in the liturgies practiced in Ruether's Women-Church. In "The Coming-out Rite for a Lesbian," which is described as a "new birth," the lesbian praises the goddess, Sophia:

It was [Dame] Wisdom who gave me true knowledge of all that is, who taught me the structure of the world and the properties of the elements, the beginning, end and middle of the times, the alternation of the solstices and the succession of the seasons, the revolution of the year and the position of the stars, the nature of animals and the instincts of wild beasts the varieties of plants and the medicinal properties of roots. All that is hidden, all that is plain, I have come to know, Instructed by Wisdom who designed them all.[57]

The themes in this prayer — knowledge of the elements, astrology, animals, herbal medicines and the joining of the opposites — are all found in witchcraft, where the manipulation of elements is known as the "Craft."

♦ Communal Ecstasy

Stories, rituals and witchcraft produce communal ecstasy. In the "first chamber" the Isis group at the *Parliament of the World's Religions* had already reached levels of spiritual ecstasy that caused me to head for the door. Another group studying new feminist rituals insisted that the doors be closed. I left that one just in time. Ruether describes what happens through the rituals:

> Awakening often occurs through mystical experiences in nature or with other women. . . . Awakening implies the ability to know or see within oneself, once the sleeping draft is refused. . . . For women, awakening is . . . a gaining of power . . . it is a grounding of selfhood in the powers of being.[58]

> Trust in yourself, believe in yourself. Bring that energy up, up, through your roots, into your body. Let it come in through the soles of your feet, rise up your body, all the way to your fingertips. That energy can handle whatever comes to you. All you need to do is call it up. Feel the power of that energy. Now allow that energy to spiral around your spinal column, rising . . . and then allow the energy to sprout out your head as branches . . . Feel your connection with the other women in the circle . . . Be aware that this circle is not complete without your energy.[59]

The spiritual experience of communal power bonds people together, and produce "conversion" or "awakening" or "altered states of consciousness."[60] "Once the individual feminist has been through the process known as 'consciousness-raising,'" says Oddie, "particularly by attending the women's groups whose purpose is to produce and maintain this psychological effect, it is not merely her understanding of social relationships which has changed, but her whole perception of reality. She has undergone a kind of *metanoia*, or conversion." Feminists themselves speak of "a *conversion* to matriarchal imagery."[61] The power of the group is an essential ingredient, but the new spirituality must also be a personal, individual encounter with the cosmic Oneness. It produces formidable energized opponents to traditional Christian faith.

The pagan Roberts describes the very heart of the pagan goddess ritual. When all is ready, the goddess Hekate enters the circle. Her presence produces healing. Roberts describes the experience: "I place my head on her lap. . . . A roar forms in my belly, catches in my throat, then tears its way out through my vocal cords. I feel the tightness leaving me. . . . I am released."[62]

The Individual Experience of the New Spirituality:
The Heart of the Matter:
Non-rational Experience

Phil Jackson, NBA coach of the year (95-96) rediscovered his faith by joining Zen Buddhism to the charismatic Christianity of his youth. In his book, *Sacred Hoops*, he credits Zen with clearing his mind of all the interference from Christian prayers and Bible verses, lodged in his brain since childhood. With his new-found "intuitive illumination of the mind and spirit through meditation," his heart is open again.[63] He teaches these winning principles to Michael Jordan, Scotty Pippen and Dennis Rodman. The formula works.

Ever heard of a charismatic Roman Catholic Hindu mystic? Here is the testimony of one concerning his disappointment with traditional forms of Christian devotion:

> I began to find mental prayer (discursive meditation) completely un-productive, and so . . . I stopped reflecting on the Scriptures during prayer . . . [which was] an immense obstacle to experiencing God. . . . Only total passivity to the kundalini experience brings serenity. Only then, too, is there a sense of God's presence.[64]

In the newly discovered Easternized form of "Christian" medita-tion, which seeks to realize the True Self, the "I Am," "there is a return to the cosmic experience of the Great Mother, as the "I" now enjoys the energies of the Dynamic Ground within."[65] "Kundalini dismantles the defense mechanisms. . . . Thus open to the Dynamic Ground, the Ego stands disorientated and eventually drops its conceptual ties."[66]

What is particularly Christian in this kind of meditation?[67] Deepak Chopra, an Indian Hindu medical doctor and immensely successful New Age guru in the USA, describes his supra-rational experience in a simi-lar way. In meditation, the higher self is "in contact with the cosmos and pure being, beyond the boundaries of rational thought and all distinc-tions which originate in nothingness and return there."[68]

This non-conceptual spiritual experience brings many into the en-slavement of spirits, for the witches have a very similar spirituality, and it indicates that one is not alone in the cosmic All. Listen to a wiccan chant:

> Know the mystery, that if that which thou seekest thou findest not within thee, thou will never find it without thee . . . For behold I Have Been With Thee From The Beginning. And I await thee now. Blessed Be.[69]

Just who is the "I" who has been there since the beginning? New Age channelers indicate that "going within" through the suspension of rational thought is the perfect means for spirit possession. The spirit entities, speaking through Ken Carey, make known their preference:

> We are unable to commune with humans whose vibrational fields are distorted by ego factors, emotional fields, excessive conceptualization, or past-future orientation.[70]

They prefer minds swept clean of rational thought. There, in the hollow promise of enlightenment, they make their abode. The mind that makes distinctions between right and wrong, true and false, good and evil has produced the mess; only a new supra-rational spirituality will save us.

Meditation

The centerpiece of the new spirituality is meditation, the individual self-discipline that allows access to the occult domain of spiritual power and liberation through the age-old techniques of Hindu practice. Though the fast track of drugs achieves the same result, passive meditation is less harmful to the body. The modern witches Sjoo and Mor tie the moon, sexual ecstasy [kundalini], and soma (a potent Indian drug) together, but the goal is the same — to reach "the still center of all."[71] Meditation silences the mind, allowing the soul to escape the body and to become one with the universe. Deepak Chopra describes the experience as being liberated from a space/time prison (the body) into the knowledge that "you are infinite and boundless."[72]

To get in touch with "unbounded reality" various techniques are used: repeated mantras (religious phrases such as "aum"), visual stimuli such as crystals, or chakra meditation, which identifies seven ascending points of energy within the body, beginning with the base chakra at the bottom of the spine and rising to a point just above the head. At this point, the soul experiences unity with the whole, with the All of the entire circle of cosmic reality, and the sense of endless time, ultimate power and total liberation and glorious immortality has been achieved.

Says Chopra:

> I . . . experience complete stillness where I am an unbounded, unconditioned, omnipresent field of awareness that transcends space and time. . . . a level of being (at which) . . . you are in touch with the cosmic computer. . . . (Meditation) take(s) a person to the level of spirit beyond the mind. . . . You actually have the direct knowledge

that you're not in your body and you're not in your mind: you're beyond both.[73]

The Moon goddess of witchcraft offers a taste of immortality in a "magic"
experience of the joining of the opposites, that is, like Chopra's experience, a sense of oneness with the all:

> The immortality promised by the Moon Goddess. . . . is *union of the
> opposites* within the psyche which brings release from the final power
> of death, which allows consciousness to pulsate from one dimension
> to another in the cosmic field [emphasis mine].[74]

Mollenkott calls her experience of enlightenment

> one distinct "holy instant" [a notion taken from *A Course in Miracles*,
> as she admits]. . . . like my Elder Brother, Jesus, I am a sinless Self
> travelling through eternity and temporarily having human experiences
> in a body known as Virginia Ramey Mollenkott. . . . Perhaps my Self
> has been on earth before in other bodies, perhaps not.[75]

Again, there is the unmistakable notion of humanity's "natural" unity
with the divine All, untrammeled by the divisive, dualistic concepts of
sin and death.[76]

Does meditation work? You bet it does. It would be a mistake to
think that people are merely staring at their navel and deluding themselves into thinking their navel is the very center of the universe. There
is occult power out there, and it can give a bogus sense of well-being.
When people talk of the "alteration of consciousness" or "conversion,"
they have had deep experiences of spiritual power. They have been
washed sometimes with hate, filled with empowerment, and their lives
are never the same again. Lazaris offers a three day intensive course
entitled "Beyond the Bridge of Belief: Achieving Permanent Change."
He boasts of power to break people of their past belief systems and open
them to create "a more beautiful present and a more incredible
future. . . of limitless possibilities." "In so many ways," he declares, "we
have already achieved permanent change. *Metaphysics works* [emphasis
mine]."[77]

Sexuality and the New Spirituality
Sex and the Spiritual Woman

Why did 2000 mostly middle-class, middle-aged women from middle
of the road, mainline Christian churches end their conference on imaginative spirituality, as they blessed the sacramental milk and honey of a

sort of Lady's Supper, with a hymn to the goddess that bordered on homosexual pornography? Read for yourself:

> Our maker Sophia, we are women in your image;
>> with the hot blood of our wombs we give form to new life.
> With the courage of our convictions we pour out lifeblood
>> for justice [a reference to abortion?];
> Our Mother Sophia, we are women in your image;
>> with the milk of our breasts we suckle the children;
>> with the knowledge of our hearts we feed humanity;
> Our sweet Sophia, we are women in your image;
>> with nectar between our thighs we invite a lover, with
>> birth a child:
>> with warm body fluids we remind the world of its
>> pleasures and sensations;
> Our guide, Sophia, we are women in your image:
>> with our moist mouths we kiss away a tear, we smile
>> encouragement:
>> with the honey of wisdom in our mouths, we prophesy
>> a full humanity to all the peoples;
> We celebrate the sensual life you give us:
>> we celebrate the sweat that pours from us during our
>> labors:
>> we celebrate the fingertips vibrating the skin of a lover.
> We celebrate the tongue that licks a wound or wets our lips:
>> we celebrate our bodiliness, our physicality, the sensations
>> of pleasure, our oneness with earth and water.[78]

While the Bible joyfully celebrates sexuality within marriage, there is absolutely no equivalent of this in the Hebrew or Christian Scriptures as a description of God, so this is "imagination" with a capital "I." How can people so much in the middle be so far into the extreme? As Donna Steichen has shown, mainline protestants "discovered" this kind of spirituality only because orthodox groups in the Presbyterian and Methodist churches blew the whistle.[79] But it has been a feature of feminist religious groups since the early eighties.[80] For some time Matthew Fox has defended sexuality, and in particular homosexuality, as playful worship.[81] For Fox, "there can be no renaissance without a mystical sexual awakening." In prose worthy of D. H. Lawrence, this "creation spirituality" theologian adds: "Love beds are altars. People are temples encountering temples. . . . Wings of Cherubim and Seraphim beat to the groans and passions of human lovers."[82] Someone has said that when beds become altars, altars quickly become beds, as ancient pagan orgies easily illustrate. But these notions are making a stunning comeback in contemporary American society and church. The modern day witch Miriam Starhawk, speaking in the name of the goddess, says: *"All acts of love and pleasure are my rituals."*[83] Virginia Mollenkott's book, *Sensuous Spirituality*, defends the spirituality of illegitimate sexual expression, while various speakers at the Minneapolis *RE-Imagining Conference* defended sex for children, and playful sex among friends as normative and healthy. These examples are but the tip of an enormous iceberg, a sort of religious/theological justification for the sexual liberation of the Sixties, and the beat goes on. Though the Presbyterian Church USA in its General Assembly of 1994, denounced *RE-Imagining*, a similar conference in June, 1994, at San Francisco's Episcopalian Grace Cathedral sounded the same note, as conferees were told to "discover and cultivate sacred Eros in all its ecstatic connections."[84]

We have reached a time when the "vain imaginations of the heathen" are masquerading as divine wisdom in the temple of God. Ecstatic perverse sexuality has always been a part of pagan spirituality. In age-old pagan witchcraft, as modern adepts recognize, "sexual magic was practiced, not for the sake of fertility, but for ecstatic self-transcendence, a sexual-spiritual fusion of the human with the cosmic All."[85] "Shamanism, inspiration, mysteries of drunkenness, vision, madness, ecstasy leading to expansions of consciousness — these are the transformative processes of the Goddess."[86] If human beings are divine, then sexual energy especially is divine energy, in whatever form it gets expressed. Sexual ecstasy is one more powerful way of accessing the non-rational experience of occult knowledge, where the mind and the conscience are put on hold. And if orgasm creates a fusion of the human with the cosmic all, is there any reason why perverse sex should not include bestiality?[87] Is this the logical conclusion of Matthew Fox's diatribes against "dualisms" which "oppose not only distinctions between mind and body but also those between creature and Creator. And between man and beast?"[88]

Snakes and Adders

Goddess worship is a continuum. Moderates have just begun to toy with this "new" faith, while radicals have plumbed its depths. At the logical end of the process is a strange but unquestionable relationship between the goddess and the snake. A major expression of ancient Gnosticism that adopted goddess worship, took the name Naasenes (Hebrew *naas* means snake), "the worshipers of the snake."[89] Also, one gnostic monistic symbol is a circle made from a snake with its tail in its mouth

— the Ouroboros, or world snake.[90] Generally, as Sjoo and Mor point out,

> Great live snakes were everywhere kept in the Goddess' temples during the Neolithic . . . she is represented carrying snakes in her upraised arms or coiled around her. Or, she was imagined as a serpent herself, with a woman's body and a snake's head. . . . The Sumerian goddess was known as the Great Mother Serpent of Heaven. . . . Everywhere. . . . the Goddess-Creatrix was coupled with the sacred serpent. . . . (in) Australia, Venezuela, the ancient Middle East . . . (the) South Pacific islands. . . . Ancient Celtic and Teutonic goddesses were wrapped with snakes" — as well as in China and Egypt.[91]

The snake symbolizes the "rebellious naughty mysteries" of the goddess, viz., "yoga, *kundalini* and spinal illumination,"[92] as well as eternal life.[93] "To the serpent was attributed power that can move the entire cosmos." And witches Sjoo and Mor add, pointedly: "And [still] does."[94] Everywhere "the serpent in paradise is pictured with a woman's head and breasts."[95] Is this possibly part of the meaning of the mysterious head of a beast carried throughout the *Re-Imagining Conference* in Minneapolis?

A radical Jewish feminist recently published a book with a strange title: *The Absent Mother: Restoring the Goddess to Judaism and Christianity*.[96] She restores Lilith, (see above) whom she describes as

> the transformatory serpent coiled round the Tree — the creature of the abyss — guardian of hidden knowledge (she knew the secret name of God) . . . [who] makes the bridge from the ineffable to the carnal.[97]

Modern witchcraft also rehabilitates the serpent as the source of spiritual and sexual energy.

> To deny the earth roots of the world tree is to deny the serpent roots of the spine. And indeed the biblical Hebrews set themselves against the serpent; in so doing, they were deliberately opposing the *kundalini* power of the spine, the sex *chakra* and the ancient brain stem.[98]

The energies generated by these techniques became power used to the benefit of all — which is the only way power can be safely used. Ancient legends speak of "the winged radiance of those who have achieved the dynamic equilibrium, the ecstatic union of the currents" — which is the description of those who have raised evolutionary energy, in the form of *kundalini*, the cosmic serpent, up through the spinal world tree of all manifest being, until it reaches the highest *chakra* of the human mind, becoming winged illumination.[99]

The amalgam of images from Genesis and Hindu meditation techniques might be unfamiliar, but the new spirituality is increasingly interested in "winged illumination." Kundalini meditation derives from Hindu Tantric yoga, which identifies the seven chakra points with sexual energy, known as Serpent energy. A serpent of sexual energy, coiled at the base of the spine, is aroused through meditation, and passes up the spine through sexual ecstasy, bringing the subject into cosmic consciousness.

Kundalini and the Holy Spirit are identified as East meets West at the base of the spine.[100] One writer explains the process: a. a sense of energy pulsating between the genitals and the base of the spine, and coming into the brain via the cerebrospinal fluid; b. an uncoiling of energy knots in the ears; c. an acute, intelligent sensuality; d. an internal energy body living in harmony with the physical body; i.e. realization of True Self, "I" (self-awareness) "Am" (Christ).[101]

The signs of kundalini at work are a "sensation of electrical energy rippling through the reproductive organs, and the inability to stay focused in logical-conceptual consciousness. . . . [as well as an] inner resistance to conceptualization."[102] In the true spiritual experience, "sexual energy becomes genitally diminished and more diffused throughout the body."[103] Clearly a mind which, through sex, goes beyond all dualisms of sexual distinctions and rational moral considerations, also gets beyond the limiting notion of sin.

A recent article in *Psychology Today*, the popular "bible" for today's well-informed therapists, offers advice for the sexually hung-up: "Throwing away the rule book and holding onto yourself can be framed as believing in the God within, believing that there is a good part of you inside. The bedroom becomes a place for spirituality to emerge. Spirituality is the application of faith to everyday life, including when you have your underwear down."[104] Of course, with no rule book, there are no limits and there is no sin.

Sin and Spirituality

> To consider nothing wrong was the highest form of religious devotion among them.[105]

This statement by a repentant member of the cult of Bacchus, preserved by the Roman historian Livy, early in the first century, A.D., could be applied with no exaggeration to the movers and shakers of the new spirituality at the end of the twentieth century. Just as in orthodox Christianity, there is a deep connection between spirituality and holiness — the Holy Spirit is the Spirit of holiness — so in a sort of distorted, perverted mirror image the new spirituality is tied to sin.

If sin has been banned from Anaheim's Crystal Cathedral — how can you talk about sin just a few miles from Disneyland? — we should not be surprised if it has been eliminated from Virginia Mollenkott's newly-minted "evangelical" faith. After employing various pagan methods of spirituality, she declares:

> Gone are traditional Christianity's emphasis on sin, guilt, and retribution; instead, we are empowered toward co-creatorship, welcomed to continual renewal on a continuous Great Non-Judgment Day.[106]

This sounds like a notable example of the "instant touch-down trick." Having difficulty scoring points? Just redefine the end-zone as the place where you stand, and lo and behold, you have won the game. With no sin, there is no guilt for Mollenkott's lesbian activity, which suddenly becomes "sensuous spirituality." She will not condemn those who engage in "promiscuous or easy [casual] sex,"[107] nor women who have abortions.[108] But the new spirituality goes beyond a refusal to judge others and oneself. It actually promotes sin.

In her book, *Pure Lust*, Mary Daly, Professor of Theology at Boston College, and perhaps the leading spokeswoman for lesbian witchcraft, in a section entitled "The Courage to Sin," points out that "sin" derives from a Latin word meaning "to be." For her, in other words, to exist is to sin. Daly is rewriting the English language in order to create her new, sinful world. One entry in her *Wickedary*, "sinarticulate" is defined as the ability to sin. For radical feminists of her stripe, "The tragedy of Christianity is that it has kept untold millions of human beings from sinning, i.e., from knowing their own souls."[109]

This new spirituality eventually demands total commitment by the committing of sinful actions, especially of a sexual nature. Our actions determine who we become, and disobedience imprisons us in sinful structures. While not all feminists are lesbians, radical feminism leads to lesbianism the way monism in general leads to androgyny and homosexuality. Daly herself believes lesbianism is "almost required by radical feminism," and admitted that "everything I write is an invitation to [lesbianism]."[110] Roman Catholic journalist and author, E. Michael Jones,[111] reports on a meeting of nuns for the purpose of promoting the ordination of women that ended with the nuns anointing each other's bare breasts with jasmine.[112] Janie Spahr, a Presbyterian lesbian minister, in her speech at the *RE-Imagining Conference*, claimed that her theology is first and foremost informed by "making love with Coni," her lesbian partner. She went on: "Sexuality and spirituality have come together and, Church, we're going to teach you."[113] This thinking is expressed by a lesbian nun in the early eighties:

> My spirituality has changed over the years. . . . my experience with feminist spirituality and the Goddess has affirmed my intuition that spirit and body are inseparable . . . Now my intimacy with Marie involves my whole spiritual/sexual self.[114]

This kind of sexual sinfulness can only lead to enslavement, to being "given over in the sinful desires of their hearts to sexual impurity for the degrading of their bodies with one another."[115] Sexual sins are called "sins against one's own body,"[116] no doubt because they sin against the image of God in the body God created for monogamous heterosexual sex.

The redefinition of sin does not involve only sexual sins. Abortion, the killing of defenseless children in their mothers' wombs, is redefined as a noble and necessary act of female empowerment, that puts blood on the hands of many, and forces them into a spirituality that can justify this modern, unprecedented "slaughter of the innocents." The following citation from radical feminism gives the ultimate explanation of the real stakes in the abortion issue — that of spiritual power:

> If it is not to be too late for all of us, all women — on a global scale[117] — have got to regain our ancient ontological power — and intuitive skill — for making life-and-death decisions. . . . This is the real challenge presented by feminist issues, including abortion rights. . . . When women begin to define our own lives, including being ontologically responsible for each life we choose to bring — or not bring — into the world, then women will become fully functioning *definers of the world.* And then we will be fully responsible for the kind of world, the spiritual and physical quality of world, into which we bring new life.[118]

The new spiritual woman claims the right to determine future life on this planet. She adopts a monist view of reality in which there are no absolutes and no clearly-defined good or evil. For her, life does not begin in the womb but always is and comes from the far recesses of the universe. It has to do with mystical power of life and death.

> Women describe experiences of being pregnant, of knowing and feeling and believing that it was not the right time or circumstance to have a child; they speak of going into meditation, or into their dreams,

and speaking to the fetus as one sacred being to another. This is not the right time or space for us to be together. Please leave now. At the right time, we will meet again.[119]

Here it is. The occult knowledge that claims to define good and evil, kills a baby in cold blood in the name of spiritual health.

This is the true face of the new spirituality, whether people realize it or not, which, through mystical *gnosis,* joins opposites,[120] stands above the moral absolutes of right and wrong, and creates a genocide. The sheep follow, fed lines like "right to choose," "right to privacy," and "the population time-bomb."

If the new spirituality, behind the warm fuzzies, makes your blood run cold, it should.

The Eschatological Re-Eating of the Apple

Inevitably, this spirituality of sin develops its own sacraments which, with hardly any attempts at subtlety, turn the biblical notion of sin on its head. Women-Church practices a new baptism where "the initiate descends unclothed" into the waters.[121] The symbolism here, as in Gnosticism is both to celebrate eroticism and to affirm human innocence. But the sacramental revisionism gets much more explicit. In a vivid playing out of the rejection of the patriarchal "myth of original sin" and Eve's "victimized" place within it, the Women-Church community celebrates the "blessing of the apple," saying:

This is the apple of consciousness raising. Let the scales of false consciousness fall from our eyes, so that we can rightly name truth and falsehood, good and evil.[122]

Here is Nietzsche's "transvaluation of values," through which evil becomes good and good evil. Incredibly, the very act of original sin in the Garden of Eden is now elevated as the sacrament of gender liberation. Under the guise of Christian freedom, sin and spirituality are ritually wedded. At the *RE-Imagining Conference,* one of the speakers held up an apple, bit into it, and then with cheers from the audience asked, "What taboo have you broken today?"[123]

A semi-"sophomoric" gesture, as one commentator condescendingly suggested?[124] Not a bit of it. In their rebellion, these women, especially the leaders, are not sophomores. Their experimental sacrament stands as a perfectly accurate symbolic expression of the neo-Gnostic feminist apostasy from biblical Christianity ravaging many of the mainline churches, from which the American church may never recover. Never have we so needed the lessons of ancient Gnosticism.

CHAPTER 15

GNOSTIC SPIRITUALITY

Anyone who "has worn the flesh" will not be saved, but the ones who "know themselves will enter the kingdom of heaven.
- *Apocryphon of James*[1]

Death: The Gnostic's Best Friend

Death is not the last enemy. It is the Gnostic's best friend. A cosmic Kevorkian, Dr. Death comes as a *spiritual* "health provider" for the termination of an unwanted physical body. In the Gnostic system death *is* victory,[2] the final triumph of the spirit over matter, the ultimate undoing of God the Creator's evil work. Death is the luminous hallway into the radical freedom of disembodied spirits who have broken free from the restraining power of the physical body. Says the Gnostic specialist, Kurt Rudolf,

> redemption . . . is first realized by the gnostic at the time of his death, for at this moment he encounters the everlasting, reawakening fact of release from the fetters of the body, and is able to set out on the way to his true home.[3]

The Mandeans, a particular sect of Gnostics, called death "the day of escape" (or "release").[4] At death the divine spark sheds the hindrances of the body and returns to its place of origin in the divine Being.[5] Says one Gnostic text: "When all the elect lay aside bestiality (bodily existence) then this light will withdraw up to its essence."[6] This moment of liberation is not simply a future hope. What the soul experiences at death is the full payment of what the Gnostic has already attained in life through gnosis — knowledge.

Gnosis

Did you gnotice? In pronouncing the word gnosis (the "g" is silent as in "gnat")[7] one is at the center of the Gnostic system. Gnosticism is a movement centered on *knowledge* (the "k" is also silent!). Of course, all systems of thought claim knowledge, but Gnostic knowledge is neither technical, scientific, logical nor philosophical. The *Tripartite Tractate* warns against Greek knowledge of "philosophy . . . types of medicine . . . rhetoric . . . music or . . . logic . . . [which leads to] confusion."[8] This text teaches that people are *incapable of knowing* the truth because they draw the line at the visible — both Jews and pagan philosophers never get beyond faith in the Demiurge (the Creator) because "the powers themselves seem to hinder them (appearing as if they were the Totality)."[9]   In other words, the God of creation fools people into thinking that there is nothing beyond his sphere of authority. The result of this subterfuge is that most people never experience true knowledge.

Gnostic *gnosis* unlocks the heavens. It transforms, redeems and liberates the human being from the hum drum world of the body into cosmic flights of spiritual ecstasy. This knowledge is not dry theory. It is religious experience.[10] As the *Gospel of Truth* states of the true believer:

> if he has knowledge (*gnosis*), he is from above. If he is called, he always hears, answers, and faces the one who calls him, and goes up to him. And he knows in what way he is called. Possessing knowledge, he always does the will of the one who called him, he desires to be pleasing to him. He is given rest. The names of each come to him. The one who will have knowledge in this way will know from whence he is come and where he is going.[11]

This is the knowledge of true spiritual reality — the knowledge of where one is going.

It is also knowledge of oneself. The "Jesus" of the *Apocryphon of James* reveals true knowledge to the disciples. Any one who has "worn the flesh" will not be saved, but the ones who "know themselves" will enter the kingdom of heaven.[12]

According to the *Gospel of Truth*, self-knowledge and knowledge of God are one and the same. Those who know the Father, the incomprehensible and inconceivable God, have discovered him in themselves.[13]

Aristotle said about initiation into the pagan mysteries of his day that at the final stage there was no more "learning" but only "experiencing," producing a change in the state of mind.[14] An expert on the ancient pagan mysteries that formed the model for Gnostic spirituality also sees the importance of transformation. "Mysteries were initiation rituals of a voluntary, personal, and secret character that aimed at a change of mind through experience of the sacred."[15]   This is what religious pagan Greeks and Romans got from their mystery rituals. A contemporary observer, the Roman historian Dio (c.155 - 229 A.D.) gives some indication of the spiritual expectations accompanying an initiation: "something is bound to happen in the soul." Thus the "initial bewilderment of the candidate is changed into wonder, and acceptance of sense."[16] This is clearly *gnosis* as transformation.

A popular writer on the New Age, without any explicit reference to ancient Gnosticism, describes the contemporary movement of mystical spirituality in just the same way: "salvation for the New Ager is equated with *gnosis* (experiential knowledge). It is self-realization or the realization that one's true Self is God."[17]

The Bible distinguishes between faith and sin; submission and rebellion. Gnosticism pits *gnosis against* faith. The *Paraphrase of Shem* speaks of "the impure practice of faith."[18] According to Rudolf "faith plays only a provisional role . . . relative to knowledge."[19] Gnosticism desires (occult) *gnosis* just as Eve desired the forbidden fruit and the occult knowledge that would make her like God — hence the Gnostic fixation with Genesis 3 and its counter-reading. She refused to have faith in the word of God, and was seduced by the promise of direct knowledge, by which the world would be reconfigured — not according to God's order, but according to the diabolically-inspired human pretention to immortal selfhood.

Disavowing biblical revelation and its divinely-created handmaid, human reason, this *gnosis* puts the believer in touch with the hidden mysteries that lie within the soul.

The Goal of Gnostic Spirituality:
Union With the Divine

And it (the end) is the receiving of knowledge concerning he who is hidden, who is the Father. From whom came the beginning, and to whom all shall return who proceeded from him.[20]

Gnosticism uses the classic terms of monism, as it holds out the possibility of full identification and union with the divine. A much-employed expression to evoke the divine reality is "the Totality," and

God is referred to as "the Father of the Totalities." The goal of existence, according to the *Testimony of Truth* is "knowledge of the All."[21] Such knowledge leads from multiplicity to unity,[22] and, hence, to union with the unknown Father. "The whole order of the aeons," says the *Tripartite Tractate*, "has a love and a desire for the perfect, total discovery of the Father and this is their unhindered union."[23]

Beyond the Polarities

The very essence of this ancient heresy is the blissful confusion of Man and God. Thus, in union with the All, one simultaneously meets oneself, for the self, as we have seen, is God. Hans Jonas speaks of the "identity or consubstantiality of man's innermost self with the supreme and transmundane God, himself often called 'Man'."[24] In other words, the search for God is the search for self. However, the *Gospel of Truth* indicates what happens when the self finally meets the Gnostic God. Such a union is ultimate personal, physical, and, no doubt, individual *dissolution*:

> Eventually Unity will complete the space. Each one will attain himself inside Unity, he will cleanse himself from numerosity into unity through knowledge, his internal substance being consumed as by fire. . . . But from that time on (death), the outward form no longer appears, but it will fade away in the union of Unity, for now their works lie scattered.[25]

This dissolving of the many into the one, the annihilation of difference and individuality is a classic theme of mystical monism. Why is it in the so-called dualistic system of Gnosticism?

The present bishop of the Ecclesia Gnostica of Los Angeles, Steven Hoeller, a twentieth century Gnostic, affirms the monistic character of his faith, describing the spiritual experience Gnosticism offers as communion in the "dark sea of deep consciousness."[26]

The Elements of Gnostic Spirituality

Destruction of the Created Order

All deviations from God's creational design must deconstruct the "natural" order and recreate life in terms of their own desires. Thus in our day, homosexuals have an influence far beyond their actual numbers in intellectual circles, in the media and the arts. In these fields that help define reality, there is the opportunity to recreate the world by bringing down "heteropatriarchy" and making normative the homosexual view of the life. A similar program is espoused by radical feminists. This deconstructive and recreative activity finds spiritual resources in the new spirituality in which marginals see themselves as "shamans." Not surprisingly, a similar program characterizes the spirituality of ancient Gnosticism.

Contemporary writer Philip Lee believes that Gnosticism has returned in our day to disfigure Christianity. He notes that

> for the gnostic personality, religious knowledge (knowledge of God) could never be discovered in terms of earthly pilgrimage. Knowledge of God required the exact opposite, *a turning away from this world.*[27]

Rudolf says the negative spiritual agenda of ancient Gnosticism included "the progressive stripping off of everything associated with the earthly body."[28] Lee sees the Church Fathers as a Scriptural model of true Christianity:

> The Fathers . . . were no less spiritual than those who claimed a higher spirituality; what so radically distinguished them from their opponents was their determination to see the eternal through the God-given temporal gifts of creation.[29]

For Gnostic spirituality to flourish, God-ordained temporal gifts, especially rationality, have to go. *Gnosis* gave the Gnostic an understanding of the "non-existent" God beyond the visible world.[30] The future for the enlightened soul, according to the *Tripartite Tractate*, would be

> an entry into that which is silent, the place which has no need for utterance nor for comprehending nor for forming a concept nor for making light but (where) everything is light while they have no need to be lighted.[31]

If this is true of the post-death existence, it is true of the spiritual life of the Gnostic on earth, as the "Jesus" of the *Apocryphon of James* commands his disciples: "Be filled with the Spirit, but be lacking in reason (logos)."[32] Non-rational spirituality is a foretaste of the Gnostic heaven. The convenient short-circuiting of reason is based upon the Gnostic's claim to supra-rational experience. This explains the mystical nature of Gnostic writings as well as the importance of mystical meditative techniques as an essential component of spirituality.

As we have noted, the rejection of reason is part of the general rejection of bodily existence. Rudolf rightly notes: "the Gnostic must prove that he is a Gnostic by the rejection of the body before he can know final redemption."[33] Some Gnostics were vegetarians for that reason.[34] Many were ascetics, as the Nag Hammadi texts show. Some engaged in sexual license, as the Church Fathers document, as a way of shaking their fist at the Creator of normative sexuality. This, of course, is where sexuality and spirituality overlap.[35] The Gnostics say this very clearly.

Not so in our day. Major changes in sexual norms and practices, pushed by a massive agenda of religious/pagan monism, are surreptitiously justified, not as issues of religion (which would be prohibited by the logic of church/state separation), but as non-religious issues of "civil rights." Many unconsciously slip into a *religious* redefinition of existence by their "political" acceptance of an egalitarian, anti-patriarchal and pan-sexual vision. The unseen religious agenda of undifferentiated sexuality is actually monistic union of the opposites within the impersonal divine.

Present Spiritual Technology

A foretaste of that union in immortality is experienced in the present, physical existence, as a "call." "Thus, if [the Gnostic believer] has knowledge," says the *Gospel of Truth*, "he is from above. If he is called, he always hears, answers, and faces the one who calls him, and goes up to him."[36] This ascent of union is anticipated even in the aborted fetus of one's body. Philip Lee notes, correctly that "The gnostics were able, at least to their own satisfaction, to accomplish in Houdini-like fashion a successful exit from the cosmos prior to physical death."[37] Filoramo identifies the "fundamental experience" of Gnosticism as "the visionary moments of ecstasy . . . [of the] divine reality [which] cannot be known through the ordinary faculties of the mind."[38] Ecstatic experiences, both communal and individual, prepare the Gnostic for that final release from the body and ascent to the Father of the Totalities.

Communal Ecstasy: The Gnostic Sacraments

Like the pagan mystery religions which they studied and frequented, the Gnostics engaged in highly secretive initiation ceremonies, the details of which are only suggested by our texts. The authors of the recent book, *Ancient Christian Magic* (1994) call these sacraments "rituals of ascent" in which the Gnostics developed their "practices of ritual power."[39] "Initiation in general," says Burkert, speaking broadly of the ancient pagan mystery cults, "has been defined as "status dramatization" or "ritual change of status."[40] The goal of sacramental initiation, in other words, is spiritual and mystical transformation. Irenaeus observes that in Gnosticism "there are as many redemptions [sacraments of initiation] as there are mystery-teachers of this doctrine."[41] The *Gospel of Philip* enumerates five such sacraments: "a baptism and an anointing and a eucharist and a redemption and a wedding chamber."[42] The very existence of five consecutive sacraments suggests progressive ascent into the depth of mystery. Nothing is known of the sacrament of redemption, so we shall comment on only four.

◆ Baptism Unto Perfection

The baptism in question is not Christian baptism, representing the removal of sins, through the death of Christ. Rather the Gnostics invented another baptism, based on the words of Jesus—"I have another baptism to be baptized with."[43] This they claimed to be a secret, mystical baptism of perfection bestowed by Christ on Jesus,[44] and revealed only to his true followers. For this reason, they argued, you could not find it described in the pages of the Bible.

◆ The Anointing

Beyond spiritual baptism "into perfection," the *Gospel of Philip* mentions the sacrament of the chrism (anointing) which is superior to baptism, "for it is from the word "chrism" that we have been called "Christians."[45] Though we are not told much about it, this anointing with oil served as a special redemption ceremony, and functioned as a prerequisite for partaking of the communal meal and entry into the *pleroma*, the highest mystery of all, "The Holy of Holies," the bridal chamber.[46]

◆ The Lord's Supper With a Twist

Not surprisingly, the Gnostics also modified the central sacrament of orthodoxy, the Lord's Supper. How interesting that today we discover a renewed desire to tamper with the Lord's Supper. In the *Gospel of Philip*, the flesh and blood of Christ, a part of the physical creation so detested by Gnostics, were re-interpreted as "the word" and the "Holy Spirit," given to the perfect Gnostics who have realized oneness with the divine.[47] In a Gnostic text not found in the Nag Hammadi Library, the *Acts of Thomas*,[48] prayer at the eucharistic table invokes "perfect compassion . . . intercourse with the male . . . and [the] hidden Mother."[49] This is theological tampering. Some Gnostics, using the same theology, went to quite radical extremes.

Epiphanius gives an account of the Ophite/Naasene (the worshipers of the Serpent) version of the Lord's Supper:

> They have a snake which they foster in a particular box; at the hour when they perform their mysteries they coax it out of the hole, and whilst they load the table with bread, they summon the snake forth.

When the hole is open, it comes out . . . crawling onto the table and wallowing in the bread: this, they claim, is the 'perfect offering.' And that is also why, so I heard from them, they not only "break the bread" in which the snake has wallowed, and offer it to the recipients, but everyone kisses the snake on the mouth, once the snake has been charmed by sorcery. . . . They prostrate themselves before it and call this the 'thanksgiving' (eucharist).[50]

To modern ears, such a ceremony appears grotesque, but one of the great fathers of modern psychology, C. J. Jung, saw in the snake a representation of the "extra-human quality in man. . . . The cold-blooded, staring serpent, express[ing] man's fear of the inhuman and his awe of the sublime, of what is beyond human ken."[51] Modern versions of the Eucharist do not include the snake, but the "re-eating the apple" at the end of the Supper in Rosemary Radford Ruether's Women-Church, in its gnosticizing inversion of the Genesis account, reveals a theology that is potentially just as radically "serpentine."

♦ **Degenerate Ancients:**[52]
The testimony of Epiphanius, the fourth century church father, concerning the "eucharistic" celebration of the Borborians, is often dismissed as exaggeration, phantasy, and vicious slander.[53] This is possible. In his favor, he expresses a strong sense of Christian piety and personal holiness, and claims to have been compelled to attend such an initiation as a young twenty year old on a visit to Egypt. In sum, he professes to being an eye-witness, and a number of independent witnesses corroborate his testimony.[54] According to Epiphanius, the Borborians began their Lord's Supper with a gastronomical agape, a lavish meal accompanied by plenty of wine. Then followed "the Agape with the brother," in which married couples split up and had intercourse with other members of the group. Since conceiving would be imprisonment in the structures of the Creator, *coitus interruptus* was practiced. The male emission was then held heavenward with the prayer: "This is the body of Christ," and then eaten. If a woman were to become pregnant, the fetus was aborted, and eaten, accompanied by the prayer: "We were not mocked by the archon of lust, but have gathered the brother's blunder up." This they called "the perfect Passover."[55]

Again, the modern reader is shocked. But today we worship a god of unlimited human freedom through condom-aided *coitus interruptus*. Fetal murder of holocaust proportions is the greatest ecological disaster the world has ever known. Our neo-Gnostic devotion only lacks Christian eucharistic terminology — and doubtless that will come. We, too, shake our fists and our twisted technology in the face of the

God of creation, radically disfiguring, with the gifts he has given us, the world he made.

◆ **The Bridal Chamber: Spirituality and Sin**

What went on in the bridal chamber was, as in the pagan mystery cults in general, a very well-kept secret. Rudolf believed that the Valentinians prepared a bridal chamber "after the image of the conjunctions (syzygies — [the joining of the opposites]) which is held in contrast to normal marriage as the "unsullied marriage."[56] In this conjunction the soul returns to "the arms of her partner or ideal prototype . . . [which] is the decisive event at the end of time."[57] Doubtless some form of enactment of this final conjunction took place in the bridal chamber.[58] Filoramo speaks of the individual Gnostics being "reconstructed in androgynous unity" in the bridal chamber.[59]

At one level, this spirituality appears ascetic and world-denying. "Unpolluted marriage," says *Philip*, "(is) a true mystery. It is not of the flesh but pure. It belongs not to desire but rather to the will. It belongs not to the darkness or the night but rather to the day and the light."[60] This claim to purity notwithstanding, what went on in these spiritual bridal chambers is anyone's guess. This, readers will remember, is the *Gospel of Philip* which recounts that Jesus often kissed Mary Magdalene, the converted prostitute, on the lips.[61] The phrase, "One will cloth himself in this light sacramentally in the union," implies spiritual and perhaps physical nakedness.[62] If the only clothes worn were "perfect light," and physical contact with a woman is held up as the model Jesus leaves his disciples, then the allegations of the Church Fathers make a lot of sense.

As noted above, *Philip* declares that the bridal chamber is reserved for "free man and virgins." In other words, like the non-Christian pagan mysteries, these initiations are secretive and private.[63] Dio, the Roman historian, also notes the secretive element to the pagan mysteries. "At best," he says, "we are in the situation of eaves-droppers, of strangers at the gate"[64] — or, in modern terms, detectives.

So, who were the "virgins?" Epiphanius in his description of the Borborians, called virgins "women who have never gone on to the point of insemination . . . but are always having intercourse and committing fornication."[65] Admittedly the Borborians who joined together the two "sacraments" of the eucharist and the bridal chamber were no doubt the most radical. But some form of sexual compromise does not appear out of the question, given the context of Gnostic theology in general. Should one be tempted to think that this was limited to the radical extreme, Epiphanius also notes that less radical groups like the followers of Basilides also practiced "promiscuous intercourse."[66] Irenaeus and Hippolytus do also. And of course, such activity began with one of the earliest of the Gnostic heretics, Simon the Magician.[67]

This lurid information is not for shock value. It illustrates the program of deconstruction of normative, marital, child-producing sexuality. Indeed such deconstruction is served by both radical asceticism and libertinism. No doubt some Gnostic sects were ascetic, particularly the group that collected the Nag Hammadi texts.[68] Perhaps most of them were. But others, according to the Church Fathers, went to sexual excess.[69] This latter option serves two functions. It flies in the face of God the creator, and it reproduces ecstasy through sexual orgasm, which is well-documented religious pagan practice. Epiphanius says of the Borborians: "They never have their fill of copulation; the more indecent one of their men is, the more praiseworthy they consider him."[70] Some Gnostics who, as Hippolytus asserts, joined in the pagan mystery religions, probably rivalled them in sexual excess. The Roman historian, Livy, recounts comparable sexual orgies in the initiation ceremonies to Bacchus. He cites their justifying principle: "To consider nothing wrong . . . was the highest form of religious devotion."[71] How incredible that a group claiming to be Christians would have had no difficulty saying "amen" to this radical pagan notion. Indeed, the Gnostic group called the Cainites said as much, according to uIaeus:

> Not otherwise can one be saved than by passing through every action, as also Carpocrates taught . . . At every sinful and infamous deed an angel is present, and he who commits it . . . addresses him by his name and says, 'O thou angel, I use thy work! O thou Power of such and such, I perform thy deed!' And this is the perfect knowledge, unafraid to stray into such actions whose very names are unmentionable.[72]

What a powerful example, in an ancient text, of the joining of sin and spirituality that we find so prevalent today.

Irenaeus further observes that

> According to their writings, their souls before departing must have made sure of every mode of life and must have left no remainder of any sort still to be performed: lest they must again be sent into another body because there is still something lacking to their freedom.[73]

Whether ascetic or libertine, such freedom stems from the rejection of God as Creator and Law-giver, and from a radical commitment to overturn creation's structures. The apostle John, who knew some form of early Gnosticism, issues a damning judgment against all such deluded people: "No one who continues to sin has either seen him [Christ] or *known* him."[74] Gnosticism affirmed the very opposite. Its religious experience is actually *generated* by acts of sin. John names this too. "He who does what is sinful is of the devil, because the devil has been sinning from the beginning."[75]

Whether sexual ecstasy was part of every Gnostic bridal chamber ceremony, ecstasy of a more spiritual nature (union of the opposites) seems to have been produced in the chamber, perhaps by the chanting of strange mantras. According to Irenaeus, the following words are pronounced in the marriage ceremony:

> [I baptize you] into the name of the unknown Father of the universe, into Truth, the Mother of all, into him who descended upon Jesus, into the union and redemption and participation of the powers.

Then follows a repetition of bizarre words: "Basyma cacabasa eanaa irramista diarbada caëota bafabor camelanthi . . . . Messia ufar magno in seenchaldia mosomeda eaacha faronepseha Iesu Nazarene."[76]

◆ Redemption: Stages/ascent though Meditation

Mantras are an important element of individual mystical meditation. *Gnosis* was also an intensely personal affair. The challenge of spirituality is immense. Gnostics saw themselves as imprisoned in a physical body and then surrounded by at least seven[77] concentric circles stretching out into the cosmos before them, each representing various levels of illegitimate authority of the principalities and powers instituted by the great Archon/Ruler, the God of Creation. According to the theory, the soul is escorted by beings of light, and goes through the seven horrific domains where Christians, monks, apostate Mandeans and other unworthies are held, until it reaches the world of light.[78] "In departing this world," recounts Epiphanius, "the soul makes its way though these archons, but no one can get through them unless he is perfect in this knowledge."[79] The knowledge serves as a password, at the passage of each circle or aeon. Irenaeus describes the soul's journey: "when they come to the Powers, they are to speak as follows: 'I am a son of Father, of Father who is preexisting. I am a son in the Preexisting one. I have come to see all things that belong to me and to others.'"[80] Each soul has its own "helper" or spiritual "counterpart" who reassures the ascending soul: "I shall cause you to ascend and keep you safe in my garment," which is a garment of light.[81] Clearly spirit guides are not the invention of New Age spirituality.

The Process:
Tasting Monistic Union Now

Again we ask, is this final journey through the stars the only journey of the soul? Certainly re-incarnation is present in the Gnostic texts,
so that imperfect souls have to do it again, and again, and again.[82] However, in the light of contemporary New Age spirituality, which gives ample
documentation concerning earthly mystical experience, it would appear
that the Gnostic soul *already in this life*, through meditation, made the
"trip," if only imperfectly. Hindu and New Age meditation, the reader
will recall, also proceed via the number seven — *seven* chakra points in
the body, whereby the spirit/soul mounts up and out of the limitations
of physical existence into the eighth domain of spiritual freedom on a
regular basis.

In the Nag Hammadi text *Zostrianos*, a document deeply influenced
by the Eastern magical mysticism of Zoroastrianism,[83] the teacher,
Zostrianos,"presents a series of revelations made by exalted beings regarding the nature of the heavenly realm."[84] Zostrianos advances from
one stage to the next through initiatory baptisms, progressing in spiritual insight through *seven* stages and then enters into the eighth and
finally the ninth of perfect knowledge. He recounts his experience of
the ascent of the soul, but in the past tense. A number of fascinating
statements have a modern New Age ring. "He (the power from a holy
spirit higher than God the Creator) came upon me alone . . . I saw the
perfect child [a "higher self?"]." Every one of the seven baptisms puts
one in "the path to the Self-Begotten One." Towards the end of the process Zostrianos states, in terms similar to the claims of those who have
successfully penetrated to the spirit world through meditation: "I was
[standing] above my spirit, praying fervently to the great Lights." He
finally arrives at the "simplicity of the invisible Spirit within the ninth
[which is] unity." At the end of this journey, Zostrianos declares: "I saw
how all these (the Hidden Aeon, Barbelo/Sophia) and the Unknown
Spirit) dwell within one."[85] In a word, the mystical experience is none
other than divinization: "I became divine."[86]

To reproduce this process, the master leads the disciple in a prayer/
chant of vowels and nonsense words: Zoxathazo a oo ee ooo eee oooo ee
ooooooooooo ooooo uuuuu oooooooooooo ooo Zozazoth.[87] After this
there follows an ecstatic state, and a vision of the divine mediated
through the master. "The Discourse closes as the master instructs the
student to write his experience in a book . . . to guide others who will
"advance by stages, and enter into the way of immortality . . . into the
understanding of the eighth that reveals the ninth."[88]

A similar use of mystical techniques, mantras and seals is found in the *Second Book of Jeu*, a Gnostic text not found at Nag Hammadi. The adept is initiated into a "baptism by fire" by saying the following prayer: "Make Zorokothora Melchizedek come secretly and bring the water of baptism of fire of the virgin of the light, the judge. Yea, hear me, my father, as I invoke your imperishable names." There then follows a list of undecipherable, mystical names for God: "Azarakaza A . . . Amathkratitath, Yo Yo Yo Amen Amen Yaoth Yaoth Yaoath Phaoph Phaoph Phaoph etc."[89] These esoteric names, of which there are many more, seem to represent a disengagement from rational speech, and thus aid in the process of the ascent through meditation. This method of spirituality is not Christian. Indeed, it is specifically repudiated by Jesus in his teaching on prayer.[90]

This journey of the soul through the heavens, similar to the one the Paul of the Gnostic texts makes to the *seventh* heaven and beyond,[91] becomes the basis for the exhortation to all Gnostic believers to follow the same path.[92] "Release yourselves, and that which bound you will be dissolved." It seems quite probable that the journey of the soul at death is therefore the final experience of the soul in life who has sought through initiations and meditations to escape the confinements of the flesh, even if for only limited periods.[93]

This mystical spirituality of present, temporal and final escape from the body is the very antithesis of Christian spirituality. As Philip Lee rightly notes about Christian discipleship: "Absolutely no escape from this tangible world of sensory perception is allowed. Salvation from the world by any other route than through the world will be called a fraud."[94]

Mystical Magic

If this spirituality is not Christian, what are its origins? We have noted that, "Christian" Gnostics frequented ceremonies of the pagan mystery cults, adopting and/or spiritualizing the sexual perversions of the Goddess cults.[95] Hippolytus states that:

> The entire system of their [the Sethian Gnostics] doctrine . . . is (de-rived) from the ancient [Greek pagan] theologians Musaeus, Linus and Orpheus, who elucidate especially the ceremonies of initiation, as well as the mysteries themselves. For their doctrine concerning the womb is also the tenet of Orpheus; and the (idea of the) navel . . . is (to be found) with the same symbolism attached to it in the Bacchanalian orgies of Orpheus.[96]

This is confirmed by Irenaeus:

> the most perfect among them shamelessly do all the forbidden things, . . . Food sacrificed to idols . . . they are the first to assemble at every heathen festival held in honor of the idols for the sake of pleasure.[97]

Much of "Christian" Gnosticism, through its contact with Graeco-Roman mystery cults, was a self-conscious variant of non-Christian mystical paganism. "Mystical thinking," says the modern polytheist, David Miller, describing its hoary history:

> begins with the mystical mathematics of Pythagoras, moves counter-culturally through metaphysical theologies and not a few heresies (gnosticisms of several sorts), comes to manifest itself in Pietism after the Reformation, and ends in various forms of Romanticism, from some nineteenth-century literatures in England and Germany to men and women fascinated by sensitivity training, Don Juan, the Yaqi sorcerer, and the *I Ching*.[98]

Hippolytus and Epiphanius accuse a number of the Gnostic systems for having taken their theories and mystical speculations from the Greek mystical mathematician, Pythagorus (581-497 B.C).[99] Pythagoras is believed to have gone to India where he was initiated into the spiritual ideas of Hinduism, and into the notion that the true self was "an occult self."[100] Through Pythagoras, in particular, and no doubt by many other connections,[101] Gnostic spirituality includes the crucial ingredient of pagan, monistic Hinduism.

The other significant element is Egyptian goddess magic. As we have already noted, Thunder/Sophia, the feminine principle of revelation, declares: "[I] am the one whose image is great in Egypt." The connection is appropriate since Isis was the Egyptian Goddess of Wisdom,[102] that is, the Goddess of magic.[103] A scholar of Isis notes that the magic of Isis is "real wisdom," since it consisted of insight into the mystery of life and death. . . . Thus wisdom was to the Egyptians equivalent to the capacity of exerting magical power."[104] Initiation into her mysteries and the ecstatic secret experiences in her temples gave adherents a foretaste of transformation into immortality.[105]

We possess but one text (already cited) from the ancient world that describes initiation into the pagan cult of Isis. In the satirical novel written by Apuleius entitled *Metamorphoses, or The Golden Ass* (first century A.D.), the hero recounts:

I approached the frontier of death, I set foot on the threshold of
Persephone [death], I journeyed through all the elements and came
back, I saw at midnight the sun, sparkling in white light, I came close
to the gods of the upper and the nether world and adored them from
near at hand.[106]

This account has all the ingredients of contemporary "new age"
experiences — light, union with the all, in a near-death experience.[107]
Such tangible occult spirituality, which appears to be the very center
of Gnostic spirituality, is dabbling in some form of pagan manipula-
tive magic.

The Witness of Contemporaries

Tertullian accused the Gnostics of meddling in magic. "They hold
intercourse with magicians, charlatans, astrologers and philosophers and
the reason is that they are men who devote themselves to curious questions (curiositati)."[108] Earlier, nIreus made the same accusation against
the Simonians. The "mystery priests" and every member of the Simonian
school "performed sorceries":

They practice exorcisms and incantations, love potions and erotic
magic, familiar spirits and dream-inducers, invoking those demon
companions (typical of Greek magic) who send dreams, and whatever
other occult things exist, and are zealously cultivated among them.[109]

While it is fashionable nowadays to accuse the "heresy-hunting"
Church Fathers of exaggeration, support for their allegations comes from
an unusual source, the pagan philosopher, Plotinus (205 - 270 A.D.),
who was scandalized that the Gnostics would use "exorcisms," "appropriate utterances," "melodies," "shrieks," "whisperings and hissings with
the voice."[110] Many Gnostics, says Rudolf, "fostered a cult of images,
even owning statues of gods such as those found among the archeologi-
cal remains of mystery cults."[111] We must conclude that the fathers were
right and that pagan magic was a significant part of Gnostic spirituality.
As Gnosticism is rehabilitated as authentic Christianity, we should not
be surprised to see a similar spirituality of magic and the occult re-enter
the church, in particular through the goddess of pagan wisdom.

Conclusion

The Gnostic revolt against the God of Scripture and the resulting
search for a "new" spirituality finally led many so-called Christians into
a demonically-inspired religious occult paganism. Stripping the Old Tes-

tament God from New Testament Christianity did not fill the church with the Spirit of Christ, but opened her doors to the religious pagan agenda of sexual ecstasy, idols and spirit-inspired magic — about which the silenced Old Testament had a lot to say. In a vision recalling what now goes on in living technicolor at the Cathedral of Saint John the Divine in New York City, and in many other places of "christian" worship, the prophet Ezekiel is taken to the Temple in Jerusalem[112] where he sees:

♦   in the entrance north of the gate of the altar, the statue of a pagan god to provoke God to jealousy;

♦   near the gate to the forecourt of the Temple, in a secret room, seventy lay elders, the official representatives of the house of Israel, usurping the function of the priests, engaging in esoteric practices of pagan worship to unclean idols;

♦   at the north gate, a woman prostrate before the Babylonian nature god Tammuz;

♦   in the sanctuary, between the holy place and the altar of burnt offerings, (a traditional place of penitence), twenty five priests,[113] with their backs to God, facing East, worshiping the pagan Sun god.[114]

There is nothing new under the sun. This worship of idols in the very Temple of Jahweh, this searching for light from the East, says the Old Testament commentator, Walter Zimmerli, represents the "unsurpassable height of blasphemy,"[115] against which God's wrath inevitably breaks out with unremitting severity.[116] To these idolaters who know the truth, and deliberately spurn it, God pronounces a woeful judgment: "I will deal with them in anger; I will not look on them with pity or spare them. Although they shout in my ears, I will not listen to them."[117]

Just as in ancient Israel, so in the early Church, the mystical pagan spirituality of Gnosticism promised believers occult knowledge and human freedom. How many, then as now, were seduced by the glittering half-truths of salvation without sacrifice, redemption without repentance, triumph without crucifixion. How many, then as now, fell knowingly or unknowingly into the power of the great seducer, the "one wiser than them all," whose wisdom masked a lie of cosmic proportions hurtling its adepts to death and destruction. How many will rise up now and warn our spiritually up-beat generation of its dead-beat direction and its foolish ways — before it is too late?

CHAPTER 16

CONCLUSIONS

Nothing is going to delay the Goddess's second coming.
- Caitlín Matthews, pagan priestess[1]

Short-Term Future — The Sophianic Millennium

The God of the Bible locked in mortal combat for the souls of men with the goddess of revived paganism — who would have imagined such a scenario in civilized, Christian America at the end of the twentieth century? In the last thirty years so many leaders in the news media, entertainment, business, national and international politics, the judiciary, academia and even the Church, have turned for personal renewal to a spirituality that they think is compatible with their past but which at every major point is diametrically opposed to Christianity. Anti-Christian forces have always stalked the church's earthly route, but rarely has religious paganism entered into the temple of God with such bravado and virulence as it has in our day — except, perhaps, at the time of Gnosticism.

What can stop the short-term triumph of this pagan religion both in its Christian and non-Christian forms, with its agenda of tolerance for all, and of planetary peace? Few in the church and the popular culture realize the enormity of the revolution going on around us. The Age of Aquarius, if one is to believe the leading spokeswomen of the movement, is nothing less than the "Second Coming of the Goddess," or the Sophianic Millennium, the era of goddess blessing and worship when all peoples and faiths will be united around the Divine Feminine. "It may be," says Isis priestess Caitlín Matthews, "that Sophia is about to be discerned in much the same way as she was in first century Alexandria: as a beacon to Christians, Jews, Gnostics and Pagans alike."[2] Sophia is the divine Savior who will lead humanity into another, more peaceful and loving civilization because She will lead us out of "the delusion of duality" and into the "marriage of humanity with Nature" and finally into marriage with the Divine.[3]

The time for this program is now. According to Matthews, "Sophia has been inching her way into popular consciousness throughout the latter half of the twentieth century." She goes on: "Those born in this century are now prospective citizens of the New Age, . . . where spiritual orthodoxy will be replaced by spiritual adventure, [and]. . . where the Divine Feminine will lead the way and where women will rediscover and enter their power."[4] This, Matthews argues, is already happening in the changes that affect gender-roles and spirituality in present Western society.

Even without the apparent help of goddess spirituality, national, tax-paid programs at all levels of society deconstruct traditional gender "stereotypes" and produce a new and profoundly egalitarian view of sex, by which, one day, women may take power. When that happens, the biblical male God will appear as an archaic anachronism revered only by right-wing marginal neanderthals. Sophia will take power, unopposed.

Queer Millennium

A minor variation on the coming age of bliss is the sophianic millennium seen through the eyes of a homosexual. The Rev. Nancy Wilson, senior pastor of the homosexual Metropolitan Community Church in Los Angeles, who calls herself a "lesbian ecu-terrorist" (ecu = ecumenical), proclaims a "queer theology" justifying all sexual choices, that can lead all Christians, gay lesbian, and straight, into the next Queer millennium.[5] Virginia Mollenkott, the "evangelical" lesbian applauds her work as a "stunningly important, both for our tribe [gays and lesbians] and for any other person, church or organization that seeks to be whole."[6]

One way or another, the star of the Religious Left, with an appealing social agenda in its train, and the support of many international organizations, is in the ascendent in contemporary American society. One of the great secular world historians, Sir Arnold Toynbee, in mid-century, at the height of the cold war and the expansion of Communism, made a surprising prophecy. He predicted that the twentieth century would be remembered as the time of the first appearance of the great universal religion of the third millennium blending Eastern religions and

Christianity.[7] Christians at ease in modern Zion should realize that there is a tide in modern history and that it does not appear to be going their way.

A New Creation or a New Fall?
Neither of the Above!

As we stand on the threshold of the new millennium are we moving towards a "new Creation?" Are we headed for a repetition of the Fall? Or will history continue with its ups and downs without any significant change of intensity? The example of ancient Gnosticism suggests that as we enter the Age of Aquarius, the eschatological Eve stands transfixed once more before the tree of forbidden knowledge, seduced by the "wisdom" of the Serpent through whom speaks the goddess. Lilith, the serpentine Sophia, dangles before the modern woman the titillating fruit of autonomous freedom and power as the modern Adam, like the first, looks on in silence, afraid to say a word.[8]

In one of the most politically incorrect statements of all time, the inspired Apostle Paul declared: "Adam was not the one deceived. It was the woman"[9] Paul surely does not mean that Eve was intellectually inferior, morally weak and spiritually immature. Rather he sees that in her role, so essential to the project of civilization,[10] and in her function as "helpmeet," so crucial for the revelation of the trinitarian God, Eve was exposed with particular force to the bewitching promise of self-liberation.

How clever the Tempter's misuse of Scripture. And Hollywood's too. In her new CD *It's A Man's World: Oh, Really?* popular singer Cher kneels in a seductive pose, her jet-black hair intertwined with a green serpent wrapped seductively around her body, clutching in her long fingers a bright-red apple. The modern Eve eats, convinced she is clarifying the true intentions of the Gospel for radical liberation. But if the original sound of the bite reverberated through the cavernous halls of the universe, signaling the imminent Fall from paradise, what will be the significance of the feminist liturgical sound bite of the eschatological "re-eating of the apple," if not the final catastrophic disobedience and deconstruction of the race?

American Dream or Planetary Nightmare?

Beyond culture wars and gender wars are *Spirit Wars*. In this ultimate struggle for mastery, the pagan goddess Sophia seeks to usurp the place of God the Creator and Redeemer. This is not colorful hyperbole. The conflict is real, the protagonists irreconcilable. Sophia is the very opposite of the God of the Bible. She represents monism as God represents theism. Her all-encompassing, encircling womb gives expression to the pagan notion of the divinity of all things, while her name, Sophia, vaunts the human claim to wisdom. With exquisite subtlety she seduces the modern mind by claiming to be tolerant and non-dogmatic. In fact she is neither, for behind the velvet glove is an iron fist; behind the neopagan rejection of doctrine is a firm commitment to a non-negotiable dogmatic belief in the unity of all things to which humanity and the planet are ineluctably headed; and behind the tolerance is a global system of unimaginable totalitarian possibilities which cannot tolerate the discordant voice of biblical theism.

Utopian thinking and the pagan spiritual experience on which it is based obliterates the truth that there *is* a cosmic conflict, that there *is* a deep antithesis between the Law of God and the ways of fallen man. The new eschatology sees history moving to its appointed evolutionary rendezvous with human liberation and "redemption." Aided by a leap in consciousness, humanity will evolve from its present immaturity into a new world order of peace and love. Of course, people who attains a "leap in consciousness" cease to perceive the need for objective salvation. Virtual salvation through human engineering and pagan spirituality will do just fine. In such a utopia, breaking the spell by the preaching of the Cross will not be tolerated.

Pagan monism is, by its very nature, an all-inclusive, totalitarian movement whose success depends upon total conformity to its view of peace. Its vision of a tolerant, all-inclusive world cannot tolerate those who believe in absolute truth, in ultimate right and wrong, and in differentiated creational structures. In the future "utopia" there will be "no place for truth." Surveying the totalitarian stance of the politically correct orthodoxy on university campuses, where dissent to the official line is just not tolerated, Philip Johnson wonders if we are not being given a chilling preview of an era of "self-righteous bullying."[11] With little ultimate harm, school bullies control the playground; adult bullies, in matching shirts, can turn a democracy into a police state, and wreak unimaginable harm on fellow human beings. The "Karma Patrol" of today could be the Great Inquisition of the Aquarian tomorrow.

While the Clinton White House describes the twenty-seven openly practicing homosexual members of its administration as "gentle people," there is another, scarier side to this sexual palace revolution. In a widely circulated article called "Gay Revolutionary," the anonymous author, "Michael Swift," warns the straight community, in prose that chills the spine:

We shall be victorious because we are filled with the ferocious bitterness of the oppressed who have been forced to play seemingly bit parts
in your dumb, heterosexual shows throughout the ages. . . . We too
are capable of firing guns and manning the barricades of the ultimate
revolution. . . . Tremble, hetero swine, when we appear before you without our masks.[12]

Psychologist Peg Thompson, author of the book *Finding Your Own
Spiritual Path,* after documenting what she calls the contemporary movement of "spiritual individualism," concludes by wishing she could be
around in a hundred years "to see how things turn out."[13] Her naive
inquisitiveness, like the optimism of many within and without the
church, does not betray the slightest fear that a return to paganism could
produce one of the most radical and costly revolutions in human history. For when people make freedom from God and his laws the highest
good, they become enslaved to the lie. This becomes obvious in the
radical expressions of the movement. Diana Beguine, once a Christian now witch, celebrates her freedom from the Gospel of the Cross
and the law of God, by singing "A-mazing Grace . . . That saved a
Witch like me. I once was lost, myself I found, was bound, but now
I'm free."[14] This freedom leads to diabolical chains.

There is another side to the picture of gentleness, peace and love.
The hubris that tries to save the self, by flaunting the laws of the Creator, leads in fact into slavery to evil. A repentant former member of a
Wicca group has described her experiences in terms that strip away any
illusion of harmlessness and genuine freedom:

When I was a witch, I performed rituals. I evoked spirits. I called
entities. I cast spells, burned candles, concocted brews. . . . But where
did it lead to? Into darkness, depression and the creation of an aura of
gloom around me. I was frequently under demon attack. The house
where I lived was alive with poltergeist activity . . . due to residual
"guests" from rituals. My friends and family were afraid of me. I
knew I had no future; all I had was a dark present. I was always
wanted. It wasn't Satan's fault. He didn't exist — or so I thought. I
gave it all up, and came to Jesus on my knees . . . .He freed me from
the oppression and gave me back my soul — the one I had so foolishly given to evil in exchange for power. . . . Our salvation was
bought at a great price and all we have to do is reach out for it. But
we cannot serve two masters.[15]

The new spirituality contains power, and for those sufficiently committed to it, it is a power that binds — with great chains. Perhaps the
most significant foremother of the new spirituality is Madame Helena

Blavatsky, a Russian princess who, at the end of the nineteenth century, sought to unite Western occultism with Eastern spirituality, and claimed she was in touch with "ascended masters." Madame Blavatsky, whose major work, interestingly, was entitled *Isis Unveiled,* left Russia for the United States where she established the Theosophical Society in New York in 1875, and then set up an ashram in India. In 1884, unburdening her soul to an old Russian friend, Vsevolod Soloviev, whom she met in Paris, she said the remarkable following words:

> I would gladly return, I would gladly be Russian, Christian, Ortho-
> dox. I yearn for it. But there is no returning; I am in chains; I am not
> my own.[16]

The trouble with this freedom is that it is slavery to the powers of evil. Its glittering promise is the same old lie. Its wages lead to personal dissolution and death. But it is a *real lie,* spoken by the Father of Lies. Those who hope to exploit it to serve ideological ends are, in the powerful image of Donna Steichen, like foolish, perverse, vulnerable children, playing with a plastic bomb as though it were Silly Putty.

The Great Conspiracy

This book is not a "conspiracy theory." It does not intend to accuse anyone, whether liberal or progressive conservative, of orchestrating a diabolical plot. If there is conspiracy, it is far greater than any individual or group of individuals could imagine. Rather, the above pages intend to set side by side the various "progressive" agendas, (whose proponents may not even see the connections), in order to indicate their deep compatibility and then to compare the result with the ancient Gnostic system for independent confirmation. Under the light of scrutiny, a profound coherence appears in the multi-hued fabric of diversity: pagan monism. This broad pattern will not account for the myriad particularities, qualifications and inconsistencies of any given position. But in a time of moral, spiritual and theological confusion there is a need to see the broad picture and the ultimate stakes.

A New Age Pope?

Vatican expert Malachi Martin sees it, from his perspective within the Roman Catholic church. In a work of fiction, *Windswept House,*[17] Martin describes an "unspoken alliance" between liberal forces in the

Vatican (who equal the traditionalists in the Curia, but hold the positions of power), and international humanist organizations like the United Nations. Their desire is to change church doctrine on divorce, contraception, women priests, abortion and homosexuality. This powerful alliance is preparing to elect a pope who shares their liberal, globalist agenda. Martin dismisses the notion of conspiracy. It is just a fact that these people inside and outside the church share the same liberal vision for the planet. It is also a fact, admits Martin, that his novel is not fictional at all.[18]

At the deepest level, the issue rending our civilization is not "commitment to change" versus "nostalgia for the past," nor is it even the conflict between proponents of heterosexuality and those who promote pan-sexuality. Rather it has to do with the age-long antithesis between the woman and her seed and the Serpent. For the "ferocious bitterness" of feminists and gays is ultimately directed not against "straights" but against God, the Creator of heaven and earth who made Man male and female. We recall the words of Abraham Kuyper regarding the deep antithesis within human history: "Do not forget that the fundamental contrast has always been, is still, and always will be until the end: Christianity and Paganism, the idols or the living God."[19]

As she covers her anemic body with a fake robe of Christ, Sophia begins to look more and more like the harlot of the Apocalypse,[20] that startling image of an apostate Church, fornicating with the kings of the earth, drunk with the blood of the saints and the martyrs of Jesus. On the threshold of the third millennium, the *Spirit Wars* have begun in dead earnest, though at present we have only seen the initial skirmishes. Sophia is only at the beginning of her reign.

Long-Term Future

I have reached the end. This has been a hard book to write. Doubtless I have stood on toes and unnecessarily offended well-meaning people, for which I humbly beg forgiveness. But I could not avoid putting pen to paper. For five years since moving to the United States, I have felt the oppression of error masquerading as truth in a land that for so long has been a citadel for the Gospel. The urge to warn my fellow brothers and sisters has been heavy upon me and kept me at my desk longer than anyone should sit at a desk. I firmly believe, though I pray I am wrong, that we are witnessing the first signs of an assault against the truth of Christ the likes of which the church has never seen before. Orthodox Christian faith, instead of being celebrated as the backbone of the West is now dismissed as its lunatic fringe. As Western civilization, with America in the lead, lurches away from its spiritual moorings, what has constituted its center for so long is now, in our generation, being dismissed to the edges as an embarrassing marginal extremism.

The burden of this book is to expose the growing apostasy around us. In that sense it is a wake up call. I have not given many answers, for I am not sure we have heard all the questions yet. This is surely not a time for quick fix-it solutions. I have not set out the Christian alternative.[21] I have rather looked into "the abyss of madness," to use the words of Irenaeus, to describe how so many professing Christians seem to be hell-bent on leading the bride of Christ into the lap of Satan. I have tried to make mine the motivations of the Church Father Hippolytus, who sought to expose the heresy of Gnosticism for two reasons:

♦ **to show Christians what is truth and what is error:**
He set out the heretical beliefs in order that believers:

will be assisted by our discourse to become more intelligent, when they have learned the fundamental principles of the heresies . . . (and that) they shall be on their guard against those who are allowing themselves to become victims of these delusions.

♦ **to win those who are themselves teaching heresy:**

by proclaiming the folly of those who are persuaded by (these heterodox tenets), we shall prevail on them to retrace their course to the serene haven of the truth.[22]

Hippolytus understood the heart of the God of the Bible. Calling to apostate Israel to forsake her "adultery with wood and stone," the Lord, with longsuffering love invites this wayward nation to turn and to repent.[23]

Post tenebras lux

The motto of our forebears in the faith, "After darkness, light," should encourage Christians to believe that the light will always triumph over the darkness, and that the gates of Hell will not prevail against the church.[24] Christians must remember that God's kingdom will not come by physical violence and the use of the sword. In the war of the spirits, the weapons are also spiritual. And among those weapons is love of our enemies. This is the way Jesus prevailed. This is the way his church will prevail.

The message of this book is ultimately not discouraging. There is great darkness in the Church today. She disregards the Scriptures, she drags the name of God the Father in the mud, she mocks and spurns the gracious redemptive work of the eternal Son and makes sin the principle of life.

But the seductive lie is not in control of the situation. In its very nature as deception and counterfeit it cannot help but cause the light of the truth to appear in greater splendor. Looking at false teaching makes the Gospel even more convincing, and examining the lie causes the truth to sparkle in all its radiance, and with greater intensity. God promises this to his people: "Even in darkness light dawns for the upright."[25]

Such is the challenge to Christians who will live and witness in the Age of Aquarius. This is a program of *action* for God's people at the threshold of the third millennium — to engage in an act of deep understanding as to the nature of truth and falsehood in our day, and to be faithful Eves and courageous, loving Adams who incarnate obedience to the God of Scripture, Creator and Redeemer, and who by the power of the Spirit celebrate the presence of the coming Kingdom in godly families, holy lives and unflagging evangelism. For, in the words of Hippolytus, those who "have learned the fundamental principles of the heresies," are the ones who will stand firm in the darkness. They will be able to "warn the sinner of his wicked ways."[26] They will stand as watchmen on the walls. They will keep the flame of the Gospel burning brightly in an hour of great apostasy,[27] until, at God's appointed time, at the certain rendez-vous of the Son with the nations, the truth will blaze forth, across the planet and the cosmos, in the final word of universal confession — in terms paternal, indeed patriarchal — that "Jesus Christ is Lord to the glory of God the Father."[28]

> Thy kingdom come that earth's despair may cease
> Beneath the shadow of its healing peace:
> Lift high the cross, the love of Christ proclaim,
> Till all the world adore his sacred name.[29]

End Notes

Preface
  1. John Lennon, *Skywriting by Word of Mouth* (San Francisco: Harper and Row, 1986), 35. I am indebted to Alan Morrison, *The Serpent and the Cross: Religious Corruption in an Evil Age* (Birmingham, UK: K & M Books, 1994), 67, for this reference.
  2. An editorial in *The New York Times*, reproduced in the Escondido *Times Advocate*, July 8, 1994, A-7.
  3. *The Los Angeles Times*, July 6, 1994.
  4. Genesis 3:15.
  5. The title of a recent book: *After Patriarchy: Feminist Transformations of the World Religions*, ed. Paula Cooey (Maryknoll, NY: Orbis Books, 1991).

Chapter One
  1. Marilyn Ferguson, "Aquarius Now . . . Making it Through the Confusion Gap," *Visions Magazine*, July, 1994, 7.
  2. Cited in Morrison, *The Serpent*, 119.
  3. The severe correction in the midterm elections of 1994 was only a ripple on the surface. A number of politicians are glad to be identified as *fiscally* right wing, but very few, even in the Republican party, are willing to call themselves *socially* on the Right. In 1996, a third of the Republican Party opposed the traditional Republican stand against abortion, and another twenty-five percent were not sure. It is here, of course, where the true revolution has taken place — in societal and human moral values.
  4. In his controversial book, *Unlimited Access: An FBI Agent Inside the Clinton White House* (Regnery, 1996), retired FBI agent Gary W. Aldrich, responsible for security at the White House during the first term of the Clinton administration, paints a picture of a new kind of presidential staff. It scorns the protocols of the past and is open to drug use. (Some staff members have histories of serious illegal drug use — see *Human Events*, July 12, 1996, 1. Symbolically, the White House abolished the drug office during Clinton's first term — ibid., 20). The staff also rejects FBI security procedures relative to personal background checks and the use of classified documents. According to Aldrich, William Held Kennedy III, Associate White House Counsel, in explaining to Aldrich why he encountered such resistance to background checks of White House personnel, said: "these people are just a little different from the crowd you're used to working with. They do not like telling strangers about their personal business. They think it's too intrusive." (See excerpts published in *Human Events*, July 5, 1996, 12-14). A strong Clinton supporter, Eleanor Clift, Washington correspondent for *Newsweek*, said on the Larry King Show of July 1, 1996, corroborating the picture Aldrich paints of the Clinton administration: "we all knew that there were hundreds of aides who did not get their clearance. This was a new generation, some of them did have a drug history, and they were lax about getting that thoroughly reported" — cited ibid., 3. According to an independent source, twenty-one White House staffers "entered a special testing program because of recent illegal drug use" — *Associated Press* reported in the *San Diego Union Tribune* (July 17, 1996).
  5. Part of the title of a sociological study by Annie Gottlieb — *Do You Believe in Magic? The Second Coming of the 60s Generation* (New York: Times Books, 1987).
  6. These are the well-crafted words of Cal Thomas, see *World*, April 23, 1994, 12. Of course, what I say in this chapter concerning President Clinton should be in no way seen as personally or politically motivated. As a person, Bill Clinton is a child of his times, and what is true of him is true of so many of his generation. For instance, the

young Clinton in 1972 ran the George McGovern campaign in Arkansas, the presidential candidate whom the Republicans at that time derided as "the candidate of the three A's: acid, amnesty and abortion." In 1972, with the nomination of McGovern, the New Left of the Sixties revolution took over the machinery of the Democratic Party. Their attempt failed but succeeded twenty years later. In 1992, finally one of their generation, "with their values" entered the White House — see Thomas J. Herron, "Aids Awareness as Established Religion," *Fidelity* vol 14/10 (October, 1995), 26, 29. That this is not a political observation is proved by the fact that the keynote speaker National Convention of the Republican Party in San Diego, 1996, was Susan Molinari, congresswoman from New York, who is pro-abortion and admitted to smoking pot in her student years.

7. Marilyn Ferguson, "Aquarius Now," *Visions Magazine*, July 1994, 7.

8. While a poll administered by *People for the American Way* in 1994 showed that more than half of the American people believe that our problems stem from a decline in moral values, and that seventy-four percent would be more likely to vote for a candidate who put top priority on returning to traditional moral values, it is also true that seventy percent of Americans no longer believe in absolute truth, so that a return to traditional values is strictly impossible — *World* (September 24, 1994), 8.

9. As an example, the government's *Goals 2000*, which sets the agenda for public education up till the year 2000, includes such noble-sounding aims as: "All children in America will start school ready to learn," and "United States students will be first in the world in mathematics and science achievement." Unfortunately, these goals and the others in the list presuppose healthy, two-parent families, and this is not the case for the majority of children.

10. Humorist Fran Lebowitz, cited by Suzanne Garment, *L.A. Times*, January 24, 1993.

11. Garry Wills, *L.A. Times*, January 24, 1993.

12. According to Ram Dass (Richard Alpert) in a public lecture in San Diego on May 18, 1993.

13. Marianne Williamson, *A Return To Love: Reflections on the Principles of 'A Course in Miracles'* (New York: HarperCollins, 1992).

14. According to the *Chicago Tribune*, Tuesday, December 20, 1994, 2.

15. *Parliament of the World's Religions: Program Catalogue* (Chicago: 1993), 119-120. In her lecture, Jean Houston described her regular meetings during her adolescence with Pierre Teilhard de Chardin, an excommunicated Jesuit priest who is considered one of the seminal thinkers of New Age spirituality.

16. Bob Woodward describes this incident in a forthcoming book, *The Choice*, recommended for reading by the White House. See Sonya Ross, "White House Defends First Lady's Use of Spiritual Advisers," *Associated Press*, reported in the *San Diego Union Tribune* (June 23, 1996).

17. Gillian Russell Gilhool, "More on Beijing," *Wellesley* (Spring, 1996), 1.

18. *Associated Press* reported in the *San Diego Union Tribune* (July 17, 1996). In a hearing before the House Government and Reform Committee several FBI agents testified that in 1993 between thirty and forty of the Clinton White House staff had recently used drugs including cocaine, hallucinogens and crack, according to *Human Events* (July 26, 1996), 1. This fact suggests a relationship with another fact. A recent report (August, 1996) indicates that during the period 1992-1996, the use of drugs by teenagers has increased by seventy-eight percent. An administration that takes drugs will not stamp out the drug plague.

19. Michael Lerner, often seen around Washington these days as one of Mrs. Clinton's ideological gurus, was the leader of the Berkeley SDS in the Sixties, and at his first marriage, the wedding cake bore the inscription "Smash monogamy." This Jewish radi-

cal reappeared at the end of 1995 as part of a the left-wing evangelical sit-in protest against the Republican project to balance to the Federal budget by streamlining the welfare system. Pushing the notion of co-belligerency to new levels of compromise, both he and Tony Campolo were arrested by the same police detail!

20. Ken Carey, *The Starseed Transmissions* (Harper, 1982), cited in Morrison, *The Serpent*, 155.

21. Marilyn Ferguson, "Aquarius Now," 7.

22. The phrase is from Roger Kimball, *Tenured Radicals* (San Francisco: Harper and Row, 1990).

23. Michael Bauman, "The Chronicle of an Undeception," *Culture Wars* 1/7 (December, 1995), 17.

24. This should in no sense be taken as defense of the misuse of patriarchal power, but the misuse of judicial power does not necessarily mean the dismantling of the judicial system, which is our only defense against the chaos of lawlessness.

25. As reported in *World*, July 2, 1994, 19.

26. See two excellent discussions of deconstruction: Gene Edward Veith, *Postmodern Times: A Christian Guide to Contemporary Thought and Culture* (Wheaton, IL: Crossway, 1994), 47-70, and Charlene Spretnak, *States of Grace: The Recovery of Meaning in the Postmodern Age* (San Francisco: Harper, 1991), 233-244.

27. Jerry Rubin, *Do It* (New York: Simon and Schuster, 1970), 249.

28. Indeed, many New Left adherents have abandoned the old ideology, but especially the political ideology — see Peter Collier and David Horowitz, *Destructive Generation* (New York: Simon and Schuster, 1990).

29. The "Stonewall" riot of 1964 in Greenwich Village where homosexuals resisted a police sweep of this famous gay bar, is revered as a defining moment for the homosexual movement.

30. In his book, *The Politics of Meaning: Restoring Hope and Possibility in an Age of Cynicism* (New York: Addison-Wesley Publishing Company, 1996), Lerner shows himself to be a true postmodern as he attacks liberalism/modernity from the Left and from the "high" ground of the new spirituality.

31. The *Los Angeles Times* (July 6, 1994) calls upon readers to let themselves fall into summertime lust, since this is only natural.

32. *Playboy*, which Hugh Hefner began in the fifties, is now one of the more conservative and mainstream of the pornographic literature available today.

33. NAMBLA (North American Man-Boy Love Association) in 1994 managed to be included in the Stonewall 25 gay/lesbian parade, sponsored by the City of New York. Meanwhile, a San Diego Superior Court judge ruled that the Boy Scouts may not exclude homosexuals as Scout leaders (see *The San Diego Union-Tribune*, July 8, 1994).

34. Genesis 15:16. I am grateful to Rev Steve Schlissel for this insight.

35. Gary L. Bauer, President of *Family Research Council*, in a newsletter of February 7, 1994.

36. See the excellent account of this religious search in Os Guinness, *The Dust of Death: A Critique of the Establishment and the Counter-Culture — and a Proposal for a Third Way* (Downers Grove, IL: IVP, 1973). He notes (284) that turning to the East opened the West to the occult again. In particular he notes that "The sixties was the decade marking dramatic growth in the occult. In fact, 1966 can be taken as the year in which the movement surfaced into popularity. Several of the more famous Satan Churches, Magic Circles and Witches' Covens were founded that year."

37. Ken Kesey, one of the bards of the movement said: "For a year we've been in the Garden of Eden. Acid opened the door to it. It was the Garden of Eden and Innocence and a ball." — cited in Guinness, *The Dust of Death*, 232. Guinness, (ibid., 233), in relation to the spiritual quest of the drug culture, also cites Aldous Huxley's com-

ment that "the urge to transcend self-consciousness and selfhood is one of the principal appetites of the soul." Guinness spoke of drugs as having "attained an almost sacramental importance, virtually the bread and wine of the new community" (ibid.).

38. Public lecture in San Diego, May 18, 1993.

39. David Miller, *The New Polytheism: Rebirth of the Gods and Goddesses* (New York: Harper and Row, 1974).

40. Cited in Morrison, *The Serpent,* 228.

41. Charles H. Simpkinson, "Civility and Building Community: Interview with M. Scott Peck," *The Light Connection,* July, 1994, 12.

42. Gary Bauer, president of the *Family Research Council,* in an article "American Family Life: Worth Exporting?" *Focus on the Family,* July, 1994, 2ff. See also William J. Bennett, *The Index of Leading Cultural Indicators: Facts and Figures on the State of the American Society* (New York: Simon and Schuster, 1994), 59: "The United States has the highest divorce rate in the world. At present rates, approximately half of all U.S. marriages can be expected to end in divorce." This, of course, is no way to construct a solid culture, for unstable families create unstable people. There can surely be no future, in spite of enormous technical prowess, for a civilization built on such shaky foundations.

43. Cited by Bauer, ibid.

44. The breakdown of the family has had enormous impact on the rest of the culture — see William J. Bennett, op.cit. In particular, the breakdown of the family is filled by the growth in government. Lyndon B. Johnson's "Great Society" was part of the Sixties answer to society's problems, but the judgment of Bennett is damning: "Never before has the reach of government been greater or its purse larger — and never before have our social pathologies been worse." See ibid., 12.

45. Ibid.

46. These are facts from the Census Bureau as reported in the *Times Advocate* (Escondido), July 20, 1994.

47. Ibid.

48. Alvin P. Sanhoff, "The Core of the Matter," *U. S. News & World Report* (March 25, 1996), 57-58.

49. Ibid., 58.

50. George Gilder, *Men and Marriage* (Gretna, LA: Pelican, 1986), 79ff.

51. No age has truly expressed the Christian faith in a radical and consistent way. No doubt the call to end racial prejudice gave the Sixties revolution an appearance of moral purity that, in part, explains the longevity of its popularity. There were elements to be criticized in the pre-Sixties American Christianity, not least its easy acceptance of racial segregation. But the Sixties was not a reactionary movement that denounced inconsistencies, insisting on a return to the sources. It turned away from those sources, finding answers in Eastern paganism.

52. The title of W. C. Roof's sociological study, *A Generation of Seekers: The Spiritual Journeys of the Baby Boom Generation* (San Francisco: Harper, 1993).

53. W. C. Roof, ibid., 126.

54. On this see W. C. Roof, ibid. Robert Wuthnow, reviewing the book says: "An important book that addresses the struggles of an entire generation to find themselves and *to define spirituality in a new way* [italics mine]." See *Harper's Torch Letter* (San Francisco: Harper, April, 1994), 32.

55. As Roof, op.cit., 249-50, notes, "The counter culture came and went, but many of the values associated with it . . . libertarian aspirations, greater egalitarianism, ecological consciousness, and an enhanced concern for the self, are all now deeply entrenched in American life . . . . What was once on the cultural margins now permeates the cultural mainstream."

Chapter Two

1. Romans 1:25.

2. For parts of this analysis, I am indebted to Professor Jeffrey Haddon of the Department of Sociology at the University of Virginia, in a public lecture on the major characteristics of the New Age Movement. For Eastern monism, see Guinness, *The Dust of Death*, 211-225.

3. The U.S. Army has recently removed the cross from the insignia worn by chaplains. In its place is a sun with its rays, symbolizing the divine in all things — see Chris Murray, *Army Times*, January 17, 1994, 12, cited in James Dobson's newsletter of February, 1994. Another version of the circle, the world egg, popped up as the centerpiece of the opening ceremonies of the Winter Olympics in Lillehammer, Norway, in February, 1994, where the organizers, in a country that has been described as ninety-five percent Lutheran, proposed to the watching world a program extolling ancient Norse paganism.

4. Asphodel P. Long, *The Absent Mother: Restoring the Goddess to Judaism and Christianity*, ed., Alix Pirani, (London: Mandala, 1991). There can be no heresy in a universe like this, except the heresy that denies its total validity.

5. See David F. Wells, *No Place For Truth; Or Whatever Happened to Evangelical Theology?* (Grand Rapids: Eerdmans, 1993).

6. Arthur L. Johnson, *Faith Misguided: Exposing the Dangers of Mysticism* (Chicago: Moody Press, 1988), 32. Johnson shows the mystical nature of this tolerance: "He may argue that since the non-mystic has not had the experience he has had, the non-mystic is therefore not qualified to sit in judgment on it. . . . Either way, the religious mystic claims to have experienced God and to have received special revelations. . . . The practical results of all this is that it is nearly impossible to reason with any convinced mystic." For a good discussion of this issue, see James W. Sire, *The Universe Next Door* (Downers Grove, IL: Inter Varsity, 1976), 178-83.

7. For a report on this parliament, see Peter Jones, "Curb Your Dogma: In the Midst of a Gloomy Week, One Bright Moment," *World* 8/17 (September 18, 1993), 22.

8. See Arthur L. Johnson, *Faith Misguided*, 35-36.

9. As the great modern Gnostic, C. G. Jung said: "The self is a circle whose center is everywhere and whose circumference is nowhere" — see Miguel Serrano, *C. G. Jung and Hermann Hesse: A Record of Two Friendships*, trans. Frank MacShane (New York: Schoken Books, 1968), 50, 55.

10. Cardinal Bernadin, highly visible in episcopal and sartorial splendor at the opening ceremonies, never once exercised his function as teacher and pastor, and remained silent with regard to historic theistic Christianity.

11. *The Light Connection*, July 1994, 14.

12. James Davidson Hunter, *Before the Shooting Begins: Searching For Democracy in America's Culture War* (Free Press, 1994).

13. Martin Marty, *The Public Church*, cited in James W. Fowler, *Weaving the New Creation: Stages of Faith and the Public Church* (San Francisco: HarperSanFrancisco, 1991) 14.

14. J. M. Robinson, "How My Mind Has Changed," *SBL 1985 Seminar Papers* (Scholars Press, 1985), 486.

15. Edited, Robert Funk (New York: Macmillan, 1993).

16. This is the term used for God in all his promotional literature and speeches. One of his seminars is entitled: "Through the Eyes of Your Soul: Utilizing the Gifts and Treasures of God/Goddess/All That Is." See *1994 Concept: Synergy*, P. O. Box 3285, Palm Beach, Fl., 33480.

17. The "New Age" free newspaper, *The Light Connection* (San Diego, April, 1994), which is looking more and more like *Good News, Etc.*, its Christian counterpart.

18. Gary Bauer, director of Family Research Council, by his own admission, is "not by nature a doomsayer." Bauer is rather a seasoned Washington insider, but in his newsletter of February 7, 1994, he states that the family is "fighting for its very life."

19. See *World*, April 2, 1994, 24.

20. *Christianity Today*, March 7, 1994, 45.

21. According to the recent *Family Research Council* newsletter (June 7, 1994), a Christian couple were encouraged by doctors to abort the child they were eagerly expecting because the woman went into labor in the fifth month of her pregnancy. Though the baby was no larger than her father's hand, weighed "no more than a pint of milk," and had translucent, blood-red skin, pre-natal technology saved her life, and now she is doing fine, with no abnormalities.

22. The California Supreme Court, as reported in the *Southern California Christian Times*, June, 1994, actually decreed as murder the killing of an unborn seven to eight week old child. At this point the fetus is the size of a peanut, but this delightful peanut gets the protection of the law — except, of course when the mother decides to kill it.

23. *The Times Advocate,* Friday, June 17, 1994.

24. See "Column One," *Los Angeles Times,* July 5, 1994.

25. In his book, *The Awakening Earth: The Next Evolutionary Leap*, a standard New Age textbook, cited in Morrison, *The Serpent,* 135, 138.

26. "The Manson Murders: Twenty Five Years Later," *Los Angeles Times*, August 6, 1994.

27. Marilyn Ferguson, "Aquarius Now," *Visions*, July, 1994, 13, refers to Ilya Progogine's model of dissipative structures.

28. Robert L. Wilken, the William R. Kenan, Jr. Professor of the History of Christianity at the University of Virginia appears to agree with this judgment when he says: "The changes we are witnessing [in our civilization] are not the inevitable alterations by which older ways adapt to new circumstances. They are the result of a systematic dismembering, a 'trashing' of our culture that is 'intentional, not accidental,' as Myron Magnet puts it in his recent *The Dream and the Nightmare*." See Wilken, "No Other Gods," *First Things*, December, 1993, 13. On the other hand, John S. Hawley, editor of the book, *Fundamentalism and Gender* (New York: Oxford University Press, 1994), 10-12, simplistically dismisses the opposition to feminism is a nostalgic attachment to the past of male/patriarchal domination. The authors do not include in their "savant" analysis the radical redefinition of society that has taken place as the result of the influence of a new, pagan world view.

29. *The Times Advocate*, Saturday, May 21, 1994. p. A1.

30. Robert Wilken, "No Other Gods," 14. Another author who sees the onslaught of paganism is Stephen Smith, "Worldview, Language, and Radical Feminism: An Evangelical Appraisal," Alvin F. Kimel, Jr. ed., *Speaking the Christian God, The Holy Trinity and the Challenge of Feminism* (Grand Rapids, MI: William B. Eerdmans Publishing Company, 1992), 258-275. Smith's analysis is even more precise, and employs the terms used in my own analysis here.

31. See Alan David Bloom, *The Closing of the American Mind: How Higher Education Has Failed Democracy and Impoverished the Souls of Today's Students* (New York: Simon and Schuster, 1987). For a longer view, see George M. Marsden and Bradley J. Longfield, *The Secularization of the Academy* (New York/Oxford: Oxford University Press, 1992). In the article by Robert Wood Lynn, "'The Survival of Recognizably Protestant Colleges': Reflections on Old-Line Protestantism, 1950-1990," p.171, the author speaks of "recognizably protestant colleges" as surviving only as "cognitive minorities" relative to their once dominant position in American education. Reflecting on the Harvard of 1945, *General Education in a Free Society*, which stated that Christianity was "no longer a practicable source of academic unity," Lynn observes that by mid-

century, "America was intractably pluralistic" (176). This academic rejection of Christianity came out on the streets in the Sixties.

The seedbed of the Sixties is another fascinating story, to which I can only allude in what follows. See David Halberstam, *The Fifties* (New York: Fawcett Columbine, 1993).

32. For an excellent documentation see Michael Medved, *Hollywood Versus America: Popular Culture and the War on Traditional Values* (New York: Harper Collins, 1992).

33. See George Grant, *Grand Illusions: The Legacy of Planned Parenthood* (Franklin, TN: Adroit Press, 1992).

34. According to pollster George Barna, reported in *World*, March 5, 1994. These statistics support the findings of W. C. Roof, *Generation of Seekers*, 130, who finds that boomer New Agers *and* evangelicals have very similar self-centered spiritual aspirations that focus much more on personal psychological health than on an "external set of behaviors, dogmas, and forms associated with organized religion."

35. Stephen Smith, "Worldview, Language, and Radical Feminism," 275.

36. Os Guinness, *The Dust of Death*, 209.

Chapter Three

1. Friedrich Nietzsche, "The Greatest Utility of Polytheism," *Joyful Wisdom*, trans. Thomas Common (New York: Ungar Publishing Co., 1960), 178-180.

2. The fatigue sometimes turns to panic. See Walter Brueggemann, "On Writing A Commentary . . . An Emergency? *ATS Colloquy* (September/October, 1992), 10-11. Brueggemann wonders what will happen as the old scientific, so-called "historical-critical method" is abandoned, and scholars become advocates of whatever turns them on. See chapter 8.

3. Of recent popular liberal theology, Carl A. Raschke, *The Bursting of New Wine Skins: Reflections on Religion and Culture at the End of Affluence* (Pittsburgh: Pickwick Press, 1978), 51, says: "popular liberal theology preached the salvation of the individual, while disregarding the meaning and worth of persons." He sees this same theology as having "so overdone the new that it has sundered its own roots and thereby withered from lack of nourishment" (24-25). See also David Walsh, *After Ideology: Recovering the Spiritual Foundations of Freedom* (San Francisco: Harper, 1990), 1, who speaks of "a shift of far-reaching significance . . . presently taking place within Western civilization. . . . A remarkable opening of the soul is taking place, as we increasingly come to realize that we are not the self-sufficient ground for our own existence. Right at the heart of secular contemporary civilization the recognition is emerging of our participation in an order of being utterly beyond our control." Walsh speaks of the "arrogance" of modernity and of modernity's "dead end" (9). Modernity is the secular ideology of which liberal theology is the "Christian" version.

4. W. C. Roof, *Generation of Seekers,* found that only four percent were atheistic or agnostic (126). He notes that this non-spiritual life style lacks any "transcendent symbol," any "overarching `sacred canopy'" (127). Such people were not satisfied with their non-religious world and life view: "secularists we talked to often expressed the lack of a broad encompassing framework for interpreting their lives and a yearning to be able to express their deepest feelings about life" (ibid., 127).

5. Benton Johnson, Dean R.Hoge and Donald A. Luidens, "Mainline Churches: The Real Reason for Decline," *First Things* 31 (March, 1993), 13. See also Milton J. Coalter, *et al*, ed., two volumes: *The Presbyterian Predicament: Six Perspectives* and *The Mainstream Protestant "Decline": The Presbyterian Pattern,* both from Louisville, KY: Westminster/John Knox Press, 1990.

6. Edward W. Farley, "The Presbyterian Heritage as Modernism," M. J. Coalter, in *The Presbyterian Predicament*, 64.

7. Arthur Matthews, "Emptying the Box," *World* (October 30, 1993), 28, gives the details. The central offices of the Presbyterian Church (USA) and the United Church of Christ, once located in the "God Box," 475 Riverside Drive, New York, have fled to the heartland; the United Church of Christ to Cleveland, Ohio, and the Presbyterian Church (USA) to Louisville, Kentucky.

8. Ibid., 14-15.

9. Ibid., 18.

10. This is all the more surprising since Dean Hoge, one of the authors of this report, was a speaker at a major conference sponsored by the Roman Catholic group Time Consultants. The conference, held in Milwaukee in 1990 dealt with the future of the Roman Church during which the radical feminist New Age agenda was proposed by leaders of Women-Church, including Rosemary Ruether. This is reported by Donna Steichen, *Ungodly Rage: The Hidden Face of Catholic Feminism* (San Francisco: Ignatius Press, 1991), 190-191. Steichen states that "in the competition for the control of Catholic feminism, Women-Church has clearly been the victor." Where Hoge sees no "major cultural shift" on the horizon, Steichen sees "much of the American Catholic Church . . . occupied by enemy forces." And what is true of Roman Catholicism is surely true of mainline liberal Protestant churches.

11. *Lambda Report* (September, 1993), 10.

12. Thomas Oden, *After Modernity . . . What? Agenda For Theology* (Grand Rapids: Zondervan, 1990), 39.

13. David A. Noebels, author of a profound critique of secular humanism in all its forms, *Understanding the Times* (Manitou Springs, CO: Summit Press, 1991) expects to see "liberalism (Secular Humanism) crumble like its twin sister (Marxism) crumbled in the former USSR." Philosophically, there is much evidence to think that this has already happened in principle. This will not signal the end of liberalism. Like a quick-change artist, liberalism is now rapidly clothing itself in the mantle of pagan spirituality.

14. Stephen Carter, *The Culture of Disbelief: How American Law and Politics Trivialize Religious Devotion* (New York/San Francisco: HarperCollins, 1993). Carter's analysis is excellent, but his "soft" Episcopalian pluralism is no match for the pagans.

15. Spretnak, *States of Grace,* 5.

16. This term is now used by Mary Daly, the radical feminist witch — see *Beyond God the Father: Toward a Philosophy of Women's Liberation* (Boston: Beacon Press, 1985), 100, showing again that Nietzsche's ideas are far from dead.

17. Interestingly, the feminist Gloria Steinem finds monotheism too stifling and narrow, the expression of "imperialism in religion" espoused by "the kind of people our ancestors came here to escape" — quoted in Donna Steichen, *Ungodly Rage*, 156.

18. James Pinkerton, Senior Fellow at the Manhattan Institute, in an article, "The Death List Has Its Roots in Philosophy," *L.A. Times* (December 26, 1993), argues persuasively that both the theories of Hegel and Nietzsche were significant elements of the Nazi ideology. Hegel, he notes, glorified the state and the charismatic leader as the powerful means whereby history advances to spiritual liberation. Nietzsche glorified "the amoral superman, the blond beast, freed from dull Christian convention to fulfill his inborn and relentless will to power . . . . It wasn't much of a jump from Nietzscheanism to Nazism." William E. Hughes, "The People Versus Martin Heidegger," *First Things* (December, 1993), 36, argues that another great German philosopher, Heidegger, who was a member of the Nazi party, supported Hitler from the basic principles of his philosophy: "Dr Heidegger's philosophy . . . justifies his National Socialism." It is therefore not without interest that Heidegger's existentialism is a major ingredient of the way our modern world thinks.

19. Nietzsche, "The Greatest Utility of Polytheism," *178-180.*

20. For the role of Elizabeth Nietzsche in posthumous renown of her famous brother, see Ben Macintyre, *Forgotten Fatherland: The Search for Elizabeth Nietzsche* (New York: Farrar Straus and Giroux,Inc., 1992).

21. David Miller, *The New Polytheism.* David Miller, Professor of Religion at Syracuse University, makes Nietzsche's sentiments his own when he says: "Attending to the rebirth of the Gods and Goddesses is an experience which can be liberating. The multiple patterns of polytheism allow room to move meaningfully through a pluralistic universe. They free one to affirm the radical plurality of the self, an affirmation that one has seldom been able to manage because of the guilt surrounding monotheism's insidious implication that we have to 'get it all together'"(ibid., ix).

22. David Cave, *Mircea Eliade's Vision for a New Humanism* (New York: Oxford University Press, 1993), 26.

23. Steichen, *Ungodly Rage,* 286.

24. Ibid., 2.

25. Certain leaders of the Joseph Campbell Society, were prominent organizers of the *Parliament of the World's Religions.*

26. Ibid., 250.

27. David Wells, *No Place for Truth,* 66, notes this tendency: "the new theologies have typically shared a disaffection with the various forms of fragmentation that modernization has produced . . . . They propose to bind up what has been torn apart, in some cases by calling for a return to pantheism or for adopting a view of God's immanence that equates divine activity with the rectification of social wrongs . . . . Such theologies thus reassert the union of nature and human nature in a whole that is religious and that gives us the ground for seeking its expression not simply as individuals but in community. In this sense, to be 'post-modern' is often to be Eastern in one's spirituality."

28. Cassandra Burrell, Associated Press, see the *Times Advocate,* November 11, 1994. According to this article, Lynne Cheney, chairwoman of the National Endowment for the Humanities during the Bush administration, finds the guidelines little more than anti-Western propaganda.

29. See chapter 8.

30. Cited by Charles Colson, "The Abolition of Truth," *World,* February, 1994. A further quote of Fish underlines this character of naked power: "someone is always going to be restricted next [by someone else's principle/preference], and it is your job to make sure that someone is not you."

31. Melanie Kirkpatrick, "Jesus in New York: A Church Yuppies Can Have Faith In," *The Wall Street Journal* (July 8, 1993), has this more optimistic read on baby boomers: "Churches have been growing all around the country as baby boomers rediscover religion."

32. See the report in *World* (October, 1993), 28.

33. Carl A. Raschke, *The Interruption of Eternity: Modern Gnosticism and the Origins of the New Religious Consciousness* (Nelson-Hall, 1980). See also James W. Fowler, of Emory University, *Weaving the New Creation,* 13: "I believe that we are in the midst of a shift in cultural consciousness of major proportions. In face of the uncertainties and the threats of the emerging era people are turning to religion, mysticism, and spirituality."

34. Lynn Willeford, "Why I Went Back," *New Age Journal* (August, 1993), 35-40. The following quotes are drawn from this short article.

35. *New Age Journal* (December, 1992).

36. Roof, ibid., 154, takes a different position from that of Benton, Hoge and Luidens, who only see decline for the mainline. "Many in Barry's generation today," says Roof, "are exploring churches, synagogues and other religious institutions." A national study, funded by the Lilly Foundation, shows that two-thirds of the church dropouts of the baby boomer generation have returned to church and synagogue — see Sandi Dolbee,

"Rediscovering Religion: Boomers Seeking a Place That Gives Moral Support to Their Children," *The San Diego Union-Tribune* (Friday, September 3, 1993).

37. Op.cit., 260ff.

38. A personal letter to Constance Cumbey, cited in *Hidden Dangers of the Rainbow* (Shreeport, LA: Huntingdon House, 1983), 147. One is reminded of the observation by Lee, *Against the Protestant Gnostics*, (New York: Oxford University Press, 1987) 4: ". . . very few gnostics were to be found outside the main body of the Church. The typical gnostic was a member, often a pillar, of the local and recognized Christian Church."

39. Ken Carey, *Starseed*, ix, xi.

40. Ibid., xv.

41. Ibid., 37.

42. Ibid., 176-177.

43. Ibid., p. 177-178.

44. Published by Westminster/John Knox Press, Louisville, KY, 1993.

45. Only the article by Morton Kelsey, "The Former Age and the New Age," ibid., defends a form of re-invigorated traditional Christianity. Harmon Bro does point to the importance of "communal and time tested" revelation over against individual inspiration (180), and the Christ outside of ourselves (195), but this is vitiated by his acceptance of re-incarnation and a relativizing of Christianity's uniqueness (195).

46. On page 98 of *New Age Spirituality*, it is true, Spangler disavows this formulation as far too flippant, claiming that he meant no more than the fact that we need to encounter both our dark side as well as our light side before we can know wholeness. Whatever Spangler might now say, it certainly is a strange way of speaking, and since Spangler really does not disavow New Age thinking, it gives a Christian great cause for concern. Finding a positive place for Lucifer was certainly a major preoccupation of the proto-New Agers, the Gnostics.

47. Ibid., 74-75, Methodist minister, Glen Olds, hopes for a rosy future as "the best of the New Age and all our religious traditions" work together to solve the global problems of the third millennium. Carl Raschke is similarly optimistic. He sees the New Ager as a model of courageous modern spirituality, someone who "does not fear taking the road not taken, because all treks converge at the Final Crossroads"(120). Vivienne Hull, cofounder of the Chinook Learning Center near Seattle considers the "entrancing and empowering vision" of New Age spirituality as the movement's major contribution: " *nothing at this time in our history may be more essential*" [emphasis mine] (141).

48. Steichen, *Ungodly Rage*, 210, 213 and 232-33, notes this same phenomenon, but argues, as I do, that despite the disclaimer, Fox is as New Age as anyone.

49. Ibid., 219.

50. Interestingly, this word is being thrown not just at orthodox protestants and hard core evangelical fundamentalists but also at orthodox Roman Catholics — see Steichen, *Ungodly Rage*, 227.

51. "Matthew Fox: 'Joy Happens,'" *New Age Journal* (December, 1992), 26-27.

52. On this term, see Virginia Mollenkott, *Sensuous Spirituality: Out From Fundamentalism*, (New York: Crossroads, 1992), 73ff.

53. See chapter 8.

54. Unfortunately the optimism of Thomas Oden does not seem to be panning out. The fascination with the future, with what Charles Colson called one of the four horses of the modern apocalypse — the illusion that utopia is around the corner — has not abated. Constantly fueled by the myth of evolutionary progress, it is clear that the Hegelian world spirit is at the root of the new liberalism. One has to wonder whether Liberalism, like Marxism, is obliged to focus on the future because the present never

quite corresponds with its ideological claims. David Wells, *No Place For Truth*, 60, speaks of "the need [in contemporary Liberal theology] to be in motion, moving toward the future, to know that we are leaving behind periods of lesser achievement and shaking ourselves free from what is obsolete."

55. Ninian Smart and Steven Konstantine, *Christian Systematic Theology in a World Context*, (Minneapolis, MN: Fortress Press, 1991), 143. It is true that the future plays a profound role in classical Christian and in the New Testament. However, the hope has to do with God's radical transformation of the cosmos by his own almighty power, not an evolutionary process caused by humans. Realizing the kingdom of God on earth has always been a theme of liberal theology, especially in the nineteenth century. The difference with this new form is its "apocalyptic" note.

56. Stephen Hawking, *A Brief History of Time* (1988), 175.

Chapter Four

1. Mary Daly & Jane Caputi, *Webster's First New Intergalactic Wickedary of the English Language* (Boston: Beacon Press, 1987), 88.

2. The title of James Davidson Hunter's best-selling sociological study published in 1991 (Basic Books/Harper).

3. Significantly, as noted above, Hunter's latest book has a much more ominous title, *Before the Shooting Starts*.

4. Tom Williams, priest of the Church of All Worlds, cited in Dave Bass, "Drawing Down the Moon," *Christianity Today*, April 1991, 17.

5. A poll conducted by Family Research Council concludes that there is "common agreement that [American] culture is decaying [but] there seems to be an absence of consensus over what to do about it." Reported in *World* (December 11, 1993).

6. A company that espouses a pro-homosexual stance in its organization and public statements.

7. See *Lambda Report* 1/5 (October, 1993), which documents that Radecic gave an address to the "S/M Leather Fetish Conference" which took place during the homosexual "March on Washington" in 1993, in the Mellen Auditorium, a federal building on Constitutional Avenue. On display in this federal building were booths selling various S/M wares such as leather hoods and body racks. In her address, she identified herself with the S/M leather-fetish community, and encouraged her listeners to be active in gay politics. "We have to be at the table of the gay, lesbian and bisexual community who are setting the agenda." Part of her agenda was to oppose the censorship of homosexual sadomasochistic art.

8. Homosexual and lesbian high government officials, along with their "straight" co-belligerents, are behind closed doors in federal departments like Health and Human Services, Justice, Housing and Urban Development and the Office of the Surgeon General. Just what they are planning for this once Christian country remains to be seen.

9. This movement no doubt has enormous financial power to be able to start a telephone company in competition with AT&T, MCI and Sprint. This power is suggested by the fact the latest ideological elaboration of the new religious liberalism, *The Universe Story: From the Primordial Flaring Forth to the Ecozoic Era; A Celebration of the Unfolding of the Cosmos,* Brian Swimme and Thomas Berry (San Francisco: HarperSanFrancisco, 1992), is dedicated to Lawrence S. Rockefeller.

10. This, on the commercial level, is the equivalent of the new governmental theory of "the politics of meaning," an ideology associated with Michael Lerner and the network of ex-Sixties radicals known as "the friends of Hillary." This ideology is everywhere. A public librarian friend passed me a publication from one of the most respected library publishers, on the subject "The Choice to Change: Establishing an Integrated School Library Media Program," by Paula Kay Montgomery (Englewood,

CO: Libraries Unlimited, Inc, 1989). The article affirms that the library media specialist must change himself, that "reality lies within," that one must "trust and use intuition," "learn to meditate," and "expect miracles."

11. Cited in Harold A. Netland, *Dissident Voices:Religious Pluralism and the Question of Truth* (Grand Rapids: Eerdmans, 1991), 196.

12. Paul Knitter, *No Other Name? A Critical Survey of Christian Attitudes Toward the World Religions* (Maryknoll, N.Y: Orbis Books, 1986), 225.

13. This is the optimistic read of Leonard Swidler, *The Meaning of Life at the Edge of the Third Millennium* (New York: Paulist Press, 1993), 4 and 116. According to Swidler, who is professor of Catholic Thought and Interreligious Dialogue, Temple University, Philadelphia, "dialogue is Christianity's formal contribution to the world of the Third Millennium." Leonard Swidler, the much quoted theologian on Jesus as an egalitarian feminist, believes that modern man "can no longer hold to an absolutist view of truth," and calls on Christians to experience other religions "from within" — see Leonard Swidler, ed., *Towards a Universal Theology of Religion* (Maryknoll, NY: Orbis Books, 1987), 12, 16.

14. Smart and Konstantine wish to "carry forward" the project proposed by Teilhard and the syncretist theologians Wilfred Cantwell Smith, Raimundo Pannikar, John Hick and John Cobb.

15. Op.cit., 144-145. Even if this terminology is complicated and elitist, it is not difficult to know what Episcopalian Ninian Smart means. His commitment to a one-world religion is evidenced by the fact that he is "presiding council member" of the "Inter-Religious Federation for World Peace," sponsored by the Rev. Sun Myung Moon, head of the Unification Church.

16. *Religious Studies,* Harper San Francisco Catalog for 1995, 2.

17. Tertullian, *De Praescriptione* 41, cited in K. Rudolf, *Gnosis: The Nature and History of an Ancient Religion* (Edinburgh: T & T Clark, 1977), 216.

18. Matthew Fox, *The Coming of the Cosmic Christ: The Healing of Mother Earth and the Birth of a Global Renaissance*, (San Francisco: Harper, 1988), 229.

19. Fox, ibid., 229. "Mysticism . . . has never been tried on an ecumenical level." Under the influence of Knitter, Fox, and others, this oversight will soon be put right.

20. Ibid. This kind of spirituality has already appeared at the World Council of Churches. In the General Assembly at Canberra, Australian, in 1991, the Korean feminist theologian Chung Hyun Kyung, in her keynote address, included a performance of Korean and Aboriginal dancers as well as a shamanistic paper-burning ritual to chase away evil spirits. What the great missions movement of the modern era managed to eradicate is now returning in the highest councils of the Church.

21. Caitlín Matthews, *Sophia, Goddess of Wisdom: The Divine Feminine from Black Goddess to World-Soul* (London: The Aquarian Press/Harper Collins, 1992), 368.

22. Katherine Zappone, *The Hope For Wholeness: A Spirituality for Feminists* (Mystic, CN: Twenty Third Publications, 1991), 39. Another example of this participative syncretism is found in the teaching of Joseph Campbell, who instructed his students to "read other people's myths, not those of your own religion . . . .(which) put(s) your mind in touch with this experience of being alive." See Joseph Campbell with Bill Moyers*The Power of Myth*, (New York: Anchor Books/Doubleday, 1988), 5.

23. R. H. Drummond, *Towards a New Age in Christian Theology*, 183. See also, on the openness to other religions, Harvey Cox, *Turning East* (New York: Simon and Schuster, 1977); Matthew Fox, ed., *Western Spirituality: Historical Roots, Ecumenical Routes* (Santa Fe, New Mexico: Bear & Company, 1981); T. M. Hesburgh, *The Humane Imperative: A Challenge for the Year 2000* (New Haven, CN: Yale University Press, 1974); Rodney R. Romney, *Journey to Inner Space: Finding God in Us* (Nashville, TN: Abingdon Press, 1980); S. J. Samartha, *Courage For Dialogue* (Maryknoll, NY: Orbis Books, 1982); by

the same author, *One Christ — Many Religions* (Maryknoll: Orbis Books, New York, 1991); L. Swidler, ed., *Towards a Universal Theology of Religion* (Maryknoll: Orbis Books, New York, 1988); *The New Universalism: Foundations for a Global Theology* (Maryknoll: Orbis Books, 1991); Maurice Wiles, *Christian Theology and Inter-religious Dialogue* (London: SCM Press, 1992). Many more titles could be added. These are just a selection of the avalanche of recently-published materials on this increasingly-popular subject.

24. Elizabeth Moltmann-Wendel, "Having Broken Camp, We Are Now On the Open Road," *Theology Today* 51/1 (April, 1994), 73.

25. Jürgen Moltmann, "Christianity in the Third Millennium," *Theology Today* 51/1 (April, 1994), 77.

26. Ibid., 89.

27. A general letter of the *Center of Theological Inquiry*, Princeton, New Jersey, dated September 29, 1994.

28. Moltmann, ibid., 88, cites gatherings of this kind as the locus where religious leaders can forge a new consensus.

29. Fox, *Cosmic Christ*, 229, says quite plainly: "Deep ecumenical possibilities emerge when we shift from the quest for the historical Jesus to the quest for the Cosmic Christ."

30. R. H. Drummond, *A Life of Jesus the Christ* (San Francisco: Harper and Row, 1989)

31. Ibid.

32. Fowler, *Weaving*, 21.

33. Cited in Steichen, *Ungodly Rage*, 92. Joachim of Fiora (A.D. 1132 - 1202) first developed the three age description of history: the age of the Father (Old Testament Faith), the age of the Son (Christian church), and the age of the Spirit, where there would be no church.

34. Rosemary Radford Ruether, *Sexism and God-Talk* (Boston: Beacon Press, 1983), 11

35. Ferguson, Aquarius Now," *Light Connection* (1993), 7.

36. Chris Griscom, *Ecstasy Is a New Frequency*, 169.

37. "Co-creating Heaven On Earth," *The Light Connection* (July, 1992), 11.

38. Ben Nova, "Future War . . . Future Peace," *Omni* (November, 1993), 65.

39. Joseph Campbell and Bill Moyers, *The Power of Myth*, xix.

40. The New Age concept of *homo noeticus* — the new rational/spiritual human being — comes from the theology of Jesuit priest Pierre Teilhard de Chardin (1881-1955). See in particular his *Le phénomène humain* (1955) published in the year of his death, and translated into English as The *Phenomenon of Man* (1959). This work contains the essence of his ideas. His christianized Evolution posits a final stage of development for mankind called the *noosphere* (sphere of the mind). In this final state man reaches a level of spirituality which joins him to Christ, the "Omega Point," producing a radical transformation of the cosmos and the end of history. Reinterpreting the biblical notion of resurrection in terms of the philosophical/scientific concept of Evolution, Teilhard's ideas, while condemned by the Roman Catholic Church, are making a remarkable comeback, both in "Christian" and "non-Christian" New Age circles. See, for instance, Hesburgh, *The Humane Imperative* , and Archbishop Dom Helder Camara, *Race Against Time* (Denville, NJ: Dimension Books, 1971). Interestingly, Hesburgh was one of the honorary presidents of the *Parliament of the World's Religions* held in Chicago in 1993. Protestant and Greek Orthodox theologians, Smart and Konstantine, acknowledge their commitment to Process Theology, (the idea that God, along with the universe, undergoes the process of evolution), to the "holy magnetism of the future." Teilhard's concept of the "noosphere," according to these authors, "daily becomes more relevant, as the various parts of the world are in virtual instant communication." See also Harvey Cox, *Many Mansions: Christianity's Encounter with Other Faiths* (Boston: Beacon Press,

1988), 211-212. Cox cites Teilhard's "religious hope." Virginia Mollenkott, the New Age lesbian "evangelical" finds great inspiration in Teilhard — see *Sensuous Spirituality*, 174. Even Southern Baptist Vice President Al Gore finds him irresistible — see his *Earth in the Balance*, 263.

41. Cited in Cumbey, *Hidden Dangers*, 111-112

42. Swimme and Berry, *The Universe Story*, 3-5. Thomas Berry associates with Matthew Fox and is known as a "creation theologian," meaning one who rejects the Fall and the need of redemption, because, quite simply, the cosmos is good and auto-redeeming.

This integration of evolutionary theory and religion is a new version of Teilhard, whose influence is enormous. Waldenbooks carries a number of New Age titles that contain the telling term "omega" and explicitly or implicitly recognize their debt to Teilhard. Kenneth Ring, expert in paranormal phenomena such as UFOs and "near-death experiences, who entitles his book, *The Omega Project* (New York: Morrow, 1992), 11, draws upon "the inspirational visionary ideas of Teilhard de Chardin. . . (who saw that) the human race is advancing to an end-state of evolution." A previous book by Ring has the title, *Heading Towards Omega* (New York: Morrow, 1984). Another "secular" New Age author, Donald Keys, is indebted to Teilhard and entitles his book *Earth at Omega:Passage to Planetization* (Brookline Village, MA: Branden Press, 1982). See also the highly scholarly work of two well respected scientists, John D. Barrow, astronomer at the University of Sussex, England, and Frank J. Tipler, Professor of Mathematics and Physics at Tulane University, New Orleans. In their 700pp book of the most technical mathematical and scientific data, *The Anthropic Cosmological Principle* (Oxford: Clarendon Press/New York: Oxford University Press, 1986), 204, they nevertheless accept the "Omega Point" theory of Teilhard, as "the only framework wherein the evolving Cosmos of modern science can be combined with an ultimate meaningfulness to reality."

43. John Randolf Price, *The Superbeings* (Quartus Books, 1981), pp. 2-3, cited in Morrison, *The Cross and the Serpent*, 156.

44. Cited in Morrison, *The Cross and the Serpent*, 157-158.

45. Ken Carey, *The Starseed Transmissions*, pp. 54-55.

46. James B. Irwin with William A. Emerson, Jr., *To Rule the Night* (Philadelphia and New York: A. J. Holman), pp. 17,18.

Chapter Five

1. K. C. Johnson and J. H. Coe, *Wildlife in the Kingdom Come* (Grand Rapids: Zondervan, 1993), 72.

2. Philip Lee, *Against The Protestant Gnostics*, xi, who notes that "while theological conservatives have often been open to my analysis of their affinities with gnosticism, theological liberals have, for the most part, found gnostic-liberal parallels to be contrived, unfair, unacademic, and overstated."

3. For other works on this general theme, see, in particular Robert N. Bellah, "Civil Religion in America," *American Civil Religion*. ed., Russell E. Richey and Donald G. Jones (New York: Harper and Row, 1974); Carl Raschke, *The Interruption of Eternity: Modern Gnosticism and the Origins of the New Religious Consciousness* (Nelson-Hall, 1980); James Hitchcock, *The New Enthusiasts and What They Are Doing to the Catholic Church* (Chicago: Thomas More Press, 1982); Donna Steichen, *Ungodly Rage: The Hidden Face of Catholic Feminism* (San Francisco, 1991); Harold Bloom, *The American Religion: The Emergence of the Post-Christian Nation* (New York: Simon and Schuster, 1992). An important early source is Eric Voegelin, Professor of Political Science, University of Munich, who was a pioneer in developing the category of Gnosticism for the understanding of Western intellectual/religious history. It would be correct to say that

his work, begun in the thirties at the University of Vienna, eventually gave rise to a school — see Ellis Sandoz, *The Voegelinian Revolution* (Baton Rouge: Louisiana State University Press, 1981), and Eugene Webb, *Eric Voegelin: Philosopher of History* (Seattle: University of Washington Press, 1981). A profound and sympathetic treatment of Voegelin's contribution is found in David Walsh, *After Ideology: Recovering the Spiritual Foundations of Freedom* (HarperSanFrancisco, 1990), 54-58 and *passim*. See also Michael Franz, *Eric Voegelin and the Politics of Spiritual Revolt: The Roots of Modern Ideology* (Baton Rouge: Louisiana State University Press, 1992, and Stephen A. McKnight, *Sacralizing the Secular: The Renaissance Origins of Modernity* (Baton Rouge: Louisiana State University Press, 1989). One should also note the important connections between the psychologist C. J. Jung and Gnosticism: see J. F. Satinover, "Jungians and Gnostics", *First Things*, 46 (October, 1994), 41-48, and Richard Noll, *The Jung Cult: Origins of a Charismatic Movement* (Princeton: Princeton University Press, 1994).

4. Philip Lee. *Against the Protestant Gnostics*, 84. Lee defines the high-ground of Protestant as Barthianism, and then identifies Protestant Gnosticism as most of what lies to his right and to his left. Lee's book deals with classic liberalism. He does not define what I have called the "new liberalism," liberalism with feeling and soul and a new spirituality. My arguments therefore compliment his and take the analysis a step further.

5. For a well-developed and detailed description of this, see H. Jonas, *The Gnostic Religion: The Message of the Alien God and the Beginnings of Christianity*, (Boston: Beacon Press, 1958), 3-27.

6. See W.Schmithals, *Paul and the Gnostics*, translated by John E. Steely (Nashville: Abingdon, 1972), who sees Gnostics behind the letters of Paul to the Galatians, to the Philippians, to the Thessalonians, and to the Romans: see also his *Gnosticism in Corinth: An Investigation of the Letters to the Corinthians*, translated by John E. Steely (Nashville: Abingdon, 1971).

7. G. Filoramo, *A History of Gnosticism* (Cambridge, MA: Basil Blackwell, 1990), 34ff, pushes behind the earlier philosophical analysis of Gnosticism by H. Jonas, seeking to uncover a sociological cause of this explosion of religious thought. Filoramo argues that while the religious texts proposed a new spiritual identity, they found fallow, fertile ground in humanity's search for a new social identity.

8. See the works of Gnostic specialists such as U. Bianchi, "Mithraism and Gnosticism," in J. R. Hinnells, ed., *Mithraic Studies: Proceedings of the First International Congress of Mithraic Studies*, l-ll (Manchester: 1975), 457-465; S. Giverson, "Der Gnostizismus und Die Mysterienreligionen," in J. P. Asmussen and J. Laessøe, eds. *Handbuch der Religionsgeschichte* (Göttingen: 1975); Mcl. R. Wilson, "Gnosis and the Mysteries," in R. van den Broek and M. J. Vermaseren, eds., *Studies G. Quispel* (Leiden: E. J. Brill, 1975), 451-457.

9. See important studies by S. Angus, *The Mystery Religions: A Study in the Religious Background of Early Christianity* (New York: Dover Publications, 1975 — originally published in 1925); A. J. Festugière, *Personal Religion among the Greeks*, Sather Classical Lectures, 26 (Berkeley: 1954); Walter Burkert, *Ancient Mystery Cults* (Cambridge, MA: Harvard University Press, 1987).

10. Just as today we can observe both secular New Age/Liberalism and "Christian" New Age/Liberalism (see below), so in the ancient world one is justified in speaking of both pagan and "Christian" Gnosticism.

11. We are not attempting to define something like a scarlet thread that runs through history showing *direct* relationships between the two. Philip Lee, *Against the Protestant Gnostics*, 6-7, makes the following helpful observation: "To trace gnosticism from ancient time through the Middle Ages down to the present would be, at best, a dubious enterprise. Because it is not essentially a historical faith — in the sense of clinging to

particular historical structures — by the very nature of the phenomenon, it defies ordinary historical study. . . . The connection between ancient and modern gnosticism can be established, however, through the identification of the gnostic *type* . . . . The very least, if we can perceive a gnostic pattern, then perhaps the danger ancient *gnosis* posed for the early Church can, in an objective sense, alert us to the dangers now being posed by a modern *gnosis*."

12. Steichen, *Ungodly Rage*, 122.

13. Elaine Pagels, *The Gnostic Gospels* (New York: Random House, 1979), 25.

14. Ibid., 175.

15. *Against Heresies*, 1:13:6

16. Elaine Pagels, *The Gnostic Gospels*, 37.

17. *Refutation of All Heresies* 5:8:2.

18. See Birger A. Pearson, *Gnosticism, Judaism and Egyptian Christianity* (Minneapolis: Fortress Press, 1990), 132 for the terms in Coptic, and references to the Nag Hammadi literature. Pearson shows that the Gnostics share with the highest God his attributes, and their conception of total freedom corresponds to the definition of the primal Father as "the Monad (who) is a monarchy with nothing above it" (*Apocryphon of John* 2:26-27).

19. Pagels, *Gnostic Gospels*, 162.

20. What an incredible opportunity for the Devil who, strangely, is the only figure surprisingly absent from the Gnostic myth, just like an author is absent from his own work. When Satan is present, he is present as the giver of truth, whereas the God of the Old Testament is identified with the demonic. So the Devil is read out of the personae dramatis in the drama of redemption — [Gnosticism would be the first attempt at "Screwtape" literature] — both by the Gnostics and by many contemporary liberal theologians!

21. Elaine Pagels, *The Origin of Satan* (New York: Random House, 1995).

22. Philip Lee. *Against the Protestant Gnostics*, 79.

23. Rudolf, *Gnosis,* 53.

24. Cited in J. Dart, *The Laughing Jesus: The Discovery and Significance of the Hag Hammadi Gnostic Library* (San Francisco: Harper and Row, 1976), 117, without references.

25. Panarion 25:2:1. I have collected a list which is surely not definitive, but which gives the reader an idea of Gnostic diversity: the Sethians, the Simonians, the Naasenes/Ophites, the Valentinians, the Manicheans, the Mandeans, the Messalians/Eustathians, also known as the Choreutes, Adelphians or Lampetians, the Satornilians, the Archontici, the Audians, the Cainites, the Marcosians, the Melchisedekians, the Nicolaitans, the Haematites, the Phrygians, the Entychites, the Peratae, the Priscillians, the followers of Simon Magus, Marcion, Basilides, Megetius, Prepon, Markos, Axionicus, Cerinthus, Dositheus, Carpocrates, Menander, Sisinnios, Euphrates, Celbes, Gabriabios, Florinus, Isidore, Cerdo, Apelles, Heracleon, Ptolemaeus, Theodotus, Assionicus, Colarbasus, Carpion, Carpocrates, Candidus, Justin, Menander, Marsanes, Monoimus, Marcellina, Helen, Prodicus, Saturnilus, Zostrianos, Pontitus, Basilicus and Hermogenes. This list would hardly begin to make a dent on the list of modern protestant denominations. It should be compared rather with the much more unified and monolithic character of the church in the first few centuries.

26. Hans Jonas, *The Gnostic Religion*, 25. I first noted this citation in Philip Lee, *Against the Protestant Gnostics*, 40. Lee observes that "The gnostics were not alone in this sort of religious plagiarism" (ibid, 41). He cites Frederick Grant, *Hellenistic Religions: The Age of Syncretism* (New York: Liberal Arts Press, 1953), p. xiii, to the effect that "the main characteristic feature of Hellenistic religion was syncretism: the tendency to identify the deities of various peoples and to combine their cults." In other

words, Gnosticism, in marked distinction to Christian orthodoxy, shared with the sur-rounding culture a love of syncretism.

27. Some leaders of the New Left who promoted rebellion against society have had second thoughts about the good it achieved. Peter Collier and David Horowitz, *Destructive Generation*, speak of the utopianism of the Left as a "secular religion" with its "promise of an earthly kingdom of heaven" (246), that ended in great failure.

28. The call for an end to racism and the genuine quest for spirituality, to name but two. The overall judgment of the Sixties, from David Horowitz and Peter Collier (ibid., 304), is quite negative.

29. Previous examples include: the evolutionary theories of Hegel and Darwin the early nineteenth century, "christianized" by F. C. Baur; the social optimism of the late nineteenth century, expressed by liberal theologians like Ritschl and von Harnack as "the social gospel"; Rudolf Bultmann's profound dependence on the existential-ism of Martin Heidegger; the marxist liberation movements in the third world and cultural revolution of the Sixties created the liberation and feminist theologies of recent years.

30. As Filoramo, the Italian specialist on Gnosticism (ibid., 24), so succinctly puts it: "the new spiritual climate positively insisted that one transcend these barriers [be-tween heaven and earth] and become a *hyperanthrôpos* (a super human). This now became the goal in a spiritual contest destined to attract increasingly numerous and enthusiastic competitors. . . . (this) was tending to become a possibility on offer, at least theoretically, to everyone, indeed to everyone able to undergo the experiences of spiritual conversion and rebirth."

31. Ibid., 34.

32. Cited in J. Dart, *The Laughing Jesus*, 132, without any precise reference.

33. James Robinson, *The Nag Hammadi Library in English*, 1. When it is recalled that the first signs of the New Age are evident in the social revolution of the Sixties, and that New Age and Gnosticism share a common view of the world (See my *The Gnostic Empire*), Robinson's seemingly off-hand remark is actually most profound.

34. Ibid., 37. The complete quote of Filoramo is as follows: "a cultural universe in which syncretism had become an ideological garment, in which oriental blood had now been flowing for centuries in the somewhat anaemic body of the West."

35. Rudolf, *Gnosis*, 14.

36. Paul Knitter, *The Myth of Christian Uniqueness: Towards a Pluralistic Theology of Religion* (Maryknoll, NY: Orbis Books, 1987), 226.

37. 1 Corinthians 10:20.

38. *The International Standard Bible Encyclopedia*, 489.

39. Giles Quispel, *Gnostic Studies* (Istanbul: Nederlands Historisch-Archaeologisch Instituut in het Nabije Oosten, 1974), I, p. 12.

40. Robert M. Grant, *Heresy and Criticism: The Search for Authenticity in Early Christian Literature* (Louisville, KY: Westminster/John Knox Press, 1993), 6.

41. Cited by J. Dart, *The Laughing Savior*, 118, without reference.

42. Still the standard work on Marcion, and not yet translated into English is Adolf von Harnack, *Marcion: Das Evangelium von fremden Gott*, 2nd ed. TU 45 (1924): see also R. S. Wilson, *Marcion: A Study of a Second-Century Heretic* (London, 1933), and R. Joseph Hoffmann, *Marcion: On the Restitution of Christianity: An Essay on the Devel-opment of Radical Paulinist Theology in the Second Century* (Chico, CA: Scholars Press, 1984).

43. A. von Harnack, *Marcion*, 235, (cited in P. J. Tomson, *Paul and Jewish Law*, 10, note 4). Harnack's praise of Marcion was certainly high: "ein Religionsstifter, ein wirklicher Reformator . . . der erste Protestant ["a founder of religion, a true re-former . . . the first Protestant"].

44. See Helmut Koester, *Introduction to the New Testament: Volume 2: History and Literature of Early Christianity* (Philadelphia: Fortress Press, 1982), 330. In true liberal fashion, Marcion argued that the gospel of redemption is only available through, and is not to be identified with a written text, so R. J. Hoffmann, *Marcion: On the Restitution of Christianity: An Essay on the Development of Radical Paulinist Theology in the Second Century*, AAR Academy Series 46 (Chico, CA: Scholars Press, 1984, a Ph.D thesis from Oxford University, 1982), 110-111. An American liberal scholar also has good words to say of these ancient heretics. Robert Grant believes they produced the first thought provoking theological works, keeping "alive the great issues of freedom, redemption and grace" (cited in J. Dart, *The Laughing Savior*, xvi).

45. Orthodox Roman Catholics might be tempted to breathe a silent "amen" to that comparison, but that would be misplaced. For while it is true that Luther, in his zeal and rhetoric, sometimes went overboard [see his impulsive rejection of James and Revelation — which he later renounced], his love for the Gospel and the Scriptures Old and New leaves most of us in the starting blocks.

46. Cited in R. J. Hoffmann, *Marcion*, 110-111.

47. Irenaeus, *Against Heresies*, 3:3:4. If Marcion is the proto-typical liberal, he may also be the first "modern." E. Michael Jones, in his fascinating study, *Degenerate Moderns: Modernity as Rationalized Sexual Misbehavior*, (San Francisco: Ignatius, 1993), claims that the locomotive driving much of modern social science has been the production of "scientific" theory and data to justify the personal deviant sexual behavior of its creators. Jones analyzes the histories of Mead, Kinsey, Keynes, Picasso, Freud and Jung, and argues that their essential methodology consisted in placing desire before truth rather than truth before desire. In this sense, Marcion appears to be the first modern, at least in his methodology. According to early Church tradition, Marcion was originally excommunicated by his own father for having seduced a virgin — see Helmut Koester, *Introduction to the New Testament*, vol. 2, 329. Koester dismisses this tradition as a "malicious polemical invention," though he recognizes its important "symbolic meaning." If this tradition were true, all Marcion's later work to demonstrate that the Old Testament law and the Old Testament God were not binding on true, spiritual Christians, would be an attempt to justify his own wrong-doing.

48. Recognition of the religious differences in today's society suggests the same radical contradictions. Wade Clark Roof, a sociologist at the University of California, Santa Barbara, in his book, *Generation of Seekers*, 119, speaks of an "enormous religious gulf. . . . two vastly different symbolic worlds . . . polar extremes" which he calls "mystic versus theistic." Though a sociologist, he demonstrates great theological perceptiveness in seeing the enormous chasm between monism and theism. He does wonder, at the end of this study, whether "baby-boomers" bridge this chasm in that, in spite of the cognitive differences, on the emotional level, there is a tendency to act and feel monistically/mystically (256-257). Ultimately, of course, the cognitive will suffer, and monism will win. Joseph Campbell sees that the two cannot co-exist for long in the same person: "You get a totally different civilization and a totally different way of living according to whether your myth presents nature as fallen or whether nature is in itself a manifestation of the divinity, and the spirit is the revelation of the divinity that is inherent in nature" (*Power of Myth*, 121).

49. Duncan Greenlees, *The Gospel of the Gnostics* (Madras, India: The Theosophical Publishing House, 1958), vii.

50. J. Gresham Machen, *Christianity and Liberalism* (New York: MacMillan Company, 1923), 2. The title itself states the thesis, though Machen, as noted, was careful to distinguish between liberalism and liberals.

51. Ibid., 160, 172.

52. Pope Pius X, encyclical on modernism, *Pascendi Gregis* (London: Burns and Oates, 1907). See also *Lamentabile Sane*, and the "Oath Against Modernism," appendices in Michael Davies, *Partisans of Error: St Pius X Against the Modernists* (Long Prairie, Minn: Neumann Press, 1983), cited in Steichen, *Ungodly Rage*, 257.

53. *Religiousstudies News* [joint publication of the American Academy of Religion and the Society of Biblical Literature], vol. 9, No. 4 (November, 1994), 15.

54. "The RE-Imagining Conference: A Report," The American Family Association, April, 1994, 19.

55. James M. Robinson, "Introduction," *The Nag Hammadi Library in English*, 1-25, see especially pp. 3, 6, 7, 16, 24. In addition, on pp. 5 and 18 he uses the term "heretical" in a similar way.

56. In the feminist *"RE-Imagining Conference"* held November 4-7, 1993, in Minneapolis, the notion of heresy was often a cause for derisive laughter. See *Good News*, January, 1994, a publication of conservative Christians within the United Methodist Church. Though this kind of heresy seems far removed from the denunciation of ancient Church Fathers, the removal of any standard of truth and the espousal of Gnosticism finally ends in the same place. Interestingly, the Nag Hammadi texts were cited with approval on a number of occasions at the Minneapolis conference.

57. As a moderate such as Philip Lee recognizes in *Against the Protestant Gnostics*, 13. Lee wonders if it is possible to speak of heresy in our time.

58. See "RE-Imagining Foments Uproar Among Presbyterians," *The Washington Post*, June, 1994. Some now describe the conservative reaction as "hostility" and "harassment" and vow to make such reactions impossible.

59. Alan Morrison, *The Serpent and the Cross*, 200.

60. Op.cit., 14. Specifically, Lee is a Barthian, and so technically, from an orthodox point of view, has one foot in the liberal camp.

61. David Remnick, "The Devil Problem," *The New Yorker* (April 3, 1995), 56.

62. Ibid., 63.

63. *Thunder, Perfect Mind* 13:16-21.

64. Thomas Jippling, "Aggressive Activism is Legacy of Clinton Judges," *Human Events* (August 9, 1996), 12.

65. Cited in an excellent short essay/letter by James Dobson, *Focus on the Family* (July 1996), 2.

66. Ibid., citing Charles Colson, "Pandora's Box," *Breakpoint*, March 11, 1996.

67. Ibid., 3, citing Russell Hittenger of Catholic University.

68. Ibid., 2, citing Justice Antonin Scalia's dissent.

69. Eugene North, "Partial Birth Abortion Jubilee: A Perverse Tribute to Leviticus," *Culture Wars* (July/August, 1996), 6.

70. The words of Jesus, Matthew 24:24/Mark 13:22.

Chapter Six

1. David Miller, *The New Polytheism*, 76.

2. Cited by Cal Thomas, "Manipulating the Bible for Political Ends," *Los Angeles Times*, October 7, 1994.

3. Alicia Suskin Ostriker, *Feminist Revision and the Bible: The Unwritten Volume* (Cambridge, MA: Blackwell, 1995).

4. James Robinson, cited by K. B. Welton, *Abortion is Not a Sin: A New Age Look at an Old-Age Problem* (Costa Mesa, CA: Pandit Press, 1987), 166.

5. K. B. Welton, *Abortion*, 67.

6. Rosemary Radford Ruether, *Womanguides: Readings Towards a Feminist Theology* (Boston: Beacon Press, 1985), ix.

7. Susan Durber, "The Female Reader of the Parables of the Lost," *Journal for the Study of the New Testament* 45 (1992), 78.

8. Ruether, *Women-Church*: Theology and Practice (San Francisco: Harper and Row, 1985) 137. These texts only "haunt" evangelical feminists. Young Lee Hertig, assistant professor at Fuller Theological Seminary in Pasadena, complains in a sermon entitled, "On Liberating Theology from Sexual, Racial Bias," that while Christian women are being swept into a more progressive view on gender, what still haunts us are phrases like, 'Women should be silent in the church,' and 'The woman should be submissive to the man." She claims that these phrases come from a "patriarchal interpretation of Scripture . . . [which] is exclusive and culturally biased. There is no culture-free theology." See *Los Angeles Times*, September 12, 1994.

9. Ruether, ibid., 47 and 142.

10. In an interview with Terry Gross, "Fresh Air," *PBS*, Easter Sunday, 1996.

11. David Remnick, "States of Mind: The Devil Problem," *The New Yorker* (April 3, 1996), 64.

12. Art.cit., 63.

13. Ibid., 63.

14. Campbell & Moyers, *The Power of Myth*, 40.

15. Danna Nolan Fewell and David M. Gunn, *Gender, Power and Promise* (Nashville: Abingdon, 1993), 20.

16. "General Introduction," *The New Testament and Psalms: An Inclusive Version*, vii.

17. Ibid., ix.

18. Just a generation ago, liberal scholars were hailing Jesus' revelation of God as Father, Abba, as the essence and uniqueness of his message: see E. Loymeyer, *"Our Father"*: *An Introduction to the Lord's Prayer*, translated by John Bowden (New York: Harper and Row, 1966), 41-42, and Joachim Jeremias, *The Prayers of Jesus*, Studies in Biblical Theology: Second Series, 6 (Naperville, IL: Alec R. Allenson, Inc., 1967), 57.

19. James M. Robinson, "How My Mind Has Changed," *Society of Biblical Literature: 1985 Seminar Papers* (Atlanta, GA: Scholars Press, 1985), 495. This might be considered one of the first attempts to apply practical deconstructionism to the Bible.

20. William Farmer, a recognized New Testament critic, Professor of New Testament at Perkins School of Theology, in his article, "The Church's Stake in the Question of 'Q'," *Perkins Journal*, 39/3 (1986), 10, acknowledges that "no one book has been more influential in setting the stage for the present upswing in 'Q' research" than Robinson's and Koester's *Trajectories Through Early Christianity* (Phila: Fortress Press, 1971). Farmer goes on to state that of the essays in that book, "none is more often cited in the 'Q' literature than Robinson's 'LOGOI SOPHWN.'"

21. Robert Funk, "Three Tributes to James M. Robinson," *Foundations and Facets* 5:2 (Polebridge Press, June, 1989), 6.

22. Specifically, Bultmann felt he could not understand the New Testament without the help of philosophy, and the philosophy in vogue in the 20s and 30s was the pagan philosophy of monistic existentialism, especially associated with Martin Heidegger. Bultmann acknowledged his great debt to Heidegger, but it was the pagan thinking of Heidegger and others that helped produce the ideological underpinning of National Socialism. See William E. Hughes, "The People . . .," 34-38. Though Bultmann refused any association with Nazism, existentialism seems to have oriented him towards the importance of Gnosticism, an ancient cousin of existentialism — see the essay by Jonas, "Epilogue: Gnosticism, Existentialism and Nihilism," *The Gnostic Religion*, 320-340.

James Robinson, "Introduction," *The Future of Our Religious Past*, 5, recognizes these connections to be part of Bultmann's contribution: "Bultmann was able to penetrate through the layers of the establishment's interpretation of the New Testament to hear and bring to expression primitive Christianity as the radical movement it origi-nally was. Moreover he was able to correlate that past with what has been called for in his own time. In this way he gave a religious past (that for many seemed irretrievably lost) a future with promise in our otherwise so chaotic world." The actual meaning of Robinson's words become clearer when one realizes that Robinson speaks of his own "early exit from orthodoxy" and identifies as positive the counter-culture rebellion of the Sixties as he sees its parallels with the counter-culture of ancient Gnosticism (see James M.Robinson, *The Nag Hammadi Library* in English, 1). Note also that in the Introduction to their book *Trajectories*, 1, Robinson and Koester claim to be involved in the "indigenization of the Bultmann tradition on American soil."

23. Robinson, *Trajectories*, 1-19.

24. They build on the work of Walter Bauer, with the telling title *Orthodoxy and Heresy in Earliest Christianity* (1934).

25. In addition to their joint work, *Trajectories*, see Helmut Koester, "GNOMAI DIAPHOROI: The Origin and Nature of Diversification in the History of Early Chris-tianity," *Harvard Theological Review* 58 ((1965), 279-318; also "One Jesus and Four Primitive Gospels," *Harvard Theological Review* 61 (1968), 203-247; James Robinson, LOGOI SOPHWN: On the Gattung of Q," *The Future of Our Religious Past: Essays in Honor of Rudolf Bultmann* (London: SCM, 1971), 84-130.

26. Koester, *Trajectories*, 270, states in the concluding essay: "The distinctions be-tween canonical and noncanonical, orthodox and heretical are obsolete. . . . One can only speak of a 'History of Early Christian Literature.'" The gray web of theological confusion is extended to the early Church.

27. Robinson, "How My Mind Has Changed," 486.

28. *The Future of Early Christianity: Essays in Honor of Helmut Koester*, ed. Birger A. Pearson (Minneapolis: Fortress Press, 1991)

29. Ibid., 473.

30. Ibid., 472.

31. Ibid., 474. The feminist theologian, Elizabeth Schüssler Fiorenza, is equally in-debted to the historical critical method for the same reasons: "I . . . had experienced historical-critical scholarship as liberating, setting me free from outdated doctrinal frame-works and literalist prejudices." She emphasizes the "connections between . . . feminist theological questions and those of historical-critical scholarship." See *Bread Not Stone: The Challenge of Feminist Biblical Interpretation* (Boston: Beacon, 1984), 94.

32. Ibid., 475-476.

33. The liberal critic Farmer sees this in "The Church's Stake," 10. In his own words: "it is Rudolf Bultmann as read through the work of Walter Bauer who lives on in the *Trajectories*." Farmer notes that the goal of the program is to deliver the con-temporary church from the moribund orthodox by restoring the Gnosticizing texts of Q and Thomas (ibid., 14).

34. See Pagels, *Gnostic Gospels*, 46 and 142.

35. *In Memory of Her: A Feminist Theological Reconstruction of Christian Origins* (New York: Crossroad, 1988), xv. See also her *Bread Not Stone*, 66-67.

36. Robert J. Miller, "The Gospels that Didn't Make the Cut," *Bible Review* (August, 1993), 21. See also Burton L. Mack, "Q and the Gospel of Mark: Revising Christian Origins," *Semeia* 55 (1991), 31, who says about the struggle of the Q community to survive: "a certain form of Christianity [orthodoxy] finally won over the others." Or-thodoxy won not because it was true but because it used social power more effectively.

37. Rosemary Radford Ruether, *Womanguides*, ix.

38. Susan Cyre, "PCUSA Funds Effort to Re-Create God," *Presbyterian Layman* 27/1 (January/February, 1994), 10.

39. Ibid., 9.

40. James M. Robinson, "Introduction," *The Nag Hammadi Library in English*, 20.

41. Caitlín Matthews, *Sophia, Goddess of Wisdom*, 338.

42. See James M.Robinson, ibid., xiii-xv.

43. See Peter Jones, *The Gnostic Empire Strikes Back* [from now on *The Gnostic Empire*] (Phillipsburg, NJ: P&R, 1992).

44. Shirley MacLaine, *Going Within: A Guide for Inner Transformation* (New York: Bantam Books, 1989), 29-30.

45. T. Roszak, *Where the Wasteland Ends: Politics and Transcendence in Post-Industrial Society* (New York: Doubleday, 1972), 262.

46. Ruether, *Women-Church*, 47 and 142.

47. K. B. Welton, *Abortion . . . is not a Sin*, 167, appealing to the *Gospel of Thomas* or the *Apocryphon of John*.

48. Long, *The Absent Mother*, 53, notes: "Gnosticism is becoming a powerful influence in feminist research into the overthrow of the female in the divine." Long refers to the earlier Nag Hammadi texts where Protennoia has a major role in the godhead, but sees a later more "Christian" influence in Gnosticism which lays the blame for the fall at the feet of Sophia.

49. For instance, the new spirituality — see June Singer, *A Gnostic Book of Hours* (San Francisco: Harper, 1992).

50. Robert J. Miller, ed. *The Complete Gospels* (Sonoma, CA: Polebridge Press, 1992).

51. Robert W. Funk and Roy W. Hoover, *The Five Gospels: The Search for the Authentic Words of Jesus* (New York: Macmillan, 1993). This title appears in the Polebridge Press Catalog, but is now published by Macmillan.

52. *Polebridge Press Catalog*, Fall/Winter 1991-1992, 3.

53. Stephen Mitchell, *The Gospel According to Jesus* (NY: Harper Collins, 1993), 10-11 has some clearly Gnostic themes — rejection of eschatology, the awakening experience to the kingdom of God within, the Gnostic toying with the sayings of Jesus and censoring what they do not like. On a popular level, this view of Jesus and Christianity is promoted through seminars and lectures throughout the New Age subculture and the diffuse movement of so-called Unity "churches." Gary Jones, dean of Education at the Unity School of Christianity, lectures on "The Credo of Jesus" that popularizes the "scientific" Jesus of left wing New Testament scholarship; Wendy Craig Purcell gives a series on "Ancient Wisdom for Modern Times," demonstrating once again that the old Gnosticism has returned.

54. Bentley Layton, *The Gnostic Scriptures* (New York: Doubleday, 1987), xxi.

55. Irenaeus, *Against Heresies*, 3:9:8.

56. *Against Heresies*, Preface, 2.

57. See Siegfried Schulz, *Q: Die Spruchquelle der Evangelistisen* (Zürich: Theologischer Verlag, 1972), 13. Paul Wernle in 1899 was the first to use the designation Q (ibid., 14-15).

58. One of the first to engage in this was James M. Robinson, in the article already cited, LOGOI SOPHWN. See Farmer, "The Church's Stake," 14, who believes 'Q' has staying power because many today are no longer interested in it as a way to explain Matthew and Luke (a thesis that has constantly been challenged), but as a way to reconstruct the history of early Christianity.

59. The reference is constructed by taking the name Q and adding the chapter and verse of Luke where Q is supposed to occur.

60. Arland D. Jacobson, *The First Gospel: An Introduction to Q* (Sonoma, CA: Polebridge Press, 1992).

61. Burton L. Mack (also a member of the Jesus Seminar), *The Lost Gospel: The Book of Q and Christian Origins* (San Francisco: Harper, 1993).

62. This is another offering by Polebridge Press — John S. Kloppenborg, Marvin W. Meyer, Stephen J. Patterson and Michael G. Steinhauser, *Q Thomas Reader* (Sonoma, CA: Polebridge Press, 1990).

64. Bertil Gärtner, *Theology of the Gospel of Thomas*, translated by Eric J. Sharpe (New York: Harper and Brothers, 1961), 30, speaks of its "unique . . . literary form."

64. Even this should be modified. The hymnic material scattered throughout the New Testament is extremely early and includes reflection on the death and resurrection of Christ — see Phil 2:6-11 and 1 Cor 15: 3ff.

65. Robinson, "Jesus–from Easter . . ." 22. For the proposed relationship between Q and the *Gospel of Thomas*, see Robinson, "LOGOI SOPHWN, 84-130, and his "On Bridging the Gulf From Q to the *Gospel of Thomas* (Or Vice Versa)," *Nag Hammadi Gnosticism and Early Christianity*, eds. Charles W. Hedrick and Robert Hodgson, Jr., (Peabody, MA: Hendrickson, 1986), 127-176; see also H. Koester and James Robinson, *Trajectories Through Early Christianity* (Philadelphia: Fortress Press, 1971), 186-187; H. Koester, "Q and Its Relatives," *Gospel Origins and Christian Beginnings*, ed. J. Goehring (Sonoma, CA: Polebridge Press,1990), 49-63; see also H. Koester, *Ancient Christian Gospels* (London-Philadelphia: London SCM Press,1990),86-99.

66. Stevan Davies, "The Christology and Protology of the *Gospel of Thomas*," *JBL* III/4 (1992), 663. Stephen J. Patterson, *The Gospel of Thomas and Jesus* (Sonoma: Polebridge Press, 1993), 116, whose book is a form of his doctoral dissertation under James Robinson, proposes a date "close to Paul." In the Koester/Robinson school Thomas has been brought into the first century and pre-dates Matthew, Luke and John.

67. *Talk of the Nation*, hosted by Ray Suarez, December 5, 1993.

68. In Robert Funk's radio interview, he assured listeners that a number of the seventy-five fellows of the Seminar were neither church members nor even Christian believers.

69. Robert J. Miller, "The Gospels that Did Not Make the Cut," 15. See also his introduction to *The Complete Gospels*, xi, where he boasts that the work is "free of ecclesiastical and religious control." Is Miller naive enough to think that Funk did not bring together a group of scholars with a religious pre-commitment?

70. The studied attempt at objectivity is undermined by the ideological homogeneity of the Seminar members assembled by Robert Funk, most of whom would doubtless call themselves theological liberals. Beyond that, one may well wonder how much these scholars are representative of world-wide New Testament scholarship.

71. As a matter of fact, it is seriously questioned whether Q and Thomas have any direct literary relationship — see C. M. Tuckett, "Q and Thomas: Evidence of a Primitive Wisdom Gospel: A Response to H. Koester," *Ephemerides Theologicae Lovaniensis* LXVII/4 (1991), 346-360.

72. Cited in Theodore Rosché, "Word of Jesus and the Future of the Q Hypothesis,"*JBL* 79 (1960), 210-220. Incidentally, Rosché concluded his article by arguing that logic was on the side of the non-existence of Q (219).

73. H. H. Stoldt, *History and Criticism of the Marcan Hypothesis* (Macon: Mercer, 1980), cited in John Wenham, *Redating Matthew, Mark and Luke: A Fresh Assault on the Synoptic Problem* (Downers Grove, IL: InterVarsity Press, 1992), 1-2.

74. John Wenham, *Redating*, xxi, cites the names of scholars of the past and the present such as T. Zahn, H. G. Jameson, B. C. Butler, P. Parker, L. Vaganay, A. M. Farrer, A. W. Argyle, R. T. Simpson, W. R. Farmer, E. P. Sanders, D. L. Dungan, R. L. Lindsey, M. -É Boismard and J. M. Rist. To these we can add James Hardy Ropes, Nigel Turner, Morton Enslin, Wilhelm Wilkens, Robert Morgenthaler, M. D. Goulder, and Edward C. Hobbs. Most of these scholars could be called moderate liberals.

75. John Wenham, *Redating*, ibid. A similar group, called the *International Q Project*, was re-organized in 1989 by the *Research and Publications Committee* of the *Society of Biblical Literature*, under the leadership of James Robinson and John Kloppenborg, with Helmut Koester in attendance — see James Robinson, "The International Q Project; Work Session 17 November 1989," *JBL* 109/3 (1990), 499-501. A similar Q Project is maintained at the *Institute for Antiquity and Christianity* at Claremont, directed by James Robinson.

76. Ibid. See also the judgment of Hobbs in 1980: "There is no serenity in the field of the sources of the Gospels, there are no longer 'assured results of scholarship.'"

77. A lecture given at Drew University in 1983, published as "The Sayings of Jesus: Q," *Drew Gateway* (Fall, 1983), 26-38, cited in Farmer, "The Church's Stake," 15.

78. Farmer, "The Church's Stake," 15. See also S. Petrie, "Q Is Only What You Make It," *Novum Testamentum* 3 (1959), cited by Wenham, *Redating*, 42. See P. Jones, *Gnostic Empire*, 105, n.34, where a portion of this article is cited. In 1989 a similar judgment about Q was made by Edward C. Hobbs, professor of theology at the Graduate Theological Union, and the Church Divinity School of the Pacific, Berkeley, California, "A Quarter-Century Without 'Q'," *Perkins Journal* 33 (Summer, 1980), 13, who says: "No reconstruction of Q has gained anything like overwhelming acceptance."

79. A. M. Farrer, "On Dispensing With Q," *Studies In The Gospels*, ed. D. E. Nineham (Oxford: University Press, 1955).

80. M. D. Goulder, a radical critic, nevertheless finds Farrer's arguments still convincing in 1980. See his "Farrer on Q," *Theology* 83 (1980), 190-195, and also his "On Putting Q To the Test," *New Testament Studies* 24 (1978), 218-234.

81. Art.cit., 10.

82. Art.cit., 19. In the judgment of Hobbs (in somewhat purple prose): "very few are owed so much by so many as Austin Farrer is owed. He is dead these ten years; the posterity of his work lives after him, to declare his wisdom and to summon his successors to honor him, as in fact we do this day." William Farmer, "The Church's Stake," 16, still cites Farrer's argument as unanswered in 1986.

83. See the following note.

84. Allan J. McNicol, with David L. Dungan and David B. Peabody, editors, *Beyond the Q Impasse — Luke's Use of Matthew* (Valley Forge: Trinity Press International, announced for December, 1996), see *Fall/Winter Catalogue*, 1996, 9.

85. Ibid.

86. Earle E. Ellis, a review article in *Southwestern Journal of Theology* 31 (1989), 66, of John S. Kloppenborg, *The Formation of Q: Trajectories in Ancient Wisdom Collections* (Philadelphia: Fortress Press, 1987).

87. N. T. Wright, quoted in *Time* (January 10, 1994).

88. Ibid.

89. See Kloppenborg/Vaage, "Early Christianity," *Semeia*, 55 (1991), 4.

90. Marcus Borg, *Jesus: A New Vision: Spirit, Culture and the Life of Discipleship* (San Francisco: Harper, 1987), 8. With slightly more nuance, Stephen J. Patterson, *The Gospel of Thomas and Jesus*, 231.

91. This is the same notion that is found in the Gnostic *Secret Book of James* which is included among the "Complete Gospels." "Heaven's domain is discovered through knowledge. . . [and the major concern of the document] lies in Jesus's teaching and the furnishing of a foundational revelation for a community of Gnostic Christians." Ibid., 324-325.

92. Burton Mack, *The Lost Gospel*, 1.

93. Patterson, *The Gospel of Thomas and Jesus*, 234.

94. Patterson, ibid., 235.

95. See Elizabeth Schüssler Fiorenza, *In Memory of Her: A Feminist Theological Reconstruction of Christian Origins* (New York: Crossroad, 1988), 124, 130ff; see also Louise Schottroff, "Itinerant Prophetesses: A Feminist Analysis of the Sayings Source Q," *Institute for Antiquity and Christianity, Occasional Papers* 21 (Claremont, CA: Institute for Antiquity and Christianity, 1991).

96. Ibid., 4-5.

97. See *Quality Paperback Bookclub* flyer.

98. Though even Fiorenza, admits that neutrality is impossible: *In Memory of Her*, xvi-xvii.

99. Robert Funk, *The Five Gospels*, 5.

100. Marcus Borg, *Meeting Jesus Again for the First Time* (San Francisco: Harper San Francisco, 1993).

101. Marcus Borg, "Me and Jesus: The Journey Home," *The Fourth R* (July/August 1993), 9.

102. Scott McKnight, "Who is Jesus: An Introduction to Jesus Studies," *Jesus Under Fire: Modern Scholarship Re-invents the Historical Jesus*, ed. Michael J. Wilkin and J. P. Moreland (Grand Rapids: Zondervan, 1995), 70, n. 22. Professor McKnight here mentions a master's thesis written under his direction at Trinity Evangelical Divinity School by Dana K. Ostby, "The Historical Jesus and the Supernatural World: A Shift in the Modern Critical Worldview with Special Emphasis on the Writings of Marcus Borg," 1991.

103. A. Morrison, *The Serpent*, 568, documents that Huston Smith is a sponsor of the Temple of Understanding (a Non-Governmental Organization in the United Nations devoted to global syncretism), was a faculty member with Assistant Secretary-General of the U.N., Robert Muller, the Dalai Lama and Marilyn Ferguson (author of the book, *The Aquarian Conspiracy)* at an interfaith gathering in Malta in 1985 and, in the same year, gave a lecture at the Theosophical Society's "Blavatsky Lodge" in Sydney, Australia on the subject, "Is a New World Religion Coming?"

104. Huston Smith, *Beyond the Post-Modern Mind* (Wheaton, IL: Theosophical Publishing House, 1989).

105. James Webb, *The Occult Establishment* (La Salle, IL: Open Court, 1976), 25 and 553.

106. Borg, "Me and Jesus," 9. In a "Program Release" from *PBS* (April, 1996), Smith is presented as "a pilgrim seeking to experience personally the spiritual to which the different religions point. . . . He remains a Methodist [like First Lady Hillary Clinton], the faith into which he was born of missionary parents in China, but he practices yoga, prays five times a day as Muslims do, [and] has endured the rigors of a Zen monastery."

107. *Catalog Spring/Summer 1994* (Sonoma, CA: Polebridge Press, 1994), 3.

108. Neil Douglas-Klotz, *Prayers of the Cosmos: Meditations on the Aramaic Words of Jesus* (San Francisco: Harper, 1993).

109. *Polebridge Press Catalog 1994*, 5.

110. See the *Vedanta Catalog 1992-1993* (Hollywood, CA: 1993), 49, which argues that the Nag Hammadi texts reveal an early Christianity which had much in common with "Eastern religions and the teachings of holy people of all times." This is an accurate description of Gnosticism but a false picture of early Christianity. This Hindu catalog enthusiastically features James Robinson's *The Nag Hammadi Library in English*, and Elaine Pagels' *The Gnostic Gospels*. New Age book stores do the same.

111. Stevan Davies, "Christology and Protology," 663-682. This article claims *Thomas* as valuable a source for the teaching of Jesus as Q "and perhaps more so than the Gospels of Mark and John." This is described as an emerging consensus of American

scholarship, though most of the names cited are associated in one way or another with the Jesus Seminar or James Robinson and the Q Seminar.

112. Ibid., 665.

113. Steve Beard, "Mainline Churches Sponsor Radical Feminist Conference: Pagan Worship Encouraged, Lesbianism Praised," *AFA Journal* (February, 1994).

114. Kurt Aland, *The Problem of the New Testament Canon* (London: Mowbray, 1962), 25-26, compare E. Hennecke and W. Schneemelcher, *New Testament Apocrypha* (Philadelphia: Westminster Press, 1963), 372 and 391.

115. Another approach is to isolate passages and ideas in the Bible and turn them in a New Age direction. See, for instance Ronald Quillo, *Companions in Consciousness: The Bible and the New Age Movement* (Liguori, MO: Triumph Books, 1994). Quillo admits, nevertheless, that on some points the Bible and the New Age may never agree, so finally the New Age does need a new Bible.

116. David Miller, *The New Polytheism*, 76.

117. Some well-known Christian liberal scholars are associated with this organization. Ninian Smart, Professor of Religious Studies at the University of California, Santa Barbara, and author of *Christian Systematic Theology in a World Context* (Minneapolis: Fortress Press, 1991), is a "presiding council member, and Leonard Swidler, Professor of Theology, Temple University, Philadelphia, and author of the much quoted and translated article, "Jesus Was a Feminist," *Catholic World* (January, 1971), is a member of the "board of advisers." Also, one of the presidents of IRFWP's "Presiding Council" is Paulos Mar Gregorius, Metropolitan of Delhi, of the Syrian Orthodox Church, and one of the leaders in the World Council of Churches. Clearly, by taking a low profile, and no doubt spending lavishly, the "moonies" have begun to live down their bizarre cultic image of a few years ago. The Rev. Moon's name is absent from all the honorary boards and councils of the movement. It does appear, however, in a modest side-bar, where the IRFWP Newsletter does note that the IRFWP "was founded in 1990 by Reverend Sun Myung Moon."

118. See *IRFWP Newsletter* 12 (Fall, 1993), 9. The book is now in print as *World Scripture: A Comparative Anthology of Sacred Texts* (New York: Paragon House, 1994).

119. *The Other Bible* (San Francisco: Harper, 1984), xvii.

120. Philip Novak, *The World's Wisdom* (San Francisco: HarperSanFrancisco, 1994).

121. *Portable World Bible,* ed. Robert O. Batlou (London: Penguin, 1994). See also the *Vedanta Catalog 1992-1993*, p. 49, which offers *The Other Bible* edited by Willis Barnstone, which contains Hermetic and Gnostic texts as well as selections from the Jewish Kabbalah, from Marcion, Mani and Plotinus.

Chapter Seven

1. According to Rudolf, *Gnosis,* 53, "there was no Gnostic 'church' or normative theology, no Gnostic rule of faith nor any dogma of exclusive importance. No limits were set to free representation and theological speculation . . . there was no gnostic canon of scripture."

2. Tertullian, *De Praescriptione*, 38.

3. Frank Moore Cross, Jr., *The Ancient Library of Qumran* (New York: Doubleday, 1961), 40.

4. See chapter 6.

5. Kurt Rudolf, *Gnosis,* 152. See also Bertil Gärtner, *The Theology of the Gospel of Thomas,* 271, who dates *Thomas* about 140 A.D.

6. Ibid., 54-55.

7. Rodolphe Kasser, *L'Evangile Selon Thomas* (Geneva: Delachaux et Niestlé, 1961), 58. Kasser lists some twenty allusions to the canonical Gospels in this one saying. See also Gärtner, *Theology of the Gospel of Thomas,* 177. Gärtner shows how the recasting of canonical material expresses the Gnostic world and life view.

8. Irenaeus, *Against Heresies* 1:8:1. This quotation is taken from a new translation by D. J. Unger, *Ancient Christian Writers* (New York: Paulist Press, 1992), 41. If this is a reference to *Thomas*, as it could well be, then Irenaeus is affirming in no uncertain terms that *Thomas* is dependent on the Synoptics.

9. See Mary A. Kassian, *The Feminist Gospel: the Movement to Unite Feminism with the Church* (Wheaton, IL: Crossway Books, 1992), 182.

10. G. W. MacRae, "Introduction to Gospel of Truth," *The Nag Hammadi Library in English*, 38.

11. Romans 3:23.

12. *Acts of Peter* 20, quoted in Gärtner, op.cit., 79.

13. Irenaeus, *Against Heresies* 1.14.1 cp Hippolytus, *Refutation of All Heresies* 6:42:2.

14. Liddell and Scott, *Greek-English Lexicon* (Oxford: Clarendon, 1968), 201.

15. Ibid., 204.

16. *Apocryphon of James* 1:1:20-30.

17. *Apocryphon of John* 31:25-32:5, translation taken from Soren Giverson, *Aprocryphon Johannis* (Copenhagen: Prostant Apud Munlsgaard, 1963), plates 70:22-80:5. All the citations from the *Apocalypse of John* in this present book are taken from Giverson.

18. John 20:30-31.

19. John 12:32.

20. *Apocalypse of Paul* 22:24-30, and 23:26-27.

21. William R. Schoedel, *The Nag Hammadi Library in English*, 242.

22. Charles W. Hedrick, *The Nag Hammadi Library in English*, 249.

23. *Apocalypse of Adam* 85:22-26.

24. *Apocalypse of Peter* 71:21.

25. Matthew 10:27.

26. *Gospel of Thomas*, prologue.

27. *Gospel of Truth* 22:38-23:15.

28. *Gospel of the Egyptians* 69:6-7, 15.

29. *Zostrianos* 132:5-8.

30. *Trimorphic Protennoia* 50:22-24.

31. *Gospel of Truth* 19:34-37.

32. John H. Sieber, in the introduction, *The Nag Hammadi Library in English*, 368.

33. Ibid.

34. Fritjof Capra, *The Tao of Physics* (Boston: Shambhala Publications, 1975), 7.

35. David L. Miller, *The New Polytheism*, viii.

36. Ibid.

37. This could, off course, be an innocuous statement of human dependence upon God, but there are many New Age tendencies in her writings that suggest a different interpretation. See Samantha Scott and Barbara. Smith, *Trojan Horse: How the New Age Movement Infiltrates the Church*, (Lafayette, LA: Huntingdon House Press, 1993), 38.

38. Virginia Ramey Mollenkott, *Sensuous Spirituality: Out From Fundamentalism* (New York: Crossroad, 1992), 21.

39. Ibid., 14 and 25. On pages 18-19 she describes her writing process and wonders if her insights, which do not come from her ego, come from "my guardian angel, a Spirit Guide, the Holy Spirit, or Jesus, or God's Self?" Christianity has come a long way when the Holy Spirit can be confused with Spirit Guides. First lady Hillary Clinton's book, *It Takes a Village* was written by a ghost writer but also with help from New Age guru channeler Jean Houston, and through her, Eleanor Roosevelt. It clearly took an odd little village to write *It Takes a Village*.

40. 1 Corinthians 12:10.

Chapter Eight

1. Burton Throckmorton, Jr. is quoted by Virginia Byfield, in "The Move to Rewrite the Bible," *Alberta Report* (April 29, 1986), 36, cited in Kassian, 169.

2. Sherry Ruth Anderson & Patricia Hopkins, *The Feminine Face of God: The Unfolding of the Sacred in Women* (New York: Bantam Books, 1991), 2-3. Anderson is described in the book as "a Jewish easterner [from the East coast] who became a serious student of Buddhism." She once chaired the Department of Psychological Research at the University of Toronto's Clarke Institute of Psychiatry "while simultaneously serving as the head dharma teacher at the Ontario Zen Center. Such a background would make one wonder if the new "Torah" really is "new" and empty, or whether it will simply be a new version of Eastern monistic paganism written from the perspective of radical feminism.

3. Alicia Suskin Ostriker, *Feminist Revision and the Bible* (Oxford: Blackwell, 1993), 11.

4. William Oddie, *What Will Happen to God? Feminism and the Reconstruction of Christian Belief* (San Francisco: Ignatious Press, 1988), 140-141.

5. Cited in Steichen, *Ungodly Rage,* 147.

6. Ibid.

7. Elliot Miller, *A Crash Course on the New Age: Describing and Evaluating a Growing Social Force* (Grand Rapids: Baker, 1989), 17.

8. David Wells, *No Place for Truth.*

9. Arthur Johnson, *Faith Misguided,* 66.

10. David Jobling, *The Sense of Biblical Narrative: Structural Analysis in the Hebrew Bible,* II JSOTS 39 (Sheffield: JSOT, 1986), 19. On a different social level, Kimberle Crenshaw, a black feminist and UCLA law professor, argues that "gender is central to the issues we in the black community consider [as] the black agenda." See "A Dilemma for Black Women," *Los Angeles Times,* August 27, 1994, A20.

11. For a helpful treatment of this subject, see Veith, *Postmodern Times,* 49.

12. Cited by Charles Colson, *World,* February 19, 1994, 22.

13. David Wells, *No Place for Truth,* 65. Wells cites David Lehman, *Signs of the Times: Deconstructionism and the Fall of Paul de Man* (London: Andre Deutsch, 1991); Brian McHale, *Post Modernist Fiction* (London: Routledge, Chapman & Hall, 1987); and Linda Hutcheon, *A Poetics of Post-modernism: History, Theory and Fiction* (New York: Routledge, Chapman & Hall, 1988).

14. *Time Magazine,* July 11, 1994, 47.

15. Ibid., 14, 15.

16. Mollenkott, *Sensuous Spirituality,* 167.

17. This method has been used to justify abortion (rape, incest and the life of the mother), and euthanasia (excruciating terminal cancer), but ends up with millions of "life-style choice" abortions, and the proposed extension of euthanasia to paraplegics and all terminal illnesses — see Peter J. Barnardi, "Dr. Death's Dreadful Sermon," *Christianity Today,* August 15, 1994, 31.

18. E. D. Hirsch, *Validity in Interpretation* (New Haven: Yale University Press, 1967) seeks to defend the importance of the author for establishing some objective meaning. He distinguishes between "meaning," which is the author's intent, and "significance" which depends upon the reader and the various readers' perspectives. "The author's intended meaning is what a text means." This study is cited in Walter C. Kaiser and Moisés Silva, *An Introduction to Biblical Hermeneutics: The Search for Meaning* (Grand Rapids: Zondervan, 1994), 30, which I recommend as an excellent introduction to the details of modern hermeneutical theory and practice. See also V. Poythress, *Science and Hermeneutics: Implications of Scientific Method for Biblical Interpretation* (Grand Rapids: Zondervan, 1988).

19. Of which there are two schools, known as New Criticism of the 40s and 50s, and Structuralism, which came later.

20. Kaiser and Silva, ibid., 29. Kaiser discusses the decisive influence of Gadamer.

21. Ibid., 31. See also a programmatic article by D. A. J. Clines, *What Does Eve Do to Help? and Other Readerly Questions to the Old Testament: JSOTS* 94 (Sheffield: Sheffield Academic Press, 1990), but especially p.9.

22. Silva, ibid., with great balance, sees the positive aspects but also the dangers: "The moment we recognize that Paul wrote something the original readers would not understand, the text then has a life of its own, subject to being understood in ways different than the author intended. This "autonomy" of the text can be positive if it brings interpreters to appreciate the literary character of the text: it is negative if the original historical setting is dismissed as unimportant. . . . We cannot avoid the place of the interpreter/reader, both for science and the humanities. An interpreter comes with a theory that seeks to account for as many facts as possible, but given the finite nature of every human interpreter, no interpretation accounts for the data exhaustively. . . . In reader-response theory there is no such thing as an objective text because every reader generates a new meaning and therefore a new text. However, we must not refuse the invaluable contributions of this movement, which underlines the role of the reader, because the Bible has been actualized in the believer's experience for two thousand years of Christian history. . . . If an omniscient and foreseeing God is the author of Scripture, then we can assume that the human authors were not aware of the significance of all that they wrote. . . . My own position . . . [is that] the meaning of a biblical passage need not be identified completely with the author's intention. It is quite a different matter . . . to suggest that authorial meaning is dispensable or even secondary." What the author meant is always a necessary question" (240, 242, 244, and 248).

23. D. T. Maurina, *Reformed Believers Press Service*, June 16, 1994, 2.

24. Mary Jo Weaver, an associate professor of religious studies at Indiana University and the author of *New Catholic Women*, a scholar who is named with reverence among Wicca feminists, cited by Donna Steichen, *Ungodly Rage*, 145-6.

25. Steichen, *Ungodly Rage*, 168, citing Fiorenza.

26. Ruether, *Women-Church*, 3

27. Ruether, *Womanguides*, cited in Mary Kassian, *The Feminist Gospel*, 182.

28. Ruether, *Women-Church*, 63.

29. Elizabeth Schlüssler Fiorenza, "Changing the Paradigms," *How My Mind Has Changed*, ed James M.Wall and David Heim (Grand Rapids: Eerdmans, 1991) 86, To what extent evangelical feminists buy into this new method remains to be seen. Patricia Gundry, *Neither Slave Nor Free* (New York: Harper and Row, 1987), 77-78, claims that a new, more sophisticated science of hermeneutics makes feminist biblical interpretation possible (pp.77-78). Hopefully she will not be seduced by the sophisticated hermeneutics of suspicion.

30. For an elaboration of this view of history see Riane Eisler, *The Chalice and the Blade: Our History, Our Future* (San Francisco: Harper and Row, 1987).

31. Oddie, *What Will Happen to God?*, 152, notes that "it is, above all, from the tortured and angry world of the secular feminist struggle that the 'feminist hermeneutics of suspicion' has been directly culled so that it may scatter broadcast its dragon's teeth of resentment and mistrust in the fertile soil of the Church's life."

32. See Ruether, *Women-Church*, 41, and Francis Watson, "Strategies of Recovery and Resistance: Hermeneutical Reflections on Genesis 1-3 and its Pauline Reception," *Journal for the Study of the New Testament* 45 (1992), 81ff.

33. Fewell and Gunn, *Gender, Power and Promise* (Nashville: Abingdon, 1993).

34. Ibid., 18 - 20.

35. Oddie, *What Will Happen to God?* 142, discussing Fiorenza.

36. Oddie, ibid., 143.

37. Stanley Fish, *Is There a Text in This Class? The Authority of Interpretive Communities,* 1980, cited in Mollenkott, *Sensuous Spirituality,* 167.

38. Moisés Silva, *Biblical Hermeneutics,* 249.

39. Ben Wildavsky, "Agency OKs New Policy on Diversity at Colleges," *San Francisco Chronicle,* February 24, 1994. I am indebted to my colleague, Dean Dennis Johnson, for showing me this article.

40. Fiorenza, *Bread Not Stone,* 147. See also p.140, where she bases her theory on earlier liberal theory.

41. When truth is power, even truth comes out of the end of a gun.

42. Thirteen learned societies, including AAR, sponsored a major multidisciplinary conference on *The Role of Advocacy in the Classroom,* in June, 1995 in Pittsburgh.

43. Quoted in Oddie, *What Will Happen to God?,* 40.

44. Walter Brueggemann, "On Writing a Commentary . . . An Emergency, *ATS/Colloquy* (September/October, 1992), 10-11.

45. Harvey Cox, *Many Mansions: A Christian Encounter with Other Faiths* (Boston: Beacon Press, 1988), 210-212.

46. Ibid., 17.

47. Cave, *Mircea Eliade,* 181. See also Fiorenza, *Bread Not Stone,* xxiii, who concludes, citing another scholar, Berstein, that "it is not sufficient to come up with some new variations of arguments that will show, once and for all, what is wrong with objectivism and relativism, or even open up a way of thinking that can move us beyond objectivism and relativism; such a movement gains 'reality and power' only if we dedicate ourselves to the practical task of furthering the type of solidarity, participation, and mutual recognition that is founded in dialogical communities." Any meaningful thought and action for the future is based on the monistic dogma of the unity of the whole, without reference to a transcendent God and special revelation.

48. Daly, *Wickedary,* 201.

49. Steichen, *Ungodly Rage,* 148, citing an address by Sister Madonna Kolbenschlag.

50. Elizabeth Cady Stanton, *The Women's Bible* (1895), certainly a significant "foremother" of this modern approach; Phyllis Trible, Baldwin Professor of Sacred Literature, Union Theological Seminary, New York, "Adam and Eve: Genesis 2-3 Reread," *WomanSpirit Rising: A Feminist Reader in Religion,* ed. Carol Christ and Judith Plaskow (San Francisco: Harper, 1979), 74-83; Carter Heyward, Professor of Theology at Episcopal Divinity School, Cambridge, MA, *The Redemption of God: A Theology of Mutual Relations* (New York: University Press of America, 1982), 150-152; At the American Academy of Religion's annual meeting in San Francisco in 1992, Heward boasted, in a public address, of being the only lesbian, pregnant [by artificial insemination] Episcopal priest in the world; Francis Landy, *Paradoxes in Paradise: Identity and Difference in the Song of Songs B & L* (Sheffield: Almond, 1983); Dorothee Solle, leading German Protestant theologian and feminist, *The Strength of the Weak: Towards a Christian Feminist Identity,* trans. Robert and Rita Kimber (Philadelphia: Westminster Press, 1984), 126-129; David Jobling, *The Sense of Biblical Narrative: Structural Analysis in the Hebrew Bible* II JSOTS 39 (Sheffield: JSOT, 1986); Mieke Bal, *Lethal Love: Feminist Literary Readings of Biblical Love Stories,* ISBL (Bloomingdale: Indiana University, 1987) 104-132; Anne Primavesi, *From Apocalypse to Genesis* (Minneapolis: Fortress Press, 1991); Frederica Halligan, "Keeping Faith with the Future: Towards Final Conscious Unity," *The Fires of Desire* (New York: Crossroad, 1992), 176-177; Francis Watson, member of the Department of Theology and Religious Studies, King's College, London, and editor of the Journal for the Study of the New Testament, "Strategies of Recovery and Resistance: Hermeneutical Reflections on Genesis 1-3 and its Pauline Reception," *JSNT* 45 (March, 1992), 79-103; Susan Niditch, Professor of Religion at Amherst

College, "Genesis," *The Women's Bible Commentary* (Louisville, KY: John Knox/Westminster, 1992); see also the works of certain Jewish scholars: Judith Plaskow, "The Coming of Lilith: Towards a Feminist Theology," *WomanSpirit Rising*; H. Bloom, *The Book of J* (New York: Grove Wiedenfeld, 1990) who argues, from an unbelieving point of view, that the hypothetical source "J" of the Pentateuch was written by an unbelieving woman of the tenth century B.C. who presents Jahweh as a bungler and favors the serpent. Bruce Waltke's estimation of J as the "most blasphemous writer that ever lived" was written before the appearance of much of this "new" exegesis — see Waltke, "Harold Bloom and 'J'": A Review Article," JETS 34/4 (December, 1991), 509.

51. Fewell and Gunn, *Gender, Power and Promise*, 18-19.

52. Ibid., 95.

53. Ibid., 23.

54. Ibid., 24.

55. Ibid., 25 and 67.

56. Ibid., 26.

57. Ibid., 24.

58. Ibid., 38.

59. Trible, cited in Mieke Bal, *Lethal Love*, 113.

60. Ibid., 127.

61. Landy, Ibid., 212.

62. Jobling, *Sense of Biblical Narrative*, 25,

63. Landy, *Paradoxes in Paradise*, 219.

64. Fewell and Gunn, ibid., 33 and 168.

65. Bal, *Lethal Love*, 113.

66. Jobling, ibid., 26. This of course is true, but the force of the Genesis text is to suggest that Adam, in such a passive role, is not functioning as the covenantal head he was supposed to be.

67. Phyllis Trible, *God and the Rhetoric of Sexuality* (Philadelphia: Fortress, 1978), 113.

68. Susan Niditch, *The Women's Bible Commentary*, 14.

69. Elizabeth Cady Stanton, *The Women's Bible,* republished as *The Original Feminist Attack on the Bible*, intr. Barbara Welton (Arno Press, 1974), 24-25. This surely is a more accurate title since Stanton herself states openly that her "reason had repudiated [the Bible's] divine authority" (ibid., 12). Stanton also recognized "general principles of love, charity, liberty, justice and equality . . . in the holy books of all religions," and worshipped the God whom she called "our ideal great first cause, `the Spirit of all Good'" (ibid., 12-13). Hopefully Christian evangelical "egalitarians," in their rush to embrace this feminist heroine of the past will recognize the pagan character of her thinking.

70. Ibid., 31.

71. Fewell and Gunn, ibid., 30.

72. Ibid., 38.

73. Ibid.

74. Ibid., 31 cp Bal, ibid., 124 and 125.

75. Bal, ibid., 125.

76. Fewell and Gunn, ibid., 31 cp Bal, ibid., 125.

77. Fewell and Gunn, ibid., 65.

78. Ibid., 166-167.

79. Ibid., 32.

80. Bal, ibid., 122.

81. Ibid., 122.

82. Jobling, ibid., 26.

83. Niditch, *The Women's Bible Commentary*, 14.

84. Bal, ibid., 116 and 109.

85. Fewell and Gunn, ibid., 30 cp Landy, ibid., 189.

86. Bal, ibid., 124.

87. Fewell and Gunn, ibid., 34.

88. Landy, ibid., 210.

89. Bal, ibid., 123.

90. Niditch, *The Women's Bible Commentary*, 14.

91. Betty Eadie, *Embraced by the Light* (Goldleaf Press, 1992), 109: Frederica Halligan, "Keeping Faith with the Future: Towards Final Conscious Unity," *The Fires of Desire* (New York: Crossroad, 1992), 176-177. "Eve was seeking truth, and it was the patriarchal church that condemned her."

92. Francis Watson, "Strategies of Recovery and Resistance: Hermeneutical Reflections on Genesis 1-3 and its Pauline Reception," *JSNT* 45 (March, 1992) 79-103. Watson teaches in the Department of Theology and Religious Studies, King's College, London [emphasis added].

93. John Richard Neuhaus, *First Things* (June/July, 1994).

Chapter Nine

1. Irenaeus, *Against Heresies*, 41.

2. David L. Balas, "The Use and Interpretation of Paul in Irenaeus's Five Books Adversus Haereses," *Second Century* 9 (April, 1992), 31, notes that "the Gnostic speculations seem to be based primarily on an esoteric exegesis of the Old Testament and the Gospels."

3. *Hypostasis of the Archons* 86:20-30.

4. Ibid., 87:24-26, 88:24-25, 89:3-16.

5. Orval Wintermute, "Gnostic Exegesis of the Old Testament," in J. M. Efird (ed.), *The Use of the Old Testament in the New and Other Essays* (Durham: Duke University Press, 1972) 252, shows that this was justified by assigning the Aramaic meaning ("teacher") to the Hebrew word HYH — "wild animal" of which the serpent was one (Gen 3:1).

6. *On the Origin of the World*, 114:3-4. See also the treatment of this theme by Birger A.Pearson, *Gnosticism, Judaism and Egyptian Christianity* (Minneapolis: Fortress Press, 1990) 43ff, a publication of the Institute for Antiquity and Christianity. In the *Testimony of Truth* the Coptic term describing the wisdom of the serpent is stronger than that used in the Bible and means "revealer of wisdom and knowledge." In this literature the serpent is the "teacher of Eve and Eve is the 'teacher' of Adam (see *On the Origin of the World*, 113:33 cp. *Hypostasis of the Archons* 89:32; 90:6). Gnosticism clearly makes the role reversals and role confusion an aspect of Gnostic wisdom.

In this same document the serpent/teacher is called "the beast" (*therion*, see 114:3), in this context, a title of nobility. Revelation uses this term for a being who is the embodiment of evil (11:7) whom the inhabitants of the earth will worship and who will make war against the saints and conquer them (13:7). His bestial successor is given the number 666 (13:18).

7. Irenaeus, *Against Heresies* 1:27:3 (p.368 in *Early Church Fathers*) suggests that Marcion believed the serpent possessed him. Marcion certainly believed in the salvation the serpent preached by which Cain, the men of Sodom and the Egyptians were saved, while Abel, Enoch, Noah, Abraham and the prophets perished. Irenaeus also recounts a tradition concerning a meeting between Polycarp and Marcion. The latter asked, "Do you know us?" and Polycarp answered, "I know you, the first born of Satan." (*Against Heresies*, 3:3:3). Hippolytus gives an extended treatment of the Naasenes who worship the serpent. Their doctrines are classically Gnostic, as for example their rejection of the Old Testament and of the sacrificial system. "The universal

serpent is . . . the wise discourse of Eve . . . this is the mark that was set upon Cain that anyone who findeth him might not kill him. This . . . is Cain, whose sacrifice the god of this world did not accept. The gory sacrifice, however, of Abel he approved of; for the ruler of this world rejoices in blood." (*Refutation of All Heresies* 40). See also the discussions in Jonas, *The Gnostic Religion*, 92-95, and Kurt Rudolf, *Gnosis*, 84ff.

8. *Testimony of Truth*, 47:15-30.

9. Hippolytus, *Refutation of All Heresies* V:xxi.

10. *On the Origin of the World* 97:25.

11. *On the Origin of the World* 113:21-114:4.

12. *On the Origin of the World* 118:25-119:19.

13. *On the Origin of the World* 120:3-6, 9-11.

14. The following texts from the Nag Hammadi collection, in addition to the ones cited, make direct use of the "reversal exegesis" of Genesis: *Tripartite Tractate* 78:14ff; *Apocryphon of John* 11:15-24:31; *Sophia of Jesus Christ* 106:25-107:15; *Trimorphic Protennoia* 40:23-27; *Second Apocalypse of James* 58:2-6; *Apocalypse of Adam* 64:9-67:14; *Gospel of Philip* 75:3-9; *Letter of Philip to Peter* 136:5-14; *Second Treatise of the Great Seth* 53:19-54:13; *Paraphrase of Shem* 19:26-21:18; *Concept of Our Great Power* 38:1-26; *Interpretation of Knowledge* 6:30-35; *A Valentinian Exposition* 37:32-38:10; *Gospel of Truth* 1:18. On Gnostic hermeneutics in general, see David S. Dockery, *Biblical Interpretation Then and Now: Contemporary Hermeneutics in the Light of the Early Church* (Grand Rapids: Baker, 1992), 45-46, 56-58.

15. Vern Woolf, *Light Connection*, June 1992.

16. Mary Daly, *Pure Lust: Elemental Feminist Philosophy* (Boston: Beacon Press, 1984), 155.

17. Plutarch, *Def.or.* 421 A, cited in Filoramo, *Gnosticism*, 47.

18. Ibid., 51.

19. Ibid.

20. Irenaeus, *Against the Heresies* 1:20:1-3.

21. Rudolf, *Gnosis*, 53.

22. Hippolytus, *Refutation of All Heresies* 5:27.

23. Ibid., 5:l.

24. Rudolf, *Gnosis*, 54-55.

25. J. Dart, *The Laughing Savior* (New York, Hagerstown, San Francisco, London: Harper and Row, 1976), 132.

26. Tertullian, *De Praescriptione* 7, 138.

27. Rudolf, *Gnosis*, 53-54.

28. Rudolf, ibid.

29. Filoramo, *Gnosticism*, 94.

30. Clement of Alexandria, *Stromateis* 3:9:2.

31. Irenaeus, *Against Heresies* 1:3:6 and 1:8:1.

32. *Panarion* 25:2.1

33. Pagels, *The Gnostic Gospels*, 137.

34. Ibid.

35. Irenaeus, *Against Heresies* 1:5:1ff.

36. I. P. Couliano, *The Tree of Gnosis* (San Francisco: Harper, 1992), 121.

37. Ibid., 124.

38. Ibid., 124-5.

39. As notes Couliano, Ibid., 88.

40. *On the Origin of the World* 116:20-25.

41. *Apocryphon of John* 22:20-23:5.

42. Klijn, in a book review of "G. A. G. Strousma, 'Another Seed: Studies in Gnostic Mythology,'" *Novum Testamentum* XXVll (July 1985:3), 278.

43. *First Apocalypse of James* 26:23-27:13.
44. *Dialogue of the Savior* 138:11-15.
45. Rudolf, *Gnosis*, 58.
46. Irenaeus, *Against Heresies* 1:9:1-5.

Chapter Ten
1. Ibid.
2. Martin Marty, *The Public Church* (1981), cited in Fowler, *Weaving the New Creation*, 14.
3. Fowler, Ibid., 21.
4. Ibid., 20. "Paradigm shifts require more than conversions of the mind and heart: they require the shifting of priorities and resources in institutions; they bring political and economic changes; and, most extensively, they require changes in the worldviews." See also Campbell and Moyers, *The Power of Myth*, 121.
5. S. Scott and B. Smith, *Trojan Horse*, 166: "The God most people are worshiping in churches and temples hasn't grown since Christ's time. He's deteriorated . . . We need a God who's big enough for the atomic age. (Madeleine L'Engle, *Camilla* [New York: T.Y. Crowell, 1965], 249-250).
6. Campbell & Moyers, *The Power of Myth*, 40.
7. Carol Christ, "Symbols of Goddess," 231. On page 250 she speaks of "enormous political and social consequences" of the reemergence of the Goddess.
8. Christ, art.cit., 249, states what she means by social transformation through the goddess. Using the term goddess rather than God the Mother or God-She, which are "hybrid symbols," "is a more clear validation of the legitimacy and autonomy of female power." Whereas the Bible always promotes human relationships in covenant, the goal of the new spirituality is autonomy.
9. Mollenkott, *Sensuous Spirituality*, 55.
10. See Steichen, *Ungodly Rage*, 92.
11. Though many of these mainline Protestant women believed they were imagining a new god/dess *ex nihilo*, Sophia had been in preparation for a number of years. In 1984 at Grailville, a retreat center for Roman Catholic feminism, in Ohio, one of the first attempts to worship Sophia on American soil was undertaken. In the ecumenical and interfaith atmosphere of Grailville, a workshop, with the title: "Sophia and the Future of Feminist Spirituality," produced a Goddess, Sophia, who became the symbol of interfaith/syncretistic feminist spirituality. Though the organizers in Minneapolis claimed that their conference was "Christian," its origins are far from Christian. It is also noteworthy that many of today's leading feminist theologians — Rosemary Radford Ruether, Elizabeth Schüssler Fiorenza, Letty Russell, Mary E. Hunt, Nelle Morton, Judith Plaskow — regularly attended Grailville in their earlier years, and some of the above were leading figures in the conception of the *RE-Imagining Conference*. For this documentation, see Patricia Miller, "Leadership at Grailville," *Women of Power* 24 (1995), 77-78.
12. Already in 1986 a group of women at Calvary United Methodist Church in Philadelphia held alternative Holy Week celebrations in which Sophia, not Jesus, was worshiped as the suffering savior — see Cady , Ronan and Taussig, *Sophia: The Future of Feminist Spirituality* (San Francisco: Harper and Row, 1986), 103.
13. "The RE-Imagining Conference: A Report," *American Family Association* (Tupelo, MS, April, 1994), 2. See *Good News*, January, 1994, a publication of conservative Christians within the United Methodist Church, and the *Presbyterian Layman* (March/April 1994), the periodic of a similar group in the Presbyterian Church USA.
14. In this statement, is clear indication that the organizers knew precisely of the Gnostic and pagan backgrounds of Sophia. Indeed, this conference, which many in the

mainline churches no doubt thought was a unique aberration, has been long in preparation. In 1975, eighteen hundred women gathered in Boston to share information about spirituality. In 1978, a conference at the University of California at Santa Cruz on "The Great Goddess Reemerging" drew a sell-out crowd of five hundred — Christ, art.cit., 247. Donna Steichen traces the movement and its many conferences in her book *Ungodly Rage*.

15. See also the apocryphal *Wisdom of Solomon* 7:22-27, 29; 8:1; 9:10-12. Here as well, personified Wisdom affirms the creative handiwork of God.

16. "The RE-Imagining Conference: A Report," 19.

17. Ibid., 3.

18. Ibid., 9.

19. "The RE-Imagining Conference: A Report," 4.

20. John 1:1-3, Colossians 1:15-20, and Hebrews 3:1-3.

21. Katherine Kersten, "The RE-Imagining Conference: A Report," 18.

22. Ruether, *Sexism and God-Talk*, 11.

23. Ruether, *Women-Church*, 169.

24. Ibid., 144.

25. Ibid., 104.

26. Ibid., 159.

27. Caitlín Matthews, *Sophia, Goddess of Wisdom: The Divine Feminine From Black Goddess to World-Soul* (London: The Aquarian Press/Harper Collins, 1992).

28. Ibid., 11 and 65.

29. Carolyn McVickars Edwards, *The Storyteller's Goddess: Tales of the Goddess and Her Wisdom from Around the World* (San Francisco: Harper, 1991), 65.

30. "The RE-Imagining Conference: Report," 13.

31. *The Politics of Women's Spirituality*, ed. Charlene Spretnak (New York: Anchor Books Doubleday, 1994).

32. Lazaris, *Concept: Synergy*, P. O. Box 3285, Palm Beach, Fl 33480.

33. Alix Pirani, ed., *The Absent Mother: Restoring the Goddess To Judaism and Christianity* (London: Mandala, 1991). See also an earlier book, Merlin Stone, *When God Was a Woman* (San Diego, New York, London: Harvest/HJB, 1976), which attempts a similar reversal.

34. Alix Pirani, ibid., 54.

35. Kathleen Alexander-Berghorn, "Isis: The Goddess as Healer," *Women of Power* (Winter, 1987), 20, cited in Z, *Another Gospel: Alternative Religions and the New Age Movement* (Grand Rapids: Zondervan, 1989), 340-341.

36. Matthew 11:19.

37. Pages 187-198 of *The Spiritual Dance* are reproduced in D. W. Ferm, *Contemporary American Theologies II: A Book of Readings* (San Francisco: Harper and Row, 1982), 208-221.

38. Miriam Starhawk, *The Spiritual Dance* (San Francisco: Harper and Row, 1979), 215.

39. On this see Mary Kassian, *The Feminist Gospel*, 54. On page 57 Kassian cites Ruether, *Liberation Theology*, 189, whose aspirations for "development towards a new planetary humanity" have a strongly New Age ring. Ruether goes on: "(the) revolution of the feminine ... sought to reclaim spirit for body and body for spirit in a messianic appearing of the body of God."

40. *Times Advocate*, August 28, 1994.

41. Anne Llewelyn Barstow, *Witchcraze: A New History of the European Witch Hunts* (San Francisco: Harper, 1994).

42. Mollenkott, *Sensuous Spirituality*, 97: "The integration and honoring of both sexuality and spirituality can be achieved in several ways: a person can walk away from

established institutions and develop a more independent form of spirituality, either through private meditation, study, and ritual, or through starting or joining an alternative spirituality group such as a witches' coven, a Course in Miracles study group, or a twelve-step group." Compare also ibid., 45: "Sometimes judgmentalism takes the form of Christian or Jewish feminists who reject the spiritualities and rituals of those who have left us to become nature-mystics or witches or Goddess-worshipers."

43. Referred to in Steichen, *Ungodly Rage,* 92.

44. S. Scott and B. Smith, *Trojan Horse,* 44: "There is a lot of emphasis today, particularly among the more extreme right branches of the church, on the evils of witchcraft. Any book that mentions witches, or magic, or ghosts is automatically to be taken from the shelves." (Madeleine L'Engle, *Trailing Clouds of Glory: Spiritual Values in Children's Books* [Philadelphia: Westminster Press, 1985], 62-63).

45. Ruether, *Women-Church,* 223.

46. Ibid.

47. Miriam Starhawk, *Yoga Journal* (May-June, 1986), 59, cited in Ruth Tucker, *Another Gospel,* 340.

48. Starhawk, *Spiritual Dance*; see also Goldenberg, *The Changing of the Gods,* and Christ, *WomanSpirit Rising,* for the same programmatic call for radical overhaul.

49. *Los Angeles Times,* Saturday, May 22, 1993.

50. As does Ruth Tucker, *Another Gospel,* 340, who devotes little more than half a page to this important phenomenon.

51. Steichen, *Ungodly Rage,* 64, cites a feminist witch who emphasizes that Wiccans are not satanists. "I don't even believe there is a Satan," she said. "And not necessarily a true good and evil." See also Sjoo and Mor, *The Great Cosmic Mother: Discovering the Religion of the Earth* (San Francisco: Harper, 1987) , 314: "Satanism is a Christian heresy." cp ibid., 298. There is a continuum in paganism that ends in Satanism, i.e., the open worship of Satan. All one can say is that some witches come very close. For a contemporary wiccan/neopagan liturgy, see Marjorie Procter-Smith, ed., *Women At Worship: Interpretations of North American Diversity* (Louisville, KY: John Knox/ Westminster Press, 1993), 145.

52. Zsuzsanna E. Budapest, *The Grandmother of Time: A Woman's Book of Celebrations, Spells and Sacred Objects for Every Month of the Year* (San Francisco: Harper, 1989), 57.

53. Ibid., 21.

54. See Hasting's *Encyclopedia of Religion and Ethics,* Vol. 7, 434.

55. See Chapter 17.

56. Carol P. Christ, art.cit., 248, citing, with agreement Nelle Morton, "Beloved Image," published as Deo/Dea immagine dilletta" in *La sfida del femminismo all teologia,* ed. Mary E. Hunt and Rosino Gibellini (Brescia: Queriniana, 1981).

57. David Miller, *The New Polytheism,* vii.

58. Ibid., 3.

59. Ibid., ix. A similar polytheistic movement was beginning in the early seventies in ecological circles. Jackson Lee Ice, "The Ecological Crisis: Radical Monotheism vs. Ethical Pantheism," *Religion in Life* 44 (1975), 207-208. In this article Ice argued: "we must temper our harsher sentiments nurtured by a radical monotheism with a more tender, vivifying, and unifying spirit expressed in pantheistic religions . . . such as Shinto, Confucianism, Taoism and the American Indian religions." Cited in William B. Badke, *Project Earth: Preserving the World God Created* (Portland, OR: Multnomah, 1991), 118.

60. Ibid., 12.

61. "RE-Imagining Conference: A Report," 7.

62. "RE-Imagining Conference: A Report," 13. Mollenkott argued that since God dwells within human beings, one must show honor to every world religion, "not just

to Christianity." This would include interaction and "mutual modification of the kind that Dr. Chung was discussing." She also spoke about worship as "interreligious."

63. *Good News*, January, 1994, 8.

64. "RE-Imagining Conference: *A Report*," 6.

65. Miriam Starhawk, "Witchcraft as Goddess Religion," *The Politics of Women's Spirituality: Essays on the Rise of Spiritual Power Within the Feminist Movement*, ed. Charlene Spretnak (Garden City, NY: Anchor Press/Doubleday, 1982), 50-51.

66. Sjoo and Mor, *The Great Cosmic Mother*, 63.

67. David Miller, *The New Polytheism*, 74. S. Scott and B. Smith, *Trojan Horse*, 164, maintain that Madeleine L'Engle was favorable to goddess notions. "While mocking 'this angry god, out to zotz us,' L'Engle glorifies the idols of the Canaanites, falsely portraying them as kindlier, female goddesses. She contrasts these loving pagans to the Hebrews who wanted "to box God in."

68. Elizabeth Cady Stanton, *The Women's Bible* (1895), 14.

69. Cady Stanton, ibid., 13.

70. Mollenkott, *Sensuous Spirituality*, 64.

71. William Oddie, *What Will Happen to God?*, 87.

72. Cady Stanton, *Women's Bible*, 13.

73. Virginia Ramey Mollenkott, in her speech at The RE-Imagining Conference in Minneapolis, see "RE-Imagining Conference: A Report," 5.

74. According to Methodist theologian James Fowler, *Weaving a New Creation*, 105. See also 107 where he ties this kind of childish faith to the belief that the Bible is the "inerrant word of God," the "absolute foundation on which [one] can stand."

75. Ibid., 113. "Beyond paradox and polarities, persons in the Universalizing stage are grounded in a oneness with the power of being or God." S. Scott and B. Smith, *Trojan Horse*, 174, document how this kind of "universalizing" faith entered the thought of Madeleine L'Engle. They state: "L'Engle constantly refers to God as the "God who is One, God who is All."

76. James Fowler, *Weaving*, 61: "we are called to holistic patterns of thinking and to metaphors that enable us to represent God's involvement and influences in unified ways in the world process in its many strands and complex unity." Fowler finds the feminist Sallie McFargue's proposal appropriate, that we image the "world" as God's body (ibid., 63). This formulation leads again to goddess worship and pagan "deep ecology" — see the following phrase, ibid., 65: "In ways reminiscent of Marney — and of Teilhard de Chardin, who influenced both Marney and McFargue — the metaphor of the world as God's body provides the basis for a rich and deep recovery of the sense of the world as sacramental. One gives regard to dogs, cats, and goldfish; one honors the Godness in each human being, from derelict to diva."

77. Cited in Constance Cumbey, *Hidden Dangers*, 45-46.

78. So Halligan, "Keeping Faith with the Future, 192: "The cooperative efforts of humankind will prevail when we are aided in our work by the essential creative action of the Deity, *who is beyond all our knowing*."

79. William Oddie, *What Will Happen To God?*, 88, shows how an influential "Christian" feminist thinker, Dorothee Solle, has adopted this monistic view of God and reality. "In the mystical tradition, she [Dorothee Solle] suggests, the emphasis is not on obedience to God, but on union with him: and this emphasis enables our relationship with God to become one of 'agreement and consent' (note the curious return to personal symbolism), and this can then become the nature of religion: 'when this happens,' concludes Solle, 'solidarity will replace obedience as the dominant virtue.'"

80. Os Guinness, *Dust of Death*, 228-229.

81. Brooke, *When the World*, 68.

82. MacLaine, *Going Within*, 100.

83. Mollenkott, *Sensuous Spirituality*, 63. Mollenkott's completed phrase is: "She is right — as long as she (and they) constantly remind themselves that everyone else and every other living thing, as well as much more we may not be aware of, is also God."

84. "The RE-Imagining Conference: A Report," 2.

85. Romans 1:24-25.

86. Cited Pirani, *The Absent Mother*, 149.

87. Isaiah 34:14.

88. Alicia Suskin Ostriker, *Feminist Revision and the Bible* (Oxford: Blackwell, 1993), 99 recounts the Jewish legend. Lilith was Adam's first wife who refused to submit to him and was banished from the garden. she was found consorting with demons in the Red Sea, Ostriker, Professor of English at Rutgers University, takes the Lilith legend as a profound symbol of the modern feminist revision of the Bible and writes poems in praise of her (ibid., 92-98).

89. Ibid., 145.

90. Ibid., 152.

91. See Judith Plaskow, "The Coming of Lilith: Towards a Feminist Theology," *Womenspirit Rising*, 198-209.

92. Ibid., 156.

93. Ibid.

94. Ibid., 160.

95. On this see the fine treatment by Morrison, *Serpent*, 229ff.

96. See the excellent critical treatment of Process Theology as it relates to feminism, by Donna Steichen, *Ungodly Rage*, 202-206.

97. See chapter 12 .

98. Sjoo and Mor, *The Great Cosmic Mother,* 321, argue that the distance between a male God and the creation "lays the basis for all further alienated relationships — between people and God, between people and people, between people and the natural world."

99. David Miller, *The New Polytheism*, 4: "There is an incipient polytheism always lurking in democracy. This polytheism will surface during the history of democracies if the civilization does not first succumb to anarchy." Pope John Paul II, on the contrary, warns in his encyclical *Veritatis Splendor* of the danger of the joining of democracy and relativism.

100. David Miller, *The New Polytheism,* 72, states: "*A polytheistic theology will be a phenomenology of all religions* [italics mine]. It may be that the works by Mircea Eliade and Gerardus van der Leeuw are clues as to the future shape of a polytheistic theology. A truly polytheistic theology would be the first theology of religions."

101. James Lovelock, *Orion Nature Quarterly* 8 (1989), 58.

102. Sjoo and Mor, *The Great Cosmic Mother*, 231: "The father is *not* of the same all-containing, all-infusing, shaping and nourishing substance, and so the relation between humans and the Father God becomes abstract and alienated, distant and moralistic.

103. William Fowler, *Weaving the New Creation*, xiii: "in dialogue primarily with Sallie McFargue, I explore possibilities for a metaphoric transformation in our depictions of God's involvement in the processes of an evolving, expanding universe. For me this marks a moving away from my long-time reliance on the metaphor of God as sovereign toward exploration of a reconfiguration of my earlier expressions of God's *praxis* in the action metaphors of creating, governing, liberating, and redeeming."

104. David Miller, *The New Polytheism,* 5, states: "Psychologically, polytheism is a matter of the radical experience of equally real, but mutually exclusive aspects of the self. Personal identity cannot seem to be fixed. Normalcy cannot be defined. The person experiences himself as many selves each of which is felt to have autonomous power, a life of its own, coming and going on its own and without regard to the centered will of a single ego. Yet surprisingly this experience is not sensed as a pathology." Miller cites an article in *Psychology Today* entitled, "Multiple Identity: The Healthy, Happy Human Being Wears Many Masks," *Psychology Today* 5 (May 1972), ibid., 59.

105. Virginia Mollenkott, *Sensuous Spirituality,* 42.

106. Ibid., 16.

107. David Miller, *The New Polytheism,* 72-73: "*A polytheistic theology* will be neither another theism nor another logic. Understanding by way of positing theistic systems and by way of intellectualistic modes of knowing is already monotheistic: it is the imperialism of the mind over the feelings and the will. Polytheistic theology is always multivalenced, never bipolar, never good versus evil, right versus wrong, finite versus infinite, light versus dark, up versus down, in versus out. There is no orthodoxy in polytheistic theology."

108. There is even a Bible text. Mollenkott, *Sensuous Spirituality,* 68, calls upon the much used text, Galatians 3:28. "Extrapolating from the pluralism already present in Galatians 3:28, we could extend it to say that the Body of Christ is *She* as well as *He,* poor as well as affluent, handicapped as well as fully abled, lesgay and bisexual as well as heterosexual, of many colors, many nations, many religions, and many interpretive communities."

109. Daniel T. Spencer, *Gay and Gaia: Ethics, Ecology and the Erotic* (Cleveland, OH: Pilgrim, 1996). Pilgrim is the publishing house of the United Church of Christ.

110. Heinz O. Guenther, "The Sayings Gospel Q and the Quest For Aramaic Sources: Rethinking Christian Origins," *Semeia* 55 (1991), 41.

111. Fiorenza, *Miriam's Child, Sophia's Prophet* (New York: Continuum, 1994).

112. This is Robinson's proposal in 1988, through an exegesis of "Q 13:34," — see "Very Goddess and Very Man: Jesus' Better Self," *Images of the Feminine in Gnosticism,* ed. Karen L. King (Philadelphia: Fortress, 1988), 113-127.

113. Marcus Borg, *Jesus: A New Vision,* 190-191. Borg is Associate Professor of Religious Studies at Oregon State University and frequent contributor to *The Christian Century.*

114. Ibid., 184.

Chapter Eleven

1. *Allogenes* 51:12: the Aeon of Barbelo is revealed as "the Perfect Youth" (51:37). Barbelo is another name for Sophia — see Rudolf, *Gnosis,* 80.

2. Cullen Murphy, "Women and the Bible," *The Atlantic Monthly* (August, 1993), 40, cites Pagels, who in her book, *The Gnostic Gospels,* shows how the Gnostics invoked the feminine in their prayers.

3. Couliano, *Tree of Gnosis,* 70. Pheme Perkins, "Sophia and the Mother-Father," *The Book of the Goddess, Past and Present: An Introduction to Her Religion,* ed. by C. Mackenzie Brown and Carl Olsen (New York: Crossroads, 1983), 98, refers to Sophia's "liminal situation" between ultimate divinity and created existence. Her situation reflects the "tensions and ambiguities of the Gnostic, . . . caught in this world and superior to its authorities."

4. Couliano, *Tree of Gnosis,* 76.

5. Rudolf, *Gnosis,* 11.

6. Ibid., 65.

7. Jonas, *Gnostic Religion,* 26.

8. Pirani, *The Absent Mother*, 53. See the radicality of today's feminist attack on western patriarchal civilization in the writings of witches Mary Daly and Emily Culpepper (why are witches so concerned to see the end of patriarchy?), as well as the exegetical work of Fewell and Gunn, who begin with a similar denunciation of patriarchy.

9. In a few Gnostic texts, Christ as the Logos takes the place of Sophia. See *Tripartate Tractate* 100:1ff The Logos created the various aeons and authorities, over which he placed the chief Archon. "When the archon saw that they are great and good and wonderful, he was pleased and rejoiced, as (101) if he himself in his own thought had been the one to say and do them, not knowing that the movement within him is from the spirit who moves him . . . he was thinking that they were elements of his own essence."

10. Filoramo, *Gnosticism*, 82, citing the Valentinian Ptolemy.

11. *Sophia of Jesus Christ* 112:19, 114:14-15.

12. *Gospel of Thomas* 101, according to the reconstruction of T. Lambdin in *The Nag Hammadi Library in English*, 128-129. According to Kurt Aland, *Synopsis Quattuor Evangeliorum* (Stuttgart: Württembergische Bibelanstalt, 1964), 528, the original text reads: "for my [mother] . . . but in truth she gave me the life." Certainly Lambdin's emendations make sense theologically from a Gnostic point of view, and fit with the general anti-creational theology of *Thomas* (see sayings 22, 52, 53, 56 and 114).

13. *On the Origin of the World* 100:5-10, 26-27.

14. *Apocalypse of Adam* 64:14-16.

15. *Apocryphon of John* 15-19 cp. 21:30: "And his (man's) thinking was superior to all those who had made him."

16. See *Prayer of the Apostle Paul* 1 A:26-27, *The Nag Hammadi Library in English*, 28.

17. *Apocalypse of James* 34:10, *The Nag Hammadi Library in English*, 246.

18. Couliano, *Tree of Gnosis*, 96.

19. See *Letter of Peter to Philip* 135:16 — God the Creator is called "Authades (Arrogance)." Arrogance became proud and "commissioned the powers within his authority to produce mortal bodies" (136:11-13).

20. See also *Apocryphon of John* 11:15-25.

21. This is the summary of Couliano, *Tree of Gnosis*, 96. For other examples from the Gnostic texts, see *Apocryphon of John* 11:25-35, 13:5, *Gospel of the Egyptians* 58:23-26, *Sophia of Jesus Christ* 108:9-11, 119:9-15, *Gospel of Philip* 75:1-10, *Gospel of Truth* 17:10-19.

22. The modern witches' version of the Gnostic rejection of Jahweh is found in Sjoo and Mor, *The Great Cosmic Mother*, 269. "Yahweh is called the jealous God. What was Yahweh jealous of? Of the Goddess, and her lover, of their sacred-sexual relation itself, and of its domination over the minds and hearts and bodies of generations of Neolithic people. This is why the God and religion of the Bible are identified so clearly from all other preceding gods and religions: The Bible God and his religion are based on a violently asexual, or antisexual morality never before seen on earth. Sex — the source of life and pleasure of love — becomes the enemy of God.

23. *Apocryphon of John* 2:15.

24. *Gospel of the Egyptians* 41:7-9. See *Trimorphic Protennoia* 37:20

25. Filoramo, *Gnosticism*, 77-78.

26. Isaiah 45:18.

27. A reference to Psalm 8:4.

28. *Apocalypse of John* 11:25-35.

29. For the text, see *Second Treatise of the Great Seth* 62:28-63:30, *The Nag Hammadi Library in English*, 335.

30. For the text, see *Second Treatise of the Great Seth* 53:28, *The Nag Hammadi Library in English*, 332. See also 55:30-56:19, 62:28-30, 62:35-37, 63:4-5, 63:12-14, 63:18-22,

63:25-27, 64:18-23. See also the theme of laughter in the *Apocalypse of Peter* where the living Jesus, on the tree, is glad and laughing for the nails are put into the flesh of a substitute whom no one sees (81:15-25).

31. The account of the Naasene Gnostics in Irenaeus (1:30:7), cited by Hans Jonas, *The Gnostic Religion*, 93.

32. *Apocryphon of John* 21:15-22:1

33. *Apocryphon of John* 10:19, 10:33-11:3.

34. For the text, see *Gospel of the Egyptians* 57:16-20, *The Nag Hammadi Library in English*, 201.

35. Cited in Couliano, *Tree of Gnosis*, 94.

36. Ephesians 2:11-13 and 1:3.

37. *Trimorphic Protennoia* 39:21, 40:23, 43:32, 43:35-44:2. In *Testimony of Truth* 70:1-4 says that David had a demon dwelling in him, the one who laid the foundation of Jerusalem and that the temple had seven waterpots with demons in them that ran away when the Romans arrived!

38. *Apocalypse of Peter* 82:18-25. These texts confirm the accuracy of Hippolytus account (*Refutation of All Heresies* 1:12), which describes a Gnostic Jesus explaining to the Pharisees that their father, a murderer from the beginning, was the Demiurge, and that the "Son is the Serpent."

39. Filoramo, *Gnosticism*, 132.

40. *Hypostasis of the Archons* 95:8ff cp *On the Origin of the World* 103:25ff.

41. For the text, see *On the Origin of the World* 126:20-30, The *Nag Hammadi Library in English*, 178-179.

42. Rudolf, *Gnosis*, 50.

43. Irenaeus, *Against All Heresies*, 11.

44. *Apocryphon of John* 3:20-25.

45. *Eugnostos the Blessed* 71:14ff, 72:3ff.

46. *Allogenes* 62:28-64:13, 65:33 and 66:26-27.

47. For the text, see *Teaching of Silvanus* 100:13-16, *The Nag Hammadi Library in English*, 353.

48. *Tripartite Tractate* 85:34.

49. *Allogenes* 48:10-11: God is "the All [located in the] place that is higher than perfect" See also *Allogenes* 48:12-49:38 with its long section on the being of the unknowable God. See also *Trimorphic Protennoia* 35:31: "I exist before the [All, and] I am the All . . . "

50. See Rudolf, *Gnosis*, 59.

51. Pheme Perkins, Professor of theology at Boston College, art.cit, 98, appears to agree with this judgment: "the whole [Gnostic] system drives towards the recovery of the primal androgynous unity. The world fractured by imperialism [no doubt of the male Demiurge] is recovered in the overwhelming monism of the Gnostic pleroma."

52. For the full text, see *Gospel of Mary* 7:4-9, *The Nag Hammadi Library in English*, 471.

53. *Gospel of Thomas* 77. An interesting variant of this pagan monism is found in unfaithful Israel. Jeremiah decries their apostasy: "the house of Israel shall be shamed: . . . they . . . who say to a tree, 'You are my father,' and to a stone, 'You gave me birth'" (Jeremiah 2:27).

54. See Irenaeus, *Against Heresies* 1:5:3.

55. Pheme Perkins, art.cit., 107, notes that Sophia "often appears as the crucial link between the human in this world and the divinity which constitutes his/her truest identity."

56. John D. Turner, *The Nag Hammadi Library in English*, 461.

57. *Trimorphic Protennoia* 35:9-18.

58. Zeus is the God of Thunder — see Sjoo and Mor, *The Great Cosmic Mother*, 169. Perhaps the choice of this name, Thunder, suggests that Sophia has taken on all the powerful prerogatives of the male God.

59. According to George MacRae, who introduces this text in *The Nag Hammadi Library in English, Thunder* is "a revelation discourse delivered by a female revealer in the first person. . . . Antithesis and paradox (are) used to proclaim the absolute transcendence of the revealer whose greatness is incomprehensible" (George W. MacRae, "Introduction," ibid., 271). This analysis is possible if Gnosticism is seen simplistically as a dualistic system.

60. See Emily Culpepper, "The Spiritual, Political Journey of a Feminist Freethinker," *After Patriarchy: Feminist Transformations of the World's Religions*, ed. Paula Cooey *et al* (Maryknoll, NY: Orbis, 1991), 155. See also the semi-humorous article by Peter Berger. "The Other Face of Gaia," *First Things* (August/September, 1994), 15-17, which includes a description of Kali.

Emily Culpepper, raised in an Evangelical Baptist church in Macon, Georgia, became involved in the counterculture movements of the Sixties. Today she is an ecofeminist lesbian witch replete with "familiar," a spirit guide from Kali that possessed her cat. Describing her Christian roots as "compost," she proposes the following agenda: Christianity should be seen as "a complex tissue of truths and lies"; the idea of the Incarnation is not only "implausible . . . (but) offensive" to feminists; she promotes the adoption of "an expanding personal pantheon of goddesses and other mythic images (as) a great psychic counterweight to the father gods of patriarchy." Through her cat, Culpepper found great inspiration from Kali who is pictured as a female deity with "red eyes, disheveled hair, blood trickling at the corners of her mouth, lips saturated with fresh blood, a dangling tongue, long sharp fangs, a gaunt, dark-skinned body. . . . Her necklace contains fifty human heads; her waistband is a girdle made of severed human arms; she is wearing two dead infants for earrings. . . . She holds a blood-smeared cleaver in her . . . left hand and a dripping severed head in the . . . right."

How can such a bloodthirsty picture inspire anyone? An expert on Kali explains that Kali has two sides. She nurtures those who respect her but destroys those who cross her: "Her bloody intoxication with rage and violence is not an indication that she is evil. Kali is 'Mother of us all' — she gives birth, dazzles with her splendor, and consumes us in the game of life. Both beneficent and terrible qualities are combined in the image of Kali")see *The Book of the Goddess*, 110-123).

This is exactly what the witch Culpepper finds so attractive — the mystical experience of the connection with all the processes of living and dying "beyond dualism." Lest readers think that I am attempting to be sensational by the use of such marginal and bizarre material, they should realize that this essay by Culpepper was required reading for bright sixteen year-olds in the Governor's School (a summer program for gifted teenagers) in Arkansas in the late eighties — see *World*, September, 1993.

61. Pirani, *The Absent Mother*, 54.

62. James Preston, "Goddess Worship: An Overview," in Carl Olsen, ed., *The Book of the Goddess, Past and Present: An Introduction to Her Religion* (New York, 1983), 38. Pheme Perkins, in an article in this same book, reflecting on *Thunder Perfect Mind*, says: "Like Isis, this female figure [who she takes to be Sophia] claims to be behind all human wisdom."

63. See the description of Sophia in the program of the *RE-Imagining Conference* as "the place where the entire universe resides." "The RE-Imagining conference: A Report," 19.

64. Cited by Sjoo and Mor, *The Great Cosmic Mother*, 253, without reference. This representation of Isis is no doubt correct. Professor Luther H. Martin of the Univer-

sity of Vermont, in his book *Hellenistic Religions: An Introduction* (Oxford and New York: Oxford University Press), 1987, states that in the Hellenistic world where Gnosticism took root, Isis was no longer seen as a local Egyptian deity tied to her consort Osiris, but becomes the "lunar Queen of heaven . . . the universal 'Mother of All Things.'"

In the ancient novel, *The Golden Ass* by Apuleius (mid second century A.D.), the hero Lucius, through the rites of Isis, which included incubation [remaining in a room for days fasting and meditating (see Martin, ibid., 60)], gained the classic monistic experience of light. "At midnight," reports Lucius, as he meditated in the Temple of Isis, "I saw the sun brightly shine, I saw likewise the gods celestial and the gods infernal, . . . and worshiped them." So Apuleius, *The Golden Ass*, translated by Jack Lindsay (Bloomingdale: Indiana University Press, 1960), 249.

65. C. J. Bleeker, "Isis and Hathor, Two Ancient Egyptian Goddesses," in *The Book of the Goddess*, 32.

66. Caitlín Matthews, *Sophia, Goddess of Wisdom: The Divine Feminine From Black Goddess to World-Soul* (London: The Aquarian Press/Harper Collins, 1992), 67.

67. Ibid., 38.

68. Ibid., 33 and 35.

69. *Trimorphic Protennoia* 45:2-6. See also *Exegesis of The Soul* and an introductory article by W. C. Robinson, Jr., "The Exegesis of the Soul," *Novum Testamentum* 12/2 (1970), especially 116, who argues that the content of this text is close to that of the Naasenes for whom the mutilation of Attis was a type of the androgynous ideal.

70. *Trimorphic Protennoia* 44:30-33. Filoramo, *Gnosticism*, 61 and 63, understands what MacRae [see above] seems not to have grasped. "androgyny is the distinctive trait of this (Gnostic) God." In the Gnostic understanding of God is "the conquest of all duality."

71. Perkins, art.cit., 107.

72. See, for example *The New Testament and Psalms: An Inclusive Version* (New York/Oxford: Oxford University Press, 1995), 9.

73. Filoramo, *Gnosticism*, 58 cp 53.

74. Genesis 3:5.

75. Irenaeus, *Against Heresies* 1.30.6.

76. *First Apocalypse of James* 27:7-9.

77. Steve Beard, *AFA Journal*, February, 1994, 1.

Chapter Twelve

1. Quoted in the *San Diego Union-Tribune*, July 4, 1994, A-4.

2. Elinor Gadon, *The Once and Future Goddess* (New York: Harper and Row, 1989). The completed quote is: "The reemergence of the Goddess is becoming the symbol and metaphor for this transformation."

3. Ruether is Professor of Applied Theology at Garrett-Evangelical Seminary, Evanston, Illinois.

4. Ibid., 57.

5. Ruether, *Women-Church*, 131, 280-281, 132, 153, 57, 61, 63, 69, 73, 74, and 125.

6. Dr. Sharron Stroud, founder of the Center for the Celebration of Life, gives classes on "Access the Wild Woman," and "Access the Wild Man," advertised in the local New Age paper. "Wild" seems to stand for sexuality liberated from Judeo-Christian creational and moral structures.

7. Virginia Mollenkott, *Sensuous Spirituality*, 73.

8. Mollenkott, *ibid.*, 12.

9. Kate Millett, *Sexual Politics* (Garden City, NY: Doubleday, 1970), 250-251. Cp the argument of Ti-Grace Atkinson, reported by Mary Kassian, that "only lesbian women

could think radically and profoundly about the possibility of social change, free from the shackles of heterosexual gender assignments" (cited in Kassian, *Feminist Gospel*, 86). As E. Michael Jones, "Lesbian Nuns," 22 notes: "Not all feminists are lesbians; however the ideological thrust of feminism naturally leads to lesbianism." He cites a statement by Mary Daly conceding that "everything I write is an invitation to [lesbianism]."

10. Patricia Beattie Jung and Ralph F. Smith, *Heterosexism: An Ethical Challenge* (New York: State University of New York Press, 1994).

11. Stanley J.Grenz and Roger E.Olsen, *Twentieth Century Theology: God and the World in a Transitional Age* (Downers Grove, IL: InterVarsity Press, 1992), 234. Patriarchy is juxtaposed with the two other unmitigated evils without any qualification. This commits the fallacy of supposing that the abuse of power disqualifies the use of power. Unscrupulous politicians do not put into question the political process. The sinful misuse of fatherly responsibility ought not to bring into question the role of authority that creation invests in fathers. While it is no doubt true that Paul would not object if we added to Gal 3:28: "neither parents nor children," patriarchy is clearly maintained in the apostle's teaching of the New Covenant church, when he calls upon children to obey their parents. He does not reject patriarchy. He calls for a just exercise of the same (Colossians 3:21).

12. *Christians for Biblical Equality: Books, Reprints and Tapes Catalog*, August, 1991. See also Rebecca M. Groothuis, *Women Caught in the Conflict: The Culture War Between Traditionalism and Feminism* (Grand Rapids: Baker, 1994), 65.

13. Groothuis, ibid., 122, denies the possibility that patriarchy can be reformed along Christian lines, for she claims their "mutually exclusive features" (the authority of patriarchy and the intimacy of Christian love) make the attempt absurd. How can a husband do both, she asks rhetorically? I detect here a flaw in the logic of her theology.

While admitting (rightly so, against radical religious feminists' denial of the fatherhood of God) that God is a true *patriarch* who "uses his power [authority] lovingly and wisely [intimacy]," thereby showing that this is finally a false dichotomy (101), she then denies this as a genuine possibility for sinful men, even though Ephesians 5:22-33 invites Christian men to do just that. At the same time, her appeal to end patriarchy presupposes that sinful men (and women) *can* exercise power justly on this earth — by bringing an end to unjust patriarchy. But if one is possible, why not the other? If she argues that the *structure* is inherently sinful, then she must bow to the radicals and eliminate the patriarchy of God. If men are inherently sinful, then why call for reform?

14. Leading, and not particularly religious, feminist theoreticians like Riane Eisler, Charlene Spretnak and New Age feminist Jean Houston were prominently featured on the parliament's program. Its ethics statement was remarkable only in the feminist flavor exhibited in part of its rhetoric.

15. See W. Roof, *Generation*, 222. See also P. Jones, *The Gnostic Empire*, 63-64. Recent Supreme Court decisions, against the will of the people, show that the new ideology of the Left can circumvent the democratic process.

16. Naomi Goldenberg, *Changing of the Gods: Feminism and the End of Traditional Religions* (Boston: Beacon Press, 1979), 41, cited in Kassian, 154. See also Sjoo and Mor, *The Great Cosmic Mother*, 197.

17. Naomi Goldenberg, *Changing of the Gods*, 5.

18. Few Christian books on the New Age broach this subject, so that great sections of the church have been swept along by a more modified, sanitized form.

19. William Oddie, *What Will Happen To God?*, 11.

20. Andrew Greeley, *Omni Magazine* (January, 1987), 98, cited in Welton, *Abortion*, 163. While the present pope, John Paul II, has opposed religious feminism, there is reason to think that the Roman Catholic church will one day become what Greeley predicts. In 1990 a well-known Roman Catholic mystic, Father Bede Griffith, who lived for 37 years in India, suffered a near-fatal stroke that gave him "a greater understanding of love, non-duality and the importance of the feminine aspects of life." The Dalai Lama hails his "acceptance of all the major religions with respect and dignity," and Cardinal Hume, Roman Catholic Archbishop of Westminster, UK, enthusiastically recognizes him as "a mystic in touch with absolute love and beauty." See the catalog of *Palisades Home Video* (Virginia Beach, 1994), 5. With cardinals like that, it only takes, as they say, one whiff of white smoke.

21. The comparison is no doubt valid, for, like the Reformation, the women's movement is a movement affecting all levels of society. Whether it will have all the benefits of the Reformation is another question.

22. Elisabeth Schüssler Fiorenza, *In Memory of Her*, xvii.

23. Mary Daly, *Beyond God the Father: Towards a Philosophy of Women's Liberation* (Boston: Beacon Press, 1973), 169.

24. Donna Steichen, *Ungodly Rage*, 9. See also the incisive article by E. Michael Jones, "What Lesbian Nuns Can Teach Us About Vatican II," *Fidelity* 5/1 (December, 1985), 16-26.

25. See above, chapter 3. New Age liberal spirituality, especially in its feminist form of gender liberation, is bringing people back to church.

26. Naomi Goldenberg, *Changing of the Gods*, 5.

27. Ibid., 2. See also William Oddie, *What Will Happen to God?*, 12.

28. See Goldenberg, "Feminist Witchcraft and Inner Space," *The Politics of Women's Spirituality*, ed. Charlene Spretnak (New York: Doubleday, 1982), 217.

29. Emily Culpepper, "The Spiritual, Political Journey", 153-154.

30. "Text of VMI Opinions," *The Chronicle of Higher Education* (July 5, 1996), A36.

31. Roof, *Generation of Seekers*, 217-219. A more recent poll confirms this trend. Seventy-six percent of all American adults, two out of three "born again Christians," eighty-six percent of mainline Protestants, and forty-five percent of "conservative evangelicals" favor women's ordination, according to figures published by the Evangelical Press Association, December 1993. This has to be classified as an enormous social revolution that has occurred in just one generation, from the Sixties through the nineties.

32. J. Gordon Melton, *The Churches Speak On: Women's Ordination* (Detroit: Gale Research Inc, 1991). xiii.

33. Madeleine L'Engle, *The Irrational Season* (New York: Farrer, Straus and Giroux, 1979), 156.

34. A report from Religious News Service appearing in the *L.A.Times*, July 24, 1993.

35. Ibid., 13. Steichen comes to a similar conclusion concerning the spread of radical feminism in the Catholic church.

36. See Mary Daly, *Wickedary*, 78 and 186.

37. Donna Steichen, *Ungodly Rage*, 330, documents that Harvey Cox, was one of three hundred scholars who signed a petition from the American Academy of Religion pleading that Daly be promoted, saying, "It is hard to imagine where the whole field of religious and theological studies would be today were it not for the contributions she has made." See Leila Prelec, "BC Campus Scene of Small Daly Protests," *National Catholic Register*, Apr. 30, 1989, 1. See also Cox's endorsement of Daly's latest book, *Outercourse: The Be-Dazzling Voyage Containing Recollections from My Logbook of a Radical Feminist Philosopher* (HarperSanFrancisco, 1992) in the 1992 HarperSanFrancisco Catalogue "Religious Studies," p.17. This book of Daly is a further promotion of ecofeminist erotic

lesbian witchcraft. In 1988 Cox is surprised by the reemergence of witchcraft (See *Many Mansions*, 195). Four years later he is the enthusiastic supporter of a witch/philosopher.

38. See Leila Prelec, op. cit., 1, cited in Steichen, *Ungodly Rage*, 330.

39. Clearly the *RE-Imagining Conference* in Minneapolis, 1993, did not appear out of the blue. See a detailed account of this feminist/pagan movement in Donna Steichen, *Ungodly Rage:*.

40. Don Feder, "What's up at the Harvard Divinity School?" *Conservative Chronicle*, April, 1994, 28. I believe the accepted plural is "shamans," but I reproduce Heder's original form, "shamen," which he no doubt intended as a pun.

41. In particular, Elaine Pagels' book, *The Gnostic Gospels*, and *The Nag Hammadi Library in English* translated under the direction of James M.Robinson.

42. Paula Cooey, ed., *After Patriarchy* (Maryknoll, NY: Orbis Books, 1991).

43. Mollenkott, *Sensuous Spirituality*, 52.

44. A speech by Jeff Levi in 1987 to the National Press Club in Washington, cited in Joseph P. Gudel, "That Which Is Unnatural: Homosexuality in Society, the Church and Scripture," *Christian Research Journal* (Winter, 1993), 10.

45. "Gays on the March," *Time*, (September 8, 1975), 43, cited by Gudel, ibid.

46. See P. Jones, *The Gnostic Empire*, 67.

47. See the front page of the *L.A.Times*, January 10, 1994, in an article, "Gay Rights Moves On Campus."

48. So writes Larry Kramer, playwright and gay activist in "Film Comment," *L. A. Times* (January 9, 1994), 30. Kramer believes that the first Hollywood movie "in which a male star like Tom Hanks, makes love in bed, naked, with another male star, like Tom Cruise, in the same bed, also naked, and they embrace and they talk to each other in an adult fashion, doing the same things straight lovers do in every single movie, TV show and commercial . . . will make a fortune." He is probably right.

49. By Jerry Z. Muller, Associate Professor of History at the Catholic University of America, in *First Things* (August/September, 1993), 17-24. "Most important in measuring the influence of homosexual thought in the academy is its impact upon women's studies, by far the fastest growing area within the humanities and social sciences, both institutionally and in terms of publications. It is estimated that there are now five hundred women's studies programs, thirty thousand courses, and fifty feminist institutes"(18). One of the leading ideas in academic feminism is that lesbianism is the most "authentic form of feminism."

50. Ibid.

51. Reported in *World*, November 13, 1993.

52. This item surely indicates the importance of NAMBLA in the homosexual movement. As John Richard Neuhaus observes, in "Table For One," *National Review* (December, 13, 1993), 57: "mainline" homosexuals "may be right when they say that NAMBLA is on the kooky fringe of the homosexual subculture [they may be wrong, too]. There is no secret, however, about the significant role that boys play in the actual and fantasy world of homosexuality."

53. Ibid., 7.

54. Robert Muller, *The New Genesis: Shaping a Global Spirituality* (New York: Image Books, 1984), 189.

55. Cited in Cumbey, *Hidden Dangers*, 111-112.

56. This term comes from the Jesuit theologian Teilhard de Chardin, whose thought informs much of modern New Age and new liberal thinking. See Halligan's use of Teilhard, *"Keeping Faith with the Future: Towards Final Conscious Unity,"* *Fires of Desire* (New York: Crossroads, 1992), 191, discussed below.

57. Some feminists claim that one must go behind the male god to and original bisexual goddess — see Monica Sjoo and Barbara Mor, *The Great Cosmic Mother: Discovering the Religion of the Earth*, (HarperSanFrancisco, 1987), 21, who argue that the original goddess originates in Africa, the Black Goddess, the Great Mother of Africa (from which Isis in Egypt), regarded as bisexual, and a witch who carried a snake in her belly. Betty Talbert-Wettler, "Secular Feminist Religious Metaphor and Christianity," a paper read at the annual meeting of the Evangelical Theological Society, Washington, D.C., 1993, 7, notes that the "Supreme Being" in witchcraft is "bipolar (male/female).

58. On second thoughts, France is not that easy to invade!

59. Frederica R. Halligan, clinical psychologist and Assistant Director of the counseling Center at the Roman Catholic Fordham University.

60. Ibid., 188-89.

61. Ibid., 192.

62. Monica Sjoo and Barbara Mor, *The Cosmic Mother*, 67: "the further back one goes the Great Mother is gynandrous — so the present day lesbian is the closest to ancient women."

63. Ibid.

64. See note 49.

65. Quoted from a lecture, in Steichen, *Ungodly Rage*, 32.

66. Ibid., 43.

67. See Rosemary Radford Ruether, *Women-Church: Theology and Practice* (San Francisco: Harper and Row, 1985), 104, where she states her goal of establishing a liturgical practice that marries Christianity to the pagan religions: "The liturgies of this book [*Women-Church*] . . . reappropriate the hallowing of nature and cyclical time of ancient pre-Judeo-Christian traditions [including Baalism].

68. Steichen, *Ungodly Rage*, 302: "Androgyny is her model for a human species liberated from "dualistic" gender into "psychic wholeness."

69. David Cave, *Mircea Eliade's Vision for a New Humanism* (New York: Oxford, 1993), 109.

70. Shirley MacLaine, *Going Within*, 197.

71. Ibid., 154.

72. G. A. Moloney and B. J. Rogers-Gardner, two Christian psychologists, in their book, *Loving the Christ Within You: A Spiritual Guide to Self-Esteem* (New York: Crossroad, 1991), 93, call people to spiritual wholeness by "thinking of yourself 'as both male and female.'"

73. Virginia Ramey Mollenkott, *Sensuous Spirituality*, 165. Mollenkott is not sure whether P. B. Jung's educated guess is accurate, but she is "certain that healthy lesbi-gay people have a lot to teach society about sex roles."

74. Scott Lively and Kevin Adams, *The Pink Swastika: Homosexuality in the Nazi Party* (Keizer, OR: Founders Publishing Corporation, 1995), 46.

75. See Mollenkott, *Sensuous Spirituality*, 74.

76. Mollenkott, *Sensuous Spirituality*, 16.

77. Mircea Eliade, *Myths, Dreams and Mysteries* (New York: Harper and Row, 1975), 174-175, and *Patterns of Comparative Religion* (New York: New American Library, 1974), 420-421.

78. In our day one could reformulate the Reformation dictum—*cuius regio euis religio* (whose region his religion) — to "whose sexuality his/her religion."

79. In the same way the attack on *mono*gamy is an attack on *mono*theism. Donna Steichen, *Ungodly Rage*, 86, gives the example of an avant-garde Catholic feminist, Tesse Donnelly, who in a presentation at Mundelein College and Seminary, maintained that virginity was not a static thing. In Greek mythology, "virginity was

renewable. . . . Hera regained hers each spring. Persephone returned each year 'younger than springtime.' Aphrodite was not a maiden; she was the lover of many, mother of many. But she was a virgin because she belonged to no man. 'One-in-herself, belonging to no man' is the *real* meaning of *virgin*."

80. Quoted in Donna Steichen, *Ungodly Rage*. 230. Steichen, 231, reports that Fox's diatribes against "dualisms" oppose not only distinctions between mind and body but also those between creature and Creator. "And between man and beast; . . ." A finer example of a monist would be difficult to find.

81. John Spong, Episcopal Bishop of Newark. Cited in *World* (November 7, 1992), 19.

82. Judy Grahn, *Another Mother Tongue: Gay Words, Gay Worlds* (Boston: Beacon Press, 1984), 44, cited in Emily Culpepper, "The Spiritual, Political Journey of a Feminist Freethinker," *After Patriarchy*, 158.

83. Quoted in a "Program Release" concerning a video series, *The Wisdom of Faith With Huston Smith: A Bill Moyers Special* (Spring, 1996).

84. Robert M. Baum, "Homosexuality and the Traditional Religions of the Americas and Africa," in Arlene Swidler, *Homosexuality and World Religions* (Valley Forge, PA: Trinity Press International, 1993), 15.

85. Ibid., 147, 150 and 158.

86. Ibid., 164, citing Judy Grahn.

87. Sjoo and Mor, *The Cosmic Mother*, 131.

88. John Ankerberg and John Weldon, *Encyclopedia of New Age Beliefs* (Eugene, Or: Harvest House Publishers, 1996), 532ff.

89. Ibid., 155.

90. Ibid., 155.

91. Ankerberg and Weldon, *Encyclopedia of New Age Beliefs*, 541.

92. *Ibid.*, 543.

93. See Randy P. O'Connor, *Blossom of Bone: Reclaiming the Connections Between Homoeroticism and the Sacred* (San Francisco: Harper, 1994). See also by the same publisher, Carter Heyward, a lesbian Episcopal priest and mother by artificial insemination, *Touching Our Strength: The Erotic as Power and the Love of God*, which argues for sacred power in sexual (in particular lesbian) pleasure.

94. Mollenkott, *Sensuous Spirituality*, 42, 166. This is becoming an acceptable mainline "Christian" theme. Judy Westerdorf, a United Methodist minister in Minnesota said in a session of the feminist conference "RE-Imagining" held November 4-7, 1993, in Minneapolis: "The Church has always been blessed by gays and lesbians — witches, shamans, artists" — see *Good News*, January, 1994, a publication of conservative Christians within the United Methodist Church.

95. Mollenkott, *Sensuous Spirituality*, 19, 24.

96. "The RE-Imagining Conference: A Report," 2.

97. Just what this "shamanistic function" could prove to be is perhaps indicated by the contemporary actions of the gay community. Gary L.Bauer, "In Front of the Children," *Family Research Council Washington Watch* (May, 1993), reports that at the April 23-25 Homosexual March on Washington, the marchers called for the persecution of Christians by chanting, "Bring on the lions." According to the Washington Post, says the same article, "10,000 hand-clapping, war-whooping lesbians erupted out of Dupont Circle shouting 'we're dykes, we're out, we're out for power!'"

98. According to Ben MacIntyre, *Forgotten Fatherland: the Search for Elizabeth Nietzsche* (New York: Farrar Straus Giroux, 1992), 92, citing remarks from Sigmund Freud and Carl Jung.

99. Culpepper, *After Patriarchy*, 149, broke with Christianity, in part through her reading of Nietzsche.

100. Chuck and Donna McIlhenny, *When the Wicked Seize a City: A Grim Look at the Future and a Warning to the Church* (Lafayette, LA: Huntington House, 1993), 18. The authors agree with this analysis when they speak of "two diametrically opposed religions," and when they say, "As a lifestyle, homosexuality represents a holistic culture under the dominion of man in rebellion against God. . . . The religion of homosexuality challenges the fundamental structure of morality, the nature of the word of God, and civilization in general" (60).

101. Ibid., 85-93.

102. Ibid., 16.

103. Mollenkott, *Sensuous Spirituality*, 49.

104. Rudolf, *Gnosis*, 257

106. See the books of Texe Marrs, Constance Cumbey, Dave Hunt/T. A. McMahon and Douglas Groothuis. This stops them from measuring the true threat of the New Age movement, not as a sect, but as a world and life view that goes way beyond the exotic expressions of New Age, and includes the optimistic new liberalism of the twenty-first century. When feminism is not seen as part of the movement, then hidden from view is the deep coherence tying the new liberalism's many themes together. Such a thoughtful book as Elliot Miller's *A Crash Course on the New Age Movement* (Grand Rapids: Baker, 1989) also does not address feminism. This is true of David Clark and Norman Geisler's excellent book, *Apologetics in the New Age: A Christian Critique of Pantheism* (Grand Rapids: Baker, 1990). Notable exceptions are *When the World Shall Be As One* (Harvest House, 1989) by Tal Brooke, who sees the dangers of feminism and the global extent of the New Age philosophy, and Mary Kassian, *The Feminist Gospel* (Wheaton: Crossway, 1992), who clearly identifies the link between feminism and New Age monism. Russell Chandler, *Understanding the New Age* (Dallas: Word, 1988) does give seven pages out of 360 to radical feminism's involvement in witchcraft and goddess worship.

107. The evangelical world, like the Church at large, is undergoing a massive assault. Charismatic fundamentalistic churches present both the pastor and his wife in the local evangelical paper as "pastors." The Baptist fundamentalistic church around the corner, in its children's Christmas pageant, features "Wise Women" instead of "Wise Men." Every one laughs. It is so cute, especially out of the mouth of babes and sucklings, but we are witnessing a cultural and theological revolution. Churches who believe the Bible is the inerrant Word of God from cover to cover, ("and the covers too"), see no problem with this rereading of the sacred text.

108. John Dart, "First Draft of Lutheran Statement Revises Teaching on Sexuality," *L.A. Times* (Saturday, December 4, 1993).

109. Ibid., 4.

110. See Mary Kassian, *The Feminist Gospel*, for a description of the slide towards paganism in those who began their feminism as a Christian protest movement. I wish in no way to imply that my egalitarian Christian brothers and sisters have become pagans or Gnostics, nor am I seeking to impugn their motives. I am merely setting forth what I see to be a dangerous route that begins by the rightful desire to right wrongs and promote the many gifts of the priesthood of all believers but arrives at the rejection of creational structures as normative in the church. This is, I believe, the first step to Gnosticism.

111. "Feminists and pagans are both coming from the same source without realizing it, and are heading towards the same goal without realizing it, and the two are now beginning to interlace," says feminist Margot Adler, *Drawing Down the Moon: Witches, Druids, Goddess-worshipers and Other Pagans in America Today* (Boston: Beacon Press, 1986), 182, cited in Kassian, *The Feminist Gospel*, 219.

112. Patricia Miller, "Leadership at Grailville," 76.

113. The power of this elite is nevertheless demonstrated in an article by Michael Fumento, "Exploding Myths," *National Review* (December 13, 1993), 42-45. Fumento documents how his book, *The Myth of Heterosexual AIDS* (Regnery Publishing, 1989), was kept off the shelves of all the major chains, how reviews were manifestly inaccurate and slanderous, how interviews on national TV were canceled at the last minute, how a research grant was denied and how he lost his job as a journalist — all because he had the temerity to argue that AIDS, while devastating the minority homosexual population, has left the majority heterosexual population essentially unscathed.

114. See above, 9.

115. Is the Christian response that of Peter Coleman, Bishop of Crediton, Devon, England, who, in his book *Gay Christians: A Moral Dilemma* (London: SCM Press, 1989), xi, presents homosexuality as "a reasonable request from a minority of the human race to live their own lives as best they can"? Or is the paradigm, *mutatis mutandis*, that of Israel and the principle that of "sin in the camp"? Because of Achan's sin, many lost their lives in a subsequent battle with the Canaanites (Joshua 7). Certainly the church takes its cue from the Old Testament people of God. Society will be a reflection of the numerical and spiritual power of Christians within that society.

Chapter Thirteen

1. Ruether, *Women-Church*, 39.

2. See Pagels, *Gnostic Gospels*, 44, and P. Jones, *The Gnostic Empire*, 31. This bridal chamber ceremony is called a sacrament of "redemption," that is, release from the God of Creation and Scripture.

3. *Sophia Jesu Christi* 119:9-15. Ialdabaoth is a mixing and punning on the Hebrew names for God. As the Prime Begetter, God is at the source of the evil process of childbirth.

4. *Sophia Jesu Christi* 118:23-119:8. This is called "the Gospel of God, the eternal, imperishable Spirit," 119:15-16.

5. Wilfred M. McClay, *The Masterless: Self and Society in Modern America* (Chapel Hill: The University of North Carolina Press, 1994). Does this not suggests why religious America, when all the other conditions are right, would be fertile ground for the return of Gnosticism.

6. *Apocryphon of John* 28:1-5 and 2:20-25. See Filoramo, ibid., and Rudolf, *Gnosis*, 220-221 and 206 where he lists their preferred names.

7. Douglas Parrot, in the introduction to his translation of *Eugnostos the Blessed* (III, 3 and V, 1), and *Sophia of Jesus Christ* (III, 4 and BG 8502, 3), *The Nag Hammadi Library in English*, 206. He refers to Sophia of Jesus Christ 108:9ff. The texts is mysterious, but speaks of the "unclean rubbing . . . that came from their fleshly part." Then comes the exhortation: "Tread upon their malicious intent."

8. *Gospel to the Egyptians* 56:5-15, 60:9-18, suggests some form of homosexuality. See also *Paraphrase of Shem* 28:25-29:34.

9. Marvin W. Meyer, *The Ancient Mysteries: A Source Book* (San Francisco: Harper & Row, 1987), ibid., 147. In particular the Naasene Gnostics, who worshiped the serpent of Genesis 3, and saw Eve as a heroine in her grasp for knowledge, were no doubt interested in these goddess cults in part because of the important place they gave to the serpent. See William M. Ramsay, *Roman History* (Oxford: Clarendon Press, 1895-7, reprinted Arno Press, 1975), 94.

10. The same testimony comes from Irenaeus, *Against Heresies*. In commenting on the fact that "some say that he [God] is without conjugal consort, being neither male nor female, . . . Others . . . a hermaphrodite," Irenaeus notes the similarity with pagan notions: "Do not these men seem to you, my dear friend, to have had in mind the Homeric Zeus more than the Sovereign of the universe (53-54)?" Irenaeus fur-

ther notes their dependence on other pagan ideas: "They accept the theories of the astrologers and adapt them to their standard of doctrine" (87). He too witnesses to their being inspired by pagan ceremonies: "they observe other rites that are just like those of the pagans" (90).

11. This same goddess is worshiped under the name of Artemis at Ephesus where Paul established a church (Acts 19). Sjoo and Mor, *The Cosmic Mother*, 126, argue that sexual perversion and perverse spirituality (of which they approve) go back a long way. The Scythian Ennares were hermaphrodites who wore women's clothes and received gifts of divination from the goddess Aphrodite.

12. Cited in Meyer, *Ancient Mysteries*, 126-128.

13. See the account of Lucian of Samosata (second century A.D.), cited in Meyer, ibid., 134. Lucian also describes the actual rites he observed: "On those days, too, men become Galli (initiates of Cybele/Rhea) . . . The youth for whom these things lie in store throws off his clothes, rushes to the center . . . and takes up the sword . . . He grabs it and immediately castrates himself. Then he rushes through the city holding in his hands the parts he has cut off. He takes female clothing and women's adornment from whatever house he throws these parts. This is what they do at the Castration" (*De Dea Syria*, 51).

14. *Metamorphoses*, 26, cited in Meyer, ibid., 143. Apuleius also describes their transvestite clothing and female cosmetics on their faces (27), as well as a gang-rape scene of a "lusty young rustic, chosen for his goodly proportions" brought in for the occasion (29).

15. See Meyer, ibid., 128-130, for a fourth century A.D. description of this rite.

16. *Against Heresies*, 5:9:10.

17. *Against Heresies* 5:7:13-15. This clearly helps explain logion 114 of the *Gospel of Thomas* which Hippolytus cites as one of their sources a few lines further on (5:7:20).

18. *Against Heresies* 5:9:11. Some modern, apparently innocuous, arguments for the ordination of women come perilously close to this form of Gnostic reasoning, when it is argued, for instance, that the headship of the husband over the wife is not carried over into church life, so that in the church a wife could be the pastor of her husband. Comments C. P. Venema, "does a married member of the church become a spiritual 'eunuch' when it comes to the life and fellowship of the church, the married relationship no longer relevant to relationships within the church?" in "Gathering Or Scrounging for Grounds?" *The Outlook* (March, 1992) 15.

19. Hippolytus, *The Refutation of All Heresies* V.xxi.

20. *Paraphrase of Shem* 28:35-29:33.

21. *Gospel of the Egyptians* 56:4-21. Rudolf, *Gnosis*, 139, in his discussion of this text, does not mention a possible homosexual reference.

22. Epiphanius, *Panarion* 27:4:5.

23. Ibid. 25.2:5. The Nicolaitans "teach their followers to engage in promiscuous intercourse with women and *unnatural acts of incurable viciousness, 23.22 it is not right to say how.*" In the light of his vocabulary elsewhere, this is likely to be a reference to homosexuality.

24. Ibid. 26:11:9-11. "These persons who debauch themselves with their own hands . . . finally get their fill of promiscuous relations with women and grow ardent for each other, men for men."

25. At an international conference in 1966, the then recognized experts on Gnosticism — G. Widengren, C. Colpe, U. Bianchi, H. Jonas and J. Daniélou — produced a "Final Document" which concluded that Gnosticism was a particular expression of the so-called mystery religions — see *Lo Origini dello Gnosticismo: Colloquio di Messina 13-18 Aprile, 1966. Testi e Discussioni* (Studies in the History of Religions, Suppl. *Numen* 12: Ed., U. Bianchi, et al.; Leiden: Brill, 1977), xxvi.

26. *Against Heresies*, 5.8.23. Rudolf, *Gnosis*, 14, shows that Hippolytus structures his *Refutatio* in such a way that he first presents the Greek heathen ideas, then gives an exposition of the Christian Gnostic heresies, attempting to show thereby that the Gnostics took their doctrines from the "wisdom of the heathen" — which incidentally they (the heretics) even misunderstand and misuse sometimes.

27. The Roman Catholic theologian, Walter Kasper, "Position of Women," 58-59 considers this modern view of sexuality as another expression of ancient Gnosticism.

28. See for instance the statement of L'Engle already quoted: "the male chauvinistic pig god of the Old Testament" or Eisler's characterization of the "powerful upstart [male] God Jehovah" to name but two.

29. *Gospel of Thomas* 75, and compare *Dialogue of the Savior* 142:18-19. See J. J. Buckley, "An Interpretation of Logion 114 in the *Gospel of Thomas*," *Novum Testamentum* XXVII, 3 (1985), 261, 266.

30. Filoramo, *History of Gnosticism*, 24, sees the "superman" theme as an element of great attraction. What had once only been the privilege of heroes and demigods — for anyone else it was hubris — now became possible for anyone who heeded the inner voice. "The new spiritual climate positively insisted that one transcend these barriers and become a hyperanthropos (a super human)."

31. *Apocryphon of John* 15-19.

32. *Gospel of Thomas* 16, commenting on Matthew 10:34-36 and Luke 12:49-53.

33. So Marvin W. Meyer, "Male and Female in the *Gospel of Thomas*," *New Testament Studies*, 31 (1985), 556.

34. *Apocryphon of John* 24:26-27.

35. *Book of Thomas the Contender* 139:8-11, 28-29.

36. Ibid., 144:9-11.

37. *Dialogue of the Savior* 144:19-20.

38. *Authoritative Teaching* 23: 18-20. See also *Gospel of Philip* 56:25, which teaches that the soul is precious but came in "a contemptible body."

39. *Paraphrase of Shem* 18:34:-35, 27:2-3, and 22:34.

40. *Zostrianos* 131:5-8. See also *Testimony of Truth* 68:6-8. Compare Gospel of Philip 82:4 which speaks of the "marriage of defilement." On this see Marvin W. Meyer, "Male and Female," 565.

41. The texts which mention this Bridal sacrament are *Teaching of Silvanus* 94:26-2, *Exegesis of the Soul* 132:12-14, *Gospel of Philip* and *Gospel of Thomas*. On the latter see chapter 15.

42. *Gospel of Philip* 68:24-26.

43. *Gospel of Philip* 70:13-20. In some forms of Hinduism, in paricular karezza yoga, sexual union "becomes a form of worship. The male and female principles unite and the opposites are transcended." Also, abstinence "is considered to be the ultimate form of oneness with the cosmos" — so Herbert J. Pollitt, *The Inter-Faith Movement: The New Age Enters the Church* (Edinburgh: The Banner of Truth Trust, 1996), 166.

44. B.Gärtner, *The Theology of the Gospel According to Thomas* (New York: Harper, 1961), 256. Bertil Gärtner was an early authority on this gospel, teaching at Princeton Theological Seminary for a number of years.

45. Pagels, *Gnostic Gospels*, 66.

46. For a careful exegesis of Gen 1-3, see Raymond C. Ortland, Jr., "Male-Female Equality and Male Headship: Gen 1-3," *Recovering Biblical Manhood and Womanhood*, 95-112.

47. J. J. Buckley, art.cit., 246.

48. Ibid., 255.

49. *Gospel of Thomas* 75. See Meyer, "Male and Female," 558.

50. *Gospel of Thomas*, 61.

51. *Zostrianos* 131:5-10.

52. Filoramo, ibid.

53. See the Hermetic Gnostic text, *Right Ginza* III: "When there was no unevenness (or: inequality) (then) we had but one form . . . . we were both made as a single mana (spirit) Now, where there is no evenness (or: equality), they made you a man and me a woman." In Poimandres, the original Anthropos is bisexual and so is his earthly counterpart who, being earthly partakes of the earth/heaven duality. From his heavenly origin he is above separation, bisexual from a bisexual father (so Rudolf, *Gnosis*. 108). "The origin of mankind results from this mixed nature, first seven bisexual men corresponding to the"nature of the harmony of the seven (planets)," which Anthropos carried in him. The separation of the sexes comes at the end of the creation period."

54. Dawne McCance, "Contemporary Feminist," 168, characterizing the works of Letty Russell, Phyllis Trible and Rita Gross.

55. Clearly a citation of Gen 3:1, referring to the serpent — *On The Origin Of The World* 113:30-114:4. *Hypostasis of the Archons* is one of the few [perhaps the only] Gnostic document that describes the Creator, in demeaning terms, as androgynous — see 94:34.

56. The androgynous instructor recalls the contemporary identification of homosexuals as shamans.

57. *Thunder, Perfect Mind*, according to George MacRae, *NHL*, 271, has no distinctively Gnostic themes. He believes the antitheses and paradoxes wish to express the absolute transcendence of the revealer. MacRae surely has not considered the important theme of the monistic joining of opposites, which, according to Filoramo, is essential to Gnosticism. See also Rudolf, 271, who says that bi-sexuality (androgyny) is an ideal of Gnosticism. See also *Apocalypse of Adam* 81:4-11.

58. John D. Turner, in the introduction to his translation of *Trimorphic Protennoia* [literally "three-formed first thought], (*The Nag Hammadi Library in English*, 461).

59. *Trimorphic Protennoia* 45:2-6. See also *Exegesis of the Soul* and an introductory article by W. C. Robinson, Jr., "The Exegesis of the Soul," *Novum Testamentum* 12/2 (1970), especially 116, who argues that the content of this text is close to that of the Naasenes for whom the mutilation of Attis was a type of the androgynous ideal.

60. H. Jonas, *The Gnostic Religion*, 257, asserts that the ascetic tendency of Gnosticism rejected marriage. See Irenaeus, *Against Heresies* 1.24.2 on the followers of Saturnilus: "Marriage and procreation, they maintain, are of Satan." Epiphanius, *Panarion* 45.2.1, cites Severus, the Marcionite, to the same effect: "Those who consort in marriage fulfill the work of Satan." See also the Nag Hammadi *Dialogue of the Savior* 144:15-21: "Judas said, . . . 'How shall we pray?' The Lord said, "He says to us, 'Pray in the place where there is no woman,' (and) 'Destroy [the] works of femaleness.'" N.B. This is not male chauvinism because the discourse is equally divided between Matthew, Judas and Miriam (Matthew asks nine questions, Judas twelve and Miriam eleven). Compare with this ancient Gnostic attitude the statement of a leading feminist, Shulamith Firestone, *The Dialectic of Sex: The Case for Feminist Revolution* (New York: William Morrow and Company, Inc., 1970), 81, "The heart of woman's oppression is her childbearing and childrearing roles." In another chilling parallel, just as the Gnostics saw the command of Jahweh the Creator to "multiply and replenish the earth" as a ploy to enslave mankind in the carnal process of procreation (*On The Origin Of The World* 114:15-24), today feminists push the notion of "zero-population growth" and encourage young women to take up a career rather than get involved in the dangerous business (for the planet) of childbearing and motherhood. See the statement of Matthew Fox: "In some ways, homosexuality is superior to heterosexuality. There's no better birth control." And there is cosmological merit in the fact that it is not "productive" (cited in Donna Steichen, *Unholy Rage)*, 230.

61. Epiphanius (Panarion, 26:5:5) describes an orgiastic cult as an example of the libertine option — eating sperm and menstrual fluid + 730 "immoral unions" by which a man is "made one with Christ." But note that like in the ascetic option, "child-bearing is avoided. If pregnancy ensues, the infant embryo is forcibly removed . . . [and] consumed after being torn apart and duly prepared." Rudolf, *Gnosis*, 248-249, finds this an example of "perverted phantasy" on the part of Epiphanius. Rudolf (ibid., 250) nevertheless gives the theological reason for doing these barbarous acts, found in Panarion 26:9,6-9: "we are doing a kindness to created things, in that we collect the soul from all things and transmit it with ourselves to the heavenly world," finding this explanation "more credible." If the theological reason makes sense, why not Epiphanius' description of the practice?

62. See below.

63. *Apocalypse of James* 41:15-18.

64. Genesis 1:27. See Meyer, art.cit, 560. Such an understanding is another example of the misunderstanding of Genesis. Genesis 1 is a general statement. Genesis 2 unpacks that statement, following typical Semitic narrative practice.

65. *On Righteousness*, by Epiphanes, preserved in Clement of Alexandria's *Stromateis* III 6.1-9.3, cited in Rudolf, op.cit, 268.

66. See Rudolf, *Gnosis,* 268. Wayne A. Meeks, "The Image of the Androgyne: Some Uses of a Symbol in Earliest Christianity," *History of Religions* 13 (1974), 185, argues that Gal 3:28 "presupposes an interpretation of the creation story in which the divine image after which Adam was modeled was masculofeminine."

67. Tertullian, *De Praescriptione* 41.

68. Rudolf, *Gnosis*, 211, 251 and 270: "The equal standing of women in cultic practice in the Gnostic communities appears to have been relatively widespread." See also Pagels, *Gnostic Gospels*, 60ff, and Filoramo, *Gnosticism*, 176. Pheme Perkins, *The Gnostic Dialogue: The Early Church and the Crisis of Gnosticism* (New York: Paulist Press, 1980), 136, argues that the *Gospel of Mary* and Mary's prominent position is not an indication of the place of women in general in the Gnostic church, but of Mary's own unique importance. The evidence, of course, does not depend upon this text alone, as the witness of the Church Fathers indicates.

69. Hippolytus, *Refutation of All Heresies* 6:35, and Irenaeus, *Against Heresies* 1:13:1-2.

70. See my discussion of this in *The Gnostic Empire*, 32-33. Rudolf, op.cit, 212, argues that the prominent role granted to women in Gnosticism was due to the important place given to Sophia and other female deities in the Gnostic system.

71. See *The Gnostic Empire*, 40, note 39 for an extended discussion of this point.

72. For the text, see *Gospel of Mary* 8:17-9:4, *The Nag Hammadi Library in English*, 472.

73. *Gospel of Mary* 9:20. For the full text see *The Nag Hammadi Library in English*, 472.

74. *Gospel of Mary* 10:7-8, 18:13-14.

75. Pagels, *Gnostic Gospels*, 66.

76. Rudolf, *Gnosis*, 212.

Chapter Fourteen

1. James Plath, ed., *Conversations With John Updike* (Jackson: University Press of Mississippi, 1994), 14. I am grateful to my colleague, Dr. W. Robert Godfrey, for this quotation.

2. Marilyn Ferguson, *The Brain Revolution: Frontiers of Mind Research* (Davis-Poynter, 1974), pp.111-113, cited in Morrison, *The Serpent*, 128.

3. Betty Eadie, *Embraced by the Light* (Goldleaf Press, 1992), 40-41.

4. Steichen, *Ungodly Rage,* 285.

5. Ibid., 309.

6. DavidWells, *No Place for Truth*, 267. Also, "The supernatural was therefore known by *experience* rather than by detached thought" (265), or, we could add, by revelation.

7. Sister Madonna Kolbenschlag, cited in Steichen, *Ungodly Rage*, 93.

8. Steichen, *Ungodly Rage*, 60, describing Sister Dorothy Olinger, S.S.N.D., who helped to organize the first Women and Spirituality Conference in 1982, in the American Roman Catholic Church.

9. Sjoo and Mor, *The Great Cosmic Mother*, 427. If this were true, and there were only the subjectivity of people's individual experience, why would one make statements of general truth and write books trying to convince people of it?

10. Sister Madonna Kolbenschlag, cited in Steichen, *Ungodly Rage*, 93.

11. Steichen, *Ungodly Rage*, 150.

12. *Times Advocate*, Monday, June 13, 1994.

13. Roof, *Generation*, 126-127.

14. Roof, ibid., 258 quoting Donald Capps. David Wells, *No Place for Truth*, 111 and 112, sees the evangelical church as deeply influenced by this modern view of the world.

15. Cited in Morrison, ibid., 186.

16. Sjoo and Mor, *The Great Cosmic Mother*, 420.

17. Sister Elaine Prevallet, S.L., cited by Donna Steichen, *Ungodly Rage*, 291.

18. Kolbenschlag, *Kiss Sleeping Beauty Goodbye: Breaking the Spell of Feminine Myths and Models* (Garden City, N.Y.: Doubleday, 1979), 184-86, cited in Steichen, *Ungodly Rage*, 92.

19. Scott M. Peck, *The Road Less Traveled* (New York: Simon & Schuster, 1978), 283.

20. Mollenkott, *Sensuous Spirituality*, 17.

21. Peter Russell, *The White Hole in Time: Our Future Evolution and the Meaning of Now* (Aquarian Press, 1992), p. 223, cited in Morrison, *The Serpent*, 140.

22. Ibid.

23. Mollenkott, *Sensuous Spirituality*, 98.

24. Quoted in *Interfaith News*, No.3, Autumn 1983, 2, cited by Morrison, *The Serpent*, 142.

25. See Genesis 2:17. Morrison, ibid., points out that the "Hebrew word translated as 'wizard' or 'familiar spirit' (A.V.) in the Bible (e.g., Leviticus 19:31; 20:6; Deuteronomy 18:11) is *yiddeoni*, which means, literally *knowing one*, . . . The English word 'wizard' also comes from the Old English root 'wis' meaning *to know*." The original wizards were proto-Gnostics!

26. *Lazaris*, 1994 Concept: Synergy. Morrison, *The Serpent*, 162, notes with regard to modern shamanism: "This Neo-Shamanism contains radical differences from the traditional tribal phenomenon. Whereas ancient Shamanism looked to a single shaman within its community, the new shamanism believes that anyone today can become a shaman."

27. Sjoo and Mor, *The Great Cosmic Mother*, 17.

28. J. Gordon Melton, *New Age Encyclopedia* (Detroit: Gale Research Inc., 1990), xiii.

29. See Steichen, *Ungodly Rage*, 36.

30. See the whole section, Genesis 3:1-7.

31. 1 Corinthians 15:26, 55.

32. Elizabeth Kübler-Ross, "Death: The Final State of Growth," cited in Morrison, *The Serpent*, 174.

33. See especially Betty Eadie, *Embraced by the Light*.

34. Elizabeth Clare Prophet, *Prayer and Meditation: Jesus and Kuthumi* (Summit Press, 1963), inside cover, cited in Morrison, *The Serpent*, 112.

35. See Oddie, *What Will Happen to God?*, 8.

36. Oddie, *What Will Happen to God?*, 143. Elizabeth Schlüsser Fiorenza, who holds the position of Professor of New Testament Studies at Harvard Divinity School, encourages women students to write 'apocryphal' texts from the perspective of leading women in early Christianity.

37. Judith Plaskow, a leading religious feminist and her committee at a 1972 feminist conference at Grailville, Loveland, Ohio — see Steichen, *Ungodly Rage*, 94.

38. Steichen, *Ungodly Rage*, 81. This program, "The Goddesses and the Wild Woman," was the first in a series presented at Mundelein, a conference center in the Mid-West, held in March 1985.

39. A poem 'For the Unknown Goddess,' by Elizabeth Brewster, for "Christian" feminist liturgies in the UK, cited in Oddie, *What Will Happen to God?*, 20.

40. Oddie, *What Will Happen to God?*, 21.

41. Cited in Steichen, *Ungodly Rage,* 145.

42. Marjorie Procter-Smith, *Women at Worship: Interpretations of North American Diversity* (Louisville, KY: Westminster/John Knox Press, 1993), on the back cover. This is the second explosive book published by John Knox/Westminster Press, which at the time, was the official publishing arm of the Presbyterian Church USA. This book contains all the radical notions that were later expressed at the *RE-Imagining Conference* in the fall of 1993.

43. As Steichen, *Ungodly Rage,* 96, sees so well.

44. See Paul Knitter and the theologians who "pass over" for new spiritual experiences in other religions. See also Virginia Fabella, David K. H. Lee and David Kwang-Sun Suh, editors, *Asian Christian Spirituality* (Maryknoll, NY: Orbis Books, 1992), who examine the great religions of Asia to show how they foster a "liberative Christian spirituality."

45. Ruether,*Women-Church*, 86, 150-151.

46. Mollenkott, *Sensuous Spirituality*, 97.

47. David Miller, *The New Polytheism*, 11.

48. A transcript from tapes of the addresses given at the *RE-Imagining Conference* in Minneapolis, 1993, published by *Good News: A Forum for Scriptural Christianity within the United Methodist Church*, January, 1994, 11.

49. S. Scott and B. Smith *Trojan Horse*, 44, show that these same four steps are promoted in Madeleine L'Engle's books.

50. I am following here the account of Donna Steichen, *Ungodly Rage*, 72.

51. Marjorie Procter-Smith and Janet R. Walton, *Women at Worship: Interpretations of North American Diversity* (Louisville, KY: Westminster/John Knox Press, 1993), 3.

52. Ibid., 4.

53. Ibid., 145.

54. Ibid., 158.

55. Ibid., 159.

56. Steichen, *Ungodly Rage*, 71.

57. Ruether, *Women-Church*, 162 and 175. For other wiccan elements, note the omnipresence of circles: the architecture is round or egg-shaped; most of the rites take place in a circle (188); the marriage rite for a lesbian couple includes a communion rite in a circle of connection (199); there is dancing in a circle (202); a "menopause liturgy" begins with women gathering in a circle and is celebrated with "witch hazel" tea (204); a "Croning liturgy" to establish an older woman as having become a "wise old woman" begins by "casting the circle" by the song (to the tune "Jacob's Ladder"):

We are casting Janet's circle . . . sisters all around
Come now, join us, cast the circle . . . sisters all around
All together, form a circle . . . sisters all around (206);
there follow four "Circle-Casting Incantations" including the following:

Spirit of air, Spirit of fire, Spirit of water, Spirit of earth, Come join us as we celebrate the blooming of one of yours.

We are in the presence of "primitive" animism (the worship of spirits) now being practiced by twentieth century American intellectuals within the precincts of the Church.

58. Ruether, *Women-Church*, 171.

59. Steichen, *Ungodly Rage*, 55.

60. Steichen, *Ungodly Rage*, 195, reports on a major Roman Catholic feminist conference, "called "Women's Spirit Bonding," which was considered so significant to the development of religious feminism that the proceedings were published in their entirety.

61. Steichen, *Ungodly Rage*, 92.

62. Ibid., 151.

63. Phil Jackson with Hugh Delehanty, *Sacred Hoops: Spiritual Lessons of a Hardwood Warrior* (Hyperion, 1996), reported via the *Gannett News Service* in the *Montgomery Advertiser* (March 23, 1996).

64. Philip St. Romain, *Kundalini Energy and Christian Spirituality: A Pathway To Growth and Healing* (New York: Crossroads, 1991), 24 and 115.

65. Ibid., 74.

66. Ibid., 129.

67. Ibid., 131: "Surrender yourself into the care of Christ, Whose Spirit is capable of guiding your kundalini energies toward a wholesome integration. Trust that a Higher Guidance is at work in the process. Ask for this Guidance when confused."

68. Deepak Chopra, *The Higher Self: Tape Series*, distributed by Conant and Nightingale.

69. Sjoo and Mor, *The Great Cosmic Mother*, 432.

70. Ken Carey, *Starseed Transmission*, 35, cited in Morrison, *The Serpent*, 124.

71. Sjoo and Mor, *The Great Cosmic Mother*, 172.

72. Deepak Chopra, Tape Series.

73. *Light Connection*, July, 1994, 14-15.

74. Sjoo and Mor, *The Great Cosmic Mother*, 234.

75. Mollenkott, *Sensuous Spirituality*, 16.

76. Mollenkott, *ibid.*, 107, is a firm believer in this form of meditation: "we desperately need meditation or some other method of paying attention to our own inner process and feeling our connection to the sacred."

77. *Lazaris, Concept:Synergy*, August, 1994.

78. A transcript from tapes of the addresses given at the *RE-Imagining Conference* in Minneapolis, 1993, published by *Good News: A Forum for Scriptural Christianity within the United Methodist Church*, January, 1994, 13.

79. In particular, The *Presbyterian Layman* (PCUSA) and *Good News* (United Methodist).

80. Steichen, *Ungodly Rage*.

81. Steichen, ibid., 220 and 229: "Fox sees abortion as a necessity that must be provided in safe facilities. He lauds committed homosexual relationships — including genital acts — as celebrations of creation. He finds the Mass less "boring" when it incorporates witchcraft chants and dances. And he calls for more irrationality, which is understandable, given what he has to say. . . . The Church has "zeroed in so much on sexuality as morality, we're not teaching young people about sexuality as mysticism." The Foxian prescription is "playful" worship: "Step out of the rational to cure the rational — get out of the box of rationality: with "sweat lodges, wilderness education, drumming, mask work" and stories that give them a vision "of their own divinity."

82. Matthew Fox, *The Cosmic Christ*, 180 and 170.

83. Cited in Steichen, ibid., 176.

84. Berit Kjos, "An Unholy Renaissance of Sacred Sexuality," *Southern California Christian Times*, July, 1994, 9.

85. Sjoo and Mor, *The Great Cosmic Mother*, 75.

86. Ibid., 173.

87. As is the case in some forms of Satanism.

88. Steichen, ibid., 231.

89. See the following chapter.

90. *Ouroboros* means literally "devourer of its own tail": compare the Latin term *carni-vorus* which has borrowed from the Greek. See Rudolf, *Gnosis*, 223. Sjoo and Mor, ibid., 62, develop the theme of the all-inclusive Great Mother who unites both life and death, good and evil in the great monistic unity of the All. In this context they refer to the ouroboros symbol, the serpent curled with its tail in its mouth "forming the perfect circle, or female O, or zero — the cycle of all and of nothing. The continuous eternal wisdom-cycle of all coming from nothing and returning to nothing."

91. Ibid., 57-58.

92. Ibid. See also ibid., 60, where the authors show how snakes were an integral part of pagan worship: "Ancient religion used snake venom as a hallucinogen which promoted clairvoyance among female shamans." They also tie the serpent to the occult, ibid., 61: "modern man" is now unaware of his primordial connection with universal life, what occultists call "the astral serpent" "which patriarchy tells us to destroy."

93. Ibid., 58. "Gliding in and out of holes, it symbolizes the dead awaiting rebirth."

94. Ibid., 59.

95. Ibid., 277.

96. Pirani, *The Absent Mother.*

97. Ibid., 229.

98. Sjoo and Mor, The Great Cosmic Mother, 234.

99. Ibid., 425.

100. 2 Corinthians 6:16.

101. St.Romain, *Kundalini Energy*, 148.

102. Ibid., 130.

103. Ibid., 128.

104. David Schnarch, "Joy, With Your Underwear Down," *Psychology Today* (July/August, 1994), 78.

105. Livy, Book XXXIX, xiii:11, in *Livy, With an English Translation in Fourteen Volumes*, translated Evan T. Sage (Cambridge, MA: Harvard University Press, 1965), 255.

106. Mollenkott, *Sensuous Spirituality*, 27.

107. Ibid., 118. She says elsewhere: "I believe that every honest attempt to relate to another human being is a good attempt, including recreational sex or sensuality, if that is all a person can achieve (ibid., 100).

108. Ibid., 139.

109. Daly & Caputi, *Wickedary*, ad loc.

110. Ibid.

111. E. Michael Jones, "What Lesbian Nuns can Teach Us About Vatican II," *Fidelity* (December, 1985), 22.

112. Ibid., 20.

113. *Good News* tape transcripts, 7.

114. Cited in E. Michael Jones, *Fidelity*, 1985, 21.

115. The Apostle Paul, Romans 1: 24.

116. 1 Corinthians 6:18.

117. The willingness of the Clinton administration to export American abortion ideology and techniques to all corners of the world takes on a macabre note in the light of this statement by witches.

118. Sjoo and Mor, ibid., 377.

119. Ibid., 388.

120. Morrison, *The Serpent*, 98, notes Carl Jung's belief that, "in the interests of wholeness, evil inclinations should be accepted and integrated into the personality rather than suppressed is also compatible with feminist neo-gnosticism of all shades." The point is that much of modern psychology follows Jung, and that Jung was a dabbler in the occult.

121. Rosemary Radford Ruether, *Women-Church*, 130.

122. Ibid., 145.

123. James R. Edwards, "Earthquake in the Mainline," *Christianity Today*, November 14, 1994, 39. This is a profound analysis of the heretical opinions voiced at the conference.

124. Ibid.

Chapter Fifteen

1. *Apocryphon of James* 12: 12-16.

2. As opposed to the Christian teaching that death has been vanquished and has no final victory — 1 Corinthians 15:54-57.

3. Rudolf, *Gnosis*, 171.

4. Ibid.

5. Ibid., 91.

6. *Book of Thomas the Contender* 139:28-30. See ibid., 115. According to Rudolf, 109, "the idea of the 'migration of the soul' is not alien to Gnosis: the "decanting" of the soul from one body into another, especially when it is of the punishment of sinful and unawakened souls." This migration is also expressed in the idea that the individual soul is part of the universal soul."

7. If you have been pronouncing the "g" up till this point, return to "Go," and read everything again!

8. *Tripartite Tractate* 110:11-23. See Rudolf, *Gnosis*, 55.

9. Filoramo, *Gnosticism*, 60.

10. Filoramo, *Gnosticism*, 38-39 speaks of a profound transformation the Gnostic brings to the word *gnosis*. In classical Greek *gnosis* is knowledge of 'what is' (*ta onta*) as opposed to what is merely sense perception — also *gnosis* is presented as knowledge obtained by discourse and dialectic, beginning with visual, direct observation." *Gnosis* "indicates a form of meta-rational knowledge . . . the gift of the divinity and has the power to save the one who achieves it. It enables one to take possession of the keys to the cosmic mystery, to solve the enigma of the universe by absorbing the *axis mundi*, or world axis, or archaic cosmogonies into the very essence of one's being . . . If it is true that the doctrinal content of *gnosis* is also cosmological and aims at revealing 'what is upon earth, in heaven,' it is also true that the acquisition of this teaching is not an end in itself, but a function of the knowledge of the mystery of human beings and therefore of their salvation. *Gnosis* is the 'redemption of the inner man,' that is, the purification of the spiritual being and at the same time knowledge of the Whole."

11. *Gospel of Truth* 22:2-15.

12. For the actual text, see *Apocryphon of James* 12:10ff.

13. *Gospel of Truth* 1:18. G. W. MacRae, "Introduction," *The Nag Hammadi Library in English*, 37, says that the *Gospel of Truth* is "about the eternal divine Son, the word who reveals the Father and passes on knowledge, particularly self-knowledge."

14. Aristotle *Fr.* 15, quoted in Walter Burkert, *Ancient Mystery Cults* (Cambridge, MA: Harvard University Press, 1987), 89.

15. Walter Burkert, ibid., 11.

16. Dio Chrysostom *Or.* 12.33, cited in Walter Burkert, *Ancient Mystery Cults*, 90.

17. Elliot Miller, *A Crash Course on the New Age*, 17.

18. *Paraphrase of Shem* 34:22-23.

19. Rudolf, *Gnosis*, 76.

20. *Gospel of Truth* 1:37-38.

21. *Testimony of Truth* 36.

22. *Gospel of Truth* 25:5-10, 38:1ff, and 42:25.

23. *Tripartite Tractate* 71:8ff.

24. Hans Jonas, "Delimitation of the Gnostic Phenomenon — Typological and Historical," in *Le origini dello gnosticismo*, p. 97, cited in Lee, ibid.

25. *Gospel of Truth* 25:1-7.

26. In a public address at the *Parliament of the World's Religions*, Chicago, 1993, at which I was present. J. J. Buckley, "The Cult-Mystery in the Gospel of Philip," *Journal of Biblical Literature* 99/4 (1980), 581, maintains that the *Gospel of Philip* moves beyond dualism when it describes the Gnostic initiate transcending the creational structures. This entrance into true liberty produces "a collapse of a dualistic worldview."

27. Lee, *Against the Protestant Gnostics*, 23.

28. Rudolf, *Gnosis*, 186-7.

29. Ibid., 44.

30. See chapter 12.

31. *Tripartite Tractate* 124.21ff.

32. *Apocryphon of James* 4:19-21. Burkert, ibid., 69, notes the very same tendency in pagan mystery religions. The pagan mysteries were "unspeakable," *(arrheta)* not only in the sense that one was obliged to a vow of secrecy, but also in the sense that "what was central and decisive was not accessible to verbalization."

33. Rudolf, *Gnosis,* 117.

34. 1 Timothy 4:3.

35. This makes for an inevitable overlap in the chapters on Gnostic sexuality and Gnostic spirituality.

36. *Gospel of Truth* 22:3.

37. Lee, *Against the Protestant Gnostics*, 26.

38. Filoramo, *Gnosticism*, 40.

39. Marvin Meyer and Richard Smith, *Ancient Christian Magic: Coptic Texts of Ritual Power* (San Francisco: Harper, 1994), 61. This book is a further project of the Institute for Antiquity and Christianity of Claremont Graduate School of which the Director is James M. Robinson.

40. Burkert, *Ancient Mystery Cults*, 8.

41. Irenaeus, *Against Heresies* 21:2.

42. The *Gospel of Philip* 67:25ff. These Christians are super-Christians with a different agenda from orthodoxy, though sufficiently close to deceive the unsuspecting. W. W. Isenburg in his introduction to the *Gospel of Philip*, *The Nag Hammadi Library*, 131, says: "The sacraments exhibited in the *Gospel of Philip* are similar to those used by Christians. . . . Thus the Gnostics who wrote and used the present text had not departed radically from orthodox sacramental practice; yet the interpretation provided for the sacraments clearly remains Gnostic."

43. Luke 12:49-50. This is the baptism of his death on the cross.

44. Irenaeus, *Against Heresies* 1:21:2. See Kurt Rudolf, *Gnosis*, 227.

45. *Gospel of Philip* 76:25ff.

46. See Rudolf, *Gnosis*, 229. See *Gospel of Philip* 69:15-25.

47. *Gospel of Philip* 75:15-25.

48. *Acts of Thomas* 50, cited in Rudolf, *Gnosis*, 242. Rudolf affirms that this text is Gnostic, as does G. Bornkamm in E. Hennecke and W. Schneemelcher, *New Testament Apocrypha*, vol II (Philadelphia: The Westminster Press, 1964), 426-437.

49. Cited in Rudolf, *Gnosis*, 242. Robert Mcl. Wilson's translation in Hennecke and Schneemelcher, *The New Testament Apocrypha*, II, 470, has the less sensational "Come, fellowship of the male."

50. Epiphanius, *Panarion* 37:5, 6-8. As a pagan parallel, the Dionysiac initiations employed live snakes — see Walter Burkert, *Ancient Mystery Cults*, 97. See also p.106, where Burkert describes another snake cult, the mysteries of Sabazius. "A snake made of metal was made to pass beneath the initiand's clothes. This is the 'God through the lap,' *Theos dia kolpou*. Scholars agree that this is a form of sexual union with the god; in the cultic myth Persephone is impregnated by Zeus in the form of a snake, and legend has associated the snakes of Dionysus' *origin* with the impregnation of Olympias, mother of Alexander, by a god. But in the Sabazius ritual this is transformed through double symbolism — snake for phallus, and artifact for snake. The ritual must have remained impressive enough, but the real dread would come not so much from sexual associations as from the anticipation of touching a snake, especially since the initiand by the light of flickering torches could hardly know for certain what was real and what was artifact. Even here, sexuality in itself is not the secret in question."

51. Cited in Dart, *The Laughing Savior*, 33.

52. This title recalls a recent book by E. Michael Jones, *Degenerate Moderns: Modernity as Rationalized Sexual Misbehavior* (San Francisco: Ignatius, 1993). At least two of the "degenerate moderns" Jones studies have also been described as "neo-Gnostics." See Dart, *The Laughing Savior*, 32. According to Dart, "Jung credited Sigmund Freud with introducing the classical motif of the wicked paternal authority into modern psychology. The evil creator God of the Gnostics 'reappeared in the Freudian myth of the primal father . . . [who] became a demon who created the world of disappointments, illusions and suffering.'" Jung, of course, was a great admirer of Gnosticism, and the Jung Institute acquired some of the Gnostic texts, the so-called Jung Codex, which includes the *Gospel of Truth, the Apocryphon of James*, and the *Treatise on the Resurrection*. Jung supplied to modern psychology another essential aspect of Gnosticism — "the primordial feminine spirit" revealing the higher God behind the God of Creation — see Dart, ibid. Jung, who devoted his life to the study of "mythical archetypes" as the source of psychological healing said, when he discovered the Gnostic texts: "All my life I have been working and studying to find these things, and these people knew already" — cited in Benjamin Walker, *Gnosticism: Its History and Influence* (Wellingborough, UK: The Aquarian Press, 1983), 187. See also Stephen Hoeller, *The Gnostic Jung and the Seven Sermons of the Dead* (Los Angeles: Quest Books, no date). Hoeller is director of the Gnostic Society of Los Angeles, a member of the Theosophical Society, an admirer of Joseph Campbell and bishop in the Ecclesia Gnostica. He was a featured speaker at the *Parliament of the World's Religions* in 1993.

53. This is Rudolf's position, *Gnosis*, 250. For defence of Epiphanius, see Robert L. Wilken, *The Christians as the Romans Saw Them* (New Haven and London: Yale University Press, 1984), 17-21.

54. See Rudolf, ibid., 250. Rudolf provides this evidence while still charging Epiphanius with fantasy, etc.

55. Epiphanius, *Panarion* 2:26:4,3-5,9. Dart, *The Laughing Savior*, 33-34, shows that Jung found important and useful "symbolism" in these extreme Gnostic rites.

56. Rudolf, *Gnosis*, 245.

57. Ibid., 246: "The pneumatics or Gnostics are understood as brides of the angels, and their entrance into the world beyond as a wedding-feast "which (according to

Clement of Alexandria, *Ex Theodoto* 63.2) is common to all the saved, until all become equal and mutually recognize one another."

58. Meyer, "Male and Female in *The Gospel of Thomas,*" 557, sees the solitary ones in the bridal chamber as being joined to their spiritual alter ego. In *The Exegesis of the Soul*, the "soul, described in its usual fashion as a woman, is conjoined to her heavenly bridegroom, her brother, and '[once] they unite [with one another] they become a single life'" [132:34-35]. cp Buckley, 266: "The bridegroom is Jesus."

59. Filoramo, *Gnosticism*, 141.

60. *Gospel of Philip* 82:5-10.

61. Ibid., 59:10. Scholars generally believe that there is no reference here to carnal union because Philip is ascetic — See J. J. Buckley, "The Cult-Mystery," 575.

62. Ibid., 70:5-10, cp. *Gospel of Thomas* 37.

63. Rudolf, *Gnosis*, 207: "the Gnostics practiced a more or less rigid code of secrecy (the so-called arcane discipline)."

64. These are the words of Burkert, *Ancient Mystery Cults*, 90, characterizing Dio's description.

65. Epiphanius, *Panarion* 2:11:9-11. See also the witness of Irenaeus, *Against Heresies*, 1:6:3: "Carnal things, they say, must be given to the carnal, and spiritual to the spiritual. Some secretly defile those women who are being taught this doctrine by them. . . . Others . . . feigned to dwell chastely with them as with sister, were exposed as time went on when the 'sister' became pregnant by the 'brother.'"

66. Epiphanius, ibid., 24:3:2.

67. See Acts 8 and Epiphanius, *Panarion* 2:21:2:2ff, according to whom Simon, "naturally lecherous," went around with a prostitute from Tyre whom he called the Holy Spirit.

68. This library is associated with the St. Pachomius monastery which is close to the site, and indicates a strong interest in asceticism. On the other hand, in the Isis initiation, there is an emphasis upon sexual abstinence, while at the same time, there is the suggestion that sexual activity is reserved for the final stages of initiation.

69. Burkert, *Ancient Mystery Cults*, 3 notes: "Certain Gnostic sects seem to have practiced mystery initiations, imitating or rather outdoing the pagans, and even orthodox Christianity adopted the mystery metaphor." The most explicit testimony is Irenaeus, *Against Heresies*, 1:21:3 (1:14:2 p.185, Harvey): "They prepare a bridal chamber and celebrate mysteries." Clement repeatedly says the Gnostics celebrate sexual intercourse as mysteries, *Stromata* 3:27:1,5, cp 3:10:1; 3:30:1. A homosexual encounter is insinuated in the "Secret Gospel of Mark," Smith, 1973, 115-117; 185; 452. See also R. M. Grant, "The Mysteries of Marriage in the Gospel of Philip," *Vig. Christ.* 15 (1961) 129-140.

70. Epiphanius, ibid.

71. Livy, Book 39:13:12.

72. Irenaeus, *Against Heresies* 1.31.2.

73. Irenaeus, *Against Heresies* 1.25.4 cp Eusebius, *Ecclesiastical History* 4:7.

74. 1 John 3:6.

75. 1 John 3:8.

76. Irenaeus, *Against Heresies* 1:21:3.

77. Sometimes even 365 — see Epiphanius, *Panarion* II.10:6-8.

78. Rudolf, *Gnosis*, 183.

79. Epiphanius, *Panarion* II.10:6-8.

80. Irenaeus, *Against Heresies* 1:21:5. Rudolf, *Gnosis*, 183, cites a text from the Gnostic Mandean literature, *Left Ginza* 1:4.The departed ascending soul is addressed by the watchers: "O Soul! You are ascending to the place of light, wherefore do you cry to the great and sublime Life? Give your name and your sign which you received from the

waves of water, from the treasures of radiance, from the great and high crater, from the great Jordan of healing powers and from the springs of light. When this soul stands in its place it opens its mouth and cries out, and presents itself, giving its name, its sign, its blessing, and its baptism and everything that this soul has received from the waves of water."

81. Rudolf, ibid., 177, citing the *Left Ginza*.

82. Rudolf, ibid., does not make anything of this aspect of Gnostic spirituality, but it is certainly there. According to the *Apocryphon of John* 68:17-69:13, souls that do not receive the spirit are taken over by "a counterfeit spirit." After death the counterfeit spirit hands the soul to the demiurgic powers. They "are flung into chains and led around (i.e. implanted in a body) until they are delivered from the oblivion and receive knowledge (and) so become perfect and are saved." See also Irenaeus, *Against Heresies* 1.25.4 cp Eusebius, *Ecclesiastical History* 4:7: "The souls in their transmigrations through bodies must pass through every kind of life. . . . This Jesus indicated with the words, "I tell thee, thou shalt not depart thence, till thou hast paid the very last mite" (Luke 12:59). . . . This means that he shall not go free from the power of the angels that made the world but has always to be reincarnated until he has committed every deed there is in the world, and only when nothing is still lacking will he be released to that God who is above the world-creating angels. Thus the souls are released and saved . . . after they have paid their debt and rendered their due." Note here the idea of *karma* — debt, due. Hans Jonas, *The Gnostic Religion*, 274, wonders if the Indian karma-doctrine and the release from the "wheel of birth" is not curiously present.

83. John H. Siebeck, "Introduction," *The Nag Hammadi Library in English*, 368.

84. Siebeck, ibid.

85. *Zostrianos* 129:6-12.

86. *Zostrianos* 53:19.

87. See also the *Gospel of the Egyptians*, "the holy book of the Great Invisible Spirit . . . i.e., the great Seth" which reveals the imperishable name: "Ie ieus eo ou eo oua! Really truly, O Yessus Mazareus Yessedekeus, O living water, O child of the child, O glorious name, really, truly, aion o on, iiii eeee eeee oo oo uuuu oooo aaaa{a}, really, truly, ei aaaa oooo, O existing one who sees the aeons! Really, truly, aee eee iiii uuuuuu ooooooo, who is eternally eternal, really, truly, iea aio, in the heart, who exists, u aei eis aei, ei o ei, eo os ei . . . Thou art what Thou art, Thou art who Thou art!" (*The Nag Hammadi Library in English*, 204). Pearson, Gnosticism, 77, shows a deep relationship between *The Gospel of the Egyptians* and *Zostrianos*. No one knows the meaning of these vowel sounds. Could they have some relationship with chakra mediation since there is a chakra technique for energy transfer that uses musical notes and vowel sounds where the base chakra corresponds to C.C# with the tone Uu; the "sacral centre" [next chakra] = D.D#, tone Oo; solar plexus chakra = E, tone Awh; heart chakra = F.F#, tone A; throat chakra = G.G#, tone I; brow chakra = A.A#, tone E . . . ; and top of head = B, tone E . . . ; above the head = High C, tone Uu . . . .[Taken from a diagram passed to me which contained no bibliographical reference, found in the copying machine of the local post office]?

88. All this material is cited from Pagels, *The Gnostic Gospels*, 165.

89. See Meyer and Richard Smith, *Ancient Christian Magic*, 64-65.

90. Matthew 6:7.

91. *Apocalypse of Paul* 22:24-30, 23:26-27, goes beyond 2 Corinthians 12 and reveals what the Paul of Scripture said was unlawful to reveal.

92. Dieter Mueller, "Introduction," *The Nag Hammadi Library in English*, 27, observes that the *Prayer of the Apostle Paul* "displays a striking resemblance not only to the prayers in the *Corpus Hermeticum* but also to invocations found in magical texts."

93. The same process can be read, certainly between the lines (and of course, that is the way one is supposed to read) in the *Gospel of Thomas*. Kasser, *L'Evangile Selon Thomas*, 29, sees in saying 2 stages of mystical advancement. Buckley, "An Interpretation of Logion 114," 251, believes that saying 11 which speaks about the "living" turning dead matter into live substance, "indicates nothing less that a transformation from death to life *here on this earthly level*." See also saying 22: "When you make the two one, . . . and when you make the male and the female one and the same, so that the male not be male nor the female; . . . then you will enter the kingdom." Buckley believes that "this is the language of transformation "which abolishes the pattern of opposites. . . . and a return to unity. . . . Such active creation as prerequisite for salvation must be understood as mandatory procedure while the disciple is still on earth, that is, the substitution must come about before the bodily death. . . . saying 22 may even — in veiled fashion — be speaking of a ritual of such 'spiritual' creation" (254).

94. Lee, *Against the Protestant Gnostics*, 25.

95. Rudolf, *Gnosis*, 14, shows that Hippolytus structures his *Refutatio* in such a way that he first presents the Greek heathen ideas, then gives an exposition of the Christian Gnostic heresies, attempting to show thereby that the Gnostics took their doctrines from the "wisdom of the heathen" — which incidentally they (the heretics) even misunderstand and misuse sometimes.

96. Hippolytus, *The Refutation of All Heresies* 5:16.

97. Irenaeus, *Against Heresies* 1:6:3. Irenaeus adds, "they observe other rites that are just like those of the pagans."

98. David Miller, *The New Polytheism*, 36. Interestingly, Virginia Mollenkott has made use of *I Ching* (a form of Chinese divination) in her exit from "Fundamentalism" — see *Sensuous Spirituality*, 16.

99. Epiphanius, *Panarion* 11:6:9, speaking of the Carpocratians, and Hippolytus *Refutation of All Heresies* 6:17-19, who argues that the Simonians and the Valentinians both derive from Pythagoras.

100. Morrison, *The Serpent*, 380, citing, in particular, Mircea Eliade (ed.), *The Encyclopedia of Religion* (London/New York: Collier Macmillan, 1987), 114.

101. Alexander the Great extended the Greek Empire to India.

102. James Preston, "Goddess Worship: An Overview," *The Book of the Goddess*, 38.

103. C. J. Bleeker, "Isis and Hathor," in Carl Olsen, ed., *The Book of the Goddess, Past and Present*, 32. The wisdom of Isis is recognized when the Egyptians call her "great in magic power."

104. Ibid.

105. Ibid., 38.

106. Quoted in Burkert, *Ancient Mystery Cults*, 97. Isis initiation may well lie behind the Gnostic bridal chamber. Burkert notes the "prominence of sexual abstinence in the preparation for the Isis ceremonies [which] draws attention to a center that is veiled. A priest of Isis from Prusa, in a recently published epigram, is praised for having arranged "the bed, covered with linen, which is unspeakable for the profane"; the word used for bed, *demnion*, does not suggest a dining couch."

107. Burkert, *Ancient Mystery Cults*, 91, refers to a text of Plutarch that attempts to describe the presumed process of dying in terms of a mystery initiation. At the moment of death, "the soul suffers an experience similar to those who celebrate great initiations . . . Wanderings astray in the beginning, tiresome walkings in circles, some frightening paths in darkness that lead nowhere; then immediately before the end all the terrible things, panic and shivering and sweat, and amazement. And then some wonderful light comes to meet you, pure regions and meadows are there to greet you, with sounds and dances and solemn, sacred words and holy views; and there the initiate, perfect by now, set free and loose from all bondage, walks about, crowned with a

wreath, celebrating the festival together with the other sacred and pure people, and he looks down on the uninitiated, unpurified crowd in this world in mud and fog beneath his feet."

108. Tertullian, *De Praescriptione* 43.

109. Irenaeus, *Against Heresies* 1:23:4. Filoramo, *Gnosticism*, 166, notes that Marcion's disciple, Apelles, wrote down the oracles of a virgin possessed, Philmena (acc to Eusebius, *Ecclesiastical History* 5:13:2-4), which is a further witness to the Gnostic use of occult pagan practices.

110. Plotinus, *Enneads* 2:9:14.

111. Rudolf, *Gnosis*, 225. Rudolf has to admit that though polemical, the Church Fathers' witness is "not wholly without foundation." Simon Magus, the founder of the Simonians, is associated with magic in Acts 8, and the Valentinian Marcus "practiced sorcery, astrology and numerical speculation — as did many Gnostics in conformity with classic pagan religion around them." Irenaeus, *Against Heresies* 1:23,4, describes the Simonians who "possess an image of Simon, made in the form of Zeus, and Helena in the form of Athena, and these they worship."

112. Ezekiel 8:1-16.

113. So Walter Zimmerli, *Ezekiel 1: A Commentary on the Book of the Prophet Ezekiel, Chapters 1-24*, Hermeneia Series (Philadelphia: Fortress Press, 1979), 243. See also 236-245.

114. Ezekiel 8.

115. Zimmerli, ibid., 245.

116. Ezekiel 9 recounts the physical destruction of the idolaters. In the theocracy of ancient Israel, such punishment was legitimate. In the time of the church, Jesus says to Peter, "Put your sword back in its place" (Matthew 26:52), and that is where it remains until God's final judgment of sin. The exercise of the "sword" in the church is limited to spiritual discipline in all its forms, from consultation to confrontation to excommunication (Matthew 18:15-18, 1 Corinthians 1:1-5, 14:36-38, 2 Corinthians 13:1-10, Galatians 1:9). "'Vengeance is mine, I will repay,' says the Lord," (Romans 12:19) is the principle which guides the church in its present pilgrimage.

117. Ezekiel 8:18.

Chapter Sixteen

1. Ibid., 332.

2. Caitlín Matthews, *Sophia, Goddess of Wisdom*, 330.

3. Ibid., 322, 327.

4. Ibid., 320.

5. See Nancy Wilson, *A Lesbian Ecu-Terrorist Outs the Bible for the Queer Millennium* (San Francisco: HarperSanFrancisco, 1996).

6. *Books for the Nineties* (San Francisco: HarperSanFrancisco, 1996), 10.

7. Cited in Herbert J. Pollitt, *The Inter-Faith Movement: The New Age Enters the Church* (Edinburgh: The Banner of Truth Trust, 1996), 13.

8. The virtual silence on this issue is surprising in our day when feminism has become a raging forest fire. Of the three evangelical books on hermeneutics to come on my desk in the last few months, two do not mention feminist hermeneutics at all, and one of over six hundred pages has a dozen lines. The same could be said for recent analyses of the theological situation. The well-known statement of Luther perhaps applies here: "If I profess with the loudest voice . . . the truth of God except precisely at that little point which the world and the devil are at that moment attacking, I am not professing Christ."

9. 1 Timothy 2:14 cp 2 Corinthians 11:3.

10. See 1 Timothy 2:15.

11. Philip E. Johnson, *Reason in the Balance: The Case Against Naturalism in Science, Law and Education* (Downers Grove, IL: InterVarsity Press, 1995), 124. Already the new inclusiveness is making its way into evangelicalism. As this present book goes to press, Trinity Press International announces in its Fall, 1996 catalogue, the forthcoming publication, *Beyond Liberalism and Fundamentalism: How Modern and Postmodern Philosophy Set the Theological Agenda*, by Nancy Murphy, Associate Professor of Christian Philosophy at Fuller Theological Seminary, Pasadena. Murphy, an evangelical scholar teaching in an evangelical school, proposes as the future agenda of theology the rejection of "the compulsion to separate the spectrum into two distinct camps," and the embracing of the notion of the "co-existence of a wide range of theological positions from left to right." While it is true that postmodernism has leveled some valid criticisms at modernism's hubris, one has to wonder, in reading this new theological agenda, what has happened to the biblical and orthodox concept of the antithesis?

12. Michael Swift, "Gay Revolutionary," *Gay Community News* (February, 1987), cited in Scott Lively and Kevin Abrams, *The Pink Swastika:* , 199.

13. Cited Sandi Dolbee, *The San Diego Union-Tribune*, Friday, September 16, 1994.

14. Cited in Daly, *Wickedary*, 133.

15. Guerra, "The Practice of Witchcraft," cited in Steichen, *Ungodly Rage*, 70-71.

16. James Webb, *The Occult Establishment* (Lasalle, IL: Open Court, 1976), 161.

17. Malachi Martin, *Windswept House: A Vatican Novel* (New York: Doubleday, 1996).

18. See Jeffrey L. Sheler, "Plotting World Order in Rome," *U. S. News & World Report* (June 10, 1996), 66.

19. Abraham Kuyper, *Lectures on Calvinism* (Grand Rapids: Eerdmans, 1931), 199.

20. Revelation 17.

21. I hope to do so in the third book of this trilogy whose title will doubtless begin *The Return of the* . . .

22. Hippolytus, *The Refutation of All Heresies*, 4:45.

23. Jeremiah 3:9.

24. Matthew 16:18.

25. Psalm 112:4.

26. Ezekiel 3:18-19.

27. Christian orthodoxy today seems but a bothersome pimple on the face of liberalism.

28. Philippians 2:11.

29. George W. Kitchin and Michael R. Newbolt, "Lift High the Cross," *Trinity Hymnal* (Atlanta, GA: Great Commissions Publications, 1990), 263.

Index

To order additional copies of

Spirit Wars

please send $18.95 plus $4.50 shipping and handling to:

Main Entry Editions
PO Box 952
Siloam Springs, AR 72761
Tel. 1-800-574-2978

Additional books by Peter Jones:

The Gnostic Empire Strikes Back @ $8.95 + $2.50 S&H
Study Guide for Gnostic Empire @ $5.95 + $2.50 S&H

Ask about current seminars.